Drug War Politics: The Price of Denial

Drug War Politics

The Price of Denial

Eva Bertram, Morris
Blachman, Kenneth Sharpe,
and Peter Andreas

UNIVERSITY OF CALIFORNIA PRESS
Berkeley · *Los Angeles* · *London*

University of California Press
Berkeley and Los Angeles, California

University of California Press, Ltd.
London, England

© 1996 by
The Regents of the University of California

Library of Congress Cataloging-in-Publication Data

Drug war politics: the price of denial / Eva Bertram . . . [et al.]
    p.   cm.
Includes bibliographic references and index.
ISBN 0-520-20309-7 (alk. paper)—ISBN 0-520-20598-7 (pbk.: alk. paper)
    1. Narcotics, control of—United States.   2. Drug traffic—Government
policy—United States.   3. Drug abuse—Government policy—United States.
4. Public health—United States.   I. Bertram, Eva.
HV5825.D7778   1996
363.4′5′0973—dc 20   95-19168
                                                                CIP

Printed in the United States of America

9   8   7   6   5   4   3   2

Contents

Figures

Preface

We came to write this book out of a deep concern over how a politics of fear, insecurity, and intolerance can crowd out the possibility of a politics of reason, care, and collective responsibility. We were also troubled by a common pattern in public policy: the persistence of unworkable policies in the face of overwhelming evidence of their failure. We saw these two concerns as connected in certain cases: when policies seeking to address social problems through the exercise of fear, coercion, and force reaped failure and further problems, the response was often to "get tougher." It seemed to be conventional wisdom that the reason force had not worked was that not enough had been applied and that the logical response to failure, therefore, was escalation—not reevaluation.

For many years, similar concerns informed our work on U.S. foreign policy, and in the late 1980s we turned our attention to the escalating U.S. drug war in Latin America. Longtime students of the region, we saw the danger that counternarcotics could become a prime driving force of U.S. intervention there, given the waning of anticommunism. Our initial research on the drug war in the Andes convinced us that this policy was senseless: it would never reduce significantly the supply of drugs coming into the United States; it was wasting billions of dollars; and it was undermining democracy and human rights in the region by strengthening the hands of repressive militaries and weakening already fragile civilian governments.[1] Evidence of the drug war's failure and harm was widely available, not only in academic circles but also in government documents and media reports. Yet the reports of failure only reinforced the resolve of public officials to "try harder," to apply a little more funding, a little more firepower—and the deeper flaws and harms of the policy were rarely part of the official debate.

It soon became clear to us that the same kinds of flaws and policy-generated harms were built into the drug war at home. Rather than ameliorating the problems of drug abuse and addiction, current policies of tough law enforcement are deepening many serious health and crime problems related to drug use. Yet the drug-policy debate is extraordinarily stultifying. It does not distinguish the harms caused by drugs from the harms caused by the social conditions in which drugs are used. It does not distinguish between the injuries caused by taking these illicit substances and those brought about by the policy solutions. It does not address the deeper reasons Americans use and abuse drugs, but instead weighs the most effective means to suppress this use.

The debate is polarized and simplistic, often phrased in terms of good versus evil, prohibition versus a free market, individual blame versus social causation. Politicians look for quick-fix solutions; many seem addicted to the idea of the drug war itself. People who want to open or expand the debate are delegitimized: there is a tendency to shoot the messenger rather than to analyze the message carefully. At home and abroad, the official response to failure has commonly been one of more fear, with calls for more force and more punishment.

Faced with such a situation both beyond and within our borders, our initial interest in the drug war shifted. Convinced by our research that the drug war strategy was inherently flawed at home and abroad, that it would not alleviate the growing problems of drug abuse and addiction, and that the war itself was exacerbating these and other social problems, we wanted to figure out why this strategy had persisted for so long and why the repeated response to failure was simply to continue the same policies. Persevering in a "march of folly," "becoming our own worst enemy," "shooting ourselves in the foot"—these were the metaphors for a puzzle we wanted to solve.[2]

So we sought not to write a book about drugs themselves or about the causes of drug abuse and addiction. Nor did we simply want to write another book about the failure of U.S. drug policy (though we will need to address the causes of failure and the harmful consequences of the drug war). Rather, this is a book about the politics of the drug war—a politics of denial—and the struggle for drug-policy reform.

By understanding this politics of denial in the particular case of drug policy, we also hope to reflect on our more general concern: how to encourage a more democratic politics, one that emphasizes dialogue and deliberation, not fear and loathing, and one that turns to force and punishment as a last, not a first, resort. We hope for a more open policy debate, with greater attentiveness to competing points of view; we hope to encourage a politics that is not simply or primarily about symbolic issues (as important as those might be) but about public health and well-being. And we hope to encourage citizens to step beyond their narrow self-interests, to assume responsibility for problems that in many cases have been created collectively.

In the course of our research, we have met many people with a great deal of experience with public policy and with the issues surrounding drug problems, and we have learned much from them. Most will disagree with something we have said, but we have tried to keep all in mind as we wrote this book. In some sense, the book is part of an ongoing dialogue with them all.

We have had much discussion, not surprisingly, with academics and analysts in the policy community. Those immersed in the drug issue will find that some of this book engages well-known debates to which they have contributed. What we would most like to share with them is what we have learned about the politics of policy choices: why it is so often difficult for analysts' sound critiques and smart ideas to be heard, to become part of the official debate, and to change the direction of policy. What is it about the politics of drugs that tends to filter or distort criticism, marginalize proposed policy reforms, and even distort seemingly plausible treatment and prevention alternatives? We have also learned that the search for policy alternatives needs to include more than reasoned arguments for particular policies that are likely to work better. It must include a search for alternative ways of conceiving the problem, alternative sets of assumptions, alternative values. And it must include an understanding of what it is that blocks other people's thinking about alternatives—hidden presumptions, the political costs of public criticism, a dominant ideology, and the workings of power.

We have many colleagues in the academic and policy community whose primary interests lie not in drug issues per se but in the deeper theoretical and policy concerns that inform this book. We hope the drug-policy case described here will help them in a number of ongoing debates—about the relationship between ideas and institutions; about the impact of culture on politics and of political struggle on culture; about the ways in which facts and reality that seem natural or given are often historically constructed (and reconstructed) as a result of political

conflict; about why reason is so often crowded out by ideology and ignorance; and about how the practical world of politics and the academic world of ideas might better inform each other.

We have also benefited from the experiences of those on the front lines
of the drug war: those in the drug-treatment and -prevention community and those in the criminal-justice system. These front liners have
taught us much about policy failure; it is part of their everyday experience and frustration.

Health and social-service professionals understand as well as anyone
the often self-defeating dynamics of the drug war. They see the problems
of substance abuse and addiction—to alcohol as well as illicit drugs—
becoming worse. They see the tragic impact of substance abuse on children, parents, and communities. They see diseases such as acquired immunodeficiency syndrome (AIDS) being spread by intravenous drug
taking. They know the drug war is doing little to ameliorate these problems and is often exacerbating them, yet they face inadequate resources
for health care, social services, and treatment. Moreover, many of them
find themselves trapped into supporting a drug war in which they do not
believe, marketing treatment to policymakers as another tool in the war
against crime and drugs in order to obtain the funds they need to deal
with these pressing health and social crises.

People in the criminal-justice system—police, judges, prosecutors, parole officers, prison and jail officials—find their resources and institutions strained by the avalanche of drug-related crimes. They fight for
more funds, understanding all the while that they are simply treading
water. They, too, are often frustrated by the dilemmas they face. If, for
example, they take seriously the strict laws against possession of illegal
drugs and the mandatory sentences they are required to impose, they will
have to arrest and imprison an enormous number of people (more than
24 million Americans were reported as having used drugs during 1993).[3]
They know that most of the people they do arrest will soon be back on
the streets because of overcrowded courts and prisons. They know that
their efforts to clear an area of drug dealers will simply mean that the
dealers will reemerge elsewhere. They realize that some of their tactics,
especially in inner-city minority communities, are deepening local resentment toward the police. Yet if they turn blind eyes to drug use and
dealing, they meet harsh criticism for not doing their job.

Having learned much about such failures and problems from those
on the front lines, we hope that some of the insights we have gained elsewhere will be useful to them—such as why many of the problems they

face are exacerbated by our drug policies and why, therefore, throwing more money at these problems will not bring significant improvement. We also hope to make more understandable the politics behind the policies whose failure they experience—to demonstrate where the entrenched assumptions and political coalitions that fuel the failure come from. Understanding this will help clarify why change will come only if these front liners are actively involved in the politics of reform—and why some of the reasonable, short-term political demands they make may, paradoxically, help perpetuate precisely the drug war strategy that helped create those problems in the first place. Ultimately, we hope to help them see better what many of them already know intuitively: there are other ways to provide treatment, prevention, and law enforcement that are not self-defeating.

We have written this book as much for concerned citizens as for specialists on public policy and the drug problem. Our research has taught us that most Americans understand that drug problems are serious, that what we are doing is not working, and they are puzzled about why. Some are convinced that we need to be tougher, more determined, and more efficient. The policy has failed because of a lack of will and commitment—and those who say otherwise are defeatists. Their response to criticism is understandable: they are fearful of both admitting defeat and seeing drug abuse and addiction spread in their homes, schools, and communities. We hope this book will help them understand the futility of escalating the drug war and how some of the policies they support are actually harming things they value deeply. We hope to encourage them to open a wider dialogue with critics, particularly those who share their concern about substance abuse and addiction.

Other Americans are convinced that the best thing we can do is to end the war and legalize drugs. For some, it is primarily a matter of principle: the choice to use drugs should be a free one, and individuals should take the responsibility and bear the consequences; the state should not interfere as long as the drug user is not harming anyone else. Others emphasize that abuse and addiction may be problems for some people but that the harm done by drug war policies is far greater—and that these problems would be more manageable if we minimized the damage done by the war itself. But, as damaging as the harms caused by policy are, legalization will leave intact another set of harms—those caused by drug abuse and addiction. Because many who favor legalization understand this risk and want to minimize the harms caused by drugs as well as those caused by drug policies, we hope our

proposals for making public health—rather than free choice—the ultimate goal of drug policy will be useful.

Many other citizens doubt there are any solutions at all. They are frequently confused, frustrated, or angry about the problem and the policies and often are left feeling hopeless or cynical about what to do. They
are tempted to pin the blame on the politicians or the moral majority or
the left or the decline in American values. There is, we argue, a partial
truth to such commonsense responses. But they leave out an important
factor: all citizens bear some responsibility for the persistence of the
failed drug war. Unless Americans can engage in the debate more effectively, unless there are voters who will demand, or at minimum support,
more workable and humane drug policies, public officials are not going
to change direction. Pinning the blame on "them" wrongly gets "us" off
the hook.

We are indebted to numerous people for their help in this project,
more than we can thank individually. Many gave of their valuable time
to share their thoughts with us. Some were kind enough to provide long
interviews, and their names are mentioned in the bibliography. We would
especially like to thank the following people For meeting with us repeatedly to share their expertise, analysis, and critiques of our work,
Carol Bergman, Susan Galbraith, Mark Parrino, Ellen Weber, and Ron
Weich. For providing insightful suggestions and comments on parts of
the manuscript or other valuable assistance, Bruce Bagley, Camile Barry,
Rosalyn Bass, Richard Brown, Charles Call, Marc Chernick, Jim Greer,
Ronald G. Hellman, Elaine Johnson, Helene Kaufman, Mark Kleiman,
James Kurth, Julie Locke, Don Mabry, Pat McRae, James Morone, Carol
Nackenoff, Ethan Nadelmann, Don Puchala, Evangelos Raptis, Lisa
Scheckel, Jennifer Shack, Peter Sharpe, Bill Spencer, Emek Ucarer,
Richard Valelly, Bill Walker, John Walsh, and Coletta Youngers. For in-
stitutional support and encouragement, the Bildner Center for Western
Hemisphere Studies at the Graduate School of the City University of New
York, Cornell University, the Institute for Policy Studies, the Institute of
International Studies of the University of South Carolina, Swarthmore
College, and Yale University. And finally, for providing an ideal place for
the collaborative work that produced this book, a special thanks to
Helen Swetland.

PART ONE

Confronting Denial

"Gentlemen, the fact that all my horses and all my men couldn't put Humpty together again simply proves to me that I must have <u>more</u> horses and <u>more</u> men."

Figure 1. Drawing by Dana Fradon; © 1978 The New Yorker Magazine, Inc. Reprinted by permission.

I   The Drug War Syndrome

Despite convincing, publicly available evidence that the war on drugs has not addressed the nation's problems of drug abuse and addiction, the U.S. government has consistently refused to engage in a serious reevaluation of the strategy or a search for a different approach. What we face is a politics of denial. This book aims to figure out why.

For all the public debate about drugs, a singular goal lies behind decades of American drug wars: stopping all drug use through a strategy of tough enforcement. The strategy is deceptively simple. Its main targets are cocaine, heroin, and marijuana, although other drugs are addressed as well.[1] Its primary aim is to prohibit supply, so that Americans cannot find or cannot afford drugs to use; its secondary aim is to discourage those who do consume drugs, mainly by penalizing them.

Concern with reducing the supply of drugs has long dominated the drug war effort. If law enforcement can restrict the growing, manufacturing, distribution, and sale of illicit drugs, the strategists suggest, these illicit drugs will become scarce, their prices will soar, and drug consumption will drop. The policy mix often changes—at times emphasizing a crackdown on domestic dealers and traffickers, at other times concentrating on foreign growers and international traffickers—but the underlying logic has remained constant.

The war on supply is reinforced by policies that target users. Since early in this century, drug policies have sought to discourage people who consume drugs by imposing sanctions against drug possession. If the war on supply aims to discourage consumption by raising the economic cost of drug use, the war on users seeks to raise the risk of drug use by imposing punitive measures ranging from jail terms to fines to loss of jobs, licenses, or housing.

Beginning in the late 1960s, drug-control efforts expanded to include programs of treatment and preventive education. These programs generally seek not to punish but to provide care for people who are drug-dependent and to dissuade potential users through education about the harmful effects of drugs. Although such efforts have helped many individuals avoid or reduce drug abuse, they have not altered the punitive thrust of the U.S. drug strategy. They have been at best a minor sideshow in the larger drug strategy, a limited supplement to the war on supply and on users that fundamentally defines the U.S. approach to drug control.

The logic behind the war on supply and users is compelling. Yet overall the strategy has reaped failure and a range of other social harms. Drug-enforcement agents seize more drugs each year, but they have not stemmed the supply of drugs coming into the country. Drugs are relatively cheap and readily available on our nation's streets. Despite a decline in casual drug use since the late 1970s, and despite the billions of dollars spent to fight the drug war, the number of people suffering from drug abuse or addiction, the level of violent drug-related crime, and the spread of diseases linked to drug abuse have all increased in recent decades. (For figures on levels of drug use and spending see appendixes 1 and 3.) Confronted with the evidence of failure, our policymakers have responded with renewed determination to fight harder—generating a maddening cycle of failure and escalation.

The pattern is not new. It began after 1914, when Congress passed the Harrison Act, which prohibited the sale of heroin, cocaine, and their derivatives except by doctors' prescriptions. In time, aggressive efforts by narcotics agents in the Treasury Department effectively ended this system of medical control of such psychoactive substances and made their sale or possession illegal. By the end of the 1920s, those who sold and used these drugs were considered criminals and were subject to vigorous, punitive law enforcement. In 1937 marijuana was added to the list, and soon after World War II the Federal Bureau of Narcotics (FBN) joined with Congress to press for even stiffer criminal penalties against those who sold heroin, cocaine, and marijuana.

Under President Richard Nixon a fierce, rhetorical campaign was launched to define drugs as a major source of crime in America and to make a war on drugs and crime a national priority. The drug war, which had been waged as a low-intensity conflict for decades, was thus born in its modern, expanded form. The battle against the drug supply continued under Presidents Gerald Ford and Jimmy Carter, though with less fanfare and public attention. When Ronald Reagan and then George Bush entered the White House, they revived and dramatically escalated Nixon's drug war as part of a broader effort to roll back what they saw as liberal, unpatriotic, and immoral social transformations wrought in the 1960s and 1970s. Bill Clinton inherited this intensified Reagan-Bush drug war when he came to office in 1993; he lowered the rhetoric but largely continued the strategy.

Over the years, the tenor of the debate has shifted, the foreign and domestic targets have been slightly altered, and the rate of escalation has varied. But the basic approach to the drug war remains the same—and the cycle of failure and escalation continues. The more U.S. policy encourages the eradication of coca crops in the Andes, for example, the more peasants simply expand production in new areas—yet time and again, drug-enforcement officials have responded by intensifying crop eradication. The result of closing one trafficking route into the United States has been the creation of new routes and more inventive smuggling techniques—yet somehow policymakers believe that more money and greater determination are the solution. The more dealers are locked up, the more potentially jailable dealers there seem to be—yet the official response is simply to build more prisons for more people arrested on drug charges. National and state leaders bemoan the spread of AIDS through intravenous drug use—and yet they outlaw proven programs that could stem AIDS transmission by teaching safe use and distributing sterile needles.

Do public officials insist on pursuing such unworkable and harmful policies because they do not see the record of failure or the flaws in the strategy? Is it that law-enforcement agencies see it as a way to demand bigger budgets? Is it that the public is demanding more force against and punishment of users and dealers?

It is not as if public officials and other critics have not put forward alternatives: in the second and third decades of this century, and repeatedly since the 1960s, reasoned critiques and plausible reforms have been advanced by policy analysts, members of the legal, medical, treatment, and prevention communities, and even presidential commissions.[2] But sound criticisms and bright ideas have generally fallen on deaf ears; they have routinely been dismissed or sidelined in public debate over policy.

We are left with two related puzzles: Why does the United States continue to pursue the same policies in the face of failure? And why have the debate and the policy prospects become so narrow and circular, denying consideration of valuable alternatives? A number of excellent books address critical questions of drug policy and drug use: some look at the sources of drug use and addiction; others look at what has failed and what has worked in the drug war. We seek to explore equally important, less familiar territory: the politics of the drug war.

We also believe that there is a better approach to thinking about drug problems, one drawn from the tradition of public health in America. But it is idle speculation to advance such a public-health alternative before we understand how the politics of denial has made an open, informed public debate about alternatives such as public health so difficult for so long.

Part 1 of this book is designed to expose the pattern of denial. Denial takes different forms. Some Americans think the failure of the drug war is due simply to lack of effort, lack of resources, or bad management; they deny the fatal defects at the heart of the strategy that systematically undermine the prospects for success at home and abroad. Other people deny the wide-ranging damage that the drug war itself is causing, damage that is often misleadingly attributed to drug use and dealing. In particular, many Americans fail to see the ways in which the drug war helps create and exacerbate problems of abuse, addiction, and crime. These issues are taken up in chapters 2 and 3.

Exposing the pattern of denial frames the question for Part 2: what are the politics behind this pattern? Evidence of the flaws and harms of the drug war strategy is publicly available for elected officials to consider—and yet they persist in the current policy. Is there another agenda at work? Are some political officials reaping benefits—symbolic gains or hidden purposes—from the continued war? To some extent, the answer is yes—but this merely begs other questions. It does not explain the persistence of the drug war for so many decades, nor does it explain how so many Americans have been convinced to support a patently unsuccessful policy for so long.

If neither well-intentioned ignorance nor conscious deceit by public officials is sufficient to explain the persistence of policy, what else is at play? We will argue that no single factor explains policy persistence in the face of failure. Rather, a number of pieces fit together, each piece working, as in a jigsaw puzzle, in relationship with the others to create a coherent picture of why we are mired in a politics of denial.

In chapters 4 and 5 we will see how a particular way of thinking about drugs—which we identify as a punitive drug war paradigm—frames the way drugs, addiction, and the connection to crime are understood. This "conventional wisdom" about drugs makes it difficult to recognize the flaws in drug policy and the damage it causes, and marginalizes many sound alternatives as politically unacceptable. The ways in which current understandings about drugs and crime were created out of political struggles and were sustained against challenges in the 1960s and 1970s provide clues to what a struggle for drug reform entails.

These punitive ideas and values became embedded in the operations of key political institutions—in the federal bureaucracy, in the presidency, and in Congress. In chapters 6 and 7 we will see how presidents and elected representatives have been able to draw on these ideas and images to mobilize popular support for expanded drug wars, how conservative groups and social forces have been able to use them to push political officials in this direction, how Democrats and Republicans have been tempted to "out-tough" each other, and how few officials have had an interest in reevaluating the failed and harmful policies. In chapter 8 we will look closely at the ways the punitive paradigm, operating through these powerful institutions, narrows the scope of public debate about drugs, ties the hands of moderate reformers who seek to shift budget priorities from punishment toward treatment and prevention, and ultimately undermines the effectiveness of existing treatment and prevention programs.

What, then, are the alternatives? We begin part 3 with an examination of the legalization approach in chapter 9. Despite its important critiques of the punitive paradigm, that approach is itself conceptually flawed: in particular, it tells us how some of the damage created by drug policies could be reduced but offers little guidance on how to heal the suffering caused by drug abuse and addiction. These flaws make it unacceptable to a broad segment of the American population. We will argue that a far better alternative is a public-health paradigm, which reconceives the problem of drug abuse and addiction in ways that offer some hope for those who are suffering and minimizes the damage created by current policies. In chapter 10 we look at the ways treatment, prevention, and law enforcement take on entirely different meanings and lead to different policy choices under a public-health paradigm.

As important as such a paradigmatic change in conventional wisdom might be, it will never come about simply through force of argument. Only a sustained political struggle will yield genuine drug-policy reform. In chapter 11 we look at current struggles for drug reform and consider the ways some of these might facilitate a transformation from a strategy that harms without healing to one that heals without harm.

2   Three Fatal Flaws in the War on Drugs

Much has been written about the dismal record of the war on drugs. Less well known are the reasons behind the drug war's failure. Three fatal flaws are built into the drug strategy itself, flaws that doom the strategy at every turn and systematically undermine efforts to eliminate the production, distribution, and consumption of illegal drugs.

Understanding the continuing cycle of failure and escalation in America's drug wars demands confronting the difference between failings and flaws in the strategy. The distinction is a crucial one, easily obscured by the polemics and rhetoric of the drug-policy debate. The failings of the drug war are familiar: both the supply of drugs and the levels of abuse and addiction remain high. But failure can be blamed on any of a range of causes—poor leadership, scarce funds, faulty implementation. A flawed strategy, on the other hand, is one that is fundamentally misconceived: it will continue to fail regardless of leadership, resources, or operational efficiency. The inability or unwillingness to see that the poor track record of the drug war is due to fundamental flaws in the strategy is one reason U.S. leaders answer failure with escalation, continuing to pour good money after bad in the fight against drugs.

FAILURE AND THE PATTERN OF DENIAL

The United States has been engaged in a battle against drugs since 1914. In the early 1970s President Nixon transformed it into a major drug war, and it was fought most fiercely by Presidents Reagan and Bush in the

1980s and early 1990s. Yet, as most Americans know, we have little to show for it.

The record of failure is sometimes obscured by the fact that the number of so-called current users—people who have taken drugs within the past month—declined between 1985 and 1993 from 22.3 million to 11.7 million. According to White House reports, however, this drop is explained largely by a decline in casual marijuana use—a decline that began in 1979, well before the drug wars of the 1980s were under way.[1] The more serious problems of drug abuse and addiction, meanwhile, are as bad as or worse than ever. According to figures from the 1995 *National Drug Control Strategy,* the number of heroin addicts is estimated to have jumped tenfold between 1967 and 1993 to about 600,000. Meanwhile, cocaine, which raised few concerns in 1967, claimed at least 2.1 million hard-core addicts by 1993.[2] Even the intensive drug war assaults of the mid- to late 1980s failed to reduce levels of cocaine or heroin abuse. One rough measure of hard-core use is the number of drug-related hospital emergencies. Cocaine-related emergencies increased by 22 percent between 1988 and 1993, while heroin-related emergencies rose by 65 percent (see appendix 3).[3]

More Americans are addicted to a wider range of harder drugs now than before Nixon declared war on drugs in the early 1970s. The common reaction of public officials and many voters to reports of this failure, however, is to call for an escalation of the war. "For those who say that we can't possibly win the war on drugs, I say we haven't tried," argued Senator Dennis DeConcini (D-Arizona) in February 1993. "If this nation expects to wage a true war on drugs," he added, "we need to mobilize every resource available to the country and spend whatever it takes until we choke off supply and reduce consumption."[4] In 1995 House Speaker Newt Gingrich reiterated the need to try harder by getting tougher, calling for "very Draconian, very real steps" to cut supply: anyone responsible for shipping narcotics into the country, Gingrich suggested, should be put to death.[5]

But we *have* tried. The annual federal drug budget for law enforcement has grown from roughly $53 million in 1970 to more than $8.2 billion in 1995: since 1970 we have invested roughly $68 billion in domestic and foreign drug enforcement—$65 billion of this since 1981 (see appendix 1).[6] The problem is not our lack of will or even the limits of our national pocketbook but, rather, our inability or unwillingness to see three fatal flaws at the heart of the drug war strategy: two undermine the war on the drug supply, and a third undercuts the war on drug users.

Failing to recognize these flaws, we look for another fix—a little more funding, a little more firepower—and delude ourselves into thinking the drug war can work.

THE FLAWS IN THE WAR ON SUPPLY

Most illicit drugs are grown by farmers in Third World countries. Cocaine is derived from the coca plant, grown largely in the Andean countries, principally Bolivia and Peru. Opium comes from poppies grown in Southeast Asia, Afghanistan, Turkey, and, increasingly, parts of Latin America. Marijuana, like tobacco, is grown in large quantities across the globe, including the United States. Processing these illicit substances is easy and inexpensive. To produce cocaine, for example, coca leaves are first refined into coca paste (a simple process of mixing coca with easily accessible chemicals, often done on site by local producers) and then shipped to jungle laboratories to be processed into powdered cocaine. The powder is then transported to the United States and other markets, where it is distributed through dealers—wholesalers, distributors, salespeople on the streets—who in turn package it as cocaine powder or turn it into its derivative, crack.

The U.S. war on supply is fought at each of the three stages in the global drug trade. First, U.S. antidrug agencies target drugs at the source by pressuring foreign governments to eliminate coca, poppy, and marijuana production (with eradication or crop-substitution programs) and to attack the refining facilities that convert the crops into heroin or cocaine. Second, antidrug agencies target drugs at or en route to U.S. borders, using planes, boats, border patrols, and customs officers to interdict drug shipments. Finally, drug-enforcement agents and local police go after drugs within the United States by trying to locate, arrest, and prosecute drug dealers and to seize drug supplies. At each stage the aim is to make it more dangerous and more costly for growers, refiners, smugglers, and dealers to produce and sell drugs—thus driving down production and availability, driving up prices, and discouraging consumers from buying and using drugs.

But the central objectives of significantly raising prices and lowering availability remain unmet. As the figures in appendix 2 show, cocaine and heroin prices have declined markedly in the last fifteen years despite the dramatic escalation of drug law enforcement. In the early 1990s heroin sold in New York City for about one-third its 1979 price, and its purity increased from 34 percent in 1988 to 66 percent in 1993.[7] Clinton drug czar Lee Brown concluded in 1995 that "drugs are readily available to anyone who wants to buy them. Cocaine and heroin street prices are low and purity is high—making use more feasible and affordable than ever."[8] Why has the strategy failed, even on its own terms?

The drug trade has been packaged as a crime problem for so long that there is a tendency among policymakers and the public to overlook its nature as a business, driven by the laws of supply and demand. Illicit drugs are so easy to grow and refine, so simple to ship and sell, so widely desired, and so extraordinarily profitable that there will always be an affordable supply. The drug trade is at root a market problem. The criminalization of the trade, however, makes it a black—and particularly pernicious—market. Black markets in various goods or services have long bedeviled government attempts to eliminate them, especially when the twin factors of high demand and high profits are at work.

The black markets in cocaine, heroin, and marijuana are very similar to the black market in alcohol during Prohibition in the 1920s and early 1930s. Then, too, the illegal products were ordinarily cheap and easy to produce, store, transport, and sell. Government policies aimed to interfere in the market and make the product scarce and expensive by outlawing it. Enforcement indeed raises prices by increasing the risks and costs faced by suppliers. But given the continued demand for alcohol and illicit drugs, this merchandise also becomes—as a result of government prohibition—extraordinarily profitable for producers and traffickers, precisely because it is scarcer and more expensive than it would otherwise be. If a gram of pure, pharmaceutical cocaine were purchased legally for medical purposes, it would cost about $15 to $20, for example; the retail black-market price is about $143.[9] The black market thus is the inevitable result of government attempts to make highly sought after commodities illegal. Equally inevitable is the crime that follows such black markets: the high profits, intense competition, and pressure by law-enforcement officials lead many black marketeers to arm themselves to defend their market shares against police and competitors.

Government prohibition has thus created the thriving black market in drugs, and the government's war on drugs seeks to suppress it. But success has been elusive: for decades the policy of prohibition has kept consumer prices far higher than the legal market price would be—and this has undoubtedly deterred some use, abuse, and addiction—but it has not been able to raise consumer prices high enough to keep drugs out of reach. And what many policymakers and citizens fail to recognize is that the attempt to suppress the drug trade through a war on supply generates two self-defeating effects—the profit paradox and the hydra effect—which together doom the effort.

The drug war has been unable to raise the cost of doing business enough to put drug prices out of range for consumers because the strategy generates a *profit paradox*: its success in artificially raising prices also inflates profits. These high profits have a paradoxical effect: they provide a steady incentive for drug suppliers to remain in the trade and for new suppliers to enter.

Because the drug war raises profits as it raises prices, the stick of law enforcement that is intended to discourage suppliers on the black market simultaneously creates a carrot of enormous profits—which encourages suppliers. As they pursue these high profits, they keep the supply of drugs up, and that keeps prices from rising too high, thus undermining the aim of policy. As Steven Wisotsky explains, "If the cocaine industry commissioned a consultant to design a mechanism to ensure its profitability, it could not have done better than the War on Drugs: just enough pressure to inflate prices, but not enough to keep its product from the market."[10]

The second flaw is the self-reproduction of the trade, or the *hydra effect*: attempts to stamp out drug production and dealing often spread the problem and make hard-fought gains short-lived. The key here is that cocaine, heroin, and marijuana are easy products to grow, refine, transport, and sell. The amount of money and skill needed to enter into the business is not high—there are low barriers to entry, an economist would say—and the business is quite profitable, especially compared with other business opportunities available to many of the farmers, shippers, and salespeople involved.

These conditions make even the success of drug-enforcement campaigns ephemeral. It is simple and lucrative for suppliers to produce more in order to offset what they might lose in seizures by drug enforcers. And there are always new recruits to take the place of those who are arrested. As a result, growing fields, production labs, and supply routes spring back to life and even expand despite repeated law-enforcement efforts. Like the mythical sea serpent that Hercules battled, the drug trade is an elusive enemy: each time one head of the hydra is cut off, two more grow in its place. Often, attempts to suppress the trade in one locale simply encourage new recruits or veteran suppliers to set up operations elsewhere to meet the demand for their product.

Taken together, the profit paradox and the hydra effect undermine the war on supply at every stage.

At the Source: The War Abroad

"The logic is simple," George Bush said in a 1988 campaign speech. "The cheapest and safest way to eradicate narcotics is to destroy them at their source. . . . We need to wipe out crops wherever they are grown and take out labs wherever they exist." This claim echoed those of Presidents Reagan and Nixon before him.[11] And a few years later the Clinton administration underlined the continued commitment to the war against foreign drug production with a strategy to shift the focus of international drug enforcement from transit zones to source-country programs.[12]

Those who support the war at the source assume that it is much less costly and difficult to locate and destroy crops and labs in the field than to intercept the finished product along smuggling routes or on U.S. streets. The most aggressive and expensive attempt to date to stop drugs at the source has been the war against cocaine production in the Andean countries of Colombia, Peru, and Bolivia. Launched in the mid-1980s and escalated under the Bush administration's "Andean Initiative," the U.S. drug war in the Andes was continued under the Clinton administration. The strategy is to cut supply by eradicating coca crops, destroying processing laboratories, blocking the transport of processing chemicals, and intercepting drug shipments. Traffickers are to be arrested and prosecuted, their assets seized, and trafficking networks dismantled.

The logic is simple—but deceptive. Consider what the drug warriors are up against in the war on cocaine. Hundreds of thousands of Andean peasant farmers grow coca. Crop-eradication efforts have rarely even kept pace with new growth; according to State Department reports, eradication had no significant effect on the volume of coca leaves produced between 1989 and 1994.[13] Coca leaves are refined in small, well-hidden, easy-to-move, and inexpensive-to-replace labs, where they are converted into tons of cocaine powder—which is moved throughout the region by large numbers of traffickers and is eventually smuggled out of South America. Figures for 1994 show that levels of coca-leaf production are sufficient to refine more than 1,000 metric tons of cocaine annually—more than three times the estimated U.S. cocaine market.[14] A U.S. embassy official in Peru concluded in late 1993, "We haven't had any real impact on the drug flow." In 1992 Peruvian government officials seized

7 tons of cocaine and cocaine base out of an estimated 650 tons produced in the country. He pointed out, "That's peanuts."[15]

The magnitude of the trade makes the prospect of drug control in the
Andes daunting enough. What makes it virtually impossible is the way
in which the profit paradox and the hydra effect work in conjunction
with the politics and economics of countries like Peru, Bolivia, and
Colombia to systematically undercut efforts to lower supply.

The profit paradox dooms the strategy through a simple market logic:
the drug-enforcement strategy in the United States keeps prices up at
black-market levels but does not significantly dent the demand for cocaine. The result is a dream for producers and dealers—a guaranteed
market, with profits kept artificially high by the U.S. government. The
incentives produced by these U.S. government "price supports" systematically overwhelm source-country efforts to reduce supply.

Consider the money earned from one kilogram of cocaine at various
stages of production and distribution. Once diluted and sold in grams,
one kilogram—2.2 pounds—of Andean cocaine powder in 1990 yielded
between $70,000 and $300,000 on American streets. These high prices
produce a ripple effect through the chain of production. The estimated
330 kilograms of Bolivian coca leaves required to produce one kilo of
the powder can bring a coca farmer $110. After the first stages of crude
and inexpensive processing, three kilograms of coca paste will sell for
$470. One kilogram of the slightly more refined cocaine base will earn
between $500 and $850. And a kilo of finished cocaine will sell for between $1,900 and $2,500 in the Andes. Once it arrives in Miami, that
kilo (assuming 80 percent purity) will bring between $16,000 and
$25,000 at the wholesale level.[16]

These extraordinary profits, particularly at the later stages, confound
drug warriors who are fighting to cut supply. Production costs are so low
that traffickers can easily pay more to refiners—who can easily pay more
to growers—when needed, in order to keep the profitable supply flowing. The inflated profits mean that "the average drug organization can
afford to lose 70 percent to 80 percent of its product and still be profitable," explains one former official of the Drug Enforcement Administration (DEA). "How do you intend to put that group out of business
with a basic policy of trying to suppress its product?"[17]

The incentives produced by the drug war's profit paradox are considerable even at the lowest levels of the trade. From the perspective of
an Andean peasant, coca brings many times the price of competing crops.
A coca farmer in the Bolivian Chapare region could net up to $2,600 per

hectare (roughly 2.5 acres) annually from coca production in the late 1980s, more than four times what he could earn from cultivating oranges or avocados, the two most profitable legal crops traditionally grown in the region.[18] What is more, coca is easy to grow on poor soil and inexpensive to process. The market is virtually assured: traffickers fly into remote areas and pay peasants up front. Lacking viable legal economic alternatives, growers and processors have little incentive to abandon it. And U.S. efforts to encourage the substitution of other crops for coca bump up against the high profits; no legal crop can compete given the "price supports" the U.S. drug war offers the coca producers.

The profit paradox, however, does more than influence the actions of drug producers and processors. It also shapes the incentives and decisions of entire governments—with devastating implications for the U.S. drug war. The U.S. strategy depends on local governments, militaries, and police forces possessing the will and ability to fight the U.S. drug war. But our would-be allies do not share U.S. interests in fighting the drug war, because their other priorities are simply overwhelming. Andean leaders, for example, are consumed with issues of economic and political survival—in which cocaine plays a vital role. The jobs and revenues generated by the cocaine trade help maintain the Bolivian and Peruvian economies. The drug economy in Bolivia employs roughly 500,000 people, about 20 percent of the workforce.[19] When Bolivia's President Jaime Paz Zamora met President Bush at the Cartagena drug summit in February 1990, he pointed out that more than half of his country's imports were financed by the coca-cocaine traffic and that 70 percent of real gross national product (GNP) was cocaine related.[20] According to Flavio Machicado, Bolivia's former finance minister, "If narcotics were to disappear overnight, we would have rampant unemployment. There would be open protest and violence."[21] In Peru, where the legal economy is extremely weak and official unemployment has skyrocketed, the coca industry provides hundreds of thousands of jobs and is the country's largest source of foreign-exchange revenues.[22]

Struggling to comply with strict International Monetary Fund (IMF) austerity guidelines and international debt-payment schedules, Andean countries are understandably hesitant to adopt economically risky drug policies. Indeed, they have created mechanisms to allow their financial systems to absorb as much foreign exchange from the drug industry as possible. Given their desperate need for foreign exchange, Andean governments have little choice but to tolerate revenue from any source, legal or illegal. A successful crackdown on the trade, in short, would threaten the immediate economic viability of both Peru and Bolivia—and the political survival of their leaders.

Likewise, the Latin American security forces charged with carrying out the U.S. drug strategy have little real interest in joining the antidrug campaign. They may want U.S. equipment and aid, but if they have any real military objective, it is in battling leftist insurgents, not drugs.[23] And for many soldiers and policemen the drug war simply serves as a way to supplement their often meager incomes: they can trade their enforcement capability for a share of the profits.

The endemic corruption that undermines the drug war is rooted in the high profits that make it a rational choice for government officials and police and military officers whose low salaries cannot compete with traffickers' bribes.[24] Retired Special Forces Commander General Robert C. Kingston described a conversation with a U.S. Border Patrol agent at a checkpoint in Peru: "A colonel from Lima said, 'I have the opportunity while I'm here to make $70,000 by looking the other way at certain times. You have a family, they are protected in the United States, you have a proper pension plan. My family is not protected and I don't have the proper pension plan and I will never have the opportunity to make $70,000 as long as I live. I am going to make it.'"[25]

A DEA official confirmed that corruption similarly "permeates all levels of the anti-narcotics forces" in Bolivia.[26] Antidrug officials, moreover, may go beyond simply overlooking drug activity and actively assist the drug traffickers: "We know as a fact that the Peruvian Army gets payments for letting traffickers use airstrips," a U.S. Special Forces commander reported.[27] Colombian trafficker José Gonzalo Rodríguez Gacha made multimillion-dollar payoffs to entire brigades of the army.[28] In mid-1995 more than a dozen Colombian congressmen, the comptroller, the attorney general, and the president's campaign advisor were indicted for accepting payoffs from the Cali cartel.[29] In some cases corruption is so extensive that the entire military, and even the president, uses state power to participate in the drug trade—as in the case of Panama under Manuel Noriega throughout the 1980s and Bolivia under Luis García Meza from 1980 to 1982.[30]

The United States can sometimes use pressure to force the removal of a corrupt official; Andean government officials will occasionally yield in order to secure continued U.S. assistance. But such steps do not address the systemic problem of drug-related corruption. Further, the more that U.S. training and equipment makes local enforcement agencies into efficient drug fighters, the more incentive there is on the part of traffickers to bribe them, and the greater the opportunity for widespread corruption. Ironically, then, the more aggressive the antidrug campaign, the more corruption may spread. "As long as the trade is illicit," explained Colombia's Prosecutor General Gustavo De Greiff in 1994, "the *narcotraficantes* will continue to receive these immense profits that allow them to corrupt everyone."[31]

The hydra effect heightens the obstacles created by the profit paradox to curbing drug production at the source. Crop eradication has simply led peasants to replant elsewhere, often in new and more remote areas. The profit incentive and the ease of growing coca create conditions for almost infinite supply. In the late 1980s the U.S. Department of Agriculture estimated that 2.5 million square miles in South America alone were suitable for coca production, of which a mere 700 square miles were used for growing coca. What is more, peasant coca producers have organized to protest government eradication and have developed sophisticated counterstrategies to circumvent enforcement efforts. Growers scale down and hide crops. Sometimes they finance new coca fields with subsidies given to them by the government to eradicate their existing fields. Processors downsize, camouflage, or relocate laboratories.[32]

As the trade disperses in response to the drug war, it becomes less detectable and more impervious to the efforts of enforcers. A congressional report concluded that increased law enforcement in the Andes has "helped lead to an ironic and undesirable result: the dispersion of the drug trade to other nations in South America."[33] Officials in the United States and Latin America put the problem more succinctly: "It's like hitting mercury with a hammer," said one State Department expert.[34] A Mexican official explained, "The more we seem to get rid of the problem, the greater it seems to grow. . . . It's like a water balloon. We squeeze one side and it goes out the other."[35]

The same counterproductive results characterize U.S. efforts against major foreign traffickers and cartels. According to the Department of Justice, the cartels have

> an ability to tap alternative sources of supply and to adapt readily to changing conditions. Thus Colombian cartels can buy their coca leaf or paste in Peru, Bolivia, Ecuador, or in Colombia itself. When Turkish authorities clamped down on the illicit cultivation of opium-producing poppies, drug organizations shifted production to the Golden Triangle region of Southeast Asia and to the mountainous regions on both sides of the Afghanistan-

Pakistan border. This flexibility enables the major traffickers to regroup and to redirect a part of their operations without disrupting the whole.[36]

Success against one trafficking organization simply guarantees more market share for others. Enforcement efforts against Colombia's major traffickers, for example, have shown periodic signs of success—but these have been short-lived. In the months following the U.S.-backed crackdown by the Colombian government on the Medellín cartel in the fall of 1989, cocaine processing and trafficking dropped significantly. But the disruption was temporary: production quickly recovered, nearly reaching previous levels within six months. The weakening of the Medellín cartel allowed the competing Cali cartel to boost its share of the cocaine market. When the government cracked down on the Cali cartel in 1995, younger and more violent trafficking groups began to replace it in the cocaine and heroin trades. Senior Colombian officials, pleased at their success against the Cali drug lords, nevertheless predicted that the hydra effect would lead to a more dispersed and deadlier drug trade and to greater problems for neighboring countries.[37]

U.S. efforts to curb marijuana and poppy cultivation have generated similar hydralike responses. Drug-control campaigns against Turkish heroin production in the early 1970s helped stimulate the growth of the Mexican heroin industry, which subsequently became a major supplier to the U.S. market. Pressure on foreign marijuana producers in the late 1970s, especially in Mexico, succeeded only in causing production to expand into Colombia—and to increase in the United States. Marijuana is now a major cash crop in the United States, with 100,000 to 200,000 commercial growers and industry earnings estimated at billions of dollars annually.[38] Search-and-destroy missions against domestic marijuana cultivation confront the same obstacles as do Andean enforcement efforts. Farmers intercrop marijuana with corn in order to avoid detection by overflights. In response to DEA eradication campaigns launched in 1982, many growers have moved their marijuana cultivation indoors, or underground into large subterranean bunkers, to avoid discovery. As a result of this war on supply in the United States, indoor growers have developed high-technology techniques, permitting them to harvest greater yields of a more potent product.[39]

A U.S. military official trying to curb drug production and trafficking in South America summed up the problem: "There's an increasing sense that this is a holding action. We're not stopping drug supply because it moves. And we could never get the resources to shut down the whole hemisphere. The evidence is that we haven't affected price or supply. Is this the way we want to spend U.S. dollars? I think not."[40]

At the Borders: The Interdiction War

On 20 May 1991 the cargo ship *President Truman* docked in Oakland, California. Customs agents checking out minor inconsistencies in the ship's manifest found and seized 1,071 pounds of heroin from Southeast Asia's Golden Triangle; it would have sold for about $2.5 billion on the street.[41] Despite such victories, the United States continues to lose the drug-interdiction war.

The interdiction program is impressive. The DEA, the U.S. Customs Service, the Border Patrol, and other forces have joined with the U.S. military and have enlisted radar-equipped Navy warships, Air Force fighter planes, and AWACS radar aircraft in the effort. But consider what interdictors are up against. Each year 574,000 airplanes, 177,000 ships and boats, 118 million automobiles, and 422 million people cross our 12,000 miles of coastal and 7,500 miles of land borders. Each could be carrying well-hidden illicit drugs. Now consider this: four Boeing 747 cargo planes or thirteen trailer trucks loaded with cocaine could satisfy American demand for a year.[42] The problem of interdiction is further deepened by the fact that drugs such as cocaine and heroin are extremely difficult to detect. Because there are many ways to package and conceal drug supplies, interdiction is the proverbial search for a needle in a haystack. Not surprisingly, Customs and the DEA interdict no more than a small percentage of the drugs smuggled in every year.

The profit paradox undermines any effort to cope with this problem. Think back to the kilo of cocaine we traced above. That kilo will sell for between $1,900 and $2,500 in the Andes. Once it arrives in Miami, the same kilo will bring between $16,000 and $25,000 at the wholesale level, a 700–900 percent markup. Thus a 100-kilo shipment (220 pounds) will gross $1.6 to $2.5 million. At these profit levels, traffickers can afford to pay enormous sums to those who transport drugs: a cargo pilot can earn an estimated $250,000 for a 250-kilo shipment.[43] "Somebody is always going to take a chance for that kind of money," said one convicted smuggler. "We didn't care if we lost a bag or two. Even if we lost a whole load, it didn't mean anything."[44] The consequences for the interdiction war are sobering. As one top analyst in Congress's General Accounting Office (GAO) put it, "The enormous profits in cocaine trafficking make interdiction losses relatively inconsequential. . . . Given this huge profit

margin, it appears unlikely that interdiction will be a significant cost deterrent to traffickers, regardless of the surveillance support that DOD
[Department of Defense] provides."[45]

Even successful interdiction efforts are undermined by the hydra effect: new smuggling routes simply spring up elsewhere. In Southeast
Asia, for example, the success of antinarcotics efforts in discouraging
heroin trafficking from Burma through Thailand en route to the United
States encouraged the development of at least three major new routes,
according to State Department officials; the routes lead through Laos
and then through southern China, Cambodia, or Vietnam. "Trafficking
routes have spread like a cancer to all these countries," said Assistant
Secretary of State Robert Gelbard in 1995. Closer to home, U.S. officials
were proud of the significant drop in smuggling after intense cocaine-
interdiction efforts in southern Florida in the 1980s. But before long,
traffickers responded by shifting to air drops over the Caribbean Sea for
pickup by boat. When enforcers caught up with this tactic, traffickers
switched to new shipping routes through northern Mexico.[46]

Successes in marijuana interdiction have also triggered the hydra effect. By raising the cost of foreign marijuana, the drug war created the
equivalent of a tariff barrier. Protected from cheaper foreign imports, domestic producers dramatically expanded their operations. The success of
interdiction efforts also encouraged marijuana smugglers to switch from
shipping marijuana to transporting cocaine, which is less bulky per dollar value and therefore easier to conceal, as well as more profitable—and
far more dangerous to U.S. consumers.[47]

Equally maddening is the progressive innovation in smuggling techniques that has made detection increasingly difficult. In response to intensified air interdiction, for example, traffickers switched to containerized
cargo shipping, a form of transport that makes smuggling far more difficult to detect. Almost 9 million cargo containers enter the United States
each year through legitimate commercial channels. By one estimate, it
would take more than 65 million agent days to inspect them all, at a probable cost of $27 billion a year (without calculating the added costs of dis-
rupting international trade).[48] Moreover, traffickers have developed a range
of creative ways to conceal drugs. Cocaine supplies have been discovered
inside such imported items as batteries, mannequins, sneakers, surfboards,
fence posts, and even live animals, from boa constrictors to racehorses.[49]

The results, not surprisingly, confirm that interdiction has had little
impact on reducing availability or on raising the price of drugs in the
United States. In 1993, for example, the GAO found that "the portion

of the federal drug budget allocated to military surveillance has nearly quadrupled over the last 5 years, without measurable goals or results to show that the increases were warranted. . . . The fact is that adding military surveillance to the nation's interdiction efforts has not made a difference in our ability to reduce the flow of cocaine to American streets."[50]

Government leaders occasionally have acknowledged the limits of interdiction. "With borders like ours, [interdiction] as the main method of halting the drug problem in America is virtually impossible," President Reagan stated in 1981. "It's like carrying water in a sieve," he concluded, before adding that even so, it was important to continue the effort.[51]

The failures of the war on supply at the source and through interdiction are thus a product of two inherent flaws in the drug strategy. The profit paradox ensures that the same drug war strategies that seek to drive suppliers out of business also give these suppliers the profit incentives to keep the drugs flowing. And the hydra effect guarantees that the trade will move and adapt to escalating enforcement in ways that continue to confound drug warriors.

An even simpler economic logic damns the entire effort abroad and at the U.S. borders. In the final analysis, what matters is whether the drug war can raise the street price of drugs in the United States enough to discourage use. The basic economics of the drug market makes this impossible, as economist Peter Reuter has shown. Even unimaginable drug war successes at the source and at the borders, Reuter demonstrates, would not significantly affect drug prices on the streets—because most of the value added to the drugs (roughly 90 percent of the street price, in the case of cocaine) is imposed after the product arrives in the United States, reflecting the risks and costs created by domestic law enforcement.

Reuter has estimated that even an inconceivable 50 percent reduction in the Latin American cocaine supply destined for the United States would raise the street price by a paltry 3 percent. Significant successes in interdicting this cocaine on its way to the United States would also have a negligible impact, because smuggling costs account for less than 5 percent of the retail price. The bottom line is as inescapable as it is distressing: even dramatic increases in the amount of cocaine eradicated or interdicted would have at best a minimal effect on the final street price.[52]

On the Streets: The War at Home

In 1989 federal and local police followed up on a complaint by a Sylmar, California, resident about heavy late-night traffic at a warehouse in his neighborhood. They found the warehouse unguarded and protected with only a $6 lock. Inside was almost fourteen tons of cocaine, worth $6 to $7 billion on the street.[53] Major drug busts are reported regularly in newspapers across the country. Yet the United States continues to lose ground in the war against supply at home.

In hundreds of cities nationwide, police comb neighborhoods for hidden drug supplies and interrogate and arrest thousands of suspected dealers. Treasury Department agents work to prevent drug dealers from hiding their profits in shell companies and banks.[54] Homes, automobiles, and other assets are seized under forfeiture laws. Convictions mean jail time, under stiff mandatory sentencing laws. But the task is enormous.

Each year tens of thousands of drug importers, wholesalers, distributors, and dealers engage in hundreds of thousands of transactions. The effort to locate and catch domestic suppliers is further complicated by the skill of many of the professional crime organizations and gangs involved and by the fact that it is a collusive crime, in which both buyers and sellers have an interest in keeping the transaction secret.[55] The sheer size and character of the trade thus make the domestic law-enforcement task daunting. The profit paradox and the hydra effect make long-term success impossible.

If the high profits generated by the drug war have a paradoxical effect on the war on supply abroad, they have equally self-defeating effects at home. Consider again the kilo of cocaine we have tracked across the various stages of production and trafficking. Once it arrives in a city like Miami, that kilo (assuming 80 percent purity) can be bought at wholesale for between $16,000 and $25,000. It is then transported by couriers to regional wholesalers in other cities. They divide the kilos into pounds to sell to dealers, who then divide these into grams for sale to smaller dealers and so on to the ultimate consumer. At each stage profits are multiplied, so that the value of this kilo by the time it is diluted and sold on the street is between $70,000 and $300,000. A $25,000 kilo, for example, might be sold in two transactions of roughly one pound for $15,000 each, yielding a gross profit of 20 percent, or $5,000. The pound dealer might cut his pound to half purity by adding cheap diluents such as inositol or mannitol, and sell 32 ounces at $750 per ounce, grossing $24,000, a 60 percent profit. This ounce will yield about 14 grams, and if the gram dealers sell a gram for $100, they make $1,400 on each ounce, a gross profit of about 87 percent.[56]

Not only are the gross profits high, but the costs of doing business are relatively low. It costs very little to enter the local supply business—a small loan (which a larger dealer may provide), a beeper, maybe a gun, and a car. These low barriers to entry and the promise of quick profits draw a steady stream of new small-time dealers. Although the earnings for those at the bottom of the hierarchy are less than is generally assumed in the popular mythology of the street (the median weekly incomes for crack dealers in Washington, D.C., may only be as high as $700, according to a 1990 RAND report[57]), they are alluring, particularly in a context of poverty and low social mobility. It is not surprising that many inner-city young people, faced with dead-end, low-paying service-sector jobs, have joined the drug trade. As one drug dealer in the Bronx put it, "Hey, there's no work. You go looking for a job, they want to pay you $3.50 an hour. New York's expensive, man. You can't live on the breeze. That's why we're selling drugs."[58]

The obstacles confronting drug-control efforts are heightened by the domestic hydra effect: as soon as one supplier is picked up, others emerge to take his or her place. Police sweeps designed to clear streets and neighborhoods of drug dealers and to break up organized gangs in local areas thus have limited effects. Such efforts often make a real difference in the quality of life of those who live in the area; breaking up criminal organizations and clearing the streets can also give local residents a chance to organize themselves and develop ways to keep the violent, overt forms of trafficking out of their neighborhoods. But these enforcement successes are severely limited by their localized and temporary character: they often spread street dealing to other areas and lead to greater sophistication among dealers who are determined to reap the high profits of the drug trade. Frequently, dealers return once the police move on to another area.

Robert Stutman, for example, oversaw a major crackdown on cocaine dealing in Manhattan's Washington Heights neighborhood while he was head of the DEA's New York office. Despite impressive arrest figures, he concedes that the operation had little long-term impact on the availability of crack in the area. "There is no way for law enforcement to keep up the kind of pressure that we applied to Washington Heights," he says.[59]

Even in cases where local enforcement succeeds on a larger scale—in reducing the number of open-air drug markets citywide, for example—the impact of this success is limited because drug dealing may continue at the same levels but in new (and often less detectable) locations. "We put all these uniformed persons on the street. It's driven the people inside," claims Capt. Collin L. Younger, head of the narcotics division in

Washington, D.C. "If you drove around the city, you'd say this stuff is gone. It's not gone. It's going underground." In areas where small-time street dealing is diminishing, according to DEA spokesperson Camile Swanson, "there are more midlevel distributors selling multi-ounce and kilogram quantities. We are seeing more activity in the suburban areas."[60] Ultimately, law enforcement can do little to counter the domestic hydra effect that keeps agents chasing drug dealing from one area to the next. It is like "throwing sand against the tide," commented Joseph McNamara, retired chief of police in San Jose, California.[61]

Abroad, on U.S. borders, and at home, the war to limit the drug supply has failed on its own terms. Drug-control efforts have succeeded in raising the black-market price for drugs far higher than the price would be in a legal market—but they are not able to raise the price high enough to discourage millions of drug users from shopping in that black market. The failure has not been for lack of trying or for lack of increased skill and efficiency on the part of enforcement agents on the front lines. There have been many short-term successes in eradicating crops, seizing laboratories, interdicting shipments, and arresting and jailing dealers. But such improved efficiency does not add up to greater effectiveness in the drug war. It will never make a large enough dent in price and supply to significantly lower the current levels of abuse and addiction. The war on supply at home is doomed by the profit paradox and the hydra effect, flaws that are built into the economics of the black market created by the drug war itself. As the DEA's Stutman concluded from his experience trying to suppress crack cocaine, all the dealers and cartel leaders are "easily replaceable if America continues to have an insatiable appetite for drugs. No cop with a gun will ever stop the craving, no occupying army can shut off the flow."[62]

THE FLAW IN THE WAR AGAINST USERS

Since its inception, the war on drugs has focused primarily on the battles against growers, cartels, traffickers, and dealers described above. But the drug war is not just a war against supply. It is also a war against users.

The war against users is sometimes obscured by a public rhetoric that contrasts the punitive "supply side" of the drug strategy with more benign "demand-side" policies intended to discourage drug use through prevention and treatment. This simple way of configuring the drug problem and drug policies is popular in official and media circles, but it is deceptive. Prevention and treatment programs indeed embody a vital, non-punitive response to problems of abuse and addiction, but their role in the larger drug strategy is limited[63]—and is often overshadowed by the harsh, punitive policies toward drug use and abuse that make up the "other war," the demand-side war against users (see appendix 1).

The logic of the war against users is straightforward: strategies to make drugs scarce and costly in order to discourage consumption should be backed by sanctions against the consumers themselves. Fear of punishment will act as a deterrent by raising the risks of drug use and will thus lead them to less use and abuse.

The war against users has generally been a secondary front in the drug war, but it is an old and enduring one. The threat of punishment has been deployed against users since shortly after the 1914 Harrison Act, when addicts and others who possessed drugs were punished for buying or possessing cocaine or heroin without a prescription. Like the war on supply, the war on users has escalated in recent years.

Policies that target drug possession are in some ways a natural extension of the war against supply. Counternarcotics agents often arrest suppliers for possession of the drugs they intend to sell. If they were limited to catching dealers in the act of selling, enforcement would be even more difficult than it now is. During the 1980s only 25 to 30 percent of drug-violation arrests were for trafficking, whereas between 70 and 75 percent were for possession.[64]

Picking up people on possession charges, however, nets a mix of offenders—dealers intending to sell for a profit, user-dealers seeking to earn money to buy drugs for themselves, and users possessing drugs for personal use only. Laws that seek to punish dealers for possession fail to distinguish between dealers who sell for a profit and user-dealers who sell to buy drugs themselves, often because they are addicted. Criminal-justice experts emphasize that the drug war's failure to draw this distinction and to systematically provide treatment to addicts arrested for drug dealing feeds the cycle of addiction-based crime.

Laws against drug possession, moreover, have often targeted not only dealers but also the millions of Americans who possess drugs simply for personal use. Beginning in the early 1950s with the Boggs bill, the amounts subject to penalty have decreased as the penalties have increased—an escalation of the war not only on small dealers but on users themselves. Historically, certain policies have had the explicit aim of threatening and punishing users. In the early 1960s, for example, Alfred Lindesmith reports being in court when a defendant "charged with having used and had in his possession one marijuana cigarette during the noon hour" and with "no previous criminal record" was given a two-year sentence to "dry up his habit."[65] In the 1960s and 1970s the war against marijuana users became particularly intense; and by the end of the 1980s some 350,000 arrests were made each year for marijuana possession.[66]

In the late 1980s administration officials began to talk of zero tolerance—urging harsh measures against anyone who possessed even a small amount of drugs for personal use. In 1988 Republicans in Congress promoted user-accountability measures that directed strict punishments at those who used drugs, including fines of up to $10,000 for possession of personal-use amounts. Others sought a marked expansion in mandatory drug testing by pushing legislation that demanded drug-free workplaces. The Bush administration's national drug-control strategies confirmed the need to threaten and punish "casual users"—those with a "still-intact family, social, and work life" who are "likely to still 'enjoy'" a "drug for the pleasure it offers." The argument was that users who enjoy the effects of a drug, in effect, proselytize drug use, tempting innocent nonusers.[67]

This view justified a range of proposed sanctions against drug users, including the withholding of certain federal benefits, publication of users' names in local newspapers, suspension of drivers' licenses, "employer notification, overnight or weekend detention, eviction from public housing, or forfeiture of the cars they drive while purchasing drugs."[68]

In some areas enforcement in the war against users has been particularly harsh. Police forces in a number of cities have launched programs that specifically target those who buy drugs. Stringent laws against drug use by pregnant women have led to many arrests, often of poorer, minority women who are arrested when they seek medical attention at public hospitals or clinics.[69]

The results of the war against users are difficult to measure. Without question, fear works to dissuade some potential drug users. Indeed, it is tempting to attribute at least some of the decline in casual use of drugs to threats against users. But much of this decline may just as convincingly be attributed to increased preventive-education efforts in schools, communities, and the media—or to factors entirely unrelated to drug policies, including the increased emphasis on health in American society, fears produced by the AIDS epidemic, and recent demographic trends that demonstrate a decrease in the number of young people at greatest risk for initiation into drug use.[70] The downward trend in casual drug use, after all, was already evident in 1979, two to three years before the

Reagan drug war began in earnest; and in 1991, at the height of the recent drug wars, indicators pointed to new increases in casual drug use.[71]
Even more troubling, the persistence and increase in hard-core drug
abuse and addiction since the late 1970s do not suggest great success in
the war against users (see appendix 3).

The inherent limits to the war against users become clear when we
consider the two mechanisms through which it is presumed to work: the
threat of punishment is supposed to deter an individual from using drugs;
and once a user is caught, the infliction of punishment is supposed to
deter future use. The logic—based on behavior modification through
punishment—is simple. Behavioral psychologists have substantial evidence for this in animals: if you put a rat in a box and offer it rewards
(like food) for making one kind of movement and punishments (like elec-
tric shocks) for another, you can train it to move the way you want. Negatively reinforcing human behavior through punishment or its threat can
also alter some behaviors, if the severity of punishment is great enough
and if the threat of punishment is certain enough. But such shock-the-
rat policies are severely limited by costs and moral decency. More importantly, such policies fail to reflect the ways in which humans are different from rats and the ways drug use is different from other modifiable
behaviors. This *punish-to-deter* fallacy is the fatal flaw in the war against
drug users.

Practically speaking, the limits are severe. By the government's estimates, nearly half of the 24 million Americans who used illicit drugs in
1993 did so at least once a month.[72] To credibly threaten millions of
Americans with jail in order to discourage use or encourage treatment
would bankrupt our treasury and demand a draconian, authoritarian
system of police and prisons that is politically unacceptable. Other moral
implications are troubling, too: many users are suffering from addiction
and need medical treatment and social support; casual users who have
done no harm to others are suffering a punishment that does not fit the
crime and are likely to be harmed by a prison experience that exposes
them to serious and sometimes violent offenders.

Another practical issue arises here: how effectively does punishment
deter use? Evidence indicates that its deterrent effect—particularly on
addicted drug users—is dubious at best. The test case is prison: locking
up people who use drugs is about as severe a punishment as our democratic system is likely to impose. The record is not promising. Review-
ing the limited evidence available, Harry Wexler and his colleagues report that "two-thirds or more of arrested heroin abusers return to

heroin-cocaine use and their diverse criminal patterns within three months after release from detention." Jeffrey Fagen's study of thousands of drug offenders found not only that punishment failed to deter but also that "the probability of rearrest *increased* with the length of the sentence." "Findings from a number of studies," Patricia Erikson concludes, "consistently indicate that the perceived certainty and severity of punishment are insignificant factors in deterring use."[73]

Although imprisonment seems to do little to deter use, there is evidence that intensive treatment of incarcerated offenders with substance-abuse problems (estimated at as many as 60 to 80 percent of the one million Americans incarcerated) would cut drug abuse and dependence and lower recidivism. Only one in six inmates, however, receives any kind of treatment—and only 2 percent receive the serious and sustained attention necessary to address their addictions.[74] What is worse, the prison environment may actually encourage drug use. Drugs are readily available in most prisons, and many people who enter prison as nondrug users end up using drugs by the time they leave. One survey of state-prison inmates found that about half of the prisoners who had used illicit drugs did not consume drugs until after their first incarceration.[75]

For hard-core users, it is not surprising that the threat of punishment will have a limited effect. Many are suffering from other serious problems, and being punished is not an overriding concern for them. For example, according to the government's Alcohol, Drug Abuse, and Mental Health Administration, 53 percent of drug abusers have a diagnosable mental disorder.[76] Many hard-core users in inner cities are already leading such high-risk lives on the streets that prison is not perceived as a much riskier or more threatening alternative.

The limits of punishment as a deterrent are underlined by research on the factors that have led heavy users to quit without having been arrested or imprisoned. Evidence suggests that many have been led to control or give up their drug use because the toll on their personal relationships and home and work lives was too high, and the rewards for quitting were attractive.

A study in the early 1970s by Barry S. Brown explored the reasons heroin addicts started and stopped their drug use. It found that not one of the adult men and women mentioned concern about punishment as the reason for their first attempt to stop using heroin, and only 13 percent of the juvenile users did. Drug-related physical or family problems, the desire to change a life pattern, or the expense of maintaining a habit were much more commonly cited reasons.[77]

In a more recent study, Waldorf, Reinarman, and Murphy reviewed the lives of 228 heavy cocaine users. About half of the people they interviewed had quit. When asked what motivated them to stop using cocaine, these former users ranked fear of arrest well behind health problems, financial difficulties, problems at work, and pressure from a spouse or lover. Most importantly, the authors observed that "what keeps many heavy users from falling into the abyss of abuse, and what helps pull back those who do fall, is [a] *stake in conventional life*. Jobs, families, friends—the ingredients of a normal identity—turned out to be the ballast that allowed many users to control their use or to return from abuse to occasional, controlled use."[78]

The evidence does not indict punishment per se. The threat of punishment may be one useful tool in helping resolve problems of drug abuse and addiction. Someone whose job performance is suffering because of substance abuse or who is caught driving while intoxicated may only come to acknowledge a drug problem and to seek treatment when confronted with the loss of a job or a license. Similarly, someone ordered by a court to enter treatment after committing an addiction-based crime may be motivated to kick a drug habit by the fear of time behind bars. Such sanctions, penalties, and incentive systems are in some cases a legitimate and effective means of preventing or reducing crime and addressing drug abuse. But there is little evidence to suggest that punishment can ever succeed as the primary tool against drug use.

The deep flaw in the war against users is its conception of what motivates and constrains human action. The market model that underlies much of the war against users (with its imperative to reduce demand) often leads policymakers to think of people as little more than individual consumers with a particular want or desire—to satisfy a craving for illicit drugs. Taking this desire as a given, they ask: how can we make filling that desire so costly that this individual will not consume? Raising the price and increasing the risk of punishment will, it is hoped, discourage consumption despite the desire. But this notion of a person as primarily an individual consumer in the drug marketplace leads policymakers to avoid more important, if difficult, questions. Why do people want to take drugs in the first place? How are these desires created and sustained? What leads people to moderate their use or to quit?

What those behind the war on drug users miss is that people are much more than isolated, atomistic consumers responding to risks, prices, and other forces of the marketplace—just as they are far more than isolated rats in cages responding to rewards and shocks. They are social beings who are shaped above all by a context of families, friends, neighbor-hoods, peer groups, jobs, and often ethnic or religious communities. As researchers have observed, this context deeply affects when, how, and where people use drugs, their ability to moderate drug use, and their ability to overcome abuse and addiction.[79]

Any strategy that makes fear, threats, and punishment its primary weapons in a war against drug use is thus doomed to fail. The profit paradox and the hydra effect similarly undercut the war against supply. Together, these three fatal flaws ensure that the war on drugs can never succeed.

Not acknowledging the fundamental flaws in the drug war leads many policymakers, law-enforcement officials, and members of the public down one of two blind alleys: they may conclude either that more effort (increases in resources, political will, efficiency) or that programmatic changes at the margins (a little more focus on local police, a little less on foreign supply) will make the critical difference, finally reversing the record of failure. Either conclusion, however, leads around a vicious circle, fueling the cycle of escalation and failure in the fight against drugs. A politics of sustaining or escalating the same basic policies in the face of a fatally flawed strategy is a politics of denial.

The mistaken belief that the failing drug strategy is somehow fixable is not the only myth that feeds the drug war. Another well-intended but misguided response to failure is also common: we may not be winning the war on drugs, but we have to do something about the drug problem, so why not keep trying a little longer—at least we are not doing any damage. Buried in this argument is another dangerous myth—that the drug war itself does little or no harm.

3   The Collateral Damage
of the War on Drugs

The drug war is not only a flawed strategy but a costly one. Measured in dollars, the price of persisting in a failed policy is staggering, topping $8 billion in federal drug enforcement (and another $12 billion in state and local enforcement) each year. The human toll is not so easily measured; it includes the legacy of drug problems left unsolved, of continued abuse and addiction, with the attendant human wreckage of broken families and blighted neighborhoods. But there are also other, far less obvious harms that are rarely considered when the costs and benefits of continuing the current course are weighed. The failure to consider these harms is part of the politics of denial.

The drug war, like any war, inflicts collateral damage. In military conflicts, collateral damage mounts when civilians are unintentionally killed, injured, or displaced and when schools and hospitals are inadvertently destroyed. The collateral costs of the drug war are the unintended harms imposed on innocent citizens and valued institutions.

Three kinds of collateral damage merit attention. First, the drug war exacerbates many crime and health problems rather than alleviating them. Second, it tears at our social fabric by deepening racial and class divisions. Third, it corrodes democratic institutions and values. In each case the evidence of the damage is not new; it is the stuff of daily news stories. What is often obscured, however, are the ways in which the cause of the damage is a direct consequence of the drug war strategy itself. Denying these collateral costs helps perpetuate the failed and flawed war on drugs.

EXACERBATING DRUG-RELATED PROBLEMS

The collateral damage of the drug war is obfuscated by a misleading turn of phrase at the heart of drug war talk—the notion of "drug-related" problems. Discussions of drug-related problems generally lump together a cluster of concerns that include serious drug abuse, crack-exposed babies, AIDS cases linked to intravenous drug use, crimes committed by crack or heroin addicts, harassment by street-corner drug dealers, shootouts between drug gangs, and the slaying of innocent bystanders. Rarely is a critical distinction drawn: some of these drug-related problems are in fact caused by the drugs themselves; but many are created, or seriously exacerbated, by drug policies.[1]

Promoting Crime

Consider drug-related crime. The phrase is so familiar that few Americans stop to think through its meaning: many people simply see crime as a drug problem and drugs as a crime problem. But what is it about drugs that is related to crime? The phrase "drug-related" implies that drug use itself causes crime. Some drugs, particularly alcohol and cocaine, can, in certain doses and in certain people, trigger or exacerbate aggressive or violent behavior; others, such as marijuana and heroin, generally do not.[2] But most of what is called drug-related crime is actually the result not of taking drugs but of the conditions under which people buy and sell drugs. And these conditions are the product of drug policies.

The idea that drug policies create or exacerbate crime is counterintuitive and deserves closer attention. In fact, three kinds of drug-related crime can be distinguished. Each is either a product of or is aggravated by the drug war. The first and most obvious category is the crime of drug use and possession. By far the largest single class of "drug criminals" is created by policies that impose criminal sanctions on the millions of people who possess or use drugs—regardless of whether they have committed crimes against anyone else. This obscures the extent and nature of drug-related crime. In the late 1970s eleven states decriminalized the possession of small amounts of marijuana. By the stroke of a legislative pen, hundreds of thousands of marijuana users were no longer criminals. When criminalization of marijuana possession was reenacted in these states in the 1980s, "crime" rates suddenly shot up.

It is the other two categories of crime, however, that most often come to mind in discussions of drug-related crime: crimes, such as robberies and break-ins, that are committed by drug users, and violent crimes, such as drive-by shootings, that are committed by drug dealers. Both are a consequence of the black market created by the war on drugs and of the incentives the war creates for both buyers and sellers to commit crimes.

Current drug policies give many buyers an incentive to turn to *addiction-based* crime. Drugs that would be relatively inexpensive if they were legal are made much more expensive by drug policies. Heavy users and addicts without sufficient income sources may commit crimes—including burglary, robbery, and drug dealing—to obtain the money to support their habits. In the early 1970s heroin users spent an average of $35 a day to support their habits; many who were unemployed or held low-paying jobs turned to such crimes to foot the bill.[3] President Nixon understood this when he provided major federal support for a methadone-maintenance treatment program, justifying it as a crime-fighting policy. Addicts who could obtain methadone free at public clinics not only would be more likely to break their heroin addiction but also would have much less reason to steal money or deal drugs in order to buy heroin. The strategy succeeded in reducing crime.[4]

Drug policies also encourage sellers to turn to *trade-based* crime. Much like the case of alcohol prohibition earlier in the century, the steep and illegal profits created by prohibitionist policies make it necessary for dealers to compete underground, where they defend their market position against other traffickers—and law enforcers—with guns. Drug dealers cannot ask the courts and police for protection against competitors or for assistance in settling potentially violent conflicts. "Tough law enforcement may break up those criminal enterprises that traffic in drugs," writes James Q. Wilson, "but it may also make such enterprises more skilled, more ruthless, and more dangerous. The more profitable drug sales are, the greater the incentive dealers have to protect their profits by arming themselves against rivals, forcibly maintaining discipline among subordinates, and corrupting or otherwise resisting the criminal justice system."[5]

The contradiction at the heart of the fight against drug-related crime is painfully evident: the very policies that seek to raise the black-market price of drugs to discourage use are, at the same time, encouraging increases in addiction-based crime[6] and generating the wholesale violence of trade-based crime. Much of what we fear and condemn as drug-related crime is in fact the product of our drug policies, not of the substances themselves.

Undermining Public Health

The war on drugs exacerbates other drug-related problems as well, notably threats to public health. AIDS is one example. The link between AIDS and drug use is familiar and disturbing. By late 1993 one-third of the 339,000 AIDS cases reported to the U.S. Centers for Disease Control and Prevention were associated directly or indirectly with injecting heroin, cocaine, or both.[7] Fifty percent of the 200,000 intravenous drug users in New York City tested positive for the human immunodeficiency virus (HIV).[8] Children born to HIV-positive drug users or their infected partners also suffer. AIDS is now one of the ten most common causes of death among American children under the age of five. In New York State it is the second leading cause of death among black children under the age of five and the leading cause of death among Hispanic children of that age.[9]

How do our drug policies make these health problems worse? The vector of responsibility seems simple: if there were no heroin users, the spread of AIDS (and other drug-related diseases, such as hepatitis B) would decline. But it is neither the drug nor its use that is spreading the virus; rather, it is the fact that the drug is injected into the veins and that many drug users share hypodermic syringes. Sharing these contaminated needles passes the HIV virus from an infected user to an uninfected one. Once a user is HIV-infected, she or he can pass the disease on to sexual partners, and infected women can pass it on to babies they bear. A major factor that leads to this deadly practice of needle sharing is the drug war.

In twelve states, including most of those with major heroin problems, drug policies make possession of syringes without a prescription illegal.[10] Addicts are left with little alternative but to reuse and share contaminated needles.[11] Several countries in Europe and Australia, in contrast, have elected not to punish drug use or forbid needles and instead allow addicts to exchange contaminated syringes for sterile ones, provide regular medical examinations and referrals to hospitals, distribute condoms, and offer methadone maintenance. The AIDS epidemic is far less severe in each of these countries.[12]

Infants suffering from the effects of drug exposure in the womb represent another health problem aggravated by current drug policies.[13] Drug war policies in many states exacerbate health risks such as fetal cocaine syndrome by threatening pregnant drug-dependent women with punishment. In some states, women who use drugs during pregnancy face arrest and conviction; in others, newborns who test positive, and their siblings, may be placed in state custody.[14] The justification is that sanctions will dissuade the women from using illicit drugs while they are pregnant. But such policies discourage drug-dependent mothers from seeking treatment and prenatal care. As Dr. Ira J. Chasnoff, founder and president of the National Association of Perinatal Addiction Research and Education in Chicago, points out, "Treatment programs for pregnant addicts are scarce enough; prosecutions only scare addicts away from seeking even basic prenatal care, for fear they'll be turned in."[15]

Drug policies also exacerbate health problems that are directly linked to addiction. The war on supply has often had the unintended effect of encouraging drug suppliers to turn to more profitable, higher potency, and more hazardous drugs.[16] The black market generated by drug policies also means that purity and content are unregulated. The result is far more—and far more deadly—drug overdoses. Ethan Nadelmann writes, "People overdose [on heroin] because they don't know what they're getting; they don't know if the heroin is 1 percent or 40 percent, or if it is cut with bad stuff, or if it is heroin at all. . . . Just imagine if every time you picked up a bottle of wine, you didn't know whether it was 8 percent alcohol or 80 percent alcohol. Imagine if every time you took an aspirin, you didn't know if it was 5 milligrams or 500 milligrams."[17] In 1993 there were almost 467,000 drug-related hospital emergency-room visits; drug overdoses were the reason for more than half of these (see appendix 3).[18]

The conclusion is troubling: in too many instances, the drug war is creating or aggravating precisely those crime and health problems it claims to solve. The burden of this collateral damage does not fall evenly on all segments of society. This points to a second hidden cost of the failed drug war: its discriminating impact along lines of race and class.

DEEPENING RACE AND CLASS DIVISIONS

It is no secret that problems related to drug abuse are particularly prevalent in urban, low-income, often black or Hispanic neighborhoods; that inner-city hospitals handle twice as many drug-related emergencies as do suburban ones; that black patients are admitted at three times the rate of white patients;[19] and that AIDS spread through contaminated needles is having a disproportionately devastating effect on minority communities.[20] Nor is it a secret that the vast majority of both petty theft and deadly violence related to the drug trade and drug war occurs in poor

urban areas and that African Americans and Hispanic Americans disproportionately fill the nation's jails, often for drug offenses.

What is rarely recognized, however, is that these conditions are not
simply a reflection of urban poverty in the United States; nor are they
simply the by-product of decades of government neglect, although
grossly inadequate social policies have set the stage for current conditions. A more proximate and insidious catalyst is the logic of the drug
war strategy: when a war against supply and users collides with the social conditions of inner cities, it will inevitably end up being a war against
the poor and minorities. And it will inevitably aggravate the conditions
that encourage drug abuse, addiction, and dealing in the first place.

The drug war is designed to raise prices and discourage use, through
a strategy of tough enforcement. In virtually any setting, as we saw in
the last chapter, this logic dooms the strategy to failure. But in a setting
of urban poverty, it does far more than fail.

Carrying out a war against supply in the inner city creates a powerful vacuum pump that draws poor and minority citizens into the lucrative trade itself—and then into the criminal-justice system. The pattern
is rooted in the deteriorating social conditions of the inner cities in recent decades. Deindustrialization in the 1970s and 1980s meant a loss
of exactly the kinds of blue-collar jobs that had provided less-educated
workers with a path upward, while the new jobs created either demanded
a level of skill and education beyond the reach of inner-city residents or
offered low-paid, part-time employment at best. By the end of the 1980s
the average poor black or Hispanic family was subsisting at more than
$5,000 below the federal poverty line. As unemployment and under-
employment increased in the 1980s, so too did cutbacks in health and
social services. Diseases such as tuberculosis spread, infant mortality increased, and drug abuse spiraled upward in many urban areas. Cutbacks
in federal housing support for the poor combined with skyrocketing
housing costs to create a crisis in low-income housing, breaking up communities by forcing many residents to search for new places to live while
condemning others to homelessness.[21]

The economic attraction of drug dealing for inner-city residents is not
surprising. The causal link between decaying conditions in the inner cities
and increased drug abuse, however, is neither direct nor mechanistic. It
is the product of a complex relationship long observed by substance-
abuse counselors across lines of race and class: alcohol and drug abuse
discriminate, seeking out and settling in homes and communities already
weakened by family instability, financial insecurity, and hopelessness.

Most inner-city residents hold jobs, raise families, and avoid drugs despite the hardships and closed opportunity structures they face. But for others, the stress and insecurity of daily life and work (or its lack), in the context of insufficient health, educational, and child-care services, make the turn to drug use more likely, while inadequate prevention and treatment services increase the chances that use will become abuse and that abuse will become addiction.[22] Worsening drug abuse and addiction, in turn, further exacerbate the social problems created by inner-city conditions, weakening families and local communities, making it difficult for drug-dependent individuals to get jobs, and discouraging new businesses—and employers—from moving into drug-saturated areas.

The impact of a drug war waged under these conditions has been to harden and widen the fault lines of class and race that lacerate, divide, and debilitate American society. In outcome if not in intent, the antidrug battle has been waged more intensely and more ruthlessly against African Americans, Hispanic Americans, and the poor.

The Face of Drug War Discrimination

The evidence of systematic racial bias in the drug war emerges in data on drug arrests and sentences. Hard-core use and its consequences may be more severe in the inner cities, but the overall drug-use figures for 1990 reported by the National Institute on Drug Abuse (NIDA) show that whites made up 77 percent of the estimated 13 million regular users of illegal drugs; blacks, 15 percent.[23] Furthermore, the participation of African Americans in the drug trade is not greater than that of whites. Although statistics do not analyze drug dealers by race before they are arrested, former DEA chief Robert Bonner has argued that it is "probably safe to say whites themselves would be in the majority of traffickers."[24]

Yet by 1991 blacks were four times as likely to be arrested as were whites on drug charges[25]—and in states such as Florida, Illinois, Massachusetts, Michigan, New Jersey, and Pennsylvania, the drug-arrest rate for blacks was seven to nine times as high as that for whites.[26] The proportion of blacks arrested increased steadily as the drug war escalated throughout the 1980s. Blacks, about 12 percent of the population, accounted for about 10 percent of all drug arrests in 1984, 40 percent in 1988, and 42 percent in 1990.[27]

Racial bias not only appears in arrests but also in sentences. Studies by the U.S. Sentencing Commission (created by Congress in 1984 to reform sentencing guidelines) and others show that black drug defendants receive considerably longer average prison terms than do whites who commit comparable crimes.[28] The conclusion is clear: although blacks are a minority of drug users and dealers, they constitute the majority of those who are arrested, convicted, and harshly sentenced for drug-related offenses.

The statistics provide a numerical summation of countless acts of discrimination and abuse. The face of the drug war, residents attest, is harsher and more violent in inner cities than in largely white, middle-class neighborhoods. It is not uncommon to witness street sweeps, in which everyone in sight is rounded up for interrogation and is searched without any evidence of wrongdoing, or to encounter routine and aggressive searches of apartments in public-housing projects, often without warrants. After one street sweep in Washington, D.C., in 1989, an agent from the Bureau of Alcohol, Tobacco and Firearms explained: "This is definitely not a method you'd want to use in Georgetown or out in the suburbs. But in a neighborhood like this we knew the probability was great that out of every ten people we detained, at least six or seven would be in some kind of trouble with the law. That was our thinking. It was that kind of neighborhood."[29]

As important as the individual cases of injustice are the ripple effects of a discriminatory drug war. Consider the fact that in Washington, D.C., on any given day 42 percent of all black men between the ages of eighteen and thirty-five are in prison, on probation or parole, out on bond, or sought by the police.[30] The existence of criminal records makes it that much more difficult for them to secure jobs or to raise and support families. "Employers will not touch anyone who has been tainted by the criminal-justice system," explained Ron Mincy at the Urban Institute in Washington. This is a major factor contributing to the large number of female-headed households and to high black poverty rates. Other effects are more subtle. "What does it do for a child to go and visit his father in a lockup?" asks Rev. Graylan Ellis-Hagler, pastor of the Church of the United Community in Boston's Roxbury neighborhood, who frequently visits black men in state prisons. "It becomes part of how they view the world. In a sense, you begin to create other generations of occupants."[31]

The Logic of Drug War Discrimination

As disturbing as this evidence may be, it is neither new nor surprising to many Americans. But what many observers fail to recognize is that the

pattern of drug war discrimination against the poor and minorities is virtually inevitable, given the logic and strategy of the war on drugs within
today's urban context.

The artificially high price of drugs created by the drug war necessarily puts low-income addicts at a disadvantage. A heroin user on Wall
Street can easily absorb the drug's steep prices, but an addict in Harlem
may turn to theft or other desperate measures to satisfy the same craving: thus the spiral of burglary, robbery, drug-related prostitution, and
other addiction-based crimes. And whereas the Wall Street addict can retreat to the privacy of home or office for a fix, his Harlem counterpart
is consigned to more visible and dangerous shooting galleries, where he
is prey not only to disease but also to semiregular searches by police seeking users and dealers wherever they can find them: thus the attendant
rise in arrests and imprisonment of low-income addicts.

Black-market prices do more than create problems for those who are
drug-dependent. They also create enormous profits, which translate into
incentives for drug dealing. In the context of the steep economic decline
of American inner cities, the drug war has given rise to an underground
industry capable of offering jobs, money, and status to thousands of unemployed or underemployed residents. Given the high profits created by
the policy, argues Clarence Lusane, poor black communities provide "a
ready-made distribution network of existing or easily created street
gangs of unemployed youth who could retail crack and other drugs. . . .
As a result . . . the illegal narcotics industry has become a major (perhaps the major) employer of Black youth."[32] It is not simply the money
that is attractive to inner-city youth: the fact that the jobs are challenging, often risky, and demand entrepreneurial skills also makes them more
attractive than menial jobs that may be available. Robert Armstrong, executive director of the Omaha Housing Authority, commented that in
his city, "[drug] gangs are offering opportunities to people who have
been left out of the mainstream. . . . What the gangs have done is taken
these same individuals, and shown them how to conduct business. . . .
The gangs are willing to do what no one else is: train these kids."[33]

Drug-enforcement policies not only combine with inner-city conditions to create a ready pool of street-level dealers but also help to ensure
that visible retail drug markets remain concentrated in these neighborhoods. The assault on crack-cocaine dealing at the national, state, and
local levels during the drug wars of the mid- to late 1980s, for example,
had a particularly pernicious effect on inner-city communities. Mark
Kleiman points out that escalating enforcement pressure in those years

channeled crack retailing into "high-crime, largely minority population, inner-city neighborhoods. The stream of automobiles with white drivers and suburban registrations that flowed through those neighborhoods, each pausing only long enough for their occupants to make a purchase, demonstrates that crack dealing is far more concentrated geographically than crack consumption."[34]

This creates a pattern in which the wholesale drug industry—the big-time dealers—are located outside poor urban neighborhoods, while these neighborhoods become the distribution centers of the less profitable and more competitive retail market. Former New York City Police Commissioner (and Clinton drug czar) Lee Brown explained the different levels of distribution: "There are those who bring drugs into the country. That's not the black community. Then you have the wholesalers, those who distribute them once they get there, and as a rule that's not the black community. Where you find the blacks is in the street dealing."[35]

Dire social conditions are thus compounded by a drug war that helps channel the retail trade into poor and minority neighborhoods. Add to this mix a third factor—thousands of law-enforcement officials and prosecutors who are desperately attempting to implement a flawed drug strategy against suppliers and users—and the formula for a grossly discriminatory drug war is complete. These conditions guarantee that poor and minority residents will be netted by the drug-enforcement system in highly disproportionate numbers. Racial discrimination need not be the intent of any law-enforcement official or policymaker, but it will be the effect. Lee Brown pinpointed the factors that generate a bias in minority arrests:

> When you look at the drug issue, you have to look at how and where the arrests are made. In most large cities, the police focus their attention on where they see conspicuous drug use—street-corner drug sales—and where they get the most complaints. Conspicuous drug use is generally in your low-income neighborhoods that generally turn out to be your minority neighborhoods. . . . It's easier for police to make an arrest when you have people selling drugs on the street corner than those who are [selling or buying drugs] in the suburbs or in office buildings. The end result is that more blacks are arrested than whites because of the relative ease in making those arrests.[36]

Other law-enforcement officials confirm this dynamic. St. Paul Police Chief William Finney explained that because his force is capable only of scratching the surface of drug activity, it targets the most visible segment: "We are ill-equipped to do more than arrest drug dealers that we see in the act," he said, adding, "We don't say, 'Let's go out and arrest a bunch of black folks.'" But the result is that 62 percent of those arrested on drug charges in St. Paul in 1991 were black, in a population that is only 7 percent black.[37]

The pattern of racial bias extends to drug prosecutions and sentences as well. The vast majority of drug offenders prosecuted in federal courts—and thus subject to harsh federal mandatory minimum sentences—are African American or Latino: in fact, a U.S. Sentencing Commission survey in 1992 shows that fully half the federal court districts that handled crack cases prosecuted *only* minorities.

Federal attorneys defend themselves against charges of discrimination by pointing to the logic and limits of the drug strategy: federal agents charged with curbing drug dealing on tight budgets are forced to target crack dealers "in the communities in which those traffickers are predominantly found—the African American and Latino communities. . . . It is this that explains the absence of federal Caucasian [crack] cocaine defendants." They have not staked out white neighborhoods, agents explain, because they can make many more arrests in the inner city with much less effort. This means that white dealers are more likely to be overlooked or to be picked up by local (rather than federal) agents—and thus channeled to state courts in which federal mandatory minimums do not apply. The result is a profound racial disparity in sentencing: in Los Angeles "black and Latino crack dealers," reported the *Los Angeles Times*, "are hammered with 10-year mandatory federal sentences while whites prosecuted in state court face a maximum of five years and often receive no more than a year in jail."[38]

The collateral damage in urban areas promises to increase with the periodic but predictable attempts by policymakers to respond to failure by getting tougher. The Bush administration's 1989 proposals to evict "first-time and casual users" from public housing, notify their employers, and suspend them from school, for example, had far more dire implications for inner-city residents than for suburban dwellers.[39] Policies that throw inner-city residents out of school, work, and homes may aim to deter drug use, but their deeper impact will be to further close the already limited opportunity structure that encourages drug use and dealing in the first place.

The Politics of Fear and Intolerance

The prime battlefront in the drug war against poor blacks and Hispanics may be the inner city, but its impact is not limited to those neighborhoods. The cumulative effect of years of discriminatory drug policies has been to entrench and deepen society-wide divisions between rich and poor, black, Hispanic, and white—and to fuel a politics of fear, anger, and intolerance.

The record of discrimination in the drug war has elicited outrage among black leaders. "It just shows how deep racism is institutionalized in American criminal justice," Jesse Jackson concluded. "It's racist, that's the bottom line," according to Rep. Charles Rangel (D-New York). Allen Webster, president of the National Bar Association, the nation's largest black legal group, sees the mounting black drug arrests as "astonishing." "Basically, it's a war against minorities." "It's almost legal genocide," charged A. J. Kramer, chief of the federal public defender's office in Washington, D.C. "We're locking up an entire generation of young black Americans." "You'd almost have to be blind not to see the time bomb we're creating," concluded former Newark, N.J., Police Director Hubert Williams.[40]

For many African Americans the resentment has turned bitter. Given the consequences of the drug war, it is understandable that many, in the words of Samuel Meyers, "believe that national drug policies are not just misguided, but intentionally directed to achieve a horrible result: the elimination of a superfluous pool of already marginalized segments of the black population. Some have argued that drugs and drug polices in the United States are the moral equivalent of genocide."[41] The contention is not simply an abstract argument but something many African Americans experience on a daily basis. In his examination of the racial implications of the drug war, *USA Today* reporter Sam Vincent Meddis wrote:

> Many blacks say skin color alone makes them automatic suspects for police— whether they're guilty or not. The result? An us vs. them mentality and what critics say are overly aggressive police tactics with the black community in urban areas nationwide. "I guarantee you I can get arrested this weekend driving in certain neighborhoods in this city at certain times of the day," says black civil rights lawyer Steven Belton of Minneapolis, in a comment echoed by many other blacks. "They're not stopping expensive foreign cars with white male drivers over 40."[42]

"The psychological toll [of the drug war] for African-American men is that we constantly have to be on guard—we always fit 'the description,'" says Norvell Laurent of the Twin Cities Coalition for Police Accountability.[43] As the toll mounts, there will also be, according to author Claude Brown, "increased hostility and suspicion of national policy-makers by black leaders, accompanied by some increasing acceptance by some of the black genocide conspiracy theory."[44]

It is not surprising that many citizens read intention into the discriminatory outcomes of the war on drugs. Those who want to argue that an objective of the drug war is to carry out a race war can certainly find evidence in American history in which punitive drug policies were supported by groups seeking to suppress racial and ethnic minorities. Earlier in this century, nativist and racist groups systematically targeted opium, because it was smoked by Chinese immigrants; cocaine, because it allegedly induced blacks to crime, rape, and violence; and marijuana, because of its purported crime-causing effects on Mexican immigrants.

Some Americans doubtless approach today's war on drugs with similar motives. Reinarman and Levine argue that the drug scare promoted by the media and politicians in the mid- and late 1980s began in earnest only when cocaine use, in the form of crack, spread from the middle classes into urban ghettos and "became visible among this 'threatening' group" of inner-city black and Hispanic young people.[45] Diana Gordon writes persuasively that continued support for the failed drug war can in part be explained by racial fears: many Americans see it as a way to control racial and ethnic minorities and other "dangerous classes."[46] Yet as the argument above demonstrates, regardless of whether the drug war is *intended* to be a race and class war, the *effect* of waging war on drugs in an inner-city context will be to divide and degrade along lines of race and class.

As apprehension and anger rise within the African American community, the drug war grips white citizens, too, with a fear and distrust of minority groups, particularly those in poor, inner-city communities. White Americans read the statistics splashed across the newspapers and erroneously conclude that drugs and drug-related crime are primarily the problems of—or even the responsibility of—blacks and Hispanics. The assumptions are reinforced by powerful media images. One congressional report concludes "Media and police characterizations of the nation's African American communities being overrun by drug addicts and drug trafficking stigmatize these communities as victims of a drug war. But the war is not of their own making."[47] "When you watch television," observes Lee Brown, "that's what you see: the African-American with his hands cuffed behind him being put into a patrol car. The media should accept some of the responsibility for that image."[48]

Discriminatory drug war policies at once reflect and entrench the deeply rooted race and class biases in American society and politics. The spiral of fear and intolerance triggered by the war on drugs is another hidden cost of continuing to pursue a failed drug strategy. It is a cost we all bear, if not in equal measure. The politics of fear and hatred fueled by the drug war forces us, as a society, to rely more on force, fear, and repression and less on reason, trust, and the democratic process to maintain civil order. By exacerbating social divisions and deepening disorder and insecurity, the drug war feeds a repressive response against entire communities and a fear and enmity between social groups. The collateral damage to the fabric of our social and political institutions, moreover, is not limited to the impact of the drug war on race and class relations.

THE HIDDEN INJURIES TO THE AMERICAN DEMOCRATIC SYSTEM

The collateral costs of the drug war described above—spiraling levels of crime and disease, division and discrimination along lines of race and class—are disturbing enough. But there is another cost to continuing the war on drugs. It is a toll that mounts incrementally but often imperceptibly, one that most Americans do not realize they are paying. It is the way in which the war on drugs threatens and undermines long-standing democratic values and traditions.

News stories detailing the excesses and abuses of the drug war are familiar. Drug-enforcement agents detain and search drug-dealing suspects without warrants. A local police force charged with fighting the drug war makes profits rather than arrests, as drug corruption spreads. A young woman with no criminal record receives a mandatory minimum sentence of more than a decade in prison for transporting a small amount of drugs for a relative. The reactions to these stories vary. They may be applauded as the kind of drastic action appropriate to confront the drug crisis. They may be regretted as an unfortunate but necessary price to pay to fight the war on drugs. But in general they are shrugged off as isolated incidents, a result of an oversight or poor judgment by an individual officer or judge; and their harmful impact is seen as limited to the small number of citizens who are directly involved in the incident.

Such drug war abuses, however, are not isolated. They are not simply a matter of individual error. Nor are they a matter of just a few corrupt policemen, judges, or federal drug agents. They are in part a product of the drug war itself: the current strategy creates enormous and systematic pressures for abuse at every level. What is more, the impact of these

abuses reaches well beyond the few unfortunate people directly involved
in each incident. The cumulative effect of such actions on the American
democratic system is "harm by a thousand cuts." How deep or permanent that harm will be is difficult to predict, but the effects must be
weighed in any evaluation of the drug war strategy.

The pattern becomes clear when we look at three basic premises of
the American democratic system, each of which is undermined by the
war on drugs. The first is that individual rights are protected in our democratic system. The second is that our democratic system safeguards us
from serious abuses of power by public officials. And the third is that
the democratic process produces fair and reasonable laws that are impartially enforced. Few Americans would argue that any of these principles is fully realized today. But most would agree that they are valued
tenets of our system—and that our policies should uphold them, not
undermine them. And most would concur that to the extent that these
principles are violated systematically, everyone loses.

A "Drug Exception" to the Bill of Rights?

In May 1994 thirteen Boston police officers burst into the home of
seventy-five-year-old retired minister Accelyne Williams in a surprise
drug raid. The unarmed Williams fled to his bedroom, where he
crouched, frightened, in a corner until he was handcuffed for resisting
arrest. The incident caused a fit of vomiting and then a fatal heart attack. No drugs were found.[49]

In the 1989 lightning raid on one block of Park Road in Washington,
D.C., agents from the Bureau of Alcohol, Tobacco and Firearms arrived
with AR–15 semiautomatic assault rifles and short-barreled shotguns.
The agents, some of whom were helmeted and masked, ordered every
bystander in the strike zone to "freeze" in a stationary position ("No
one is allowed to move on this street. No one!"). Twenty male and fe-
male suspects near or in one apartment building were rounded up, laid
face down on the sidewalk, and searched. A computer check was done
on their records. An hour later, all but one were let go.[50]

What is at stake here is not simply the personal harm to those arrested, or the ineffectiveness of the tactic. Also at stake is the Fourth
Amendment right to protection from unlawful search and seizure. All
U.S. citizens have a right to assume that police will not detain or harass
them at will: police are required by law to obtain search warrants or
show probable cause before searching and arresting someone.

It would be easy to blame these violations of constitutional rights on individual law-enforcement agents. But the problem runs deeper than that: the logic of the drug war creates extraordinary pressures to circumvent or transgress such constitutional rights. To conduct the war against supply, law-enforcement officials must carry out the almost impossible task of first locating and then seizing hundreds of thousands of traffickers, dealers, and their drug supplies. The crimes are largely well hidden. No one involved in the acts of possessing, buying, or selling drugs is likely to report the crimes, let alone bring charges. The potential targets of a drug raid will disappear if they know or suspect the police are coming—and they are likely to return after the police leave.

The problems inherent in finding and seizing so many elusive targets create a rationale for speed, secrecy, and the element of surprise— unannounced raids on drug suspects or frequent surprise street sweeps such as the one described above. Such enforcement tactics are made much more difficult by the need to obtain search warrants, to show probable cause, or to protect other legal rights. "By demanding that police do a job that cannot be done effectively without violating constitutional rights," argues law professor Randy E. Barnett, our drug laws "ensure that more constitutional rights will be violated."[51]

The pattern of circumvention and violation extends to a wide range of domestic drug war tactics: individuals are picked up simply because they fit a drug-courier profile created as a guide for police; drug offenders are denied the right to legal counsel.[52] Each abuse is a rational response by frustrated law-enforcement officials to an infeasible task; each is a threat to fundamental principles of constitutional democracy. Taken individually, these abuses often appear limited in impact and innocent enough. But taken together they risk creating what Steven Wisotsky has called a "drug exception" to the Bill of Rights.[53] Supreme Court Justice Hugo Black recognized the danger: "Narcotics traffic can too easily cause threats to our basic liberties by making attractive the adoption of constitutionally forbidden shortcuts that might suppress and blot out more quickly the unpopular and dangerous conduct."[54]

What is more, the harm caused by these constitutional abuses reaches well beyond those involved in the drug trade. The Reverend Williams in Boston, the nineteen people who happened to be on Park Road in Washington, D.C., at the time of the drug raid: these are a fraction of the innocent citizens whose rights have been caught in the cross fire of the drug war. Many more citizens, moreover, stand to lose from the spillover effect. The damage to individual rights that began with the drug war is no

longer limited to drug enforcement. Civil liberties attorney Harvey Sil-
verglate of Boston concludes that "the way the courts treat drug cases is
leaching over into the way they treat criminal cases in general. The
seizure of suspects' assets before trial and the easing of requirements for
searches and of the rules of evidence all started in drug cases and spread
to other matters."[55]

Drug Corruption and the Abuse of Power

In the early 1990s five police officers from Harlem's 30th Precinct were
assigned to a neighborhood unit. Local residents provided tips on who
was dealing drugs and where. But instead of using the information to
make arrests, the officers used it to reap profits.[56] By the time New York
City's "Dirty 30" scandal crested in late 1994, twenty-nine officers from
the precinct had been arrested on charges ranging from drug conspiracy
to lying under oath. The episode in the 30th Precinct was only the lat-
est: scandal had erupted in Brooklyn's 73rd Precinct in 1992 and in the
77th Precinct in 1987.[57]

The story is familiar: drug corruption in federal and local agencies has
made headlines from New York City to Los Angeles to Miami in recent
years: "Greed, Drug Dealers Bring Down Top Federal Agent"; "Ex-
Guardsman: I Stole, Sold Drug-Fight Plans"; "Metro Police 'Lost' Drugs
Stored in Property Room"; "Drug Probe in Navy Snares Nearly 40 Here;
Cases Involved Some in Presidential Unit"; "Former DEA Agent Gets
5-Year Sentence."[58]

Ultimately, the responsibility must be laid at the feet of individual officers who put private gain before public duty. But a less proximate and
more disturbing source of drug corruption also exists: our current drug
strategy creates enormous opportunities and incentives for corruption,
thus making such abuses much more likely.[59] The problem is the character of the black market, with its high profits, and the collusion among
producers, sellers, and buyers.[60] The very laws that create this black market put law-enforcement agents in the position to trade their enforcement power for the extraordinary payoffs drug dealers can afford to
make. On the front lines of the drug war, these officials possess "a highly
marketable service—the sale of nonenforcement of the law."[61] And the
more effective law enforcers are in fighting the dealers, the greater the
bribes the dealers will offer.

How do these incentives work, in concrete terms? The secrecy and
complicity of drug crimes ensure that the only officials who are likely to

know of a drug crime are the agents who conduct investigations—and if they choose not to complete an inquiry or make an arrest (in return for a payoff), only the drug dealers will be the wiser. So some agents simply "neglect" their duties. "If you look the other way," a fellow officer told former Los Angeles narcotics detective Robert Sobel when he joined the unit, "I can make you a rich man." Sobel made $140,000 over two years.[62] Sometimes the corruption involves more direct involvement: agents may give dealers information on informants and surveillance operations, sell favorable testimony at a hearing or a trial, rob drug dealers' profits, or resell seized drugs.[63]

The incentives for corruption are increased by attempts to crack down harder on the drug trade. Serious cases of corruption have emerged prominently during times of drug war escalation. In the late 1960s, as Nixon's drug war was heating up, corruption became so pervasive in the New York City office of the Bureau of Narcotics and Dangerous Drugs that almost every agent was fired, transferred, or forced to resign. In the early 1970s the Knapp Commission exposed pervasive corruption in the New York City Police Department's narcotics section. Indeed, J. Edgar Hoover resisted the entry of the Federal Bureau of Investigation (FBI) into drug-related investigations for years, partly because he feared the corrupting influence it would have on his agents. As the drug war escalated in the 1980s and early 1990s, the impact of this corruption was again deeply felt: Harlem's "Dirty 30" was a case in point. The 1994 Mollen Commission report concluded that a more vicious form of corruption had replaced the bribery schemes that had plagued the New York City Police Department a generation before, with police now "acting as criminals, especially in connection with the drug trade."[64]

The implications are clear: creating a drug war apparatus riddled with operations that are free from routine public scrutiny—and in which tens of thousands of dollars can secretly pass into the pockets of law enforcers in return for violating the law—encourages the abuse of power.

Who is hurt by such corruption? At first glance, only the drug dealers and trafficking organizations seem to pay a price. In the words of one agent, a Los Angeles corruption scheme amounted to "informal taxation of the Colombian cartels."[65] A closer look at the pattern, however, shows that the damage runs far deeper.

A principle is at stake, one that seals a fragile bond of trust between communities and those who serve them. The principle is the rule of law. The American democratic system assumes that power corrupts and tries to correct for this tendency by ensuring that the power of public officials is checked by impartially enforced laws and regulations. When these democratic checks are undermined (by the incentives and lack of scrutiny created by the drug war, for example), the danger increases that officials will abuse their authority and violate the rights of the citizens they serve—for private gain or other purposes. When that happens, the citizens' confidence is in jeopardy.

The impact of such violations is immediate. Months after New York City's "Dirty 30" scandal broke, the precinct chief spoke to Harlem residents in a church basement. His officers had arrested eighteen suspected dealers in the preceding five weeks, he reported proudly; murders were down; and drug arrests had risen 53 percent. But the bonds of trust were not so easily mended. Several residents heckled and rolled their eyes. One woman shouted, "Residents of the 30th Precinct have been victimized by the police!" "It was a deep betrayal," concluded Pastor Lenton Gunn Jr. "It will be a long time before the policemen of the 30th will be trusted."[66]

Nor is the impact limited to local neighborhoods. The barrage of local and national headlines feeds a broader public cynicism. Drug-corruption scandals, explained the chief and deputy chief counsels for the Mollen Commission, "can destroy the public confidence and credibility the police need to fight crime. When jurors disbelieve police testimony and citizens lose faith in their cops, the fight against crime becomes tougher still."[67] Such an erosion of citizen confidence risks further damage. If police come to feel isolated from those they serve and to sense that they are obeyed out of fear, not respect and legitimacy, an important internal restraint on their arbitrary or self-serving exercise of power is removed.

Drugs and the Threat to Criminal Justice

Nineteen-year-old Brenda Valencia drove her aunt to a drug dealer's home in Palm Beach County, Florida. She was arrested, convicted, and sentenced under mandatory sentencing laws to more than twelve years in prison, even though she had no prior convictions and there was no evidence that she was involved in selling drugs. The injustice of the drug law that condemned Valencia was not lost on Federal District Judge Jose Gonzales Jr., who sentenced her; the sentence was, he declared, "an outrage."[68]

Sadly, such outrages are not uncommon. They are the direct result of the get-tough response to the failed drug war. As harsh penalties fail to cut supply and raise prices, federal and state lawmakers have legislated increasingly harsh mandatory minimum sentences requiring judges to impose rigid, no-escape sentences for certain drug offenses. The Anti-Drug Abuse Act of 1986, for example, requires ten-year sentences for 11 pounds of cocaine, 2.2 pounds of heroin, or 1.7 ounces of crack; in a 1988 law, Congress mandated a federal minimum sentence of five years without parole for a first offender convicted of possessing just five grams of crack cocaine—an amount that weighs about as much as a quarter and is worth a few hundred dollars on the street.[69]

The result is that the punishments meted out in the drug war often do not fit the crime. Mandatory sentences for particular drug offenses mean that judges can no longer take into consideration the particular circumstances of the offense or the character and history of the accused. Harsh sentences are given to nonviolent, often first-time offenders.[70] U.S. District Judge Richard A. Gadbois handed down a mandatory ten-year prison sentence to a mother of four on a limited income, who was paid $52 to mail a package that—unbeknown to her—contained crack. "This woman does not belong in prison for 10 years," Gadbois said. "That's just crazy." Judge J. Lawrence Irving of Federal District Court in San Diego quit the bench in 1991 over the tough sentencing laws: "You've got murderers who get out sooner than some kid who did some stupid thing with drugs. . . . These sentences are Draconian. It's a tragedy."[71]

Judge Irving is not alone in denouncing these sentences as unjust. Ninety-two percent of U.S. federal judges have registered their opposition.[72] Mandatory minimums are opposed by the American Bar Association (ABA) and by the U.S. Sentencing Commission; in 1993 Attorney General Janet Reno also voiced criticism and ordered a Department of Justice evaluation.[73]

Who is harmed by such abuses? Only individuals who are unwise or unfortunate enough to become caught in the tangled web of the drug trade? Certainly the Brenda Valencias of this world pay a high price—and there are many like her. But again, the collateral damage of the drug war has a longer reach. Here too, a principle is at stake. Our democratic lawmaking process is supposed to produce fair laws; our democratic judicial system is supposed to inflict fair punishments. On this principle hangs the fairness of the legal system as a whole. When the system works, we assume that citizens' collective judgments about acts of wrongdoing will be largely reflected in our laws and our punishments: murder, for example, will be punished more severely than will burglary. When a policy—such as the drug war's mandatory minimum sentences—

undermines this principle, the system is distorted: drug possession becomes a more heinous crime than rape, robbery, or even murder; and the Brenda Valencias are hunted and punished more aggressively than are the violent criminals from whom we most need protection.

Concretely, the high price we pay translates into a serious drug war–generated overload on our criminal-justice system. By 1990 drug cases accounted for 44 percent of all criminal trials and 50 percent of criminal appeals.[74] In the courts the result has been overburdened prosecutors and public defenders and overcrowded court dockets. The large volume of cases means that the court system is in a perpetual state of crisis, trying to process far more drug offenses than it can possibly absorb.

The prison system is similarly overloaded. The dramatic increase in the number of Americans imprisoned in recent years has made the United States the world's number-one jailor, and much of the overload is a consequence of the drug war. Drug offenders as a percentage of inmates in federal prisons increased from 25 percent in 1980 to 61 percent in 1993, and state and local prisons are also facing heavy burdens.[75]

The overload of the criminal-justice system generates the distortion of justice described above. Because mandatory minimums force judges to jail guilty drug offenders, those who have committed more serious crimes (including murder and rape) may end up with lighter sentences. There is simply not enough space for everyone convicted, and those receiving mandatory sentences are given spaces first. Between 1980 and 1990 the average sentence imposed for robbery, rape, and kidnapping fell, while the average drug sentence almost doubled, and the proportion of persons imprisoned for drug offenses increased while those imprisoned for violent crime decreased.[76]

The overcrowding of prisons has led many states to pass cap laws that limit inmate populations. Under these regulations, every time a new drug violator is imprisoned in a facility that has reached its cap, someone else must be freed. Thus an individual imprisoned for drug possession may force the release of another individual convicted of a crime perhaps as serious as rape or murder. Miami Drug Court Judge Stanley Goldstein explained: "Our prisons are so overcrowded, we end up releasing really violent guys doing time for robbery or assault to make room for others."[77] San Francisco Sheriff Michael Hennessey put the problem bluntly: "We desperately need the limited space in our nation's jails and prisons to house violent offenders, not minor league dope addicts and dealers."[78]

Justice under the law will always be an unrealized American principle. But the mandatory and ever-harsher sentences against users and dealers—a response to the continued failure of the punitive strategy of the drug war—are widening the gap between the reality and the ideal of justice. Harsh sentences for nonviolent, first-time offenders; violent criminals being released to make room for people guilty of possessing drugs— the drug war makes a mockery of just laws and impartial enforcement.

CONCLUSION

If we total the price we pay for continuing a failed and fatally flawed drug war, it becomes clear that the nation's drug users and dealers are not the only people who are suffering the consequences of this punitive strategy. We all pay a high price for the health and crime costs exacerbated or created by drug war policies. The twin burdens of substance abuse and poverty, compounded by a discriminatory and ineffective drug war, are shouldered by communities in our inner cities, and their burdens are generating deeper social divisions within our society. Democratic institutions and values we ought to be strengthening, meanwhile, are being corroded.

The collateral costs of the war on drugs are often overlooked. Or blame for such problems is placed on drugs themselves, on deeper social problems, or on the poor judgment of drug-enforcement agents. Such factors undoubtedly contribute. But what is routinely denied are the roots of the collateral damage in the logic—if not the intention—of the war on drugs.

It may be tempting to brush aside the drug war's collateral damage as a necessary trade-off—a needed sacrifice if we are to win the war. But this is a dangerous illusion, because the war against supply and users will never be won. Seizures and arrests may increase, prices may fluctuate, casual use may decline, but the drug war strategy itself is fatally flawed: it cannot boost drug prices, reduce their availability, or raise the risk of use enough to put drugs out of the reach of most Americans. Nor can it significantly ameliorate drug abuse and dependence. As long as the drug war continues, therefore, the collateral damage will mount and the sacrifices will have been in vain. And because failure is built into the punitive drug war strategy, there will be pressure to persevere in this madness. Denying the fatal flaws and the collateral damage, the response to continued failure will be stubborn persistence and at times escalation.

Why this pattern of denial? If the war against the drug supply and drug users is fatally flawed and is also causing serious collateral damage, why has the response of policymakers—backed by the public—been to escalate rather than reevaluate the strategy?

It would be comforting if simple exposure of more facts and analysis were the key to a change in public thinking and public policy. In fact, most of the information is already widely available. The real question is why most policymakers and much of the public are unwilling or unable to confront the evidence. Why is it that public officials presume that incremental increases in sanctions will eventually reverse the pattern of failure and significantly reduce levels of supply and addiction? Why is the collateral damage of the drug war kept off the political agenda, and why are those who do cite these concerns routinely disparaged as defeatists or considered "soft on drugs"? Why has it become conventional wisdom that getting tough on drugs is the best way to deal with the nation's drug problems?

Confronting our national denial of a flawed and costly drug war is difficult. The ways of thinking that misguide us are deeply embedded in our political culture and institutions. They became entrenched because individuals and groups with power fought to make them dominant and keep them that way. And they became rooted in political institutions and bureaucracies with vested interests in continuing the pattern. Changing course demands making sense of this politics of denial.

PART TWO

Paradigms, Power, and the Politics of Denial

Suppose we approached the proverbial "average American" to ask her reaction to a new government plan. For $8 billion a year, the federal government would fund a system in which millions of ill and suffering Americans would receive little care but would instead be forced underground into criminal activity because of their health problems. These Americans would help finance a violent black-market network extending from their neighborhoods all the way to the Third World. Every effort of the government to bring the criminal activity under control would help guarantee the persistence and in some cases expansion of the black market, spreading crime to new areas. Before long, this system would crowd our courts and prisons with those who suffered from health problems and those who preyed off of them. Posed this way, such an insane scheme would earn the support of few Americans. Yet we saw in Part 1 that this is exactly the kind of costly and harmful drug war policy that has persisted for decades. In Part 2 we aim to figure out why.

At the height of President Bush's drug war, *Harper's* editor Lewis Lapham wrote that "the premise of the war is so patently false, and the hope for victory so obviously futile, that I can make sense of it only by asking the rhetorical question *cui bono?* who stands to gain by virtue of Bush's lovely little war, and what must the rest of us pay as tribute?"[1] Lapham's suspicion is a common one. Someone powerful must be benefiting from the continuing drug war, and those powerful interests help explain its persistence. The suspicion has led some analysts to search out the deeper foreign- or domestic-policy interests served by a continuing, if failing, war on drugs.[2] It is difficult, however, to pin the persistence of the drug war on a particular set of interests, because the war has been perpetuated for more than eight decades by both political parties and by presidents with diverse interests.

Lapham's own explanation is a more subtle one, emphasizing the symbolic benefits the drug war bestows on politicians:

> The war against drugs provides them [politicians] with something to say that offends nobody, requires them to do nothing difficult, and allows them to postpone, perhaps indefinitely, the more urgent and specific questions about the state of the nation's schools, housing, employment opportunities for young black men—i.e., the condition to which drug addiction speaks as a tragic symptom, not a cause. They remain safe in the knowledge that they might as well be denouncing Satan or the rain, and so they can direct the voices of prerecorded blame at metaphors and apparitions. . . . The war on drugs thus becomes the perfect war for people who would rather not fight a war, a war in which the politicians who stand so fearlessly on the side of the good, the true and the beautiful need do nothing else but strike noble poses as protectors of the people and defenders of the public trust.[3]

The claim contains an element of truth: the drug war is indeed about defending and reaffirming symbols far more than it is about substance abuse and health issues. Diana Gordon argues persuasively that many politicians manipulate these symbols to gain and acquire power. They are able to do so because behind the symbols lie popular concerns about particular groups—minorities, immigrants, youth, cultural liberals. Controlling drugs is often about controlling these groups—who are blamed for social disorder, material insecurity, and family instability—and is thus about deflecting attention from the deeper roots of social problems.[4]

Identifying the symbolic character of the drug war helps us understand why its failure to deal with real drug problems and the collateral damage it inflicts are often denied. Yet this conclusion leaves important questions unanswered. Where did the symbols of the drug war come from, and how did they come to assume so much power? Why did these and not other symbols become dominant? What sustains them, and what would it take to change them? Understanding the politics of denial demands a response to such questions. Central to our answer are the notions of paradigm, power, and political struggle.

For our purposes, a paradigm may be understood as a framework of reigning ideas and values that guides conventional wisdom on a particular issue. A dominant paradigm functions much like a pair of eyeglasses, leading us to see certain things and dismiss or distort others. Often unconscious that we are wearing these lenses, we assume we are perceiving and responding in the only logical—or even imaginable—way. Historically, shifts in a dominant paradigm have led to profoundly new ways of understanding previously unquestioned phenomena.

A classic example is the pre-fifteenth-century belief that the earth was the center of the universe and that the sun and other planets revolved around the earth. This was seen not as one "theory" among others but as simple fact, confirmed by the everyday experience of watching the sun move across the sky; it was simply "the way things were." The "Copernican Revolution"—bitterly resisted by the religious and scientific communities—eventually changed the dominant paradigm, placing the sun at the center of the universe and permanently transforming our understandings of the universe, the world, and our role within it.[5]

Many Americans approach questions of drug use and drug policy with standard-issue drug war eyeglasses, made of lenses crafted from particular beliefs and values rooted in American political culture. When they hear the word narcotics, they hear danger and crime; when they see someone who is drug dependent, they see an "addict" and a lawbreaker. When they think about addiction, they assume a bad choice by an ignorant or misguided person; when they hear she has been punished, they think she deserved the punishment. When they consider how the government should respond, they think "get tough"; and when the problem does not improve, they conclude that more force and more threats are needed.

Different eyeglasses, to continue the metaphor, might be devised out of lenses ground from other elements in American political culture—pragmatism, free choice, a concern to protect the vulnerable and disadvantaged among us. In chapter 4 we see that the punitive drug war paradigm took hold only in the early twentieth century, and in Part 3, we examine two very different drug paradigms, the legalization paradigm and the public-health paradigm.

The punitive paradigm plays a critical role in shaping the nation's debate, strategy, and policies on drugs. As the dominant paradigm, it informs the conventional wisdom about drugs. It tells a causal story that provides a particular definition of the drug problem (how to stop all use of illicit drugs), posits the source of the problem (drugs are too cheap and easily available), and suggests the appropriate solution (coercion and punishment).[6] By fashioning conventional wisdom, the paradigm also shapes the drug war strategy adopted by national leaders. The strategy translates the problem defined by the paradigm into a coherent policy plan: make it difficult for individuals to consume drugs by making them scarce, raising their price, and making it risky to buy or possess them—thus the war against supply and the war against users described in Part 1. Drug war policies then define the particular instruments that are used to carry out the strategy: they determine where and how to try to cut supply, what kinds of sanctions should be imposed, which smugglers and dealers should be targeted, and what punishment drug users should be made to suffer.

A closer study of the drug war reveals that these policies have varied significantly over the past century. Thus historian David Musto, in his classic *The American Disease,* emphasizes the often cyclical character of the American concern about drugs—the swings back and forth between periods of great intolerance, inflammatory rhetoric, and severe enforcement and periods of less enforcement, less public attention, and greater tolerance.[7]

Since the early 1900s, however, an extraordinary continuity in the drug war strategy and the punitive paradigm beneath it has underlain these changing policies. This persistence is our concern in Part 2: where did this punitive paradigm and drug war strategy come from, and what sustains them? These questions take us first to history and then to contemporary politics.

We turn to history not because we think another history of drugs in America is needed; excellent historical accounts of drug policy, including Musto's work, are already available. Rather, we plumb the past to understand the ways in which ideas and institutions that today seem given and unchangeable were actually created by earlier political struggles.

These political battles over drugs were fought out in the context of competing strands in American political culture. The punitive paradigm is drawn primarily from one deep vein: the streak of moral self-righteousness that led to zealous crusades against corruption and vice long before the struggle over drugs.[8] But this self-righteousness is not the whole of American culture, and other strands might have grounded other paradigms. The thread of pragmatic realism (try it; if it does not work, change it) in American political culture might have encouraged a more scientific, perhaps medical approach to addiction. The deeply held values many Americans share about the importance of free choice and their antipathy toward state authority could have anchored a more libertarian—or a legalization—paradigm. Conversely, the expectation among Americans that the state should provide for public safety and welfare could have rooted a paradigm of state regulation of drug markets.

The punitive paradigm thus became dominant not simply because of America's cultural traditions but also as a result of a struggle among powerful actors, particularly well-organized social groups, the drug-control bureaucracy established to carry out the government strategy, and elected officials. Chapters 4 and 5 tell this story of cultural and political conflict and development. Once the punitive paradigm became dominant, it set the agenda for continued drug war policies—and continued failure. We see in chapters 6, 7, and 8, finally, that the decisions and actions of key institutional actors—presidents, members of Congress, bureaucrats, and the electorate—are what have continued to fuel the politics of denial.

4 The Punitive Paradigm

The Early Struggles, 1900–1930

To many Americans, certain ideas about drugs such as cocaine and heroin seem commonsensical: that use of these drugs is wrong or dangerous; that ingesting or distributing them is criminal; that seeking to eliminate their supply is sensible; and that relying primarily on punitive law enforcement is the most effective way to stop consumption and dealing. But this set of ideas has not always held sway in the United States.

In 1900 opium and its derivatives morphine and heroin, cocaine, and cannabis (marijuana) were all legal substances, readily available to anyone who wanted to acquire them. Not only were they prescribed by doctors to relieve pain and sleeplessness, but they could be purchased in grocery and general stores as well as by mail order. They were found in numerous unregulated patent medicines, claiming to cure everything from stomach aches to head colds to corns. Cocaine was a favorite ingredient of soda pop (Coca-Cola until 1903), medicine, and wines. The Parke Davis Company "sold coca-leaf cigarettes and coca cheroots [cigars] to accompany their other products, which provided cocaine in a variety of media such as a liqueur-like alcohol mixture called Coca Cordial, tablets, hypodermic injections, ointment, and sprays."[1] The 1897 Sears Roebuck catalog offered hypodermic kits—a syringe, two needles, two vials of morphine, and a carrying case—for $1.50.[2]

The common use of such drugs led to problems of addiction. In 1895 informed estimates placed the number of Americans addicted to morphine at 2 to 4 percent of the population.[3] A small percentage of addicts—especially those who were black (in the South) or Chinese (in the West)—were considered social pariahs and were feared. But most addicts in the latter half of the century were middle or upper class, with women outnumbering men. Called habitués, these addicts were not stigmatized. They were not thought of as degenerates and certainly not as criminals. The idea that a national policy was needed to handle problems of addiction—let alone that such addicts should be punished under federal law—was nowhere in evidence. Rather, "the victim was regarded as one afflicted with a physiological problem, in much the same way as we presently regard the need of a diabetic for insulin. . . . His acquaintances and his community could know of his addiction, feel somewhat sorry for his dependence upon *medication,* but admit him to a position of respect and authority."[4]

By the 1930s, however, all this had changed. Drug use was publicly condemned. Support was widespread for prohibition and for punishing those who sold, possessed, or used heroin or cocaine. Drugs and crime were tightly linked in the public mind; drug users and dealers alike were seen as threats to society. Stopping all drug use and curbing the supply of drugs were unquestioned as goals of government policy; and punitive law enforcement was seen as the sine qua non for accomplishing this mission.

Over time, these ideas about drugs and drug policy hardened into a conventional wisdom that frames our present understanding and response to drugs and drug problems. Protracted political struggles beginning early in the twentieth century established a punitive, prohibitionist paradigm, setting the agenda for subsequent public-policy debate on drugs in America.

PRAGMATISTS VERSUS CRUSADERS

By the early 1900s concern about drug use was rising, although it did not generate the same organized fervor as did alcohol consumption.[5] Groups in the medical community, reformers in the Progressive Movement, moralistic antivice crusaders, muckraking journalists, and racist and nativist groups who feared that America would be mongrelized and contaminated by drug-consuming "inferior peoples" were all intent on establishing some kind of regimen for drug control. Their various struggles merged in the early decades of this century to forge a new public judgment on drug use.

Physicians had begun to pay attention to the problems of addiction in the aftermath of the Civil War, when wounded soldiers who were given morphine for pain became addicted in large numbers. But warnings about the dangers of drug abuse were not reflected in medical-school curricula and textbooks until the turn of the century. Of particular concern were the problems that resulted from the casual prescription of drugs to relieve aches and pains and from consumers' unwary exposure to these substances in popular patent medicines with unlabeled contents.

The emerging medical professions, anxious to protect their members' interests, argued that medical officials should regulate the supply of drugs and decide what treatments were appropriate. In 1903 the American Pharmaceutical Association said that cocaine and opium derivatives should be given only under prescription and that laws should regulate—but not prohibit—drug use.

The aim must be to "prevent the creation of drug habits, rather than to reform those who are already enslaved, however desirable that latter might be," concluded the American Pharmaceutical Association's lawyer-pharmacist James H. Beal in 1903. Habitual users should not be prohibited from using these drugs if a "lawfully authorized practitioner" deemed them "necessary for the treatment of such habit."[6]

Pragmatic reformers in the Progressive Movement joined the doctors and pharmacists. Seeking to protect the public interest against greedy corporations and corrupt politicians, they echoed the medical community's call for close regulation of patent medicines. "Gullible America," wrote one muckraking journalist, "will spend this year $75 million in the purchase of patent medicines. . . . It will swallow huge quantities of alcohol, an appalling amount of opiates and narcotics, a wide assortment of varied drugs ranging from powerful and dangerous heart depressants to insidious liver stimulants; and, far in excess of other ingredients, undiluted fraud."[7]

The efforts of the reformers and the medical community paid off in the enactment of the Pure Food and Drug Act of 1906, which required that all narcotic ingredients, as well as cannabis, be listed on the labels of any patent medicines shipped in interstate commerce. The legislation dramatically reduced the patent-medicine market.

Health and professional interests were not the only concerns that motivated drug reform. An explicitly antidrug crusade had also emerged as part of a broader movement against vice—drinking, gambling, prostitution—at the turn of the century. It was rooted in a puritanical strain in American culture that demanded that public control be exercised to foster moral and upright behavior. The antivice crusade was intensified by concerns that rapid urbanization in the early twentieth century was corrupting the family and undermining traditional values.[8] "The morbid craving of morphia," railed one commentator, "ranks amongst the category of other human passions, such as smoking, gambling, greediness for profit, and sexual excesses."[9] These moralistic crusades were often based on the beliefs of rural nineteenth-century Methodism, Baptism, Presbyterianism, and Congregationalism, which "emphasized individual human toil and self-sufficiency, while designating the use of intoxicants as an unwholesome surrender to the evils of an urban morality."[10]

Since they first emerged, moreover, antidrug crusades in the United States have been linked to deep-seated racist and nativist fears. The campaign against vice and urban immorality at the turn of the century was fueled in part by widespread concerns that the wave of immigration from eastern and southern Europe between 1880 and 1917 threatened America's moral (and economic) well-being. Crusaders insisted that the power of government be enlisted to protect America's moral superiority and progress. For some this meant protecting vulnerable racial minorities as well as "old-stock" society from the temptation of drugs—which led to criminality, immorality, and death—by seeking to ban these habit-forming products. In its less genteel form, the fear "that immigrant narcotics consumption would undermine cherished values"[11] was combined with violent prejudices against blacks, Chinese, and Mexicans to spur local antidrug laws aimed specifically at these minorities.

In the South, for example, cocaine was linked to deep-rooted prejudices against blacks. Its euphoric and stimulating qualities were feared for their presumed ability to make Negro cocaine users "oblivious of their prescribed bounds" and to lead them to "attack white society."[12] There were accusations that cocaine use "gave blacks superhuman strength, improved their marksmanship, and made them difficult to kill."[13]

The West saw a parallel campaign against Chinese immigrants. In 1875 San Francisco forbade opium smoking, a practice closely identified with Chinese Americans. Between 1877 and 1900 antiopium legislation was enacted in eleven western states. A 1902 American Federation of Labor (AFL) pamphlet foreshadowed what decades later would become a widely accepted "contagion" theory. Chinese opium smokers had spread the "deathly habit" to "hundreds, aye thousands, of our American boys and girls," the AFL declared, demanding, "Is it right or just to knowingly expose our children . . . to such dangerous contamination."[14]

Those who pressed for narcotics controls did not always win without a struggle. Both the motives and the effects of the new bans were questioned. In assessing the constitutionality of an opium-prohibition measure, an appellate court in Oregon openly acknowledged the racial prejudice that motivated the ban, concluding: "Smoking opium is not our vice, and therefore, it may be that this legislation proceeds more from a desire to vex and annoy the 'Heathen Chinese' in this respect, than to protect the people from the evil habit."[15]

Despite the widespread antidrug rhetoric and the local bans, opium smoking and the use of other drugs did not disappear. Users either went underground or were tolerated in limited locations. Antinarcotics groups reacted by pressing Congress to restrict supply at the national level. In 1883 the tariff on opium had been raised; four years later restrictions were imposed on the importation of some forms of opium, and Chinese immigrants were prohibited from any importation of the drug; and in 1890 the manufacture of smoking opium was limited to American citizens. Not surprisingly, these efforts also failed to stop the trade; instead, they stimulated smuggling.[16]

MISSIONARY DIPLOMACY

The drive for a more punitive drug strategy was propelled by other forces at work abroad. Since the late 1800s American missionaries in China had been appalled at what they saw as the moral and social degeneration resulting from the British opium trade. They circulated horror stories of opium's impact back home and began to urge the government to take a leading role in an international effort to control or eliminate drug trafficking. In a symbolic gesture of support the Senate passed Henry Cabot Lodge's resolution in 1901 calling for international action to ban the sale of opium and alcohol to "aboriginal tribes and uncivilized races."[17]

The full impact of missionary diplomacy became evident after 1898, when the United States gained control of the Philippines in the Spanish-American War. The United States was suddenly faced with the question of what to do about narcotics addiction in the territory: under Spanish rule, addicts had been licensed and opium was provided to them legally. The War Department turned to the Right Reverend Charles Brent, the Episcopal bishop in the Philippines. Bishop Brent saw the problem as a moral issue above all, and one of global concern. He convinced President Theodore Roosevelt to call an international conference on regulating the opium trade in 1906.[18] Perhaps more important than their impact abroad, the resulting meetings (in Shanghai and The Hague) became vehicles for organizing a campaign for stricter drug control in the United States.

In 1909, for example, Secretary of State Elihu Root convinced Congress to ban the importation of all forms of smoking opium in order to secure "legislation on this subject in time to save our face in the conference at Shanghai."[19] Other prohibitionists wanted much more. Spearheading the campaign was Dr. Hamilton Wright, who had joined Brent in representing the United States at the international conferences. Wright and others argued that Washington should not only support an international agreement to ban the production, export, and use of cocaine and opium abroad but should also pass federal legislation to ban all imports of these drugs. Such prohibitions, they hoped, would reduce supply, thereby reducing the domestic drug problem. They were quick to join their campaign to the rising domestic tide of racist fears about narcotics and their effects. Wright drafted a bill and persuaded House Foreign Affairs chair David Foster (R-Vermont) to introduce it in 1910. Wright then used the ominous conclusion of the Shanghai Commission to win the support of southern Democrats, who were hesitant to cede to Washington police powers reserved to the states: "It has been authoritatively stated that cocaine is often the direct incentive to the crime of rape by the Negroes of the South and other sections of the country."[20]

In 1910 the Foster antinarcotics bill was seen as a radical measure and was opposed by the medical and pharmaceutical communities. Health professionals were open to the idea of regulation but not to outright prohibition. Wright fought against compromising, and the bill never made it out of the committee.

THE HARRISON NARCOTICS ACT

Conditions had changed by 1914. At home the antidrug crusaders had been promoting their agenda to an increasingly receptive public and were preparing for a pitched battle over legislation. Dr. Charles B. Towns, who wrote widely for the cause, warned his readers that they would find "solid and organized opposition to any bill restricting the sale of habit-forming drugs."[21] Dr. Wright, meanwhile, continued to push tirelessly for restrictive legislation and skillfully recruited the secretary of state and the secretary of the treasury in the effort.[22] Avid in his support of prohibitionist and missionary pursuits, Secretary of State William Jennings Bryan pressed for passage of legislation to meet the requirements of the international agreements the State Department supported.[23]

Rep. Francis Burton Harrison (D-New York) eventually agreed to sponsor legislation. In the wake of a reported near tripling in the use of opium between 1870 and 1909,[24] he expressed a now-familiar logic for control of the drug supply: "This enormous increase in the importation of and consumption of opium in the United States is startling and is directly due to the facility with which opium may be imported, manufactured into its various derivatives and preparations, and placed within the reach of the individual. There has been in this country an almost shameless traffic in these drugs. Criminal classes have been created, and the use of the drugs with much accompanying moral and economic degradation is widespread among the upper classes of society. We are an opium-consuming nation today."[25]

Harrison's initial draft resembled the defeated Foster bill and was received with a similar storm of opposition, just as Towns had predicted. But a new draft emerged, as all sides now proved willing to compromise. The major pharmaceutical associations accepted the need to control narcotics, although they were opposed to the harsh penalties, complex record-keeping procedures, and the ban on even small amounts of narcotics in patent medicines in the earlier Foster bill. The drug industry and the medical profession also played a major role in shaping the bill, exacting assurances important to their interests: "The medical practitioner was assured that his professional duties would not be infringed upon, and the drug industry salvaged many of its cough and other medicines from control."[26] Even producers of patent medicines would be limited only in the amount they could put in their concoctions.

There was no mass movement, as in alcohol prohibition, to support Harrison's bill; nor was there broad public opposition. Public opinion had gradually swung to accept the view that addiction was a problem and that it was legitimate to control drugs. And, unlike alcohol users before and during Prohibition, cocaine and heroin users mounted no organized opposition to control.

The legislation did not sail through Congress, however. Many southern Democrats wanted no part of legislation that might lead to the federal use of police powers constitutionally vested in the states, and some thus argued that the bill would be unconstitutional. The compromise was to ground federal drug control in the constitutional power to tax—which meant that enforcement fell to the Treasury Department. Along with a series of other compromises, this move made possible the passage of the Harrison Narcotics Act in December 1914.

This first national drug-control law would prove momentous. But what exactly did the new law mean? Legally, the act set three major requirements for those who produced or distributed drugs: they had to register with the federal government, keep a record of all their transactions, and pay a purchase or sales tax. The Harrison Act also required that unregistered persons—drug users—could purchase drugs only with a prescription from a physician who "prescribed [it] in good faith" and did so "in the pursuit of his professional practice only."

On its face, the Harrison Act appeared to be a victory for the medical-treatment model of drug control espoused by moderate physicians and pragmatic progressive reformers. It aimed to prevent the widespread distribution of drugs to a public unaware of the dangers of addiction by controlling the drug supply in order to limit use. The major enforcement mechanisms—registration, taxes, penalties—were designed to keep drugs under the control of the medical community. Sanctions were aimed at those who sold drugs outside legal channels (by failing to register and pay the tax), not at doctors. The law did not tell doctors how to practice medicine by specifying what "good faith" or "professional practice" meant. Nor did the law criminalize addicts or brand them as morally wrong. Using drugs was not made a crime: users were simply required to turn to doctors for prescriptions to buy drugs; and there were no sanctions specified for possession or use without a prescription. The antivice crusaders, despite their rhetoric and pressure campaigns, appeared to have lost their fight: the law did not reflect their prohibitionist desires, nor did legislators believe they were passing a prohibition law.[27]

The battle to define the terms of national drug policy, however, had only begun. The language of the law left open several central questions: Over whom should control be exercised? How should that control be exercised? For what purpose should it be exercised? How were drug users to be regarded and treated? More than any other, the provision requiring doctors to prescribe drugs "in good faith" and only "in pursuit of their professional practice" was to become the point of contention around which the major struggles over administrative and judicial interpretation would be waged well into the 1920s.

In the end, prohibitionists would transform this largely medical model for controlling drug use into a punitive law-enforcement paradigm for outlawing drug use through coercion and force. Three factors helped tilt the balance of power in the direction of the antivice crusaders. Powerful government agents joined them in their quest. They were aided by an increasingly fearful and vengeful social context shaped by such events as the struggle over alcohol prohibition, World War I, and widespread fear of immigrants and foreign influences. Finally, the implementation of the Harrison Act did not strengthen and galvanize the forces in support of the medical model it embodied, but instead exposed and exacerbated divisions and weaknesses within the medical community.

TREASURY TAKES THE OFFENSIVE

The Treasury Department was charged with administering the Harrison Act, and its agents took the lead role in transforming it into a prohibitionist law. The department (first its Bureau of Internal Revenue and then, after 1920, the Narcotics Division of its Prohibition Unit) engaged the battle on three fronts, bringing pressure to bear through its power to issue regulations, through the courts, and through Congress.

Shortly after the bill had been signed into law, Treasury officials began to issue regulations interpreting it as forbidding the maintenance of addicts on drugs. Prescriptions for the treatment of addicts, a May 1915 Treasury Department regulation said, "should show the good faith of the physician in the legitimate practice of his profession by a decreasing dosage or reduction of the quantity prescribed from time to time." The department also began an "aggressive enforcement" campaign, arresting physicians and druggists in order to stop them from providing prescriptions to help maintain addicts and arresting addicts for illegal possession.[28]

This prohibitionist maneuver was rejected by the lower courts and eventually by the Supreme Court, which argued that the Harrison Act gave the government the power to enforce tax laws but did not contain language prohibiting physicians from maintaining addicts. The Court found no grounds for arresting addicts; possession was neither criminal nor subject to punishment. When the Treasury and Justice Departments brought a test case against an addict for possession to the Supreme Court (*United States v. Jin Fuey Moy*) in 1916, the Court rejected by seven to two the government's arguments for exercising such broad police powers.[29]

The Treasury Department persisted. In each of its annual reports to Congress in 1916, 1917, and 1918 it made strong, if futile, requests for new legislation to allow the punitive prohibitions the Court had ruled out. For a time the forces that insisted on regulating, not outlawing, drugs were strong enough to resist prohibitionary legislative reforms. But the Treasury Department was eventually able to take advantage of a changing social context, increasingly shaped by the antivice movement.

In the years immediately following the Harrison Act, antivice crusaders, often supported by urban dailies and popular national magazines, sought more stringent prohibition and punishment of physicians and addicts and continued to warn of "the drug evil." Mass organizations pushing for alcohol prohibition had created a moral atmosphere that condemned such vices: to argue that addicts should be treated with drugs by doctors became akin to advocating the maintenance of alcoholics on doses of alcohol. The Treasury Department also helped turn public opinion against doctors and their addicted patients: each time a doctor was arrested and accused of irresponsibly dispensing drugs, the existence of a drug problem was advertised, magnified, and portrayed as a criminal problem. Antivice crusaders and many journalists seized on such opportunities to project an image of "dope doctors" responsible for the nation's drug problems.

The growing antidrug sentiment rode the tide of other national fears. World War I and the 1919–1920 Red Scare fanned fears about foreign threats.[30] Press stories circulated about drugs being smuggled into U.S. Army training centers by Germans and about Germans "exporting drugs in toothpaste and patent medicines in order to hook innocent citizens of other countries on drugs."[31] The enactment of alcohol Prohibition in 1919 further boosted the antivice crusade, and in the early 1920s a number of antinarcotics groups formed. Some of the most vocal were created by a star orator of the Prohibition movement, Richmond P. Hobson. They included the International Narcotic Education Association (1923), the World Conference on Narcotic Education (1926), and the World Narcotic Defense Association (1927). The *Journal of the American Medical Association* and other medical publications complained about Hobson's exaggerations and distortions, but they were nevertheless broadcast widely. Hobson not only grossly exaggerated the numbers ("1 million heroin addicts") but also argued that heroin caused crime and that addicts were "beasts" and "monsters" who spread their disease like medieval vampires.[32] "Drug addiction is more communicable and less curable than leprosy," he warned, asserting that "drug addicts are the principal carriers of vice diseases." Hobson direly concluded that "upon this issue hangs the perpetuation of civilization, the destiny of the world, and the future of the human race."[33]

The antinarcotics organizations were joined by lodges and service clubs, including the Knights of Columbus, Moose, Kiwanis, and some Masonic orders. Hobson sent millions of pamphlets to these clubs, and fighting narcotics soon became a common and respectable lodge activity. Policymakers who were club members, such as Republican Rep. Stephen G. Porter of Pittsburgh, used fraternal contacts to build national support for tough antinarcotics measures.[34]

Very few voices rose in opposition to the prohibitionist tide. Groups such as the White Cross International Anti-Narcotic Society eschewed punishment in favor of treatment at the local level, advocating drug clinics at which addicts could receive their daily supplies. Some critics in the medical community pointed to the increased health risks and growing crime that prohibition would create.[35] But these groups were relatively weak, and their appeals were swiftly rejected by the Treasury Department.

The public campaigns of the antivice crusaders and the government's narcotics-control agency, meanwhile, profoundly shaped the emerging national consensus on drug addiction: over time, addiction came to be regarded with disgust and fear, and "addicts were perceived as an immense evil which should be blotted out of society."[36]

THE MEDICAL MODEL UNDERMINES ITSELF

Equally important in the collapse of the medical-treatment model was the failure of its advocates to rally and consolidate support in its favor. Ironically, their failure was facilitated in part by the Harrison Act itself.

By creating a monopoly over legal supply in the hands of doctors and druggists, the act assured that any continued drug problems were to be laid squarely at the feet of the medical profession. Soon after the act passed, some physicians began to dispense drugs to large numbers of addicts without examining them thoroughly or providing them with adequate individual care. The antidrug crusaders and Treasury officials attributed this to corrupt, profit-seeking doctors who were hiding behind their profession to make a quick profit. Some undoubtedly were, but much of the problem was the result of the legislation itself. Because the law turned addicts overnight from individuals who could legally buy drugs on the open market into patients requiring prescriptions, "hundreds of thousands of law-abiding addicts suddenly materialized outside of doctors' offices. It was inconceivable that the relatively small number of doctors in the country could so suddenly handle over half a million new patients in any manner, and certainly it was impossible that they might handle them individually. The doctor's office became little more than a dispensing station for the addict, with only an infinitesimal fraction of addicts receiving personal care."[37]

Thus responsibility for the nation's addicts was invested in an unprepared and ill-equipped medical community. Rather than galvanizing doctors in support of treatment for addicts, moreover, the Harrison Act exposed deep divisions, old and new, among medical professionals. Liberals in the medical community favored state regulation and public-health promotion, while an increasingly powerful conservative wing opposed any federal intervention in medicine.

More importantly, stark divisions emerged over the question of drug addiction and its appropriate treatment. Support for the medical-treatment model advanced by the Harrison Act was neither widespread nor well organized. The medical community itself had long distinguished between two classes of addicts: the nefarious underworld user who was to be dealt with severely, and the respectable, average addict who was to be pitied and medically treated. Many physicians shied away from treating addicts and "shared the prevailing view that addiction led to moral degeneracy and crime."[38]

Disputes over the true nature of addiction were also deep. The medical reformers who shaped the Harrison Act believed that addicts should be treated as patients because they had a disease. But was it curable or incurable? If it was incurable, addicts needed doctors who would prescribe drugs (just as insulin is prescribed today for diabetics) to enable them to lead normal lives. On the other hand, those who believed that addiction was curable (through phased withdrawal, for example) had a very different view of appropriate treatment and argued that permanent maintenance on drugs helped perpetuate a disease.

Medical professional groups represented the only organized community capable of defending the medical-treatment approach reflected in the Harrison Act—but these divisions made that impossible. They also served to fuel the efforts of the prohibitionists. Antidrug crusaders such as Levi G. Nutt, head of the Treasury Department's Narcotics Division after 1920, seized on the arguments of those doctors who claimed that addiction was curable.[39] This view justified the government crackdown on physicians who were maintaining addicts by dispensing drugs to them and who could not prove they were curing the disease.

The fact that no reliable and acceptable cure for addiction was available—or even known—sharpened the debate within the medical community, but it in no way deterred the Narcotics Division from its self-appointed task. With only 170 agents, Nutt's forces not only arrested and convicted large numbers of physicians and pharmacists (1,583 in 1921 alone) but also threatened and intimidated thousands of doctors who were legally registered to dispense drugs.[40] Doctors quickly came to fear that any drug prescription for an addict could be interpreted as maintenance and not treatment. Harassment and intimidation took their toll: unwilling to invest the effort required to fight the charges or endure the attendant social stigma, large numbers of physicians elected to stop prescribing opiates and cocaine.

The attack against private physicians was expanded into an attack on public drug clinics in the early 1920s. Created as part of a broader public-health campaign to stem the spread of disease in rapidly growing cities, the clinics were run by city or state health professionals to dispense drugs to poor addicts. By the 1920s at least forty-four drug clinics were operating.[41] Many of these clinics had emerged in response to the demand created by the Harrison Act for medically prescribed drugs. The Treasury Department's success in intimidating doctors had led city and state officials to further expand the clinics as a way of dealing with the thousands of addicts on the streets with no legal source of drugs.[42]

Except in New York City, the clinics never enjoyed a very large clientele, but they did provide a glimpse of an alternative to criminalization and incarceration. Although they could not claim many "cures," they were able to alleviate suffering among their drug-dependent clients, keep them out of the criminal underworld, and allow them to lead relatively normal lives. The clinic in Shreveport, Louisiana, for example, earned the support of the federal district judge (who claimed that it had lessened crime), the city judge (who claimed that providing care for incurable addicts enabled them to work rather than become city charges), and the sheriff, chief of police, and U.S. marshal (who said that crime and petty thievery had lessened since the clinic opened because addicts did not have to steal to buy drugs).[43]

But the clinics created a problem for the Treasury Department: they were not "curing" addicts any better than were physicians, and they were therefore promoting the maintenance of addicts—a practice Nutt's Narcotics Division staunchly opposed. In 1920 Nutt began an intense campaign to close the clinics, an effort supported by the anticlinic forces that then controlled the American Medical Association (AMA). By the end of 1921 most had been shut down.

As physicians and pharmacists backed away from prescribing cocaine and opiates and as clinics closed their doors, those drug users who were unable to break their addiction had little choice but to enter the underworld, supporting the black-market dope peddlers who had replaced doctors and pharmacists and sometimes stealing to meet the high prices created by prohibition.

The success of the Treasury Department in shifting the terms of debate to frame drug addiction not as a medical concern but as a law-enforcement problem thus transformed suppliers from pharmacists into drug dealers and turned addicts from patients who deserved treatment into criminals who deserved condemnation and isolation.

THE COURTS ENDORSE PROHIBITION

From 1915 to 1919 narcotics agents faced legal limits in their campaign to intimidate doctors with the threat of legal action for dispensing drugs to addicts: the courts refused to accept the Treasury Department's prohibitionist interpretation of the Harrison Act, and Congress was unwilling to amend the law.[44] The department's strategy was to continue to bring forward cases in the hopes of eventually swaying the Supreme Court to outlaw drug maintenance and thus consolidating the punitive approach to drug control.

In 1919, in *Webb v. United States,* the strategy finally bore fruit. Narcotics agents had arrested Dr. Webb for indiscriminately selling prescriptions by the thousands for fifty cents apiece.[45] The case was made to rest on the issue of whether the legitimate practice of medicine could include Dr. Webb's provision of morphine to maintain addicts with no intent to cure them. The Supreme Court concluded that to call "such an order for the use of morphine a physician's prescription would be so plain a perversion of meaning that no discussion of the subject is required."[46] The department wasted no time in reacting to the decision. It quickly put its personnel on notice that the Supreme Court now supported the prosecution of physicians who were distributing drugs "to a person popularly known as a 'dope fiend,' for the purpose of gratifying his appetite for the drug." Such acts, the Treasury memorandum said, put physicians in violation of the Harrison Act.[47]

In 1922 the Court again delivered a verdict supporting the Treasury Department's position. The Harrison Act, declared the Court in *United States v. Behrman,* only allowed "the dispensing or distribution of such drugs by a registered physician in the course of his professional practice." Dr. Behrman's patient "did not require the administration of either morphine, heroin or cocaine by reason of any disease other than addiction." Behrman's provision of the drugs was therefore not a legitimate act within the context of "his professional practice only."[48] The Court established that a narcotics prescription for such an addict constituted a crime independent of the intent or "good faith" of the physician. Thus any doctor would be in trouble for prescribing a drug to an addict unless he or she had some other ailment requiring treatment with narcotics.

By 1922 court rulings had transformed the Harrison Act into a prohibition law, and a punitive paradigm, backed by legal precedent and a counternarcotics bureaucracy, was dominant. The splits in the medical community on the issue of maintenance versus treatment, the abuses by some doctors (exaggerated and advertised by antinarcotics forces), and the further stigmatization of the addict as criminal had all helped weaken and divide the already limited opposition to the punitive approach. Continued pressure by the antidrug crusaders and the Narcotics Division had helped create a context in which the Supreme Court had finally given the Treasury Department the precedent it needed to enforce its vision.

The social and political tide toward punitive prohibition of drugs had turned so decisively by the mid-1920s that even a reversal of position by the Supreme Court in 1925 had little effect on enforcement practices or policy. In *Linder v. United States* the Court argued that the Behrman decision of 1922 "cannot be accepted as authority for holding that a physician who acts *bona fide* and according to fair medical standards may never give an addict moderate amounts of drugs for self-administration in order to relieve conditions incident to addiction. Enforcement of the tax demands no such drastic rule, and if the Act had such scope it would certainly encounter grave constitutional difficulties."[49] The Court took the position that drug addiction is a disease and that relieving the "conditions incident to addiction" is a perfectly appropriate medical response; thus the physician's actions did not constitute a violation of the act. The decision should have called into question the practices of the Treasury Department, but so entrenched was the punitive approach that few were willing to challenge Treasury's actions politically or in court, and the ruling had little real impact.[50]

A LOST OPPORTUNITY

There was a brief moment in the 1920s when the U.S. Public Health Service might have seized the initiative on drug treatment and might have set in motion an important counterweight to the punitive prohibitionists in the Treasury Department who controlled U.S. drug policy. The attack on maintenance by physicians and clinics still left a problem acknowledged by many doctors and public officials: what was to be done to treat the addicts denied prescriptions or clinic care?

Even the Treasury Department was not anxious to have thousands of addicts in need of drugs roaming the streets. A special narcotics committee of the Treasury urged in its 1919 report that something be done for the addict who would be made desperate when maintenance was cut off. Federal and local governments needed to enact legislation to provide for medical care, said the committee. The Treasury's Bureau of Internal Revenue proposed the "use of Public Health Service hospitals for treatment of addiction, Public Health Service officers for liaison and consultation with the various states, matching funds to the states for the care of addicts through institutions, leading to definitive cure."[51]

In July 1919 Senator Joseph I. France (R-Maryland) introduced legislation, which the bureau helped prepare, requiring congressional appropriations and the active cooperation of the Public Health Service. But the Public Health Service was less than enthusiastic. The Treasury Department's definition of legitimate treatment—treatment that would cure addiction—made service officials leery. They were dubious that such treatment was possible, and they did not want to become involved even in the temporary hospital treatment proposed in the France bill.

The AMA's more liberal wing supported the France bill, but the power of this faction had been waning. More conservative physicians who generally opposed any legislation that increased federal activity in health care (for maternal and child health, for example) were gaining influence and made clear their opposition to the bill. The Republicans who dominated Congress, meanwhile, were facing an economic recession and wanted to trim the budget before the next election. Perceived budget constraints, a divided medical community, and a reticent Public Health Service thus doomed what might have been the beginning of a serious federal effort at drug treatment.[52]

Others in Congress did come forward to advocate federal treatment during the 1920s. But when such proposals emerged they envisioned treatment as a minor appendage of the punitive approach and severely limited its scope. Rep. Stephen G. Porter (R-Pennsylvania), long an advocate of federal narcotics hospitals, crafted a "narcotics-farm" bill that became law in January 1929. The Justice Department and the wardens at federal penitentiaries had pressed Congress for action on this issue, because their prisons were equipped neither to handle the overflow of prisoners nor to deal with the addicts rounded up by the Treasury Department. The narcotics farms were to be separate facilities for such convicted drug users, run by Public Health Service officials but with cells, bars, and maximum-security provisions. Treatment was thus conceived not as an alternative to enforcement but as an alternative way of handling the consequences of enforcement and as a way of taking the pressure off the federal prison system. Two narcotics farms were established. The first was opened in Lexington, Kentucky, in 1935; the second, in Fort Worth, Texas, in 1938. The Lexington facility was not turned into a recognizable hospital until the late 1960s, when the steel bars were removed from the cells.[53]

By the end of the 1920s the punitive, prohibitionist paradigm had taken hold. Legal sources of drugs had largely been eliminated. Dope peddlers and smugglers—forerunners of today's dealers and traffickers—were defined as the key problem and became the targets of government policy. The only legitimate interpretations of addiction, meanwhile, both pointed toward harsh, punitive measures. If addiction were a disease, the carrier must be confined to prevent contagion. If addiction were not a disease but a "weakness in character which could be overcome by righteous and right-thinking people," addicts who did not quit on their own or did not seek treatment were weak willed or morally wrong and deserved punishment.[54] Old distinctions between nefarious addicts and respectable addicts had been erased—and the addict as patient was replaced by the addict as criminal. Furthermore, a consensus arose that any nonmedical narcotics use—even nonaddictive use—was a vice and that users should be punished. Laws began to sanction not just suppliers but also users themselves. The criminalization of possession was solidified in the 1932 Uniform Narcotic Drug Act, which was adopted by most states in the next decade.[55] Twenty years later, possession of drugs was a felony punishable under federal law by a minimum sentence of two years for the first offense.

5   The Punitive Paradigm

Entrenchment and Challenge, 1930–1980

The Harrison Act had turned drug addiction into a national problem and had framed the central policy question in medical terms: how should doctors treat drug problems? During the ensuing political struggle the Treasury Department and the antivice crusaders changed the question from *how* to *whether* doctors should treat addiction, and in the end they succeeded in eliminating the role of doctors. By 1930 the punitive paradigm had set the contours of a new drug-policy agenda: how should the government control drug smugglers, dealers, and users? Other pieces of today's punitive paradigm, however, were not yet in place. In particular, key assumptions about the relationship between drugs and crime had not taken hold. Antivice crusaders had long sought to associate certain addicts—particularly urban poor and minority addicts—with crime and the underworld. But the even stronger assumption that the physical consumption of drugs in itself causes crime was not widespread.

It took the institutionalization of the drug war in an expanded drug bureaucracy to further consolidate the punitive assumptions of the paradigm. And it took another political conflict to seal the drug-crime link in the public mind: the debate over marijuana. At the center of this conflict were government bureaucrats and a new generation of zealous antidrug crusaders. Playing on racist fears, they secured a ban on marijuana. In the process, they helped forge a central tenet of the current punitive paradigm: drugs cause crime.

THE FIRST DRUG CZAR

The 1930s brought a significant expansion in the institutional apparatus for drug control. Efforts in Congress to establish an independent drug-control agency paid off in July 1930, with the creation of the Federal Bureau of Narcotics (FBN) in the Treasury Department. President Hoover appointed Harry Anslinger, a high official in the Prohibition Unit, as its first commissioner.

Anslinger soon became the J. Edgar Hoover of drugs, America's first "drug czar." He believed that the primary enforcement challenge was to control the drug supply, particularly from abroad. But he was responsible for local police-enforcement work as well—and his budget and force were small. He needed to defend and expand his bureaucratic turf (against Depression budget cutbacks, for example) and to protect the FBN from reorganizational attempts to merge it with other law-enforcement agencies in the Treasury Department.[1]

To generate the support necessary to protect and expand his agency and its mission, Anslinger undertook a sweeping and aggressive campaign in the 1930s and 1940s to shape public antidrug attitudes. He "wrote scores of articles for professional journals, newspapers, and magazines fervently promoting narcotics control and linking certain ethnic, foreign, and ideological groups with the country's addiction problem. He supplied information and encouragement to other authors willing to produce likeminded books and essays; and he included the resultant narcotics-limitation rhetoric in his testimony before congressional committees."[2] The FBN's efforts to control what Americans saw and heard about drugs extended to censorship. In one instance, a documentary film on addiction prepared by the Canadian Department of National Health and Welfare in 1949 was banned in the United States because of Anslinger's maneuvers—despite the fact that it had won a National Film Award in Canada and was praised by the United Nation's Division of Narcotic Drugs as "the best technical film relating to the control of narcotic drugs." Anslinger objected to the film's portrayal of addiction as a disease, not a crime; he argued that the actors (played by actual addicts) were too personable and attractive; and he insisted that the role of the police was underemphasized.[3]

Anslinger not only proselytized and imposed censorship but actively enlisted the support of state officials and civic-reform groups to bolster the FBN's punitive drug-control campaign. Beginning in the 1930s, he sought to convince the states to assume more responsibility for drug control. Working through the National Conference of Commissioners on Uniform State Laws in 1932, he pursued a Uniform State Narcotic Law that was eventually to be enacted by almost every state.[4] At the same time, he developed and maintained close working relationships with some of the country's most zealous reform groups, giving numerous talks to temperance organizations, church groups, women's clubs, and parent-teacher associations.[5] The result was a rising chorus of demands from sources within and outside government that argued for punitive sanctions against the sale and use of opiates and cocaine. Out of this increasingly moralistic and drug-intolerant social context emerged a political struggle over another drug—marijuana.

THE BATTLE OVER MARIJUANA

Early drafters of the Harrison Act had tried to outlaw marijuana but had found little organized support for their efforts—and much opposition from the pharmaceutical industry.[6] By the mid-1920s, however, fear of marijuana was growing in the South and West, spurred by rapidly increasing legal and illegal Mexican migration. Although employers welcomed Mexicans as a source of labor, the new immigrants, like the Chinese and others before them, triggered fears of crime and social corruption.

Racist and nativist suspicions about the Mexican immigrants came to focus on the use of marijuana by some Mexicans. Before long, local residents had attributed mythical crime-producing powers to the drug. As the Great Depression made the Mexicans an unwelcome surplus labor force in the 1930s, the identification of Mexicans with both crime and marijuana deepened. Studies produced by New Orleans officials, for example, blamed marijuana for much of the region's crime and quickly captured national legislative and media attention. The articles charged that marijuana was sexual stimulant that removed civilized inhibitions and transformed users, according to the New Orleans coroner, "into the most crime-producing individuals that we have."[7] Pressure on Washington to do something mounted from several quarters, including local police forces, citizens' groups, state governors, and the Hearst newspaper chain (whose stories and cartoons detailed the ways the drug enslaved its users).

Anslinger, faced with budget constraints in the early 1930s, was not keen at first to have his FBN lead a battle against marijuana. Although he was opposed to its use, he believed that its dangers did not compare with those of heroin, that it would be very difficult to control, and that reports of its alarming spread were exaggerated.[8] By 1933, however, heightened public concern led the FBN to conclude that marijuana had "come into wide and increasing abuse in many states."[9] The agency's response was to pressure state officials for enforcement of existing local laws and for new state laws. The absence of federal legislation, Anslinger announced in his 1935 report, meant that states and cities must engage in "vigorous measures for the extinction of this lethal weed." He called on "all public-spirited citizens . . . [to] earnestly enlist in the movement urged by the Treasury Department . . . [for] intensified enforcement of marijuana laws."[10]

By 1936 Anslinger had joined the battle for federal legislation prohibiting marijuana. He and his agency had helped forge the public consensus against marijuana; they now assisted in crafting and securing passage of legislation and lent vocal support in the debate in Congress. The Marijuana Tax Act passed in the summer of 1937 and took effect on 1 October 1937. By that time forty-six states and Washington, D.C., had placed antimarijuana laws on the books.

The Marijuana Tax Act was modeled on features of the 1914 Harrison Act and a recent tax law controlling gun possession.[11] Only the non-medicinal, untaxed possession or sale of marijuana was outlawed. "Illegitimate transfers" were taxed at $100 a pound—a steep tax considering that marijuana purchased legally cost $2.00 a pound. Violations meant a fine of $2,000, five years in prison, or both.[12]

These laws and sanctions were not the only means used by the FBN and its allies to shift public debate on marijuana. By the end of the 1940s, for example, they had effectively erased marijuana from the annals of legitimate medicinal substances. Anslinger went as far as to convince the chairman of the committee revising the United States Pharmacopeia to have marijuana deleted from the publication—despite the fact that marijuana had been widely used in medical practice and the Pharmacopeia had listed it in all of its editions from 1850 until 1942.[13]

At the same time, the antimarijuana campaign had succeeded in adding the substance to the public's list of serious law-enforcement threats: by the time marijuana was outlawed, "common sense" linked its use to deadly crimes. Even after the act passed, Anslinger and others repeatedly asserted that consumption of marijuana caused criminal actions. A person under the influence of marijuana could, as Anslinger put it, be provoked by "the slightest opposition, arousing him to a state of menacing fury or homicidal attack. During this frenzied period, addicts have perpetuated some of the most bizarre and fantastic offenses and sex crimes known to police annals."[14]

Little opposition surfaced to Anslinger's efforts to define marijuana as a crime-causing "killer weed" and to ban its use; and in the fearful and moralistic mood of the day, few spoke out against the general trend toward a punitive policy of drug prohibition. The government discouraged opposition by blocking critical testimony, disparaging those who publicly questioned policy assumptions, studiously ignoring damning evidence, and straining to defend the many faulty claims about drugs propounded by prohibitionists and the media.

During the hearings on the 1937 Marijuana Tax Act, for example, opposing views were available to Congress from within government and the medical community—but with Anslinger's help such opinions were dismissed or sidelined. When the Treasury Department requested the written opinion of the Public Health Service, for example, Dr. Walter L. Treadway responded that in the case of marijuana, "there is no dependence or increased tolerance such as in opium addiction. As to the social or moral degradation associated with cannabis, it probably belongs in the same category as alcohol. . . . Marijuana is habit-forming although not addicting in the same sense as alcohol might be with some people, or sugar or coffee."[15]

But the Treasury Department buried Treadway's arguments, and he was not asked to testify. Dr. William Woodward, representing the Board of Trustees of the AMA offered mild opposition to the act in his testimony, pointing out that the evidence against marijuana was incomplete. His arguments were ignored, and he was so shabbily treated that he did not return for the hearings in the Senate.[16] Meanwhile, Anslinger, a chief witness at the hearings, related graphic and detailed stories of atrocities attributed to marijuana use.

The major criticism of the antimarijuana movement came later, in the form of a medical rebuttal from a committee of doctors and city officials appointed by New York City's Mayor Fiorello LaGuardia in 1939. Based on a pharmacological study, a clinical study, and a sociological study, the LaGuardia Commission's 1945 report challenged most of the FBN's claims. The report concluded that marijuana was not addicting, did not seriously disturb mental or physical functioning, and did not lead to violence or harder drugs. As the early findings of the report were released, some articles began to downplay the hazards of the drug—but the FBN responded by roundly and repeatedly condemning the report.[17]

If few questioned the criminalization of marijuana, almost no one challenged the basic assumptions of the overall drug strategy. One exception was the former president of the International Association of Chiefs of Police, August Volmer, who in 1936 argued to no avail that "the first step in any plan to alleviate this dreadful affliction should be the establishment of Federal control and dispensation—at cost—of habit-forming drugs. With the profit motive gone . . . the drug peddler would disappear. New addicts would be speedily discovered and through early treatment some of these unfortunate victims might be saved from becoming hopelessly incurable."[18]

The only outspoken opposition in Congress in the 1930s and 1940s came from John M. Coffee (D-Washington), a five-term representative who arrived in Washington in 1937. Coffee failed to pick up support for his 1938 House Joint Resolution, which called simply for the U.S. Public Health Service to review and evaluate the drug situation. Implementation of prohibitionary drug policies, he pointed out, had led to the "persecution of perhaps a million victims of the diseased condition known as drug addiction, the great majority of whom had been law-abiding, self-respecting, self-supporting citizens, but who now became human derelicts and were thrust by thousands into jails and prisons simply because they could not legally secure the medicine upon which depended their integrity of mind and body."

Coffee pointedly condemned the Harrison Act and the federal government for creating a vast smuggling industry: "If we, the representatives of the people, are to continue to let our narcotics authorities conduct themselves in a manner tantamount to upholding and in effect supporting the billion-dollar drug racket, we should at least be able to explain to our constituents why we do so."

The intent of the Harrison Act had been undermined, the congressman pointed out, because "the prohibitory mandate of the Narcotics Bureau effectively denies treatment to the vast majority of narcotic addicts"—despite the fact, he reminded his audience, that the Supreme Court "has declared that narcotic addicts are diseased and proper subject for medical treatment." The solution was to go back to the law's original intent, bringing addicts under medical supervision to secure the supply they needed legitimately at low cost.

> Morphine which the peddler sells for a dollar a grain would be supplied, of pure quality, for 2 or 3 cents a grain. The peddler, unable to meet such a price, would go out of business—the illicit narcotic drug industry, the billion-dollar racket, would automatically cease to exist. . . . Almost as certain is that

the army of narcotics derelicts would be reduced to the vanishing point. Courts would cease to be crowded with delinquents who owe their downfall to the necessity of meeting the dope peddler's exorbitant demands. Jails would be emptied; Federal prisons would lose a quarter of their population.[19]

THE POSTWAR ESCALATION

That critical arguments such as Coffee's were so rarely advanced—and were disregarded or derided when they were offered—underlines the reach of the punitive conventional wisdom on drugs. This widening consensus made further gains for the prohibitionists easier in the 1940s and 1950s. So did developments abroad.

As the cold war began in earnest, the FBN shrewdly tied drugs to the foreign threat of communism. "Red" China was accused of trying to destroy Western society and of securing hard cash through heroin sales to U.S. drug pushers.[20] The political atmosphere of the 1950s created a Congress receptive to Anslinger's designs: Americans were absorbed by hearings on the Mafia and organized crime and were consumed by fears of Soviet aggression and subversion, heightened by McCarthyism.

The FBN seized the opportunity to launch a campaign for mandatory minimum sentences for first-time drug convictions. Anslinger found an eager congressman in Hale Boggs (D-Louisiana), whose 1951 bill passed by overwhelming margins to establish the most severe federal law to date, imposing a mandatory minimum two-year sentence for a first conviction of possession, five to ten years for the second offense, and ten to twenty years for third-time violators.[21] In the Senate the subcommittee chaired by Texas Democrat Price Daniel embraced Anslinger's argument about the Chinese communist threat, concluding that "subversion through drug addiction is an established aim of Communist China."[22] Daniel's subcommittee recommended still further escalation of punitive policies, arguing that the offenses of "heroin smugglers and peddlers" amounted to "'murder on the installment plan,' leading not only to the final loss of one's life but to others who acquire this contagious infection through association with the original victim."[23] The resulting Narcotic Control Act of 1956 raised mandatory minimum penalties (five to twenty years for the second offense; ten to forty years for the third offense) and permitted juries to impose the death penalty on any adult who sold heroin to a minor.[24]

Anslinger's legislative gains confirmed the broad acceptance of new, more punitive assumptions about drug control. Drug consumption, a

matter of little public concern early in the century and a concern primarily of doctors after the Harrison Act, had become a law-enforcement
concern by the 1920s and a serious criminal problem demanding draconian measures by the 1950s. It had become conventional wisdom that
any drug use, even of relatively mild drugs such as marijuana, would
likely cause crime; that use of milder drugs would in any case lead to
harder and more dangerous drugs, particularly heroin;[25] and that punishing users as well as dealers was therefore perfectly legitimate. Such
thinking discouraged any discrimination between drug use and drug
abuse (the first was presumed to lead "naturally" to the second) or between more or less harmful drugs (they were all seen as dangerous and
morally wrong). The instinctive response to continued drug problems,
finally, had become almost universal: get tougher.

THE TREATMENT CHALLENGE

The dominance of the punitive paradigm did not mean an end to political struggles over the nature of drug problems and their appropriate solutions: the paradigm was not monolithic. Beginning in the early 1960s
and throughout the 1970s, important social forces emerged to challenge
two assumptions of the punitive paradigm: the idea that the best way to
discourage drug problems was to punish dealers and users, and the idea
that marijuana was dangerous, criminal, morally wrong, and legitimately illegal. These forces drew on beliefs and ideas as deeply rooted
in American culture as those that had anchored the punitive approach.

One challenge came from treatment advocates. Drug problems, they
argued, were health, not criminal, concerns; addiction should be
treated, not punished. By the end of the 1970s their efforts had established a firm place for treatment in drug control—but they did not
undermine the punitive paradigm or its law-enforcement emphasis.
Rather, treatment was largely tolerated by those who favored the punitive approach, as an adjunct to law enforcement, another tool in the
war against drug use and crime.

Signs of discontent had emerged in 1955 when the ABA, concerned
with the harsh mandatory sentences enacted by the Boggs bill, called for
a congressional investigation of the narcotics problem and created a joint
committee with the AMA to study it. The committee's 1958 *Interim Report* argued that even though "stringent law enforcement has its place"
in narcotics control, "it is by no means the complete answer to American problems of drug addiction." The report questioned whether threats

of prison could deter addicts from using drugs and suggested that the faith in punishment "rests upon a superficial view of the drug addiction process and the nature of drug addiction."[26] The committee recommended relaxing the law-enforcement approach by lifting restrictions— to allow doctors to prescribe drugs, for example, and to permit out-patient clinics to dispense narcotics to addicts.

The initial government response to arguments such as these was harsh and unsympathetic. But things began to change by the early 1960s. Most important, Anslinger's power came to an end in 1962, when President John F. Kennedy and his brother, Attorney General Robert F. Kennedy, secured his resignation as FBN chief. Furthermore, the antivice movement, so critical a few decades earlier, had died down. Meanwhile, opposition to the war against addicts began to coalesce within the medical- and social-research communities. Progressive voices, such as that of nationally known psychiatrist and drug authority Dr. Karl M. Bowman, began to reach a wider audience.

> For the past 40 years we have been trying the mainly punitive approach; we have increased penalties, we have hounded the drug addict, and we have brought out the idea that any person who takes drugs is a most dangerous criminal and a menace to society. We have perpetuated the myth that addiction to opiates is the great cause of crimes and violence and of sex crimes. In spite of the statements of the most eminent medical authorities in this country and elsewhere, this type of propaganda still continues, coming to a large extent from the enforcement bureaus of federal and state governments.[27]

Academic research backed these claims. A comprehensive study of drug addiction by a team led by psychologist Isidor Chein argued that existing policies did little more than force "the addict from degradation to degradation" and concluded that "every addict is entitled to assessment as an individual and to be offered the best available treatment in the light of his condition, his situation, and his needs," including treatment programs that "continue him on narcotics."[28]

The retirement of Anslinger and a changing social context created a new opening for such critiques in the debate on drugs, and arguments for treatment began to echo in the mainstream media and among social organizations. An April 1963 editorial in the *Wall Street Journal* urged the country to "start searching for ways in which the tragic incurables can be put on sustaining doses that will keep them from desperate acts."[29] A February 1965 editorial in the *New York Times* argued that "the best hope for smashing the illicit traffic in narcotics lies in the dispensing of drugs under medical controls—particularly at hospitals in the

search, treatment, and prevention. Within a year and a half of SAODAP's creation, the number of cities with federally funded treatment services had jumped from 54 to 214; the number of addicts assisted in these programs tripled in little more than a year, reaching 60,000 by December 1972.[38] There were fewer than 200 local clinics in 1966 and more than 3,000 by 1975. For a time the federal government sought to meet all requests for treatment, although after 1976 cuts in federal spending reduced levels of service.[39]

Four approaches to treatment emerged during this period; the primary concern of each was with heroin addicts.[40] The therapeutic communities argued that drug abuse was a psychological and social disorder, best treated by intensive individual and group counseling in residential treatment programs. The counseling sessions, frequently employing former addicts who had been rehabilitated, aimed to increase participants' responsibility for their own lives and to enable them to function better in the community. Outpatient drug-free treatment was a second, less intensive form of therapy. A variety of such nonresidential programs sprang up, aimed not simply at heroin addicts but at abusers of other drugs, including alcohol. Often modeled on the approach of community mental-health centers, the programs provided counseling for drug abusers as well as services such as family therapy and vocational and educational assistance.[41]

Methadone detoxification was a third form of therapy. These one-to-three-week programs were aimed at helping addicts to give up heroin. Withdrawal symptoms were mitigated by administering decreasing doses of methadone, a synthetic opium derivative that blocks the desire for heroin but does not have the deleterious physiological or psychological effects of heroin. Such programs helped patients take the initial step in ending addiction; on their own, however, the programs had little long-term effect, and an extremely high percentage of participants relapsed.

The fourth and most widespread form of therapy also involved methadone but provided long-term maintenance, not short-term detoxification. Patients who took oral methadone regularly in clinics could stop injecting heroin and thereby dramatically reduce the risk of disease and other harms that came from intravenous drug use. Because it was legal and inexpensive or free, low-income addicts had less reason to turn to crime to support their habits. Patients were not only maintained on methadone but also provided with counseling and with vocational, educational, and legal assistance. Although critics attacked the program for substituting one kind of drug dependence (methadone) for another (heroin), professionals in the methadone-maintenance programs saw their first task as moving addicts out of a life on the streets and helping them create satisfying work and family lives. Such changes, they argued, gave many former addicts the support and incentive to end their methadone maintenance; those who could not were still able to lead healthier and more productive lives.

Widening concern over the need to prevent—not just treat—drug-abuse problems moved drug prevention onto the policy agenda in the early 1970s. NIDA created a Prevention Branch in 1974, and small budgets were granted to prevention programs. A 1975 executive branch white paper on drug abuse made the case for prevention: "Treatment is a response to a problem which has already developed. Given the difficulties of successful treatment, it is obvious that effective programs which prevent the problem before it develops are highly desirable. Similarly, vocational rehabilitation during and after treatment which enhances the probability that a former abuser will not return to drug use should be given priority."[42]

The fear-provoking public-information programs of the Anslinger years were largely replaced with education programs that provided drug information, taught problem solving and communication skills, and encouraged peer counseling. The white paper stressed the importance of providing factual information to young people: "Future Federal media efforts aimed at this audience should: provide basic information about drugs and their effects, not in a 'scare' sense, but with an objective presentation of 'best information'; and emphasize successful productive lifestyles of non-drug users."[43]

Reform and Its Limits

Why was there so little public or bureaucratic resistance to the rise of treatment and prevention in the 1960s and 1970s? The emergence of a growing health bureaucracy and a less vocal enforcement bureaucracy (after Anslinger's departure) was one reason, but the interests of key actors in avoiding confrontation were also important.

Treatment supporters chose not to launch a more frontal assault on many of the assumptions behind punitive drug control. They could, for example, have attacked the consensus that all drug use was equally wrong and harmful: many people in the treatment community distinguished between marijuana and heroin, for instance, arguing that heroin was addictive and far more dangerous. They might have argued for a treatment continuum that sought not only total abstinence but also more modest goals, such as reducing drug dependence, stemming the most harmful patterns of drug taking (such as intravenous drug use), and increasing addicts' ability to function in the community. Indeed, these were the stated goals of many treatment advocates. But instead of publicly challenging the consensus that the only legitimate goal was "no use" of any drug, they argued primarily that treatment was more effective—and humane—in stopping use than punishment was. Nor did most treatment supporters publicly attack the war on supply. They accepted this as one legitimate way to lower use. Their claim was more limited: at least some portion of federal funds might be better invested in treating users or in preventing drug use through education.

Treatment advocates might also have challenged the deeper premises of the punitive paradigm by arguing that the fundamental causes of use and abuse were rooted in part in social structures and that treatment was therefore a matter of social responsibility and urban reform, education, and other government social policies. But many supporters instead promoted a concept of treatment that drew from the same deep strand in American culture that underlay the punitive paradigm: the premise of individual responsibility. Many enforcement and treatment advocates shared the notion that the solution to the drug problem lay primarily at the individual level; whereas enforcers looked to punishment to dissuade the individual user, treatment supporters looked to therapy to assist and empower the user. For those who saw addiction as a disease, the focus was on treating (perhaps even curing) the individual, not on changing the social conditions that had encouraged drug abuse and addiction in the first place. For those who saw addiction as a problem of individual will, therapeutic communities were required to reform "addictive personalities" and provide the supportive, drug-free environments needed to enable addicts to break their reliance on drugs. Behind such programs was a dominant ethic of individual responsibility, work, and self-help.

The position taken by the most likely opponents of drug treatment—law-enforcement agents—was also important in shaping the public response to treatment. Law-enforcement officials were well positioned to mobilize public opposition to programs that challenged their punitive approach. But despite the skepticism some felt about the claims of treatment and prevention, many in the criminal-justice system saw treatment as a useful adjunct, not a threat, to punishment. They understood that under prohibition, many drug users would continue to commit crimes as long as they remained addicted. Indeed, it was in the federal narcotics farms in the 1950s that methadone detoxification was first attempted. Not only were enforcement advocates willing to recognize that treatment could reduce crime, but they saw a way to marry the two strategies: the threat or exercise of punishment, they believed, could be used to encourage or force drug users into treatment—and thus permanently off drugs. In 1961, for example, California began a large-scale "civil-commitment" program in which thousands of actual or alleged addicts were sentenced to treatment.[44]

There was also a political reason for the limited resistance met by treatment advocates. When President Nixon chose to embrace treatment as a crime-fighting tool, an alliance was forged between anticrime conservatives and protreatment liberals. Nixon, we will see in the next chapter, made the fight against crime a central issue of his first administration, specifically identifying drug addiction as a major cause of crime. His war on crime became a war on drugs, and in this context he and his advisors embraced treatment—specifically, methadone maintenance—as one effective instrument in fighting crime. In 1970 Nixon's Domestic Council staff justified methadone maintenance in these terms: "In 1972 [an election year] citizens will be looking at crime statistics across the nation in order to see whether expectations raised in 1968 have been met. The federal government has only one economic and effective technique for reducing crime in the streets—methadone maintenance."[45] The 1970 Drug Abuse Act simultaneously launched Nixon's punitive drug war and dramatically escalated spending on treatment, with particular emphasis given to methadone.[46] Those in the treatment community, meanwhile, recognized the benefits of packaging treatment as an instrument in Nixon's war on crime and drugs. Treatment as a crime-fighting tool promised to net far more funding than did treatment packaged as a health and rehabilitation measure.

The theory and practice of treatment that took hold in the 1960s and 1970s thus did not seriously threaten the punitive paradigm and policy agenda. But it did hold within it the seeds of an alternative paradigm. It constituted an important criticism of a central element of the punitive strategy: primary reliance on the punishment and criminalization of addicts in order to discourage use. Despite the cautious tone of many of its advocates, the treatment approach represented and publicly reinforced an important strain in American political culture that was quite distinct from the punitive moralism of the dominant drug paradigm. It emphasized the physiological and psychological harms caused by drug abuse and addiction, not the moral wrongdoing or criminality of the drug taker; it implied the need to extend care and help to those who were ill, not condemnation and punishment to those who were bad.

There was an even more radical critique implicit in methadone maintenance, but it was underemphasized by methadone advocates, often for political reasons. Methadone maintenance conceived of the drug problem not as drug use per se but in terms of the harms caused by drugs (addiction) and by drug policies (which encouraged criminality); long-term maintenance of patients on drugs such as methadone was legitimate because the central issue was reducing harm and enabling those with health problems to control the consequences of these problems and lead productive lives.

But if an inchoate health paradigm was implicit in the treatment approach, it was never forged into a coherent alternative to the punitive paradigm; and there was no political movement in the treatment community to challenge the dominant paradigm. Treatment—and eventually prevention—became a legitimate but minor supplement to threats and punishment in the effort to stop all drug use. In the end, a potentially transformative political struggle over the nature of drug addiction instead became a pragmatic conflict over how funds were to be allocated—with treatment supporters pressing endlessly for a larger share of a federal budget dominated by law enforcement.

THE MARIJUANA CHALLENGE

More than the campaign for treatment, the movement to decriminalize the possession and use of marijuana directly threatened central premises of the reigning paradigm. In the 1960s and 1970s large sectors of the population, the media, and even some public officials began to dispute the notion that use of a drug—marijuana—was morally wrong or caused crime, or that moderate consumption was dangerous to users or society. Widespread use of marijuana, particularly by middle-class youth, generated a wider level of experience and familiarity with the drug. Other drugs, including lysergic acid diethylamide (LSD),[47] were also used, but no other drug triggered the broad-based campaign for decriminalization that marijuana did. A popular distinction emerged between "soft" drugs that did not create drug dependence (like marijuana) and "hard" drugs that did (like heroin); and a broad consensus arose that harsh penalties such as jail time should not be enforced against marijuana users.[48] During the Carter administration, the president himself supported legislation to decriminalize possession of small quantities of marijuana.

The Roots of Opposition

Criticisms of the war against marijuana varied: some wanted to legalize sales, some merely wanted to decriminalize possession and use. But most critics shared an antipathy to the moral righteousness that had long informed antidrug zealots and the reigning punitive paradigm, and they drew on various powerful strains in American culture.

One critical position was anchored in the American tradition of tolerance of difference, in the principle that the personal behavior of a minority must be tolerated if others are not being harmed. Another criticism drew on American pragmatism, arguing that the war on marijuana was ineffective and was causing more harm than good. A third and more pointed form of criticism came from supporters of marijuana—often white, middle-class, and young—who felt they were challenging the materialism and rigid social norms of the dominant culture. But even this middle-class counterculture drew on themes in American culture—not the least of which was the embrace of immediate gratification, a value that was actively promoted by mid-twentieth-century consumer capitalism.

Perhaps the most powerful criticism of the war against marijuana use, however, was rooted in the deep strain of individualism and free choice that runs through American culture. The decision to use marijuana, argued many antiprohibitionists, was at heart a question of individual freedom to make private choices. They argued that marijuana use did not harm the user and, more importantly, that it did not cause the user to harm others—and thus the government had no more right to interfere with it than with other personal, "self-regarding" actions.

Libertarian conservatives, liberals, and many on the left joined forces in a campaign for freedom from state authority—with marijuana as its symbol. Conservative columnist James J. Kilpatrick, for example, favored decriminalization: "I don't give a hoot about marijuana, but I care about freedom!"[49] Richard Cowan, writing in the conservative *National Review,* argued that "the hysterical myths about marihuana . . . have led conservatives to condone massive programs of social engineering, interference in the affairs of individuals, monstrous bureaucratic waste."[50] Those identified with the left-leaning counterculture, meanwhile, frequently tied their use of marijuana to an individual right to "do their own thing" and to rebel against a "higher" authority—the authority of parents, the authority of the state—that arbitrarily imposed its values on them. Their rebellion had echoes of the rugged individualism and rejection of state authority of America's mythic past. Those who took a more political position often held that the authority of elders and of the state could be flaunted because it was unjust and therefore illegitimate: they viewed the "power structure" as not only conducting an immoral war in Vietnam and denying minorities at home their rights but also enforcing harsh penalties on marijuana users that were senseless, unjust, and obviously hypocritical, because far more dangerous practices, such as alcohol consumption, were permitted.

Such claims resonated with many Americans, but these deep cultural roots do not by themselves explain the movement for reform. It took organized political opposition, together with mass resistance to legal sanctions, to transform these cultural ideals into a challenge to the punitive prohibition of marijuana.

One source of political opposition came from scientists, health officials, and professional organizations, who presented evidence that marijuana was not addictive and that harsh penalties were both unjust and ineffective. By the late 1960s such criticism was widely broadcast in the media and in congressional hearings. Legislative action followed, expanding the attack. Of particular importance was congressional authorization of a new National Commission on Marijuana and Drug Abuse, advanced by Rep. Ed Koch (D-New York) as a provision of the Comprehensive Drug Abuse Prevention and Control Act of 1970. Nine of the commission's thirteen members were appointed by President Nixon. Its March 1973 report emerged as one of the most comprehensive official studies—and critiques—of government policy to date. On the marijuana issue, the commission challenged fundamental assumptions of the punitive policy, arguing that "there is no evidence that experimental or intermittent use of marihuana causes physical or psychological harm. The risk lies instead in the heavy, long-term use of the drug, particularly the most potent preparations. Marihuana does not lead to physical dependency. . . . No brain damage has been documented relating to marihuana use, in contrast with the well-established damage of chronic alcoholism."[51] The commission recommended that growing and selling marijuana for profit should remain a criminal offense but that possession and use should be decriminalized.[52] The proposals were endorsed by a long list of mainstream news and professional organizations, including the ABA, the AMA, the American Public Health Association, the National Education Association, the Consumers Union, the National Council of Churches, the National Conference of Commissioners on Uniform State Laws, and the American Academy of Pediatrics.[53]

These reports and arguments might have been deflected despite their scientific grounding—as were the LaGuardia report in the 1940s and the arguments by Dr. Treadway and Rep. Coffee in the 1930s—but two factors forced policymakers to take notice. The experience of millions of Americans with marijuana, first, had led them to question some of the myths of the punitive paradigm. The national survey conducted in 1971 by the National Commission on Marijuana and Drug Abuse estimated that 24 million Americans over the age of eleven had used marijuana at least once.[54] Many of the parents of youthful users also began to think differently about the user-as-criminal assumption when their sons or daughters were arrested. They were receptive to expert opinions such as that of the American Orthopsychiatric Association, which suggested that such "criminal penalties . . . could lead to branding as criminal a portion of American youth to whom we look for constructive social contribution and leadership."[55]

Equally important was the social composition of marijuana users and their families: marijuana use was popular among white American adults and young people across classes, from business professionals to factory workers.[56] A sizable number of middle-class and professional users were willing to employ their education and economic clout to defend marijuana publicly and politically. The result was significant pressure for reform. Had marijuana use skyrocketed only among poor urban blacks and Hispanics, Jerome Himmelstein points out, it "hardly would have led to the myriad changes in stereotypes, political forces, and arguments that actually resulted in the reform of marijuana laws and the reformulation of its dangers."[57]

The reform-oriented atmosphere of the 1960s and 1970s provided a receptive political context for these advocates to exercise their clout at the polls and through newly created organizations. Local and national groups were established to promote the decriminalization or legalization of marijuana, the most prominent of which was the National Organization for the Reform of Marijuana Laws (NORML), founded in 1970. By 1978 eleven states had decriminalized possession of small amounts of marijuana.[58] These reforms were in part the result of campaigns by groups like NORML, which lobbied hard, seeking out sympathetic legislators and flying in expert witnesses to testify. In a number of states, prominent local citizens and legislators took the initiative. In some states, such as California, a critical factor was the young Democrats committed to marijuana-law reform who were swept into office in the November 1974 elections, three months after President Nixon resigned over the

Watergate affair. In other states, such as Oregon, Ohio, and Colorado, strong support and even leadership by prominent Republicans helped produce decriminalization legislation.[59]

The push to decriminalize marijuana was first tolerated and then actively supported by the White House. President Ford did not share President Nixon's vehement contempt for drug users. President Carter put the issue on the legislative agenda soon after he was elected. Two months after Carter was inaugurated, his special assistant for health issues, Dr. Peter Bourne, testified before Congress and argued for the decriminalization of marijuana. He was supported by officials from the DEA, the State Department, NIDA, NIMH, the Justice Department, and the Customs Service.[60] In August 1977 Carter sent his own message to Congress: "Penalties against possession of a drug should not be more damaging to an individual than the use of the drug itself; and where they are, they should be changed. Nowhere is this more clear than in the laws against possession of marihuana in private for personal use."[61] Following the recommendations of the National Commission on Marijuana and Drug Abuse, he urged that possession of small amounts of marijuana be decriminalized.

Defeat and Backlash

Despite the broad reach of the marijuana reformers—both in government and among the public—the movement was defeated. The effort was undone in part by personal attacks on Bourne by the leadership of NORML, which was angered by his support for antimarijuana measures in Mexico. Their success in discrediting Bourne lost them a major ally in the administration. President Carter, meanwhile, was unwilling to use further political capital to spearhead reforms. The proposed federal legislation ultimately died in Congress.[62]

More important than the immediate legislative defeat, however, was the conservative resistance to the marijuana reform movement that had been brewing throughout the 1960s and 1970s and was coalescing into a powerful counterattack. Throughout this period, prohibitionist forces still had a strong hold on enforcement agencies and the legal system. Despite reform efforts, law-enforcement agencies continued to enforce punitive policies, at times aggressively. Marijuana arrests rose from 18,000 in 1965 to 188,000 in 1970.[63] Some government officials, such as FBI Director Hoover, used marijuana arrests as a strategy to attack and weaken the left.[64]

But it was outside government, among moralistic, conservative groups, that the strongest reaction to the decriminalization movement was mounting. Unlike the more libertarian conservatives who decried state intervention in individual affairs, these antivice conservatives organized as a movement in the 1970s, anxious to reverse the new trend toward tolerance for drugs. They saw the marijuana reformers as part of a larger threat from the left and from the countercultural movement; they sought to roll back protest and permissiveness and to rearm America morally at home and militarily abroad. Many such conservatives identified marijuana with threats to patriotism and American security. It was no coincidence, they believed, that many of the people who were protesting the Vietnam War were also using and promoting marijuana: at the root of both was a fundamental contempt for traditional American values.[65]

These antivice conservatives rejected the defense of decriminalization in the name of free choice and antiauthoritarianism. They saw drug use not as private and self-regarding but as contagious and criminal. Furthermore, it corrupted the values they wished to teach their children—values that hinged on the authority of parents, the state, and the law. Unable to resuscitate the killer-weed myth—widespread marijuana use had put this to rest—the new moral conservatives resurrected and modernized other antidrug symbols. The college crash pad was equated with the opium den of the past, and the passive and unproductive "hippie" replaced earlier images of blacks, Chinese, and Mexicans in the drug debate.[66] The seriousness of the perceived threat was reflected in the words of Henry Gordano, head of the U.S. Bureau of Narcotics, who told a congressional committee in 1967 of the campaign to legalize marijuana: "I am afraid this is just another effort to break down our whole American system."[67] Conservative S. K. Oberdeck described the nub of the problem in similarly dire terms in a 1971 National Review article: "The weed is an adjunct, forcing tool and instrument of initiation for a lifestyle that generally rejects or seeks to bring down 'ordered life as we know it.'"[68]

The images and rhetoric circulated by zealous, moralistic, conservative groups fell on fertile ground as the 1970s came to a close, for several reasons. The defeat of the marijuana reform effort in Congress had weakened the reform movement and its public influence. Particularly among conservative Americans, the harsh law-and-order platform of the Nixon administration, combined with long months of urban riots and social unrest, had left an enduring legacy of fear of street crime and of a broader breakdown of order. Above all, the idea embedded in the punitive paradigm that drugs were dangerous and morally wrong had been so deeply ingrained in American minds by decades of official reinforcement that it was difficult for many to embrace the notions of drug tolerance circulated for a brief period by the marijuana reformers.

By the end of the 1970s concerned parents had organized a national antidrug campaign in reaction to the spread of marijuana use. Groups like the National Federation of Parents for a Drug Free Youth (NFP) began to monitor government publications in an effort to censor what they saw as prodrug statements, such as reports about the varying dangers and addictive properties of different drugs. Such information, they felt, was dangerous because it could be interpreted as condoning drug use. Echoing familiar assumptions of the punitive paradigm, they insisted that all illegal drugs must be equally excoriated for their dangers. By 1980 such groups helped form the backbone of the self-described moral majority, joining forces with other political conservatives to sweep Ronald Reagan into power. Their support, as we see in the next chapter, helped fuel Reagan's war on drugs—a campaign that dwarfed Nixon's drug war in scope as well as severity.[69]

The marijuana challenge had been subverted—but its evolution and collapse are instructive, particularly when compared with the treatment challenge. Treatment was able to coexist with a war on supply and users. The marijuana challenge, however, threatened the core of the punitive paradigm, attacking the claims that drugs such as marijuana were intrinsically wrong or dangerous, that they caused crime, that drug users and sellers were criminals, and that harsh punishment was the best way to stop use. Although the main goal of reformers was to remove marijuana from the punitive paradigm—not to challenge the punitive approach to other drugs—the marijuana reform movement did sow the seeds for the more full-blown alternative approach, the drug-legalization paradigm, which plays an important (if marginalized) role in political debate today.

The political movement to decriminalize marijuana also took a very different form than did the movement for treatment reform. Initially emerging from the popular resistance of largely middle-class youth, it was unorganized and had little official voice or support in the national government. Eventually, supporters of decriminalization did organize, and professional organizations and even some elected officials publicly pressed for marijuana reforms. Their impetus and clout stemmed from the changes in practice already under way; law enforcers, the organizers pointed out, were simply bucking the tide. The supporters of treatment, in contrast, never had such a mass base. They came from the health-care and legal professions and counted from the start on support within the government, primarily in the health-care bureaucracy.

Treatment advocates, moreover, were successful in creating drug-treatment institutions, within and outside federal and state bureaucracies—institutions parallel to but not directly threatening to the drug-enforcement bureaucracy. This meant that the treatment bureaucracy was often overshadowed by its much stronger enforcement counterpart and by the reigning punitive paradigm. But it also meant there was ongoing support for funding and continued emphasis on treatment. Although the movement to decriminalize marijuana did for a time succeed in changing laws and reducing penalties, it was never institutionalized in state or local bureaucracies; it did not develop sustained support in the Democratic Party; and it never successfully dismantled elements of the drug-enforcement apparatus or the embedded antimarijuana orientations inside these institutions. As a result, it ultimately became vulnerable to the counterattack by the right in the 1980s.

CONCLUSION

The history of U.S. drug control clarifies that nothing is inevitable or "natural" about the conventional wisdom that informs the current approach to drugs. The punitive paradigm is the product of protracted political struggles that set the agenda for an increasingly impoverished and narrow public debate. Although battles over how to define and confront America's drug problem have continued throughout the century, the past illuminates an important characteristic of these struggles: the arena of political struggle was progressively narrowed, particularly early in the century, as successive rounds of conflict consolidated elements of the punitive paradigm.

Certain questions about the causes, character, and response to drug use that were open in the early 1900s were no longer open a few decades later. The political struggles that produced the Harrison Act put regulation of drug use on the national agenda for the first time. But the act left control in the hands of physicians and pharmacists and did not criminalize addicts or punish possession or use. The question of how to understand and address addiction and abuse remained open; the option of medical treatment was as alive as the option of punishment. It took a sustained campaign by antivice crusaders and Treasury Department officials to further constrict the agenda—and prohibition and punishment by law-enforcement officials replaced treatment by the medical community as the acceptable mode of drug control. The central issue for debate was narrowed from how to enforce the regulation of drugs by doctors to how to suppress suppliers and users. By the late 1930s the previously open question of how to deal with marijuana, a drug with milder effects and less addictive qualities than heroin and cocaine, was also closed: the ban on marijuana collapsed such medical distinctions between mind-affecting drugs, and all fell under the punitive model. The central drug-policy question by the 1950s was how tough to make punitive sanctions in order to eliminate supply and use.

The challenges of the 1960s and 1970s demonstrated that the dominant punitive paradigm was by no means monolithic. Powerful social forces could still be mobilized to challenge some of its basic assumptions. But substantial reform was exceedingly difficult. By the time the treatment movement gained force, critical assumptions about addicts and abuse were already solidly in place. Had such a movement emerged at a different historical moment—when fundamental questions about how to respond to addiction and abuse remained open—it might have altered the direction of the nation's approach to drugs. Instead, treatment came to coexist uneasily within a punitive antidrug strategy, as a limited supplement to law enforcement. The marijuana challenge was a more frontal assault on the assumptions of the paradigm: unlike treatment, decriminalization could not be reconciled with the punitive law-enforcement approach. Once again, had such a movement emerged at a different time—in the late 1930s, for instance, when prohibitionists were rallying support to outlaw marijuana—its impact might have been quite different. By the 1970s the principle of prohibition was deeply rooted, and the legalizers were deflected.

This is not the end of the story. The paradigm does not fully explain the politics of denial; it merely sets the stage for it. It shapes the interests and interpretations of those who craft, vote on, and implement policy. Other political and institutional dynamics are also at work in setting drug policy: presidents seeking public approval, bureaucrats seeking increased funding, members of Congress seeking reelection. It is the conjuncture of the punitive paradigm and these political dynamics that generates the politics and policies of drug control, past and present. In the following chapters we look at how this particular way of thinking about drugs combines with the processes of key American institutions—the presidency, the bureaucracy, and the Congress—to perpetuate a politics of denial.

6 Presidential Drug Wars and the Narco-Enforcement Complex

The reigning drug war paradigm frames America's drug problem and its solution, and most Americans today simply accept it as conventional wisdom. It defines any use of any drug as criminal and morally wrong; it delineates stopping all drug use as the government's task; and it sees coercion and punishment—against dealers and users alike—as the appropriate means toward this end. These premises have informed the U.S. government's particular approach to drug control since the 1920s.

This framework of ideas and assumptions, however, cannot alone account for the persistence of American antidrug policies. Understanding what fuels the drug war demands attention not only to the paradigm but also to the politics behind drug war policies—in particular, to the ways key institutions (the presidency, the federal bureaucracy, and the Congress) work to perpetuate a failed strategy.

Most Americans learn several simple notions about government and policy in school. Our institutions of government should, over time, correct for policies that consistently fail. The federal bureaucratic system should provide the president with the resources and expertise to evaluate and implement effective policy. The system of checks and balances is designed to allow Congress to check and redirect misguided executive-branch policies: Congress's oversight powers allow it to scrutinize the policies of the president and the activities of the bureaucracy; its more potent power of the purse gives it the ability to cut off poorly conceived federal policies. The American system of party competition should encourage debate and deliberation and ensure that the merits of alternative policies are aired and advocated. Finally, our system of electoral accountability is designed to keep both executive-branch and congressional officials honest: the voters have the power to reject failed policies by making their voices heard at the polls.

Of course, these institutional mechanisms are imperfect at best. But what is striking in the case of drugs is that *none* of these mechanisms has produced rational debate or reevaluation.[1] Rather, the president, the federal bureaucracy, and the Congress have each helped fuel the cycle of failure and escalation. Why?

Part of the answer became clear in previous chapters. Social groups and well-positioned individuals have exerted pressure on particular presidents and members of Congress to sustain the drug strategy by maintaining or expanding tough antidrug policies. But there is more to the story than these external demands on policymakers. The internal dynamics of these institutions also help sustain the politics of denial.

Institutions of government have their own internal rules of behavior, which influence the individuals within them; many of these rules are familiar. Presidents must win popular and congressional approval to implement their political agendas. Bureaucrats must secure continued funding, and that may lead them to perpetuate outdated programs and bloated budgets. Members of Congress must seek reelection; and in a two-party system, that may lead them to minimize competition over certain issues as Democrats and Republicans converge on the center to appeal to the median voter. On the drug issue, these institutional dynamics are shaped by the punitive paradigm. Electoral politics, for example, may tell us why the positions of Democrats and Republicans alike may cluster close together at election time. But it is the influence of the paradigm that explains why they cluster around harsh, punitive policies rather than around health or social policies.

Joined with the punitive assumptions of the paradigm, we will see, these institutional dynamics work to perpetuate the politics of denial. Presidents who seek stiffer sanctions are more successful than are those who seek pragmatic reforms of a failed drug war strategy. Drug-enforcement officials find it is in their bureaucratic interest to chase the drug supply rather than look to address the reasons Americans use and abuse drugs. And Democrats and Republicans in Congress believe they will win votes by "out-toughing" each other on drug policy.

THE ROLE OF THE PRESIDENT

With the passage of the Harrison Act in 1914, the executive branch was formally charged with implementing a national drug-control policy. But until the late 1960s executive officials above the rank of Federal Bureau of Narcotics Chief Harry Anslinger rarely occupied themselves with drug-control issues. It was then that President Nixon made drugs a central national-policy concern and the drug war as we know it today began in earnest.

Not all presidents since then have been eager to pursue a punitive drug war strategy. Some, such as Gerald Ford, Jimmy Carter, and Bill Clinton, pursued lower-profile, more pragmatic, and occasionally reformist drug policies. Ronald Reagan and George Bush, in contrast, took Nixon's drug war to new heights. Yet behind the differences in presidential policy agendas lies a troubling continuity: after each escalation, beginning with Nixon's, the drug war has persisted at a new and expanded level of resources and severity. Presidential power, it seems, has played a major role in ratcheting up or maintaining the war on drugs— but not in reversing it.

Since Richard Nixon, presidents have relied on three primary instruments to set drug policy: the power of public persuasion (the "bully pulpit"), the power to launch legislative initiatives, and the power to direct the federal bureaucracy. But the drug-policy legacy each president has inherited—a punitive paradigm, a web of existing antidrug laws, and a growing drug-enforcement bureaucracy—favors those who want to perpetuate or escalate the drug war.

Nixon, Reagan, and Bush relied heavily on use of the president's bully pulpit and control of the federal bureaucracy to expand the drug war. The influence of the punitive paradigm ensured that presidential rhetoric to "get tough" on drugs and drug-related crimes fell on fertile ground; long-standing institutional support for punitive policies in the federal bureaucracy and Congress provided a ready-made base for bureaucratic expansion and tough new laws. Presidents seeking drug-policy reform, meanwhile, have had a much harder time. They have had to fight against entrenched interests in Congress and the federal bureaucracy to redirect drug-control institutions and dismantle legislation. Their attempts to rally the needed popular support have been thwarted, because the bully pulpit is not easy for drug reformers to use: their power to persuade is limited by the deep-seated public beliefs about drugs that characterize the paradigm. In the end—sometimes unintentionally—every president since Nixon has contributed to the persistence of the failed drug war.

Nixon Declares War

In 1969 Richard Nixon catapulted the abuse of drugs to the center of the political stage, declaring it a "national threat." Nixon helped spearhead new laws, pushed for dramatic funding increases, launched crime-fighting treatment programs, and expanded the small federal antidrug bureaucracy into a "narco-enforcement complex." Nixon's legacy was not only a larger drug war with deeper roots in the bureaucracy but also a reinforcement and expansion of the punitive paradigm.

Nixon drew on the long-standing association between drugs and crime in the public mind to heighten popular concerns and forge a new consensus for action. Antivice crusaders had railed against the crime-causing effects of drugs since the turn of the century; and the campaigns of Anslinger and his allies had solidified the conceptual link between drugs and crime in the 1930s. But if drug use was linked to crime in public thinking, the general phenomenon of crime was not automatically linked to drugs—until the Nixon years. From the beginning, Nixon identified drugs as a major source of crime. His decision to place crime at the top of his domestic-policy agenda thus made drug control a central issue.

"Law and order" was a key domestic theme for Republicans in the 1968 campaign. With the nation reeling from urban riots and FBI reports confirming rising street-crime rates, Nixon's line on crime was harsh and unyielding. The candidate sought explicitly to shape the terms of debate on crime: "I say that doubling the conviction rate in this country would do far more to cure crime in America than quadrupling the funds for [Hubert] Humphrey's war on poverty."[2]

Soon after his election Nixon became master of the presidential bully pulpit. By July 1969 he was addressing the nation on the grave dimensions of the national drug and crime problem: "Within the last decade, the abuse of drugs has grown from essentially a local police problem into a serious national threat to the personal health and safety of millions of Americans," he announced in a major address to Congress. "A national awareness of the gravity of the situation is needed; a new urgency and concerted national policy are needed at the Federal level to begin to cope with this growing menace to the general welfare of the United States."[3] The pressure mounted as the administration organized a media campaign to dramatize the problem. In June 1971 the president informed Congress, "The problem has assumed the dimensions of a national emergency."[4] Media executives received a similar call to arms: "Drug traffic is public enemy number one domestically in the United States today and we must wage a total offensive, worldwide, nationwide, government-wide, and, if I might say so, media-wide."[5]

Nixon's public message succeeded in making not only drug dealing but also drug addiction a symbol of crime. The White House used numbers that dramatically overestimated the heroin-addiction problem (reporting a tenfold increase in the number of addict-users from 1969 to 1971). The president then emphasized that "narcotics addiction is a major contributor to crime" because addicts "often turn to shoplifting, mugging, burglary, armed robbery, and so on" to feed their addiction.[6]

The president backed his rhetoric with legislative initiatives. The Comprehensive Drug Abuse Prevention and Control Act of 1970 merged previous federal antidrug regulations under one statute. Whereas the 1914 Harrison Act based jurisdiction of drug control on the constitutional power to tax, the 1970 act based jurisdiction on the much more expansive interstate-commerce powers of the Constitution. A particularly harsh punitive measure in the act allowed federal agents to seek "no-knock" warrants from judges, which permitted them to enter private homes and buildings for drug searches without giving notice of their "authority and purpose."

Nixon's legislative initiatives not only escalated domestic law-enforcement efforts but also permanently expanded the nation's drug war effort to include an ambitious campaign abroad. The foreign drug war was designed, in Nixon's words, to "strike at the 'supply' side of the drug equation—to halt the drug traffic by striking at the illegal producers of drugs, the growing of those plants from which drugs are derived, and trafficking in these drugs beyond our borders."[7] The concern over foreign supply had its origins in the international drug-control efforts of American missionaries in the last century and had remained a point of focus for nativist and other antivice crusaders. But before Nixon the government's approach was largely rhetorical, diplomatic, and low in profile. Nixon turned foreign supply into a prominent issue: drug traffickers from abroad became national enemies, and the war against foreign supply became a critical plank of U.S. antidrug policy.

Operation Intercept was Nixon's first attempt to strike at the source. The operation deployed two thousand agents on the Mexican border in September 1969 to search automobiles and trucks crossing the border in what was officially described as "the country's largest peacetime search and seizure operation by civil authorities." It netted little except Mexican animosity. Nixon then targeted Turkey, one of a number of countries that produced heroin aimed for the U.S. market. Turkey, however, was "the only country where we could expect dramatic results, and that was what the president wanted," explained a Nixon official—particularly before the 1972 elections. The United States applied strong diplomatic pressure, threatening to cut off aid if the Turkish government did not stop drug exports and offering reimbursement for losses resulting from reduced poppy cultivation. The Turks complied—and Nixon declared success. The temporary scarcity of heroin in 1972 and 1973, however, was soon reversed as the slack was taken up by supply from Mexico, Afghanistan, Pakistan, and the Golden Triangle in Southeast Asia.[8]

As Nixon's war-on-drugs campaign succeeded legislatively, antidrug spending ballooned. Spending on drug enforcement alone climbed from $43 million in fiscal 1970 to $321 million in fiscal 1975.[9] A vast new antidrug bureaucracy emerged with the rise in federal spending.

The previous thirty years had seen only a slow reorganization and growth in the drug-control apparatus. By the late 1960s the Federal Bureau of Narcotics (FBN) still had a relatively modest budget of $6 million (about twice its 1932 budget) and a staff of some 300 agents (roughly the same number as in 1932). A second agency, the Bureau of Drug Abuse Control, had been created in the Department of Health, Education, and Welfare in 1965 to regulate hypnotics and stimulants. And in 1968, the last year of the Johnson administration, the two agencies were merged to form the Bureau of Narcotics and Dangerous Drugs (BNDD). The new agency was placed in the Justice Department, ensuring that drugs would continue to be defined as a criminal problem, not a health problem.[10]

Nixon moved forcefully to expand the bureaucratic base for his war on drugs. When the BNDD resisted the Nixon administration's attempt to shift its enforcement focus from the higher levels of the drug-distribution system to street-level dealers, Nixon countered with an executive order establishing a new agency under direct White House control, the Office of Drug Abuse Law Enforcement (ODALE).[11] The harsh enforcement tactics of ODALE's agents—particularly their no-knock raids on the homes of innocent families—gained it notoriety and eventually helped lead to its dissolution.[12] In 1973 the Nixon administration consolidated the BNDD, ODALE, the Office of National Narcotics

Intelligence, and the Customs Service Drug Investigation Unit into a new drug superagency: the Drug Enforcement Administration (DEA).[13]

Alongside the escalation in drug war rhetoric and policies during the Nixon years was a significant escalation in funding for drug treatment.[14] As we saw in the last chapter, there was no contradiction here for Nixon: punishment and treatment were simply two instruments for fighting crime, which was his central concern. He became convinced that treatment—particularly methadone maintenance—would reduce the rate of crimes committed by addicts seeking to buy drugs. Nixon's crime-fighting logic had an enduring impact: in succeeding years, treatment advocates would frequently sell their budget requests in crime-reduction, not health-promotion, terms.

If Nixon succeeded in expanding the punitive antidrug strategy far beyond its previous limits, he also demonstrated that presidents are capable of moving the drug issue off the public agenda. Eighteen months after the Congress passed his Drug Abuse Office and Treatment Act in 1972 and only ten months after his reelection, Nixon signaled a change, announcing, in September 1973, "We have turned the corner on drug addiction in the United States."[15] The president's address was a clear statement of victory and of his intention to deescalate the rhetoric of the drug war. The evidence the president provided as a rationale for declaring victory—a decrease in the heroin supply and the number of heroin users—was hotly contested. A more plausible explanation, by many accounts, was the fact that the 1972 election was over. Anxious to level off spending, government budget- and policymakers found it necessary "to make major changes in the federal drug effort in order to prove that a victory had been won."[16] The federal antidrug effort was toned down: programs were moved from the White House into the federal bureaucracy; public campaigns against street dealers and users were abandoned; and many drug-programming responsibilities were shifted to the states, as part of the administration's "new federalism" efforts. In short order, the visibility and controversy of the federal effort was dramatically reduced.

Yet the laws, institutions, and logic of the Nixon drug war remained in place, even as the issue was quietly moved off the national agenda. Funding levels remained high: although the rate of expansion slowed after the president's turn-the-corner speech, the federal drug budget never fell to its previous level. Agencies created to fight the Nixon drug war continued to operate and expand. And the drug-crime link that

Nixon seared into the public mind did not disappear with his declaration of victory.

Ford, Carter, and the Limits to Change

An aggressive war on drugs was not a priority for the two presidents who followed Richard Nixon. Neither the political agendas nor the electoral coalitions of Gerald Ford and Jimmy Carter were served by a high-pitched campaign against drugs and crime. Yet each lacked the will or the ability to significantly reverse the course Nixon had set.

The Ford administration toned down the warlike rhetoric of the Nixon period. In a major departure, a white paper issued by the Domestic Council to the president urged acceptance of the fact that drug problems would always be with us. "We must be realistic about what can be achieved and what the appropriate Federal role is in the war against drugs," the paper stated. "We should stop raising unrealistic expectations of total elimination of drug abuse from our society." At the same time, the Ford paper confirmed "the validity of the basic strategy of balancing mutually supportive supply reduction and demand reduction activities."[17] The approach instituted under Nixon was not reversed.

Jimmy Carter sought not merely to deemphasize the tough enforcement approach to drugs but to roll back elements of it. Like Nixon, Carter turned to the presidential bully pulpit (if less aggressively) and to the legislature to make his case for reform. But he met with little success. The focus of his strategy was presented in an August 1977 speech to Congress: "My goals are to discourage all drug abuse in America—and also discourage the excessive use of alcohol and tobacco—and to reduce to a minimum the harm drug abuse causes when it does occur." Carter argued that penalties for possession of marijuana for personal use were more damaging to an individual than was the use itself. After four decades, "efforts to discourage its use with stringent laws have still not been effective." Carter proposed the decriminalization of marijuana and sought to replace criminal penalties for possession of the drug with civil fines.[18]

His proposal was limited. "We can, and should, continue to discourage the use of marijuana," Carter announced, "but this can be done without defining the smoker as a criminal."[19] He was seeking not to rewrite the nation's drug strategy but to alter the law controlling one particular drug. Nevertheless, it was a direct challenge to assumptions entrenched in the punitive paradigm that branded all drug use—including marijuana use—as wrong, dangerous, and criminal.

Carter's challenge drew fire, both from the public and from Congress. Legislatively, it went nowhere. In 1978 a variant of the president's proposal was incorporated into the Senate bill revising the criminal code (possession of less than 150 grams of marijuana was to be classified as a misdemeanor; possession of less than 30 grams a mere infraction under which no imprisonment could be ordered). It was among the most controversial of the bill's proposed provisions. The entire bill died in the House of Representatives.[20]

Despite the shifts in rhetoric and the fact that the drug war did not serve the political agendas of either Ford or Carter, neither president stemmed the continued expansion of the federal antidrug apparatus. Drug law-enforcement budgets continued to escalate, first to $382 million in fiscal 1977 under Ford and then to $855 million by fiscal 1981 under Carter.[21]

The experiences of these two presidents underline the inherited constraints—institutional and ideological—that restrict presidents interested in even minor drug-policy reforms. Both were able to deescalate the drug war rhetoric and remove the issue from the top of the agenda but were unwilling or unable to dismantle the drug war bureaucracy, to stem the rise in drug-enforcement spending, or—in Carter's case—to reverse elements of the strategy. Deeply rooted institutional interests created centers of resistance in the bureaucracy and Congress. Equally tenacious were the widely shared assumptions about the nature of the drug problem, its links to crime, and the need for a tough enforcement response led by the government.

Not surprisingly, the same institutional and ideological framework that inhibited change made escalation easy for Ronald Reagan and his successor, George Bush.

Reagan, Bush, and the Ease of Escalation

Nineteen eighty-one marked a watershed in the war on drugs: over the next twelve years the drug war escalated as never before, with budgets for drug law enforcement surging from $855 million to more than $7.8 billion in 1993.[22]

When Reagan took office, he confronted a social and political context quite different from that of Nixon, Ford, and Carter. The incoming president's drug-policy agenda was shaped by a sizable and vocal national constituency that had grown impatient with the permissive attitudes toward drug use and other counterculture activities of the previous decade. At the center of his domestic agenda was a set of social policies, articulated most powerfully by the so-called moral majority, which embodied a defense of traditional family values, conservative Christian morality, and patriotism.

The Reagan antidrug campaign was also shaped by a change in drug-use patterns. Although marijuana and heroin were still widely used, cocaine became the number-one enforcement priority by the early 1980s. Cocaine use had begun to rise in the late 1960s and early 1970s, in part as the result of stricter federal controls over other stimulants (such as speed and other amphetamines).[23] By 1979 the National Institute on Drug Abuse estimated that cocaine use had nearly tripled in two years.[24] And by 1980 "the number of cocaine powder sellers [in New York City] outnumbered that of heroin sellers by two to one."[25]

Initially, many users were middle class and affluent—powdered cocaine was a relatively expensive "status drug"—although large numbers of lower-income drug users were inhaling cocaine when they could afford it.[26] Cocaine was considered by users, and even by many medical authorities, as nonaddictive, for habitual users did not experience the physiological symptoms of heroin withdrawal.[27] By the mid-1980s a new, highly addictive cocaine derivative had hit the market: crack. Smokable cocaine had been around since the late 1970s as cocaine "free base," but not until the mid-1980s was this product packaged and mass marketed as crack, with a relatively affordable price that made it popular in poor urban neighborhoods. There was an important racial and class dimension to the reaction to crack: as use became visible in urban black and Hispanic neighborhoods, the rise of this new drug was tied to negative images of poor and minority Americans.[28]

The Reagan administration initially saw drugs as one of a number of issues that could garner and sustain support among the moral conservatives so important to the popular right-wing base of his electoral coalition. A campaign for total abstinence—Nancy Reagan's "Just Say No" drive—not only appealed to parents' groups that had organized to do something about drugs in schools but was a powerful symbolic attack on the left, the counterculture, and permissive liberal humanism. And the antidrug campaign promised to win even broader support when joined with an anticrime platform.

The national context—marked by a resurgence of conservatism in the early 1980s, the organizational strength of the moral majority, and

relatively weak antiprohibitionist forces—was thus ripe for Reagan's escalation of the drug war. Reagan was positioned to draw on the widely
shared assumptions of the punitive paradigm that had survived the 1960s
and 1970s and to gain legislative and bureaucratic support from the
drug-enforcement apparatus that Nixon had put into place.

The president moved quickly, using his executive power first to revise
executive-branch regulations, organization, and lines of authority. An
aggressive public-relations and legislative campaign followed. By the end
of his first year in office, Reagan had issued an executive order drafting
the entire federal-intelligence apparatus—including the Central Intelligence Agency (CIA)—into the war on drugs and ordering them to provide guidance to civilian drug-enforcement agencies. The president also
opened the door, for the first time, to the military's involvement in the
war on drugs by securing an amendment to the Posse Comitatus Act,
which had outlawed military involvement in civilian law enforcement
for more than a century. The Reagan administration argued successfully
that the Navy be allowed to join civilian agencies, such as the Coast
Guard, in interdicting smuggling vessels at sea, and all branches of the
military were empowered to assist Customs, the Coast Guard, and the
DEA with training, equipment, and information. Funding for the military's role in drug enforcement was $4.9 million in 1982, but it would
skyrocket to more than $1 billion by the early 1990s.[29]

In January 1982 Reagan created the South Florida Task Force, under
the leadership of Vice President George Bush, to coordinate drug-
enforcement efforts in the region.[30] This program became a prototype
for the Organized Crime Drug Enforcement Task Force Program, a centerpiece of the domestic drug strategy. Thirteen such task forces were set
up by 1984, each bringing multiple federal agencies into the drug war
effort in different regions of the country, including assistant U.S. attorneys and agents from the DEA, Customs, the FBI, the Bureau of Alcohol, Tobacco and Firearms, the Internal Revenue Service (IRS), the Coast
Guard, and the U.S. Marshals Service.[31]

In June 1982 Reagan put the federal bureaucracy on notice that the
drug war was to become a priority mission. The heads of eighteen federal agencies, the vice president, several military leaders, and the commissioner of the IRS were ordered to the White House for a special address: "We're rejecting the helpless attitude that drug use is so rampant
that we're defenseless to do anything about it. We're taking down the
surrender flag that has flown over so many drug efforts. We're running
up the battle flag. We can fight the drug problem, and we can win."[32]

Brilliantly employing the power of the executive bully pulpit to galvanize public attention, the president used speeches, radio addresses, and special events to bring his declaration of war to the halls of Congress and directly into American homes. Pledging in October 1982 "to do what is necessary to end the drug menace,"[33] the president announced a "legislative offensive" to make it easier to convict those involved with drugs and to keep them behind bars longer. In his 1983 State of the Union address, Reagan confirmed, "It is high time that we make our cities safe again. This administration hereby declares an all-out war on big-time organized crime and the drug racketeers who are poisoning our young people."[34]

The media helped fuel the Reagan effort, providing extensive coverage that built up the drug threat beginning in 1982.

> The national television networks broadcast news or documentary programs of at least one hour in length, including "Pleasure Drugs: The Great American High" (NBC) and "The Cocaine Cartel" (ABC). NBC embellished its drug awareness with the melodrama "Cocaine—One Man's Seduction." Weekly news magazines were particularly active purveyors of drugs-on-the-American-scene reportage. *Time* magazine did three cover stories on cocaine: "Cocaine: Middle Class High" (1981), "Crashing on Cocaine" (1983), and "Getting Straight" (1984). The tone of these stories left no doubt about the attitude of the writers or editors—this was bad news.[35]

For much of the next year the president pressured Congress—particularly the Democratically controlled House of Representatives—to act on his proposed legislation. In several Saturday afternoon radio speeches, he condemned House Democrats for not joining the fight against crime and drugs. Democratic representatives grew more concerned about these attacks as the November 1984 elections closed in, and they took up the president's challenge.[36]

In most respects the president's policy offensive was a political success. The administration sought and won congressional approval for a stiffening of the criminal-justice process and aggressive enforcement by a mobilized and expanded antidrug bureaucracy. The administration intended to use "a scorched-earth policy" in drug enforcement, according to former Associate Attorney General Stephen S. Trott, not only to send traffickers to jail but also to lay claim under the new forfeiture laws to "everything they own—their land, their cars, their boats, everything."[37]

The war on drugs was further intensified by Reagan's successor, George Bush. President Bush's first televised address to the nation, on 5 September 1989, set an unmistakable tone: "This is the first time since taking the oath of office that I felt an issue was so important, so threatening, that it warranted talking directly with you, the American people," the president began. He quickly declared a national consensus on the primacy of this issue—"All of us agree that the gravest domestic threat facing our nation today is drugs"—and then declared war, calling for "an assault on every front." Urging Americans to "face this evil as a nation united," Bush proclaimed that "victory over drugs is our cause, a just cause."

In a single speech the president effectively marginalized a significant proportion of the population, defining the enemy in the drug war in extremely broad terms: "Who's responsible? Let me tell you straight out. Everyone who uses drugs. Everyone who sells drugs. And everyone who looks the other way." The president laid out a clear policy agenda of tough enforcement against producers, dealers, and users. "The rules have changed: if you sell drugs, you will be caught; and when you're caught, you will be prosecuted; and once you're convicted, you will do time. Caught, prosecuted, punished." He added, "American cocaine users need to understand that our nation has zero tolerance for casual drug use." Bush proposed that "we enlarge our criminal justice system across the board. . . . When requested, we will for the first time make available the appropriate resources of America's armed forces." The president called for a $1.5 billion increase in domestic law-enforcement spending in the drug war and $3.5 billion for interdiction and foreign-supply reduction.[38]

Bush took unprecedented steps to widen the authority of federal agencies to fight drugs. Like his predecessors, he used executive orders and administrative regulations to expand the reach of drug enforcement. A 1989 executive order, for example, directed all federal agencies to check for drug violations before awarding hundreds of federal benefits.[39] To a degree unmatched by previous presidents, he used his power as commander in chief to draft the U.S. military into the drug war, elevating what had been a sporadic and relatively minor role in assisting in civilian enforcement into a major national-security mission for the armed forces. In the fall of 1989 Secretary of Defense Dick Cheney declared drugs to be a high-priority mission of the Department of Defense.[40] The fiscal 1989 National Defense Authorization Act charged the Defense Department with three new responsibilities. It was made the lead agency for detecting drug traffic into the country; given responsibility for integrating all command, control, and communications for drug interdiction into an effective network; and told to approve and fund state governors' plans for using the National Guard in state interdiction and enforce-ment.[41] Funding for the military's drug-enforcement activities increased from $357 million in 1989 to more than $1 billion in 1992.[42]

With the creation—under congressional mandate—of the president's Office of National Drug Control Policy (ONDCP) in 1989, Bush had an official arm within the executive branch to carry out his agenda. He ap-pointed William Bennett to head the office as his drug czar. "Bennett showed no hesitance," notes *Congressional Quarterly,* "in using the of-fice as a bully pulpit for pressuring Congress, state and local govern-ments and the private sector for stronger action against use of illegal drugs." By 1990 the office had a staff of 130, with a budget of $16.5 million, and was conducting public relations with Congress and the press for the president's growing war on drugs.[43]

Words and images emanating from the Oval Office were important in fueling a climate of rigid intolerance of drug use and in consolidating support behind the Bush drug war: the result was a more deeply en-trenched punitive paradigm. Presidential addresses not only raised the specter of a nation ravaged and destroyed by drugs but also legitimized a particular response to the problem, one that emphasized intolerance, enforcement, and punishment to the highest extent of the law. Televised images of the president holding up a bag of crack in a prime-time ad-dress sent a powerful message: crack can be purchased across the street from the White House; this poison is in your neighborhood, too.

The effect on the public mood was palpable. Nationwide surveys by the *New York Times*/CBS showed that in July 1989 only 20 percent of those polled considered drugs the most important problem facing the na-tion. In the wake of the president's speech two months later, 64 percent declared that drugs were the country's greatest problem.[44] The shift in public opinion was no accident. In mid-August the White House let it be known that Bush would be delivering a major speech on drugs. The media responded: in the two and a half weeks prior to the speech, the three major networks ran an average of almost three news stories a night on the issue; and in the week following the speech an average of four drug stories a night were aired—in contrast to less than one a night be-fore the president's plans were announced.[45]

In pursuit of a drug-free America, the Reagan and Bush administra-tions created a climate in which public officials insinuated that "any-thing goes." The president's drug czar told a national radio audience that he saw nothing "morally" wrong with beheading drug traffickers.[46] Los Angeles Police Chief Daryl Gates testified before Congress that casual drug users "ought to be taken out and shot." The administration argued that the death penalty should be used against large-scale dealers, and a majority in the House of Representatives nodded. Planes that were even suspected of carrying drugs should be shot down, declared a former U.S. Customs chief, and forty-eight U.S. senators agreed.[47]

This government support for extraordinary measures was paralleled by a public willingness to sacrifice fundamental democratic freedoms in pursuit of the drug war. A *Washington Post*/ABC News poll taken after Bush's 1989 speech revealed that 62 percent of those polled were willing to give up "a few of the freedoms we have in this country" for the war on drugs. Fifty-two percent said they would approve of homes being searched for drugs; 67 percent were willing to have cars stopped and searched without court orders; and 82 percent would permit the military to join the war on drugs.[48]

By the end of the decade Presidents Reagan and Bush had effectively built on the ideological and institutional groundwork laid by previous presidents—particularly Richard Nixon—to create a harsher, more expansive antidrug strategy. The war against supply, both at home and abroad, reached new heights. Marijuana-liberalization reforms of the 1970s were rolled back, and decriminalization of marijuana was taken off the policy agenda. The distinctions that had emerged in the 1970s, between hard and soft drugs and between casual users and addicts, no longer informed mainstream policy debate; and as these distinctions were erased, the war against all users—including casual users—reached unprecedented levels. The notion of prevention was seized from drug reformers who sought increased funds for education and usurped to justify increased funds for punishment of casual users, under the argument that fear was the most effective way to prevent the spread of drug use. Mounting evidence of the policy's inability to produce results and of its serious negative effects was of little consequence.

Clinton and the Limits to Reform Revisited

If drug policy under Gerald Ford and Jimmy Carter demonstrated limits to presidentially led reform, the experience of Bill Clinton confirmed them. Like Ford and Carter, Clinton believed that his electoral constituency and political agenda were not served by a high-profile war on drugs. Whereas Ford had limited his reform efforts to deescalating the drug war rhetoric and Carter had challenged a central premise of the punitive paradigm by supporting marijuana decriminalization, Clinton chose to steer a cautious, moderate path, offering up limited and modest proposals for reform. Like his predecessors, he failed to significantly alter the course of U.S. drug policy: by 1995 the drug war budget was larger than ever, and the proportion devoted to enforcement was essentially unchanged.

The new administration wanted to deescalate the Reagan and Bush drug wars—to soften the rhetoric, to downsize and streamline the drug war bureaucracy, and to advance a policy that placed greater emphasis on treatment and prevention. But the drug war legacy Clinton inherited severely limited his prospects for winning even this modest reform without a fight. The public had grown accustomed to hearing a get-tough line on drugs and crime; and although the economy had replaced drugs and crime at the top of America's worries, the public was in no mood to be generous toward drug users and dealers. Moral conservatives, mobilized during the Reagan / Bush years, remained organized and vigilant. The sweeping network of drug war laws and institutions, created by former presidents and Congresses, was solidly in place.

The constraints facing a new president with a reformist drug-policy agenda—but no organized political constituency pressing for reform—were formidable. Change would take a prolonged and visible struggle; it would demand expending political capital. And the Clinton administration had no stomach for a fight on this issue. Not surprisingly, drug policy quickly became a low priority for the administration. Clinton's efforts to use the instruments of executive power to affect drug policy were cautious, modest, and halting; and when they met resistance, the president tended to back down rather than wage a costly political battle.

From the outset the drug-policy message emanating from Clinton's bully pulpit was both mixed and muted. As a candidate Clinton had leveled a strong attack on his opponent: "Bush confuses being tough with being smart, especially on drugs," he said in 1992. "[He] thinks locking up addicts instead of treating them before they commit crimes . . . is clever politics. That may be, but it certainly isn't sound policy, and the consequences of his cravenness could ruin us." Clinton argued for a policy of drug treatment on demand. "Without it," he said, "the criminals will revert when they're released, and the problem will just get worse. Emphasizing treatment may not satisfy people fed up with being preyed upon, but a President should speak straight even if what he advocates isn't popular. If he sticks to his guns, the results will prove the wisdom of his policy."[49]

At the same time, Clinton had no desire to challenge the role of law enforcement in drug control. His campaign literature emphasized the tough positions he had taken while governor of Arkansas, touting the state's successful drug-interdiction program and its harsh, extended sentences for those caught selling drugs near schools. At the Democratic National Convention in July 1992, Clinton sought to further establish his hard-line credentials: "[President Bush] hasn't fought a real war on crime and drugs; I will."[50]

The new administration's positions and policy priorities on drug control emerged more clearly as the Clinton cabinet took shape. Clinton himself issued few statements on drug problems, but within months top Clinton appointees—notably drug czar Lee Brown and Attorney General Janet Reno—began to articulate a view of the drug problem and drug policy quite distinct from that of Clinton's immediate predecessors. Brown, who had promoted community policing and crime prevention as head of the New York City police department, sought to change the terms of debate. "You won't hear us using the metaphor 'drug war,'" he announced. "We should help those who need help and arrest those who are trafficking in drugs. But I don't think we should declare war against our own people."[51] The new drug czar argued the importance of seeing substance-abuse addiction as a health problem, "a chronic relapsing disease," and asserted that treatment should be judged by criteria other than total abstinence: "Partial success can be found when former heavy drug users reduce their consumption . . . decrease their involvement in criminal activity, and generally impose a smaller burden on society. They may still use drugs on occasion, but the damage they inflict on society has been minimized."[52] In interviews and testimony Brown emphasized the importance of an approach that takes seriously the individual needs and social context of each patient. "If you have a person who may go through a counseling program but there are other problems in that person's life—they can't find a job, they go back in the same trap that got them in trouble to begin with—then you haven't accomplished your objective."[53]

Under Brown's leadership, the Office of National Drug Control Policy released a national drug strategy that articulated a clear shift in emphasis: "Treating America's drug problem must start with an aggressive effort to finally break the cycle of hard-core drug use."[54] Hard-core users, explained Brown, are "about 20 percent of the drug-user population. Yet they consume about 80 percent of the cocaine that's sold in the streets of our cities. They commit much of the crime and put a burden on our health care costs. It's a major problem. Previous strategies did not address the hard-core user."[55]

Early in the new administration, Attorney General Reno offered her own critique of the nation's drug war, arguing that drug policy needed to be reevaluated and that drug abuse was a symptom of deeper problems. The limited resources of the justice system, according to Reno, should be directed against violent offenders—not against addicts who were caught selling drugs and who needed treatment more than punishment. Shortly after taking office, Reno ordered a review of mandatory sentences for drug offenses. She was concerned that nonviolent offenders were often serving mandatory ten- or fifteen-year sentences, filling up the nation's prisons "while we watch dangerous offenders going free."[56] The report found the impact of mandatory minimums to be severe: 60 percent of inmates in federal prisons were drug offenders, and a third of these were low-level dealers or couriers with no record of violence.[57]

Such early statements by administration officials quickly drew fire from conservatives, however, and it soon became clear that the White House did not want a political battle over the drug issue. After hearing the conclusions of Reno's mandatory-sentencing review in late 1993, White House officials worried that it would make Clinton look soft on crime, so they tried, unsuccessfully, to withhold the report.[58] Before long, Reno had toned down her statements.

White House reluctance to confront deeply rooted assumptions about drug policy emerged again a few months later, when Surgeon General Joycelyn Elders suggested that much drug-related crime might be caused by drug-enforcement policies—and that legalization should at least be studied for its potential to reduce such policy-generated harms. The surgeon general's statements triggered a political firestorm and eventually contributed to her dismissal by the president. The release of the annual *National Drug Control Strategy* in February 1994, soon after Elders's remark, was carefully staged to correct any public misperception about the administration's position: Clinton took his vice president and half of his cabinet to a county jail in Maryland to unveil his plan to combat crime with money for drug treatment while continuing a tough law-enforcement policy. He was, reported the *New York Times,* "plainly sensitive to the possibility of being seen as too eager to coddle drug users rather than punish them," and Clinton emphasized that his plan was both "tough and smart."[59]

The backlash from those early statements led the administration to further lower its reformist rhetoric. Concern about the health and criminal consequences of hard-core drug abuse continued to surface in official statements and documents, but there was little attempt to promote an alternative approach to drug control among the public. Clinton's drug czar—though widely admired for his intellect, principles, and experience—lacked the political savvy and forceful style needed to use the bully pulpit effectively to convey his message. More importantly, the White House decision to avoid a political fight limited the impact of the administration's reform-oriented policy positions: "I've been frustrated at the lack of attention the president has paid to drugs," explained an administration official who worked on the issue. "Unfortunately, the White House sees drugs as a no-win issue."[60]

If Clinton's use of the bully pulpit was cautious and largely ineffective, his attempts to turn the operations of the federal bureaucracy to his own purposes were equally limited. Within his first year Clinton had learned one of the limits of drug-policy reform: it was one thing to deescalate the rhetoric of the drug war and quite another to dismantle or reorganize federal drug war agencies. Clinton sought changes in the federal drug bureaucracy for two reasons: he wanted to meet his campaign pledge to downsize the federal government, and he wanted to make federal drug-control efforts more efficient and effective. His efforts were widely perceived as an expression of the low priority his administration placed on fighting the war on drugs, however, and they met resistance from lawmakers of both parties as well as from agency officials.

Within weeks of entering office, Clinton made a bold move to downsize the ONDCP, which by many accounts had become a dumping ground for Republican political appointees. In February 1993, in an effort to meet his campaign promise to reduce the White House staff by one-quarter, Clinton eliminated all but 25 of the agency's 146 positions—an 83 percent reduction. The move quickly drew fire. Members of Congress from both parties demanded to know how the administration would conduct an effective drug war given the cuts. In the end, Congress rejected the president's proposal, requiring the office to retain at least 40 staff and doubling his proposed budget for the office.[61] Rep. John Conyers (D-Michigan) called the action "a wake-up call to alert the administration that Congress wants real authority vested in the drug czar's office if the office is to continue."[62]

Another attempt at bureaucratic reform came when Clinton backed an FBI-sponsored proposal to merge the twenty-year-old DEA, a product of Nixon's drug war, into the FBI. A national performance review conducted by Vice President Al Gore promoted the change as an effort to end costly duplication and turf wars in the antidrug effort; Gore also suggested that the proposed merger would eventually save some $84 million.[63] Under the proposal the DEA, a separate entity within the Justice Department, would become a division of the FBI. The idea was not new—it had first emerged under the administration of another would-be reformer, Jimmy Carter.

The DEA, in a white paper submitted to Attorney General Reno, objected strongly: "Downgrading the United States government drug enforcement effort from a single-mission agency to just one of ten divisions within the FBI would greatly disrupt our nation's drug effort." The paper pointedly added that the merger "would also trigger the perception of a serious reduction in the federal government's commitment to this crime problem." The DEA was joined in its criticism by the 8,000-member Federal Law Enforcement Officers Association, representing officers from fifty agencies. The proposal met further resistance on Capitol Hill, particularly from House Democrats. Charles Schumer (D-New York) condemned any move that would "wipe out the only federal law enforcement agency focused exclusively on fighting drugs." William Hughes (D-New Jersey) called the merger proposal "a hostile takeover" and reminded the administration that "such a policy must not proceed, and cannot succeed, without the express approval of the Congress."[64] In the end the administration backed down. Reno announced in October that she would seek to enhance coordination through other, more modest means.

Like his bureaucratic initiatives, Clinton's early attempts to enact reforms in the legislative arena were modest and ultimately limited in impact. By the end of the 1980s the punitive approach to drug control had seen expression in a welter of tough new laws; many of the lawmakers still sat on Capitol Hill. Clinton learned quickly how controversial even modest drug-policy reform would be in the early fight over interdiction. Interdiction budgets had been declining in the last years of the Bush administration, and Clinton proposed further funding cuts in 1993, arguing that it is "an expensive high technology endeavor, and its effectiveness has been undercut by increased drug production and the continued high profitability of the trade."[65] But the small cuts he proposed in the interdiction budget (7 percent, or about $94 million) were blocked by Congress. Instead of defending the cuts—and risking the appearance of weakness in the war against drugs—the administration retreated. Not only did the President choose not to push for the proposed cuts, but a new position, interdiction coordinator, was created by administration officials who were anxious to reassure conservative critics in Congress that they took interdiction seriously. The new coordinator (who was also the head of the Coast Guard) immediately began to press for more funding.[66]

The main thrust of Clinton's reforms, however, lay elsewhere. The administration's 1994 *National Drug Control Strategy* articulated a shift in policy priorities to address the need for adequate treatment and health services, particularly for chronic hard-core drug users. The administration saw three vehicles for such a policy shift: health-care reform, increased federal funding, and new treatment programs within the criminal-justice system. The first was a bold—if doomed—initiative. It challenged the drug-use-as-crime premise at the heart of the punitive paradigm by identifying drug abuse as a health problem demanding government intervention. The goal was to "enact the first-ever guarantee of basic drug use treatment services as part of the President's Health Security Act. At a minimum, this will provide basic substance abuse treatment benefits to the more than 58 million Americans who have no coverage at all."[67]

A modest but important provision for treatment was built into the proposed Health Security Act, guaranteeing every American 30 days a year of inpatient treatment, 60 days of intensive outpatient treatment, or 120 days of less-intensive outpatient treatment. The provisions were the result of intense efforts by treatment advocates, health officials in substance-abuse agencies, and the vice president's wife, Tipper Gore. The defeat of the health-care bill (for reasons unrelated to the substance-abuse provisions) cut this initiative short.

The second vehicle was the federal drug-treatment budget. Clinton did not seek to shift funds from law enforcement to treatment, a move that would have confronted the long-standing enforcement emphasis of the drug war and triggered a political battle. Instead, he chose to request a $355 million increase in spending in his 1994 drug strategy, to be targeted for treatment of hard-core drug users. The sum was relatively modest, given the scope of the problem: the administration estimated that 2.5 million Americans in need of such treatment (other experts put the estimate at 4 to 6 million) faced a capacity of only 1.4 million treatment slots. The budget request sought to increase capacity by an additional 140,000 slots.

The move drew no strong objections—and even some support—from the Democratically controlled Congress. But with Capitol Hill anxious to cut deficit spending, such a proposal demanded the active and forceful intervention of the administration: members of Congress needed a clear signal that this was a high-priority initiative for the president. When no such message came, congressional appropriators who were struggling to meet budget ceilings chipped away at the treatment initiative in order to save other programs. In the end Clinton won a mere $57 million of his proposed $355 million increase—and lost the stipulation that the funds would be restricted to treating hard-core users.[68]

The failure to reorient national policy in ways that addressed the health problems of hard-core users was also reflected in an important administration "nonaction." Clinton's health and drug officials were well aware that contaminated needles shared by intravenous drug users were a major source of HIV transmission—and that needle-exchange programs had emerged to address this public-health threat. But when the Centers for Disease Control and Prevention issued a report in 1994 concluding that such programs diminish transmission of the AIDS virus without increasing drug use, the administration refused to release the report. Clinton officials feared that a study advocating the reduction of harm through safer drug use would trigger a political backlash. Peter Beilenson, the health commissioner of Baltimore, a city that has successfully implemented such programs, explained that the government was "overly cautious" because "the conservatives would use this to paint the administration as soft on drug abuse and crime." When a draft was finally leaked to the press in February 1995, Dr. Peter Lurie, the principal researcher in the University of California study on which the report was based, accused administration officials of cowardice "when the lives of drug users, their sex partners and their babies are at stake." He added: "This has nothing to do with science. It's politics, pure and simple."[69]

The third vehicle for Clinton's proposed drug-policy reforms was the 1994 Crime Control Act. Working with congressional allies, the administration sought major new treatment initiatives in the criminal-justice system. In particular, the administration advocated prison treatment programs for substance-abusing inmates and funding for "drug courts" to divert nonviolent drug offenders to court-mandated treatment as an alternative to incarceration.

Clinton's record on reforming drug policy through the crime bill was mixed at best. The administration was successful in building such programs into the Crime Control Act but much less successful in securing funding: of the $200 million it requested for drug courts, it received only $29 million; Congress appropriated no funds for prison treatment for fiscal 1995.[70] Even as it acknowledged the need for treatment in the criminal-justice system, the crime bill broke new ground as a get-tough initiative, mandating—for the first time—federal funding for state prisons and local law-enforcement agents. And when conservative House Republicans attacked the Democrats' crime-prevention programs and threatened to hold up final approval of the bill, the administration permitted House Democrats to bargain away millions of dollars of funding for preventive social programs.

A look at the bottom line of the drug budget confirms that the Clinton administration's early efforts to redirect the nation's drug policies yielded meager results. Federal funds appropriated for treatment and prevention in both 1993 and 1994 totaled 33 percent of the budget, only slightly more than the 31 percent share in the 1992 Bush budget. Despite Clinton's concerns with treatment and prevention and despite Democratic majorities in both houses during his first two years, the administration was able to do little to transform the overall thrust of the national drug strategy.

If the Clinton administration had little political interest or success in pursuing drug-policy reform under a Democratically controlled Congress, the arrival of a conservative Republican regime on Capitol Hill made serious reform far less likely. The administration's 1995 drug strategy reflected a further retreat on several policy fronts. The rhetorical emphasis on hard-core treatment remained, but the total increase requested for treatment programs was $180 million, only 14 percent of the total $1.3 billion drug-budget increase requested—and a far cry from the previous year's $355 million request.[71] Overall, Clinton's proposed drug budget for fiscal 1996 brought the proportion of spending for treatment and prevention back to the 31 percent reflected in the final Bush budget.[72]

The new conservative Congress voiced strong opposition to Clinton's modest reforms, and the release of the 1995 *National Drug Control Strategy* occasioned a flood of sharp criticisms from drug warriors. The president was attacked, among other things, for his emphasis on hard-core users (he was accused of abandoning young, casual users and of wasting money on hard-core addicts whom conservatives classified as largely untreatable, unredeemable, and undeserving of care)[73] and for the minor cutbacks in interdiction (a reported rise in casual drug use was blamed on these reductions, despite the fact that the increase had begun in 1991 at the height of the Bush drug war). Above all, Clinton was condemned for deescalating the drug war rhetoric and for failing to use the president's bully pulpit to wage a zealous battle against all drug use.[74]

Such opposition underlined the political costs a reform-minded president faces in promoting drug policies that run against the punitive grain. To argue for meaningful reform demands challenging the logic and symbols of the punitive paradigm—and drawing fire from drug war advocates.

To justify dramatic cuts in interdiction, for example, Clinton would have had to demonstrate the futility of programs that seek to raise the street price of drugs by stemming the flow of drugs across U.S. borders. But such reasoned arguments would have run up against the paradigm's symbolic images: the cuts would have been decried as opening our borders to allow poison to flow onto our nation's streets, or, as conservative Senator Phil Gramm (R-Texas) characterized the cuts, as rolling out "a welcome mat for drug thugs."[75] To make the case for more money for hard-core treatment without raising taxes (a political taboo) or taking money from law enforcement ("soft on drugs"), Clinton would have needed to argue that addicts deserve federal treatment assistance. But it is difficult to argue for any government aid to those who are stigmatized as degenerates and criminals, let alone to justify shifting funds from other social programs to assist such people. Similarly, to make a strong case for needle exchange, Clinton would have had to argue that reducing harm from AIDS is more important than prohibiting drug use—and therefore challenge the paradigm's central principle. Clinton's mixed record on the crime-control act, finally, shows that he largely lost his fight for prevention programs and that he made gains only when he packaged treatment as an effective crime-fighting tool (drug courts, for example, or inmate programs).

Drug reform under Clinton failed because he was unwilling to pay the political costs of doing battle; but such costs would be high for any president—and this makes the hope for presidentially led reform very slim. In the end, Clinton succeeded only in moving drug policy off the political agenda and out of the public spotlight. This created the public impression that the drug war was largely a thing of the past, a Reagan-and-Bush-era campaign that had ended in 1992. The impression was misleading.

THE ROLE OF THE NARCO-ENFORCEMENT COMPLEX

The inflamed rhetoric of the Bush drug war subsided when Clinton entered office. There were fewer public speeches, fewer congressional debates, and fewer media stories on the issue. Yet the war itself continued, unabated. At the height of Bush's get-tough-on-drugs campaign in

1990, some 1,089,500 people were arrested for drug-abuse violations. In 1993 Clinton was emphasizing the need for increased funds for treatment and prevention, but drug agents were on the streets rounding up more dealers and users: 1,126,300 Americans were arrested that year. At home and on our borders, meanwhile, interdiction agents steadily continued to tally their drug seizures: 107 metric tons of cocaine and 815 kilograms of heroin were seized in 1990, under Bush's watch; three years later, under Clinton, 110.7 tons of cocaine and 1,600.9 kilos of heroin were netted.[76]

The source of this continuity in drug war activity is an often overlooked presidential partner in the drug war: the sprawling drug-enforcement bureaucracy, whose mission it is to implement the welter of tough antidrug laws and policy directives enacted over the years. When presidents such as Nixon, Reagan, and Bush wanted to escalate drug enforcement, this drug-control apparatus provided them with a firm basis and allies in the federal bureaucracy to help justify a new offensive. But even during times of relative calm, when Presidents Carter, Ford, and Clinton chose not to lead a charge against drugs, the drug-control bureaucracy has exerted pressures to sustain and even expand the drug war. Its role in feeding the pattern of persistence becomes clear once its scope is revealed.

From a Narcotics Bureau to a Narco-Enforcement Complex

Today's drug-enforcement bureaucracy began in 1914 as a small bureau in the Treasury Department, charged with ensuring that only doctors and pharmacists sold cocaine and heroin-based drugs. As late as the 1960s the federal drug-control bureaucracy was a relatively small operation, with only a few hundred agents. It was President Nixon who began to transform that operation into a sprawling narco-enforcement complex. The Bureau of Narcotics and Dangerous Drugs (BNDD) he inherited from Johnson had a budget of $14.5 million in fiscal 1968. After Nixon launched his drug war in 1969, the BNDD budget began to swell (it had more than quadrupled, to $64.3 million, by 1972), and other agencies were brought into the drug war. Nixon consolidated a number of these agencies into the DEA in 1973, and by 1981 its budget had reached $219.4 million.[77] But this was only the beginning.

Under the Reagan and Bush administrations, the DEA budget more than tripled, totaling $756.6 million by fiscal 1993.[78] By 1990 there were 3,050 special agents—nearly two and a half times the 1972 number—and a total of 6,098 employees in more than 170 offices throughout the United States and in 48 foreign countries.[79] The escalation continued under the Clinton administration, with a 1996 budget request of $857.4 million.[80]

By the mid-1990s, however, the DEA was only the lead agency in the federal drug war, and its roughly $800-million budget accounted for only a fraction of the total budget for drug-law enforcement, which topped $8.2 billion in 1995.[81] As the budget increased, so too did the number of drug war agencies. Roughly forty federal agencies or programs—in seven of the fourteen cabinet departments—were involved in drug enforcement.

A review of the 1994 *National Drug Control Strategy* and budget provides a glimpse into the role and activities of the drug war bureaucracy. Agencies in the Justice and Treasury Departments commanded the largest shares of the nation's drug-enforcement budget. At the Justice Department the DEA was by 1993 only one of fifteen agencies or programs involved in drug enforcement. Justice Department agencies had a striking range of missions. The FBI conducted investigations into organized trafficking groups. The Immigration and Naturalization Service detected and apprehended drug smugglers and illegal aliens at or near the border. The U.S. Marshals Service received funds for judicial security, prisoner transportation and detention, fugitive apprehension, and seized-assets management. The Bureau of Prisons provided custodial care for federal drug offenders and other inmates nationwide and constructed and maintained prison facilities.[82]

At the Department of the Treasury, meanwhile, seven agencies were involved in drug enforcement. The U.S. Customs Service, for example, was charged with interdicting and disrupting the illegal flow of drugs by air, sea, and land. Even the IRS was involved: its role was "to identify and impede the transfer of drug-generated funds and to disrupt and dismantle—through select investigation, prosecution and asset forfeiture—the country's major narcotics and narcotics money-laundering organizations."[83]

The next highest share of the drug budget fell to the Department of Defense, whose mission was to provide "support to the law enforcement agencies that have counter-drug responsibilities."[84] The military's budget for drug enforcement grew from $4.9 million in 1982 to more than $1 billion in 1992, before being cut back under the Clinton administration to $700 million by 1995.[85] To carry out its drug war mission, the Pentagon created three new joint task forces.[86] Fifty percent of the time of the North American Aerospace Defense Command, a command originally created to track incoming Soviet bombers and missiles, was redirected to targeting drug smugglers. The U.S. Southern Command (SOUTHCOM) in Panama was reorganized to fight the drug war in Latin America; its responsibilities included training local security forces for counternarcotics operations.[87] The military's role in the drug-control effort extended to the National Guard as well. Guard units were involved in interdiction and eradication campaigns in all fifty-four U.S. states and territories; guardsmen searched cargo, patrolled borders, flew aerial surveillance, eradicated marijuana crops, and lent expertise and equipment to law-enforcement agencies.

The reach of the narco-enforcement complex extends far beyond the Justice, Treasury, and Defense Departments. At the Department of the Interior in 1994, the Bureau of Land Management received antidrug moneys to eradicate illegal drugs grown on the approximately 270 million acres of public land under its control.[88] The National Park Service and the Fish and Wildlife Service were also charged with fighting drug production and smuggling on the vast lands they control.[89]

Within the Department of Transportation, the Coast Guard was mandated to eliminate "maritime routes as a significant mode for the supply of drugs to the U.S. through seizures, disruption and displacement."[90] And the Federal Aviation Administration helped identify "airborne drug smugglers by using radar, posting aircraft lookouts, and tracking the movement of suspected aircraft."[91]

At the Department of Agriculture the Forest Service received antidrug funds to investigate marijuana production and drug trafficking within the 156 national forests and other lands under its control—some 191 million acres; and the Agriculture Research Service was funded to develop herbicides to eradicate illegal drug crops, especially coca.

Beyond the executive-branch bureaucracy, the vast system of federal, state, and local courts adds a further dimension to the complex. Consider the federal judiciary alone. The U.S. courts' main purpose is to decide criminal and civil cases, a significant number of which are drug related: in total, an estimated 27 percent of all criminal cases at the district-court level were drug related in 1994, involving some 25,500 out of 69,000 criminal defendants.[92] U.S. courts are also responsible for individuals who receive drug treatment under U.S. court supervision. In 1994 this meant handling an estimated total of 65,194 individuals for drug-related reasons in pretrial services or probation. The federal judiciary had to dedicate 4,255 full-time personnel positions to processing its drug cases, for which it received an estimated $296.3 million for prosecutions and another $109.8 million for corrections.[93] Adding the resources invested by state and local judicial services, needless to say, would vastly expand the picture.

The Narco-Enforcement
Complex and the Logic of Expansion

Drug war agencies, like other government bureaucracies, have a strong interest in protecting and expanding their organizations. The logic of bureaucratic politics in the drug war—particularly when compounded with the inevitable failure of the antidrug strategy—generates its own powerful dynamics for the entrenchment and expansion of drug war policies. These bureaucratic forces are at work even when the president and Congress are not actively promoting the drug war.

One familiar pattern is the bandwagoning effect. Bureaucrats will jump onto promising political bandwagons—such as the war on drugs—in order to sustain or increase their budgets. During periods of drug war escalation, bureaucratic bandwagoning has helped produce a wider drug war. The 1973 National Commission on Marijuana and Drug Abuse noted the pattern during the Nixon years: "The rapid increase in federal spending made 'drug abuse' a 'hot' area, where money was available with little exercise of control. Persons involved in other big government spending programs whose funds were drying up (for example, poverty programs) switched into the drug field and became instant 'experts'. . . . Almost anything that could be characterized as anti-drug . . . had a reasonable hope of receiving funds."[94]

Some fifteen years later a former Reagan official in the Pentagon commented on a similar reaction among some in the Defense Department to the waning years of the cold war—and to pressure from Congress and the Bush administration. "Getting help from the military on drugs used to be like pulling teeth. Now everybody's looking around to say, 'Hey, how can we justify these forces.' And the answer they're coming up with is drugs."[95] One two-star general observed in an interview: "With peace breaking out all over it might give us something to do."[96] Although many military officials continue to oppose deeper Pentagon involvement in the drug war, the Pentagon inspector general found that a large number of officers consider drug control "as an opportunity to subsidize some noncounternarcotics efforts struggling for funding approval."[97] In 1990, for example, "the Air Force wanted $242 million to start the central sector of the $2.3 billion Over-the-Horizon Backscatter radar network. Once a means of detecting nuclear cruise missiles fired from Soviet submarines in the Gulf of Mexico, Backscatter was now being sold as a way to spot drug couriers winging their way up from South America."[98] Once new funding is secured and new programs are established, powerful resistance mounts within bureaucracies to any attempt to discontinue or defund the programs—and such institutional expansions often become more or less permanent.

"Turf wars" are another pattern of bureaucratic politics that leads agencies to protect or expand their missions and their budgets. Among drug agencies, turf battles are given a particular character by the drug strategy itself. They reflect the way the strategy fragments the war on supply and users into multiple missions, assigned to dozens of agencies with separate interests and diverse operational approaches. More importantly, the flaws in the drug strategy ensure that the drug-budget "pie" will never be large enough and that dozens of agencies will find themselves with ill-conceived and overlapping missions. Bureaucratic competition for drug war turf can be intense: agencies point fingers, question allocations to other agencies, and even refuse to cooperate. Each is maneuvering not only for a bigger piece of the drug-budget pie but also for turf control or even a lead role among other agencies with similar missions.

Rivalry between the Coast Guard and the Customs Department in 1987 led the chair of one congressional committee to express outrage that "agencies cannot agree over who has jurisdiction over the land, the sea, or even which coast or border" and to admonish to little avail, "We are in the midst of a war. This is neither the time nor place for turf battles, misplaced agency loyalty, or false bravado."[99] When budgets were drawn up for the Andean drug war in the late 1980s, the State Department (which claimed overall responsibility for U.S. government activities overseas) and the DEA (which claimed responsibility for all antidrug operations abroad) were frequently at loggerheads, each denouncing to congressional committees the incompetence of the other.[100]

Competition for funds and leadership rages not only among federal agencies but also between federal and local law-enforcement agencies. An exasperated Justice Department official told a congressional committee in 1987, "We need resources everywhere. We need Marshals, we need Customs agents, we need IRS people, FBI, DEA, courts, we need a lot of additional Federal resources. For every $250 million that goes to the State and local [levels], that's in our view $250 million that probably could have been spent to help the Federal effort."[101]

Two years later a local law-enforcement leader appeared before the same congressional committee with a different appeal: "There is no way to emphasize strongly enough that drug use, abuse and trafficking should be attacked with local police in the forefront of the offensive. Local law enforcement welcomes the involvement of federal agencies . . . but local police departments *must* be the lead agency. . . . Funds have been given to federal agencies that should have been earmarked for localities. Most of us in local law enforcement are baffled by the recent allocation of substantial funds to the National Guard. The front line in this war is desperate for resources."[102] One common consequence of such turf conflicts is expanded funding for all sides—and thus an even larger drug war.

Beyond fueling the competition among agencies, the fragmentation and flaws of the drug strategy feed another pattern of bureaucratic politics: a distorted process of evaluation. By discouraging evaluation of the overall drug strategy and obscuring evidence of failure, bureaucratic drug war politics further contributes to the strategy's persistence.

Like agencies in other bureaucracies, each drug agency is concerned only about its discrete mission—seizing shipments, arresting smugglers, prosecuting dealers—not with the policy as a whole. When drug war bureaucrats find that they must demonstrate progress in their individual missions in order to justify continued funding, they turn to indicators for measuring success that obscure the larger picture of failure—and policymakers do little to challenge such assessments. Thus the DEA, Customs Service, and State Department use statistics such as seizures, laboratories destroyed, and number of arrests to show their effectiveness. Yet, as the GAO reported in 1993, these data mean little without other measures.[103] Because U.S. officials do not know the amount of cocaine being shipped out of Colombia into the United States, for example, indicators about increased seizures are misleading: if the overall supply of cocaine to the United States is expanding, then an agency's reported increase in the number of seizures is hardly a measure of success. Little official data is gathered on the impact of interdiction efforts on the price and availability of drugs on U.S. streets.

The lack of evaluation and the use of partial indicators is nothing new. Back in 1973 the National Commission on Marijuana and Drug Abuse explained, the drug-control "funding mechanism is so structured that it responds only when 'bodies' can be produced or counted. Such a structure penalizes a reduction in the body count, while it rewards any increase in incidence figures and arrest statistics with more money. Those receiving funds thus have a vested interest in increasing or maintaining those figures. The statistics, in turn, fuel public and bureaucratic concern, and assure that the problem continues to be defined incorrectly."[104] Such figures, concluded the commission, "are dramatic, but do not really tell what is happening." Increased numbers of arrests, for instance, "may simply mean more violators, rather than more effective enforcement." Similarly, "the quantities of drugs seized may reflect only the size of the illegal market."[105]

Such partial and misleading indicators are not scrutinized in part because there is no body within the federal government with the mandate, power, and resources for overall evaluation and coordination of the drug war. The Office of National Drug Control Policy operates as a small oversight body within the executive branch, with a staff of fewer than fifty in 1995. Although Clinton granted drug czar Brown cabinet status in 1993, the ONDCP lacks the authority and the means to control the actions of the seven powerful cabinet departments charged with implementing the drug war.

These patterns of bureaucratic politics—bandwagoning, turf wars, distorted evaluations—characterize many large bureaucracies. These universal bureaucratic problems, however, are exacerbated by the flaws in the drug strategy. As we saw in chapter 2, drug-control agencies have been given a "mission impossible." The strategy's flaws guarantee that there will never be enough resources to accomplish the central objectives of the drug war: to stop drug production abroad, to seal the borders here at home, to clear the streets of dealers, and to prevent users from buying or possessing drugs. This creates a built-in logic for drug war departments and agencies to continue to press Congress for more money or new agencies in an endless if futile effort to accomplish their assigned missions.[106] The result is another powerful dynamic for persistence and expansion.

That the operational failures of particular drug agencies lead to increased funding—so that they can "try harder"—is no surprise. But given the flawed strategy, even operational successes create pressure for an expanded drug war. Consider an agency's response to the hydra effect described in chapter 2, for instance: success in clearing a city block of its open-air drug markets means that enforcement officials will need more, not less, funds as they are forced to chase dealers who have moved underground or dispersed to other city blocks. Or take an example of successful interdiction. In 1991 the Bush administration reported that "the success of interdiction forces in the southeastern United States and the Caribbean islands and Sea has caused drug smugglers to shift their focus towards Mexico as a primary transfer point into the United States." As a result, "resources have been enhanced along the Southwest Border." Concretely, that meant 175 new Customs Service inspectors, 200 more Border Patrol agents, 23 more canine drug-detection teams, and increased funds for "capital assets such as fencing, ground sensors, traffic checkpoints, aerostats, and other equipment to detect smugglers," as enforcement agents expanded their efforts westward while maintaining pressure in the southeast.[107]

Operational successes by one agency or program area often create pressure on other parts of the drug-enforcement system, which leads to institutional expansion "upstream." Warren G. Woodfork, superintendent of police in New Orleans, told a congressional committee in 1989 about the success of his police department in "impacting the [drug] problem by maintaining a high arrest rate" (up nearly 50 percent in one year). But his success at arrests demanded expansion at the next level of drug enforcement: prisons. Increased arrests, Woodfork explained, keep "all of the correctional facilities in the state full. . . . We cannot help but recognize the strain we are placing on corrections with our increased enforcement efforts. The simple answer to this question is an expensive one. More facilities must be built for both adults and juveniles. The revolving door has to be slammed shut."[108]

Bureaucratic politics and the fundamental flaws in the drug war strategy thus generate a logic of entrenchment and expansion within the drug-control bureaucracy. The institutional operations of the narco-enforcement bureaucracy do not ebb and flow with the level of public interest or the degree of political commitment to the drug war by the chief executive: even during lulls in drug war rhetoric and policymaking the drug war machine embedded in dozens of federal agencies grinds on, in a perpetual effort to implement existing antidrug laws and policies.

In the absence of bold presidential leadership to cut budgets, close down agencies, alter missions—in effect, to redirect the federal bureaucracy—the drug war persists. Yet given the dominance of the punitive paradigm, there is a high political cost for those presidents who want to reverse course—just as there is great political gain for those who want to escalate the war. Faced with the inertia of a narco-enforcement complex that routinely carries out its missions, even a reform-minded president with little interest in fueling the drug war ultimately helps to ensure its persistence.

7   Congress, the Electorate, and the Logic of Escalation

The executive branch has been center stage since the inception of the drug war, but the president does not act alone. Only Congress can appropriate the funds that have fed the drug war habit. And it is to Congress that the obligation falls to check and redirect misguided executive-branch policies. Congress can assess the failings of policy through its oversight authority, and it can kill costly and ineffective presidential initiatives through its power of the purse.

Yet Congress has done more than go along with the president: it has been an active participant—indeed, often the initiator—in expanding the punitive approach in drug policy. It was Rep. Francis Burton Harrison who fought for and won passage of the first national law to control the drug supply in 1914—following the failed attempt of Rep. David Foster to secure tougher legislation. Twenty years later Congress bowed to pressure from Harry Anslinger's Federal Bureau of Narcotics (FBN) to pass the Marijuana Tax Act, over the lonely opposition of Rep. John M. Coffee. In 1951 Rep. Hale Boggs successfully sponsored a bill to establish a federal antidrug law of unprecedented severity. Attempts at decriminalization by Jimmy Carter were soundly defeated by tough-minded members of Congress in the late 1970s.

The most striking example of Congress's role in fueling the drug war emerged during the policy fights of the 1980s. Throughout the decade Congress took steps to evaluate and shape national drug policy. Even in the face of mounting evidence from committee hearings, GAO reports, the media, and policy analysts that the drug war was failing, Congress acted not to challenge or change policy but to prod the president to do more and to spend more in the war on drugs.

FRAGMENTED POLICYMAKING

Congressional committees often share jurisdiction over a single issue, and drugs is no exception. But drug policymaking is also shaped by the way the drug problem and its solution have been defined. Guided by the punitive assumption that all drug use must be suppressed, the federal government has set itself the task of stopping the drug supply at every level—from production overseas to transnational trafficking to street dealing to consumption. Defining the policy problem this way has created a rationale for dozens of congressional committees, from Foreign Relations to Judiciary, to become involved. As a result of this fragmentation, committees that address one aspect of drug policy are often unaware of the actions of other committees on related questions, and members are afforded little opportunity for serious evaluation of the policy as a whole.

Fragmented policymaking has increased as the drug war has escalated. Only two Senate committees and one House committee held hearings on proposed drug legislation in 1972, for example. By the mid-1980s the sweeping mandate of drug policies cut across the jurisdictions of some seventy-four congressional committees and subcommittees. Budget decisions were divided up among thirteen appropriations subcommittees.

A further source of splintered drug policymaking in the 1980s was the way in which drug policy was formulated through catchall omnibus drug or crime bills. Such omnibus bills generally emerged in bits and pieces, as the various committees sharing jurisdiction over drugs submitted provisions. In 1986 and 1988, for example, the legislative packages that finally reached the House floor were compilations of proposals from approximately twelve committees.[1]

The creation of the 1988 House omnibus drug bill provides a glimpse into the process. The bill began to take shape in early June. The Banking, Finance and Urban Affairs Committee was the first to approve language for the omnibus bill on 9 June; among other measures, it adopted new money-laundering controls designed to detect drug smugglers who collected cashier's checks from several banks. On the same day, in a separate committee hearing, the Ways and Means Committee voted to create five hundred new positions for the Customs Service and to increase the penalty for failing to declare a controlled substance. Several days later, the House Foreign Affairs Committee endorsed initiatives that required the State Department to revoke the passports of convicted drug offenders and reauthorized the Agency for International Development to withhold economic and military aid from countries known to be involved in narcotics trafficking. On 21 June the Merchant Marine and Fisheries Committee approved provisions that would allow the United States to prosecute U.S. citizens aboard drug-carrying vessels that were seized outside U.S. territorial waters and authorized $346 million in additional funds for new helicopters, patrol boats, and other drug-enforcement needs of the Coast Guard. Also on that day, the Public Works and Transportation Committee voted to give the Federal Aviation Administration a role in stopping the flow of drugs entering through U.S. airspace. Two days later the Education and Labor Committee approved funds for the Department of Health and Human Services to establish drug-abuse prevention and education programs aimed at youth gangs. Additional proposals came from the Judiciary, Government Operations, House Science, Energy and Commerce, and other committees.

The draft of the 1988 House bill was 400 pages long when it reached the floor on 11 August. A few months later, on 3 October, an entirely different 600-page drug bill that had wound its way through the process in the Senate was introduced on the floor. Once they reached the floor, omnibus drug bills were often subjected to marathon amending sessions. Because this was the only opportunity for individual members to make their mark, amending sessions on drug bills regularly turned into free-for-alls, in which members tried to outdo each other with the toughest proposals.

Foreign-aid, defense, and other bills have also been frequent staging grounds for new drug laws. Throughout the 1980s the defense-authorization bill was repeatedly loaded with amendments that required use of the military in drug interdiction. In 1988, for example, the House voted 385–23 to amend the defense bill by ordering deployment of the U.S. military within forty-five days of enactment to "substantially halt the unlawful penetration of U.S. borders by aircraft and vessels carrying narcotics"[2]—even though the Defense Department made it clear that this was impossible.

The fragmentation and occasional chaos of drug policymaking have prompted reactions from members of Congress. Describing the 1986 Anti-Drug Abuse Act, Rep. Michael Oxley (R-Ohio) observed that "the effort on the omnibus bill last session as you know was a difficult one . . . and I think a lot of us felt with the [Claude] Pepper [D-Florida] amendment and some of the other amendments that passed in a flurry on the floor with very little debate and really no effort to try to vote it to a moderate level because obviously we were in a state of euphoria, I guess, of passing major drug legislation, and sometimes when that happens we tend to get a little carried away."[3] Such a policymaking process hardly lends itself to careful evaluation or assessment of effectiveness. "It's quick-hit, image over substance, and nobody cares if it's going to work," commented Rep. Charles Schumer on the debate over a 1988 drug bill. "The attitude ranges from a little crazy to severe panic."[4]

ELECTORAL AND PARTISAN POLITICS

The fragmented policymaking process helps explain why it is difficult for Congress to challenge the drug strategy: the process leaves little room for careful evaluation of the costs and benefits of the policy or its alternatives. But such fragmentation fails to explain why Congress has chosen not to challenge the drug war strategy and has even actively encouraged its escalation.

An important clue to this pattern lies in when drug policy is made. For more than two decades, virtually all major drug legislation has been enacted in election years.[5] As early as 1970 *Congressional Quarterly* observed, "Spurred by election-year considerations and the Nixon administration's declared 'war on crime,' the 91st Congress in 1970 compiled an impressive record in the passage of crime control measures." The measure that drew the widest margin of approval was the Comprehensive Drug Abuse Prevention and Control Act of 1970, passed overwhelmingly by Congress on 14 October, at the end of the session and the peak of the campaign season.[6]

The pattern was particularly clear in the mid- to late 1980s: with one exception, each of the major battles over drug legislation was fought and settled in the last days of the congressional session, at the height of the campaign season. What was the electoral logic behind the growing drug war?

Reagan had made the war on drugs a national crusade in the early years of his presidency, and the effects of White House rhetoric and media coverage were reinforced when crack took hold in urban neighborhoods in the 1980s and drug-related violence rose. By the mid-1980s public-opinion polls showed that drugs topped the list of America's concerns; the issue was rated the most important problem facing the country repeatedly in polls taken between 1986 and 1992.[7]

Each election year this reading of the nation's pulse set in motion a dynamic in which Congress and the president vied for the initiative in escalating the drug war, and members of Congress in both parties competed among themselves to stake out the hardest line on drugs. Many in Congress sought to claim credit for out-toughing their opponents. Even drug war skeptics and pragmatists looked to avoid the blame for the nation's drug problems that was heaped on those charged with being "soft on drugs."[8] The out-toughing contest took place not only in campaigns in congressional districts but also on Capitol Hill, as new policies were formulated. The result was a further expansion of the punitive drug war.

Drugs and Electoral Politics in 1986

The story of the Anti-Drug Abuse Act of 1986 is a good example of the interplay of voter concern, electioneering, and drug policymaking during election years. Public-opinion polls in 1986 placed drugs at the head of the list of public concerns. Throughout the summer and fall President Reagan and Congress competed for the public spotlight with dramatic antidrug initiatives. The result was a sweeping antidrug measure—passed by Congress at the peak of the midterm election campaign and signed by the president days before voters went to the polls.[9]

The drug problem had gained visibility and momentum in the summer months preceding the election. The cocaine-related deaths of two popular athletes—University of Maryland basketball star Len Bias and Cleveland Browns football player Don Rogers—raised the pitch of public concern as members of Congress returned to their districts to begin campaigning in earnest. In late July, House Speaker Tip O'Neill—who represented Boston, where Bias had signed on with the Celtics—announced a major bipartisan antidrug initiative. All House committees with jurisdiction over the drug issue were to submit policy recommendations for an omnibus drug bill by mid-August.[10] President Reagan entered the fray on 4 August with a nationally televised speech calling for a "mobilization" in "what we hope will be the final stage in our national strategy to eradicate drug abuse." While Congress frantically prepared a large-scale legislative package that authorized major new funding, the president sent a message to the American people demonstrating his commitment to a drug-free nation. In early August he, the vice president, and several dozen presidential assistants submitted to urine tests to set a moral example—and triggered a spree of urine testing dubbed by some "dueling beakers."[11]

The race for a bigger, better drug war moved to the House floor in September, where members voted 392–16 to authorize more than $6 billion to fight the drug war. Lawmakers approved amendment after amendment to stiffen penalties and add federal dollars to the effort. Without exception, every amendment put forward that authorized more money or expanded antidrug efforts in any way was adopted; every amendment seeking to cut spending or programs was rejected. "In football there's a thing called piling on," said Rep. Patricia Schroeder (D-Colorado). "I think we're seeing political piling on right before the election." The House bill that emerged authorized the death penalty for traffickers, gave the military the authority to pursue and arrest smugglers in the United States, and ordered the president to seal the borders against drug smugglers within forty-five days.[12]

The president reentered the scene with a televised address to the nation on 14 September, three days after the House bill was passed. With the first lady at his side, Reagan called on Americans to join in "a national crusade against drugs" and laid claim to the nation's moral heritage as only a president can: "Drug abuse is a repudiation of everything America is. The destructiveness and human wreckage mock our heritage." Nancy Reagan added, "There's no moral middle ground. Indifference is not an option. We want you to help us create an outspoken intolerance for drug use. For the sake of our children, I implore each of you to be unyielding and inflexible in your opposition to drugs."[13] The next day the president sent Congress his own proposed initiative, the Drug-Free America Act of 1986, and issued an executive order requiring drug testing of certain civilian federal employees.[14]

The Republican-led Senate incorporated a number of the president's proposals in its bill. The measure passed 97–2 on 27 September. The entire Congress acted on a final version of the package a few weeks before the election. Serious disagreements over issues such as the death penalty were set aside in the rush to clear a drug bill; the war on drugs played prominently in so many election campaigns that neither side was willing to run the risk of killing the measure. The final bill sailed through the House by a 378–16 vote and through the Senate by voice vote.[15]

The out-toughing on Capitol Hill, meanwhile, was matched by intense competition over the issue on the campaign trail. The 1986 race between Florida's Republican Senator Paula Hawkins and Democratic Governor Bob Graham was one example. When Sen. Hawkins described herself as "the general in the Senate's war on drugs," Gov. Graham countered with a television advertisement. In it the governor is portrayed first in a police helicopter, giving a tough line on drug enforcement, and then beside a captured traffickers' airplane, calling for a larger military role in the war on drugs and assailing Hawkins for voting against increased funding for the Coast Guard's drug war effort.[16] *Congressional Quarterly* commented on the election-driven escalation: "In the closing weeks of the congressional election season, taking the pledge becomes a familiar feature of campaign life. Thirty years ago, candidates pledged to battle domestic communism. . . . In 1986, the pledge issue is drugs. Republicans and Democrats all across the country are trying to outdo each other in their support for efforts to crush the trade in illegal drugs. Rivals are challenging each other to take drug tests and competing to see who can propose the most stringent punishments for drug infractions."[17]

Some politicians were candid about the extraordinary election-year posturing. Rep. Dave McCurdy (D-Oklahoma) conceded that the 1986 drug bill was "out of control" but added, "Of course, I'm for it."[18] The dynamic was not limited to 1986. Two years later, Rep. Tim Valentine (D-North Carolina), after voicing concern over what he saw as the "seeds of a national disaster" in a drug-free workplace amendment, cast a yes vote regardless. "Rather than have people say, 'Well, that guy, he's in favor of drugs,' I'll hold my nose and go along with the others."[19]

Senator John McCain (R-Arizona) spoke for many in Congress. "This is such an emotional issue—I mean, we're at war here—that voting no would be too difficult to explain," McCain said of Senate efforts to increase the military role in the drug war in 1988. "By voting against it, you'd be voting against the war on drugs. Nobody wants to do that."[20]

Drugs and Partisan Politics in 1988

The election-year logic that fueled the drug war in the 1980s was exacerbated, ironically, by partisan battles over drugs. Competition between Democrats and Republicans might be expected to clarify differences, sharpen debate, and provide policy alternatives to a failing drug strategy. Instead, party competition throughout the 1980s further expanded tough antidrug policies. At the root of this pattern was the broad reach of punitive thinking on drugs, both among the electorate and among elected officials in both parties.

Throughout the 1980s the Democratic agenda on drugs differed from that of the president and congressional Republicans in certain important aspects. These differences were reflected in the two parties' platforms in 1988. The Republican platform located the source of the drug problem in the moral degeneration of American society. The appropriate government response was to deliver a message of absolute intolerance of any and all drug use, backed up by sanctions: "The Republican Party is committed to a drug-free America. Our policy is strict accountability, for users of illegal drugs as well as for those who profit by that usage. The drug epidemic didn't just happen. It was fueled by the liberal attitudes of the 1960s and 1970s that tolerated drug usage. Drug abuse directly threatens the fabric of our society. It is part of a worldwide narcotics empire whose $300 billion business makes it one of the largest industries on earth. The Reagan-Bush administration has set out to destroy it."[21]

All but one of the fourteen points in the Republican plan concerned the need for strict enforcement and sanctions to eliminate drug use. "We support stronger penalties, including the death penalty for major drug traffickers. User accountability for drug usage is long overdue," the statement read. Only point 13 strayed from the enforcement theme, to acknowledge the need for drug education as a complement to enforcement.[22]

The Democrats saw an equally serious drug threat. Enforcement, however, was only one of many components of their proposed response. They emphasized a balance between enforcement and assistance, both at home and abroad: "We believe that this effort should include comprehensive programs to educate our children at the earliest ages on the dangers of alcohol and drug abuse, readily available treatment and counseling for those who seek to address their dependency, the strengthening of vital interdiction agencies such as the U.S. Coast Guard and Customs, a summit of Western Hemispheric nations to coordinate efforts to cut off drugs at the source, and foreign development assistance to reform drug-based economies by promoting crop substitution."[23]

The most striking programmatic difference in the party positions lay in their relative emphases on and approaches to prevention and treatment. Preventive drug education, virtually at the bottom of the Republicans' fourteen-point program, was first on the Democratic agenda. The approaches to drug prevention were also distinct. The Republican view was clarified in the platform's sections on health and education:

Most of the health problems of young people today stem from moral confusion and family disruption. Republicans are ready to address the root causes of today's youth crisis. We will assert absolutes of right and wrong concerning drug abuse and other forms of self-destructive behavior. . . . A free society needs a moral foundation for its learning. . . . Our "first line of defense" to protect our youth from contracting AIDS and other sexually communicable diseases, from teen pregnancy, and from illegal drug abuse must be abstinence education.[24]

The Democrats, in contrast, advocated an approach to drug education that emphasized not simply abstinence but a range of strategies for minimizing dangerous abuse of drugs, including alcohol.

Even more noticeable was the relative emphasis on treatment. Treatment was not mentioned in the Republicans' antidrug platform, whereas the Democrats highlighted its role. A proposal submitted by House Democratic leaders to the party's National Platform committee in May 1988 urged, among other measures, a policy of treatment on demand to address the AIDS link and other harmful health effects of drug abuse, new efforts to communicate AIDS warnings to addicts, and a federal commitment to expand community-based treatment programs.[25]

This focus on treatment and prevention was a leading component of the Democratic legislative agenda in the 1980s. Senator Edward Kennedy (D-Massachusetts) expressed the view of many Democrats on the issue: "Drug use is a crime, but it is also a disease. We must respond to this disease with two tried and true weapons in the public health arsenal—treatment and prevention."[26] Treatment for all who sought it was an important step toward this end: "In my state of Arizona, it's a six to eight month waiting list," complained Senator Dennis DeConcini (D-Arizona). "We ought to have in my opinion a system of treatment on demand." Many Democrats sought to even the spending balance between enforcement and treatment from the roughly seventy-thirty split to fifty-fifty, a reallocation opposed by Bush administration officials.[27]

Another component of the Democrats' legislative agenda involved key constitutional issues. Democrats had long been concerned that an unrestrained war on drugs at home threatened civil liberties that were protected by the Constitution. Almost twenty years earlier Sam Ervin, a conservative southern Democrat and longtime defender of constitutional protections, had led the opposition to Nixon's no-knock warrants. The battle over making drug war exceptions to the Constitution was particularly heated and protracted in the 1980s, when Republicans were pushing their get-tough agenda to its limits, and strong Democratic opposition arose over threats to individual privacy, such as mandatory drug testing. Moreover, liberal Democrats, who for years had opposed a federal death penalty, resisted efforts to legislate its use for drug-related crimes.

Given these clearly articulated and sustained concerns of the Democratic majority in Congress,[28] it is striking how little impact the Democratic agenda had on drug policy during the Reagan and Bush years. Over time, most substantive differences between the parties' policy approaches were lost. The contest between the parties in 1988 reveals the central reason: the Democrats sought to seize the drug issue from the Republicans as a way to beat them on historically Republican ground— getting tough on crime and drugs.

Early in the campaign, Democrats like Jesse Jackson began to raise questions about both the direction and the seriousness of the Reagan administration's war on drugs. The Republicans quickly saw that a long-standing symbolic issue was being usurped: since Nixon's 1968 campaign for law and order, Republicans had repeatedly used the crime issue as a club against Democrats. The Republicans sprang to action.

Reagan's Health and Human Services secretary, Otis Bowen, warned the president about Jackson in May 1988: "One of the two remaining Democratic candidates for president is getting some of his highest marks for his passionate and creative oratory on the drug epidemic and is poised to steal from our party what has been a traditional Republican issue—law enforcement."[29] Rep. Robert Dornan (R-California) had an even stronger message for the administration's drug-policy staff: "You'd better take back to the Cabinet of this Republican administration that . . . I can smell it coming, that the Republican Party is going to lose this issue. I see the presidential candidates already trying to beat George Bush . . . they are going to beat him around the head with this drug issue."[30]

Partisan accusations and tough talk began to fly in the months that followed. On 15 June 1988—at the height of the campaign season— Vice President Bush appeared with Republican leaders in the House of Representatives as they presented a comprehensive antidrug proposal. Arguing for an increase in the "certainty and severity" of punishment for both dealers and users, Bush said, "I challenge the Democrats to stand up on this point. You say this is war—then treat it as such. Don't let these killers back on the streets." The following day, in the Senate,

Rev. Jesse Jackson—the Democrats' most outspoken representative on the drug issue—was the lead witness before a Labor and Human Resources Committee hearing on drug abuse. His emphasis was different—he pointed to the need for education and treatment on request as well as for local law enforcement and interdiction—but his tone was equally harsh: "I go out and talk to kids in schools, and they don't see drugs as a killer. We have to convince them that drug pushers are terrorists," he testified.[31]

The Republican antidrug campaign was part of a broader strategy for out-toughing the Democrats on crime. Indicative of the Republican attack was the insidious and effective "Willie Horton" television-advertising campaign. The Democratic presidential candidate, Massachusetts governor Michael Dukakis, was unable to blunt the effect of these pro-Bush campaign advertisements, which effectively blamed Dukakis for crimes committed by Horton, a black murderer and rapist furloughed from a Massachusetts state prison. The fact that the furlough program had originated under a Republican governor did little to counter the television image of dangerous criminals emerging from a revolving door as a result of Democratic policies.[32]

The Democrats attempted to counter the soft-on-crime charge by projecting an even tougher agenda on drugs and crime—but they failed miserably. The lead question in the first debate between candidates Bush and Dukakis took up the drug issue: "The polls say the number one domestic issue to a majority of voters is drugs. What is there about these times that draws so many Americans to use drugs?" George Bush was on solid Republican ground: "I think we've seen a deterioration of values. I think for a while, as a nation, we condoned those things we should have condemned. . . . And one of the things that I think we should do about it, in terms of cause, is to instill values into the young people in our schools. . . . We can do better on interdiction. . . . And we have to be tougher on those who commit crimes. We have to get after the users more."

Dukakis sought to challenge Bush's tough-on-drugs-and-crime credentials and to establish his own, but he was not convincing. Democratic themes of treatment and prevention were largely submerged: "I've outlined in great detail a program for being tough on enforcement at home and abroad; doubling the number of drug enforcement agents; having a hemispheric summit. But we also have to take demand seriously," he commented, interjecting a few comments on his state's record on prevention and treatment. Later he added: "I'm opposed to the death penalty. I think everybody knows that. I'm also very tough on violent crime. You know, the Vice President says he wants to impose the death penalty on drug traffickers, and yet his administration has a federal furlough program which is one of the most permissive in the country, and which gave, last year, 7000 furloughs to drug traffickers and drug pushers—the same people that he now says he wants to execute."[33] Ultimately, the Democrats failed to out-tough the Republicans in the 1988 elections, but the partisan conflict over drugs had a heavy impact on the drug legislation then being crafted.

The Democrats' push for a tougher drug war during the election campaign had the unintended consequence of pushing the Republicans to search out ways to distinguish themselves with still harsher legislative positions on the drug issue. By mid-June House Republicans were pushing for a new definition of drug-use prevention that went far beyond education in the classroom. User-accountability measures would make law enforcement a central tool in prevention by imposing severe sanctions against those who used drugs—fines of up to $10,000 for possession of amounts for personal use and denial of such federal benefits as school and housing loans. Others sought a marked expansion in mandatory drug testing by pushing legislation for drug-free workplaces.

The partisan conflict during the campaign also weakened the Democrats' resolve to hold the line on constitutional issues. Most significantly, they caved in to Republican pressure to impose the death penalty for serious traffickers. "In past years, opponents have been able to stave off capital punishment provisions, but the political heat was too intense this time," observed the *Congressional Quarterly.* "Vice President Bush's continued attacks on Democratic nominee Michael S. Dukakis, a death penalty opponent, for being soft on crime left few in Congress eager to invite the same criticism." The death penalty "became kind of a litmus test for being tough on crime, and opponents could find no way to bring down the emotional pitch."[34]

The only bright spot for the Democratic agenda was the concession they managed to wring out of the Republicans to split antidrug funds for 1989 evenly, giving 50 percent to treatment and prevention and 50 percent to supply-side enforcement strategies. But even this proved illusory: it covered only the new allocations to the multibillion dollar drug budget—about $500 million for fiscal 1989[35]—so it had little effect on the overall skewing of the drug budget.

Some Democrats did generate heated debate on these issues, but their influence on legislation was marginal at best.[36] When the dust cleared over the 1988 drug bill, it was clear that both parties had escalated the drug war and that there were few advances toward the broader Democratic agenda of increasing treatment and prevention and stemming constitutional abuses. After months of partisan negotiation Congress passed a bill that dramatically reinforced the strategy's punitive approach—with a few minor concessions to the Democrats.

In the end, the decision by the Democrats to out-tough the Republicans on drugs and crime in 1988 pushed the Republicans into more extreme positions on the issue, as they sought out ways to distinguish themselves as being tougher on crime and drugs than the Democrats were. The decision also locked the Democrats into a more rigid position on crime and drugs, as they internalized the lesson never again to appear soft on these issues. Not only was the war on drugs escalated, but a chance for a broader policy debate on drugs was lost, and the primacy of policies of fear, force, and punishment reaffirmed.

This partisan dynamic continued through the early years of the Bush administration.[37] When Bush released his new drug plan in September 1989, Senator Joseph Biden (D-Delaware), then head of the Judiciary Committee, spoke on behalf of the Democratic majority in Congress. The Bush strategy, he argued, was "not tough enough, bold enough, or imaginative enough. The President says he wants to wage a war on drugs, but if that's true, what we need is another D-Day, not another Vietnam, not a limited war fought on the cheap and destined for stalemate."[38] Biden boasted that the Democrats in 1989 more than doubled the funds sought by Bush for the antidrug program. In pushing this tough line, Biden conceded in 1990 that figuratively, "one of my objectives, quite frankly, is to lock Willie Horton up in jail."[39] According to one Democratic aide, the Democrats intended to seize the initiative and "de-Dukakisize" the issue in the next round of anticrime legislation.

THE 1990S AND BEYOND

The policy fights of the 1980s demonstrated how presidential drug war initiatives and partisan competition set in motion a bidding war during each election season, between Democrats and Republicans and between Congress and the president. The result was the steady escalation of the drug war through the 1980s. But by the early 1990s the electoral and partisan competition had reached a stalemate. With both parties committed to similarly tough positions, party leaders and individual members of Congress came to realize that there was, for the moment, little electoral gain in making drugs a central issue on the campaign trail or on Capitol Hill. Public attention had shifted to the economy and to health care. Incoming President Bill Clinton, meanwhile, had no interest in spurring Congress either to escalate the drug war or to take on serious drug-policy reform. Without pressure from the president or from the public, Congress quietly dropped drug policy from its core legislative agenda.

The policy battles of the 1980s left a legacy on Capitol Hill, however. The parameters of the debate on drugs narrowed and hardened as a result of the decade's drug war escalations. The policymaking patterns and partisan fights of the 1980s, furthermore, created a logic for both parties to maintain the status quo on drugs in the early 1990s—even as historic shifts occurred in party control of the White House and Congress.

Congressional Democrats had staked out such a hard-line position on the issue by the end of the 1980s that they risked appearing inconsistent by arguing for a shift in focus from enforcement to increased treatment and prevention. Even as the issue faded in public debate in the early 1990s, there remained "enough anxiety and sensitivity in the political arena to the accusation of 'soft on crime' that no one out there seems willing to take the leadership for a shift [in policy]," explained criminologist Alfred Blumstein. Policymakers had learned that when it came to drugs, "being tough works—not on the drugs, but on the public. It at least abates demand for a response."[40] The fact that a Democrat now sat in the Oval Office, moreover, meant that key congressional leaders on the drug issue tended largely to fall into line behind their party's leader in the White House. "After four years of proposing my own drug strategy," Biden testified in February 1994, "I am gratified that this administration has offered a drug strategy that needs no alternative."[41]

Congressional Democrats thus took little initiative on drug policy; and without presidential leadership, politics as usual reigned on Capitol Hill—and the drug war continued. Even when faced with the opportunity to fight for modest presidentially led initiatives that advanced the party's drug-policy agenda, Democrats failed to rally. Clinton's 1994 hard-core drug-treatment initiative, which sought a $355 million increase in funding, was a case in point. The proposal gained only nominal support from congressional Democrats; few members were prepared to fight for the funding increase in the prevailing antideficit climate. Absent the strong leadership and coordination of reform-minded members, fragmented budget making doomed the proposal. When the initiative was taken up by the Appropriations Committee on Labor, Health and Human Services, and Education in the Senate, for example, members were forced to weigh funding for drug treatment against funding for the Headstart preschool program and a range of other non-drug-related social programs—while drug-enforcement programs were considered separately, by other committees. Given the low priority placed on drug policy (and particularly drug treatment) by the electorate, by the White House, and by legislators, it was not surprising that committee members facing tough choices whittled away the treatment initiative to one-fifth of the original request.

Republicans in Congress, meanwhile, sought new opportunities to gain political capital by attacking Democratic commitments to social programs for drug treatment and prevention. Senator Phil Gramm echoed a familiar partisan attack on the treatment emphasis in Clinton's 1994 drug strategy: "Not surprisingly, [the Clinton strategy] reflects a fundamental view of most Democrats that when things go wrong, society is to blame, and more social programs are the answer."[42]

The 1994 crime bill was one staging ground for Republican-led partisan politics. When the Democrats incorporated provisions in the bill for social programs (such as after-school activities and urban sports leagues) designed to prevent drug dealing and other criminal activity, Republicans attacked them as "social pork." Then House minority whip Newt Gingrich denounced the Democratic measure as "a fat-loaded, stupid bill." When the measure ran into trouble in the House, the Republicans seized the opportunity to score partisan points. Gingrich agreed to supply enough Republican votes to secure passage—but only after winning a number of concessions. By the end of the negotiations, House Republicans had forced the Democrats to toughen the bill by trimming $2 billion in prevention spending from the measure. Gingrich claimed a partisan victory: "We strengthened the House Republican Party. . . . We cost our political opponents a lot."[43]

Partisan attacks increased markedly when the Republicans won control of Congress in 1995, once again pitting a congressional majority from one party against a president from the opposing party. One month after the 1994 congressional elections, incoming Senate Majority Leader Robert Dole (R-Kansas) and Senator Orrin Hatch (R-Utah), incoming chairman of the Senate Judiciary Committee, declared their party's intention to seize the initiative in a letter to Clinton drug czar Brown: "Two years of decreased prosecutions, increased hand-wringing about treatment and hard-core addicts, retreat on interdiction efforts, and an abandoned bully pulpit have led to more drugs on our streets, increased drug use and a darker future for our younger citizens. Reversing these trends will be a priority for the Republican Congress and should be a priority for the Clinton administration."[44]

Less than two months after the new Congress had arrived in Washington, William Clinger (R-Pennsylvania), the new Republican leader of the House Committee on Government Reform and Oversight, announced hearings on the president's 1995 drug strategy. His attack on Clinton was unsparing: "President Clinton has been virtually silent on the drug issue from day one—save for his gutting of the drug policy office by 85 percent and tolerating remarks on legalization by his former surgeon general." Justice subcommittee chair Bill Zeliff (R-New Hampshire), noting recent increases in youthful drug use, asserted that the gains of the late 1980s had been lost and condemned the "shocking disinterest by the Clinton Administration in pursuing the drug war. The time has come to show leadership again," he declared, adding, "The drug war is not over."[45] Zeliff arranged a lineup of witnesses featuring prominent Reagan-and-Bush-era drug war figures—from Nancy Reagan to William Bennett—to assail Clinton for his emphasis on hard-core treatment and his failure to lead more zealous attacks against drug use.

The lull in partisan drug war rhetoric on Capitol Hill had not lasted long. Nor had two years of Democratic control of the White House and Congress spurred a reevaluation or reform of failed drug war policies. Whether the Congress was poised to reinvigorate the rhetorical and policy battles over drugs remained unclear in late 1995. Certainly the punitive assumptions of the drug war paradigm and the expanded drug war bureaucracy remained entrenched and available for these or future lawmakers to launch a new escalation of the war on drugs.

Despite the continued failure of the drug war and its mounting collateral costs, such an escalation would not be surprising. The pattern of drug policymaking in the 1980s and early 1990s left little reason to believe that the politics of denial would soon be abandoned. Several puzzling questions remain about this pattern of denial, however. Why were fundamental criticisms of the drug war strategy—of its structural flaws and the harms it causes—repeatedly dismissed or sidelined in debates over the war? Why did the Democrats abandon their early positions on drug reform and instead back the escalation of enforcement policies? And why were policy options such as treatment and prevention marginalized and packaged as limited supplements rather than as legitimate alternatives to an enforcement-driven drug war?

8   The Punitive Paradigm
Revisited

We began this book with a puzzle: how is it that decades of a bankrupt drug war strategy have not led administrators, elected officials, or the public to demand fundamental policy reevaluation and change? What is clear from the last two chapters is that it is not simply presidential politics, bureaucratic politics, electoral politics, or partisan politics that drive the drug war forward, although all contribute. These institutional interests and political dynamics are given meaning and direction by a punitive conventional wisdom on drugs. The drug war paradigm locks the political sights of government officials on suppressing drug use by focusing on two targets—the drug supply and the drug users. It leads them to turn to threats and coercion as a solution, creates a powerful incentive for denying the flaws in the strategy, and makes it rational for them to respond to failure with escalation rather than reevaluation.

To clarify the ways in which political interests and the punitive paradigm work together to perpetuate the politics of denial, we examine three common patterns: how the paradigm filters out disturbing evidence and narrows public debate; how the paradigm has helped create political traps for moderates in Congress; and how potentially effective treatment and prevention alternatives are not only underfunded but also undermined by the punitive approach.

HOW THE PARADIGM DEFLECTS CRITICISM

In chapter 2 we saw that the drug war strategy is not simply failing but fatally flawed. As long as profits and demand run high, law-enforcement efforts at best are ephemeral and at worst may produce a hydralike effect, spreading the trade and increasing its sophistication and ruthlessness. And although enforcement does raise prices by raising the risks of producing, smuggling, and dealing, it also creates a profit paradox, sustaining the high profitability of the trade—and thus ensures its continuation. In chapter 3 we saw that drug war policies are not only financially costly but also socially harmful and in some respects counterproductive. They contribute, for example, to the crime problem they are designed to combat and to the overload of the criminal-justice system.

These problems should raise questions and stir controversy over the drug strategy. But they rarely penetrate the debate: they are deflected in public discussion by the protective armor of images, symbols, and myths surrounding the punitive paradigm. When they are raised, a common response is to ignore, dismiss, or attack evidence of the strategy's failure, flaws, or harms—or to malign those who present such evidence. Consider first the following examples of the ways in which public officials deny failure.

In 1992 U.S. ambassador to Bolivia Charles Bowers was interviewed by Peter Jennings of ABC News:

Jennings: Where do Americans look to see progress?

Bowers: Well, I think they look to see it in terms of are there less hectares being grown? And the answer is yes here. Are we interdicting the product that's coming out? And the answer is yes.

Jennings: Stop for a second right there. The State Department Inspector General says less than one percent coming out of Bolivia is being seized and the GAO—the General Accounting Office of the Congress—says no reduction.

Bowers: Well, I don't know where the State Department Inspector General got his figures. I don't know how much is coming out. I don't think anybody knows how much is coming out, because there's nobody out there checking on it. So the alternative. . . .

Jennings: But then how do you know you're making progress?

Bowers: Because I know we're seizing some, and the alternative is to seize none, to say we are not going to fight this thing. The alternative is to throw up your hands and say, "you can do whatever you want, let the drug flow into the United States."[1]

This exchange is revealing. When Jennings lays down a reasonable criterion for the success of interdiction (what percentage being shipped out of Bolivia is being interdicted), Bowers sidesteps the question, thus refusing to acknowledge the record of failure. His argument that we should keep interdicting whether it works or not echoes the position articulated by the Bush administration. Assailing "those who argue that interdiction is a hopeless endeavor," the White House insisted that "a civilized society does not leave its border totally open to those who would harm its citizens. Interdiction has both symbolic and real value. It demonstrates our national will to oppose drug traffickers on every available front."[2] Thus even when the "real" value of interdiction is challenged by evidence of failure, government officials are able to retreat to its "symbolic" value—and to condemn those who disregard it. Under the punitive paradigm, interdiction has become not simply a means to an end (supply reduction) but also an end in itself. There is therefore no way to actually prove that it does not work.

The response of former DEA administrator Robert Bonner to columnist George F. Will provides another example. Will expressed skepticism in June 1993 at efforts to seal U.S. borders against the flow of drugs.[3] Bonner condemned Will for joining "the prophets of doom" who believe that interdiction "is hopeless and that our drug control policies may cause more harm than good."[4] Bonner's ad hominem attack illustrates a common impulse to shoot the messenger when confronted with reports of failure.

Equally revealing is the evidence Bonner cites to counter Will's argument. He points to U.S. success in working with the French in the 1970s to close down French heroin-trafficking operations (the "French connection"). The ending to this "success" story, however, supports Will's point. No sooner was this source of heroin stemmed than other sources (Mexico, Afghanistan) replaced it—demonstrating that interdiction had not curbed the supply of heroin to the United States. "There is nothing the matter with an agency head defending his agency," commented Senator Daniel Patrick Moynihan (D-New York) after reading Bonner's response, "but there can be a good deal wrong with denial in the face of failure."[5]

Policymakers have requested numerous internal government studies to assess the progress and prospects of the drug war. Yet when their findings are negative, even these internal reports meet a wall of denial. Reports issued by Congress's own investigative arm, the GAO, are illustrative. The GAO submitted a report to a Senate subcommittee in June

1989 stating that interdiction efforts had failed. Seizures were having little effect on the important indicators of the drug problem. GAO official
Arnold P. Jones cited as evidence of failure a decrease in the price of
drugs, an increase in their purity, and a rise in drug-related hospital emergencies. The response of congressional officials was to deny the message
and to "shoot the messenger" by condemning the report and the investigative agency. Rep. E. Clay Shaw (R-Florida) simply asserted that in
his South Florida district "there is absolutely no question interdiction is
working." Rep. Duncan Hunter (R-California) called the report "one of
the poorest reports GAO has ever made," claiming that it was based on
incorrect information and assumptions. "It is absolutely wrong for the
GAO to say that, based on a couple panels of the interdiction fence that
are now up, the fence is not working."[6]

Some public officials are willing to admit that current drug policies
are not succeeding, but they deny that the policies are fatally flawed and
insist that a stronger commitment or more resources can make them
work. Two key presumptions behind the punitive drug paradigm often
underlie such arguments: first, political will is all that is required; and
second, force works if enough of it is used. Similar presumptions have
long guided government policy in other areas as well, including U.S. foreign affairs and domestic crime fighting. Deep-seated images and im-
pulses to strike back forcefully against foreign enemies (international
traffickers) and dangerous street criminals (domestic dealers) are a predictable response from policymakers who are faced with the criticism
that their wars at home or abroad are failing.

When the GAO, therefore, pointed to conceptual flaws "inherent" in
the interdiction program and argued that further investment would be
fruitless, Rep. Charles Rangel (D-New York) joined others in dismissing
the report by arguing that what was needed was the political will to make
the program work. Rangel said it was "ridiculous to stop funding interdiction because it's a failure. . . . The truth of the matter is, it's . . . been
a failure because it's not being coordinated and there's no commitment
from people in charge of the departments."[7]

A similar theme is expressed in the "can-do" response that emerges
repeatedly in debates about funding the war against supply in the Third
World. When assessments by government agencies and policy analysts
raise concerns about the feasibility of the war abroad, many in Congress
have responded to the evidence of failure with calls to action similar to
that of Representative Shaw. Shaw insisted in 1988 that "we have not
yet begun to fight. . . . We will not be able to take credit for a war against

drugs until we bring the war to the fields where marijuana, cocaine, and poppies are grown. . . . I believe the drugs grown in those fields are a greater threat to the future of this country than all the Russian missiles. If we can go in and take out a Soviet landing strip in Grenada, I believe we can go in and take out the crops that are hurting our children."[8]

General Maxwell Thurman is an unusual example of a government official who understood the critics who pointed to the hydra effect: suppressing the Latin cocaine trade in one area, he recognized, leads it to reemerge elsewhere. Thurman, who headed the U.S. Southern Command in Panama in the late 1980s, liked "to use the analogy of the Pillsbury Doughboy: poke him in the stomach and he just expands someplace else." So too with the cartels, he argued: if attacked in one area, they simply moved to another. While he recognized the problem, his professional training and his institutional position within the antidrug effort led him to reject the idea that this flaw was fatal. His point of reference was the "successful" 1989 U.S. invasion of Panama, which he engineered. The answer to the mobility of the drug traffickers, he argued, was not to abandon the effort as fruitless. Rather, the challenge was to use enough force skillfully: to attack the narco-trade operations everywhere and at once.[9]

Even policymakers who are distressed by the record of failure frequently see few alternatives to simply "trying harder" and investing more resources. Consider the logic of Rep. Benjamin Gilman (R-New York), who questioned top DEA official David Westrate in a May 1990 hearing:

Mr. Gilman:	Has there been any reduction in supply?
Mr. Westrate:	What we are seeing is disruption. And I think there are a lot of signs out there.
Mr. Gilman:	I know that you are disrupting, and I know that you are interdicting, and I know that you are raiding, but I am asking you, Mr. Westrate, has there been any reduction in supply?
Mr. Westrate:	I cannot say at this point.
Mr. Gilman:	So we are spending $7 million and we are in the second year of [the] Snowcap [cocaine-reduction program] or the third year?
Mr. Westrate:	The third.
Mr. Gilman:	You have not had any reduction but yet you do not feel that we need any additional agents to do any more than what we are doing?[10]

Thus Gilman, like others, is not led by the evidence of failure to suggest that the program should be abandoned for its ineffectiveness, or even that a more careful evaluation might be needed—but instead presses Westrate on whether he needs additional resources to increase his agency's efforts.

Public officials are periodically confronted not simply with the fact of failure but with direct and carefully demonstrated evidence that the strategy is fatally flawed. In several reports and studies and in repeated testimony before congressional committees, economist Peter Reuter described the futility of interdiction efforts. He went far beyond arguing that a war on foreign supply is doomed to failure and demonstrated that even if interdiction were more successful than the most optimistic projections—achieving, for example, an inconceivable 50 percent reduction in the cocaine supply—this would not raise the domestic price very much, the aim of the war on supply. He carefully articulated the reasons. Only a very small part of the ultimate price of drugs is determined abroad; most of the price of drugs is added on in the United States. Therefore, making the foreign price higher, through interdiction, will not have much effect on the street price of drugs. The reaction of one subcommittee chair, Nicholas Mavroules (D-Massachusetts), was not unusual: he dismissed the analysis out of hand as "defeatist."[11]

Occasionally, a member of Congress publicly questions the underlying logic of the war on supply. Rep. James Scheuer (D-New York), for example, argued:

> We have a failed system in our country, a totally failed system. Seizures, arrests, convictions, going up, yes, and violence and rates of addiction and increases in a drug like crack . . . also going up. How can we preen ourselves in the accomplishments of the former when the latter is really the ball game? . . . I think we have to have the intellectual honesty and the guts and the courage to say, "All is not well. We have a failed system, and by golly, we ought to do something about it."[12]

The reaction to such challenges is telling. When Scheuer pressed John Lawn, then head of the DEA, on this point, Lawn admitted that the enforcement strategy was not solving serious problems and that interdiction efforts were showing limited results. Scheuer was even able to extract agreement from Lawn that there are structural limits to the battle against the drug supply:

Rep. Scheuer: We are now interdicting somewhere in the process before the drugs come to the neighborhoods, as I understand it, maybe 10 or 15 percent of the drugs. . . . Now, I have been on this Committee under Charlie Rangel's leadership for close to 15 years, and it has been at that level all the time. . . . And it is easy enough for the drug lords to shove in another 10 or 15 percent . . . in the pipeline just as a cost of doing business. So there has been no reduction at all. . . .

Mr. Lawn: . . . In point of fact, if we miraculously could stop cocaine and heroin from entering the country, we manufacture enough drugs right here in this country to satisfy the appetites of every drug user in the country. . . . So the interdiction thing is part of the effort, but it is not a critical part of the effort.

Yet when Scheuer pushes to a powerful conclusion—the fundamental failure of a war against supply to cut drug availability, violence, and addiction—Lawn deflects criticism of law enforcement's role by pointing to the number of seizures, arrests, and other misleading indicators of success:

Rep. Scheuer: . . . Mr. Lawn, you would agree that anybody in any town, hamlet, or village in America can get any kind of drug that he wants up to the quantity and quality that he wants? And I think it was you who said we have never had so many drugs of such high quality at such a low price. Wasn't it you who said that?

Mr. Lawn: I was talking specifically of cocaine, yes, sir.

Rep. Scheuer: Okay. Cocaine. But when you say that, aren't you really telling us that law enforcement hasn't really made much of a difference?

Mr. Lawn: No sir, not at all. I can tell you, for example, that law enforcement has seized 1800 percent more cocaine than we did in 1981 . . . and 44 percent of the federal inmate . . . population has been convicted of trafficking offenses.

Rep. Scheuer: Mr. Lawn, that goes back to the business of rating this system on how many busts you make and how much cocaine you pick up and how many arrests you make and incarcerations you make. What I am asking you, for goodness sakes, is to look at another indication, a far better indication of the success or failure of interdiction in what you are doing, and that is to look at what is happening in the neighborhoods. And when I tell you, and you don't contradict me, that any kid in any town, hamlet, or village in America can get all the cocaine he wants at a higher purity and a lower price than we have experienced, doesn't that tell you something about the failure of law enforcement?

Mr. Lawn: That tells me, Congressman, that you are prone to use hyperbole, because that is not accurate.

Here Lawn interprets Scheuer's response as an attack on the ability of the DEA to do its job, not as a statement about the failure of the drug war strategy as a whole to reduce the price and availability of drugs. And Lawn's institutional position leads him to defend his agency's role—pointing out that the DEA *is* successful at performing its appointed task of seizing cocaine and arresting traffickers—and to sidestep the broader failure of the drug war strategy. Scheuer begins to rephrase his question:

Rep. Scheuer: My question is this: Let's say we are all disappointed in the impact of law enforcement on restricting the flow of drugs and the complete availability of drugs in all of the neighborhoods. . . . Can you gentlemen think of any re-jiggering of the system, any change in the system, any approach that's new and different that you think might enhance society's devoted wish to keep drugs away from our kids? . . . And I'm not talking about tinkering around the edges. I'm talking about something that's new and different. I'm talking about taking a trip to the mountaintop and looking at the entire length and breadth of the system by which we're trying to keep drugs away from our kids.

At this point, Chairman Rangel impatiently interrupts, thus ending the line of questioning: "Mr. Scheuer, we do not have the time for the trip to the mountaintop."[13] Scheuer's isolation is reminiscent of that of Congressman Coffee in the 1930s. He is unable to engage either a top drug-enforcement official or his own congressional colleagues in a discussion of the fatal flaws of the drug war strategy.

The broadly shared assumptions of the punitive paradigm not only allow officials to deflect criticism of the feasibility of the drug strategy but also lead them to deny the costs and harms generated by the drug war. When Congress wanted to know what it would take for the U.S. military to halt the drug flow, for example, it asked for a Pentagon assessment. The September 1989 report made it clear that Pentagon officials saw sealing U.S. borders as an unacceptably costly and near-impossible task. An effort to "substantially halt" the flow of drugs, the report concluded, would require over one-third of the Navy's fleet (210 of a total of 568 ships), more than three times the number of aircraft-hunting planes the Air Force had, and another 120 Navy radar and search aircraft. The effort to stop land-based smuggling would require about half of the Army's inventory of combatants and helicopter companies (96 infantry battalions, or more than 50,000 troops, and 53 helicopter companies, or about 1,000 helicopters). The annual price tag would be $18 billion and would require that many long-standing Pentagon missions be abandoned.[14]

The congressional response? "That list is absolute bunk," said one House Armed Services Committee aide. "We're just trying to reorganize priorities and make the Pentagon realize some things have to be done less well, or not at all, so they can help us fight drugs." The reaction echoed that of Rep. Larry Hopkins (R-Kentucky), who had assailed Pentagon officials earlier that year for dragging their feet in a hearing of the House Armed Services subcommittee on investigations: "We are serious about your active role in this war on drugs, even if it means we have to drag you kicking and screaming every step of the way." Hopkins drew on the powerful imagery of the drug war to argue for military involvement, explaining, "This is war. And they are going to have to lace up their combat boots and get involved."[15]

Within weeks, the Pentagon's evaluations were quietly shelved. Secretary of Defense Dick Cheney announced in mid-September 1989 that the military's role in the fight against drugs would be expanded. He was willing to declare the U.S. military an "enthusiastic participant" in the antidrug effort. Members of Congress were satisfied: "The Defense Department finally has enlisted in the war on drugs. For more than a year it's been AWOL."[16]

Punitive assumptions also help deflect criticism of the other harmful effects of the drug war—such as the ways the war against supply and users in part causes many of the crime and health problems that drug warriors seek to address. The causal connection provided by the paradigm seems clear: drugs cause crime and health problems, and drug enforcement is designed to solve these problems, so the logical response to continued problems is more enforcement.

This reasoning has been repeatedly challenged by medical and criminal justice experts and others. They point out that incarcerating drug users (including user-dealers) criminalizes people with health problems, diverts money from other social needs, and fails to solve the core problems of abuse, addiction, and addiction-based crime. These arguments, however, cannot reach people who accept the automatic link between "drugs" and "crime" that is implicit in the punitive paradigm. Anyone who uses or sells drugs, they reason, is by definition a criminal, and punishment must naturally follow—whether or not it really helps reduce drug-related crime or disease. Given this outlook, it makes little sense to argue that punitive policies against addicts are not working, because punishing drug criminals is an end in itself.

The willingness to deny the harms caused by the strategy's answer to addiction and crime is nothing new. In 1969 Dr. Stanley Yolles, director of the National Institute of Mental Health, testified against mandatory minimum sentences for addicts before a subcommittee of the House Select Committee on Crime:

> This type of law has no place in a system devised to control an illness. It has no place being used for individuals who are addicted to drugs.
> This type of law angers us as doctors, because it should not apply to people who are sick. It destroys hope on the part of the person sentenced—hope of help, hope for starting a fresh life. It's totally contradictory to the whole concept of medicine. A prison experience is often psychologically shattering. . . . He may for the first time in his life learn criminal ways. Such mandatory sentences *destroy* the prospects of rehabilitation.[17]

The response of Rep. Albert Watson (R-South Carolina) demonstrated how such arguments are deflected and twisted by the paradigm's drug-crime link: "Dr. Yolles's views are an affront to every decent, law-abiding citizen in America. At a time when we are on the verge of a narcotics crisis, a supposedly responsible Federal official comes along with the incredibly ridiculous idea of dropping mandatory jail sentences for those who push dope."[18]

A public official who goes as far as to suggest that the drug war itself may exacerbate crime faces enormous political risks. Surgeon General Elders suggested in December 1993 that in the search for solutions to drug-related crime, legalization should at a minimum be studied. "I do feel that we would markedly reduce our crime rate if drugs were legalized," she said in response to a reporter's question, observing that in countries that have experimented with some forms of legalization, "there has been a reduction in their crime rate and there has been no increase in their drug use rate."[19] Elders recognized that the issue was politically charged but stressed the importance of open debate and deliberation: "There are a lot of things that are sensitive subjects, but that does not mean that we should ignore them when they are destroying the very fabric of our country."[20] The response from the drug war front was swift and uncompromising. *New York Times* columnist A. M. Rosenthal accused her of surrender in the drug fight.[21] Eighty-seven Republican House members signed a letter to President Clinton demanding her resignation.[22] The National Association of Police Chiefs also called for her resignation. Former drug czar Bennett called Elders "nutty, just plain nutty."[23] President Clinton and his top drug officials publicly disassociated themselves from the remark and strenuously claimed that they were against legalization. Elders, however, continued to insist that she thought the issue should be studied.[24] That position, among others, eventually cost the surgeon general her job: Clinton fired her in December 1994.

Legalization, we argue in the next chapter, is not a solution to the problem of drug abuse and addiction. But Elders's concern about the connection between punitive prohibition and a high crime rate is a valid one. The power to silence a Yolles—or to dismiss an Elders—is the power to protect deeply held punitive assumptions from scrutiny and to bury the kinds of sensible questions citizens and legislators should be asking. What effect does elevating the price of drugs have on the crime rate? Does tougher punishment encourage or discourage treatment? What are the effects of mandatory sentencing on rehabilitation and on crime, and what are the costs to the criminal justice system and the taxpayer?[25]

These examples show how the assumptions and logic of the drug war paradigm inhibit fundamental reevaluations of the strategy by imposing a set of lenses on policymakers and citizens that make it difficult for them to see the failures and fatal flaws in the strategy and to recognize the costs and harms caused by drug war policies.

Although the particulars differ, the pattern of denial is clear. Faced with evidence of structural flaws in the policy and with challenges to its core premises, decision makers frequently act to deflect or deny the evidence, to shoot the messenger, or both. When evidence of failure is heard and accepted, a common tendency is to reject its implications or draw wrongheaded conclusions—focusing on the need for better coordination, greater force, or more resources. Those who understand the full implications and attempt to challenge the policy and its premises are met with misleading indicators of success from officials in the narco-enforcement complex who are defending their institutional interests and with impatience and dismissal by peers who are anxious to win the war.

By discouraging criticism and reevaluation the punitive paradigm locks in the current policy debate, focusing on a single goal: how do we stop all drug use? The paradigm defines not simply the ends but also the primary means of policy: through a punitive law-enforcement strategy abroad, on our borders, and at home, directed at both sellers and users. With neither the ends nor the means of the policy open for debate, policy dialogue circles maddeningly around a narrow set of issues. Who can get the job done? What level of funding and firepower are needed? How do we instill in the naysayers the can-do attitude they need to win the war?

If the record of failure were confronted rather than denied and fundamental questions about policy assumptions were pursued aggressively rather than aborted, the debate would open up dramatically. Evidence of failure would lead to studies of the sources of failure rather than to knee-jerk escalation; evidence of the structural flaws and costs of the strategy would create pressure to redefine the ends of policy. A more open debate would make possible a reexamination of our national purpose in drug control and a focus on the central question: what is the best way to address drug abuse, addiction, and related crime? A full range of strategies would merit consideration, and the means employed would be judged pragmatically on their effectiveness.

HOW THE PARADIGM TRAPS MODERATE REFORMERS

The shared assumptions of the paradigm not only influence the dialogue of policymakers in Washington but also shape the political conflicts that arise over drug policy even within the limited parameters of the present debate. Many of the issues that remain on the drug-policy agenda have been hotly contested. The conflicts of the 1980s are a case in point. The policy battles analyzed in chapter 7 were not simply driven by electoral and partisan considerations. What made it politically logical for members of Congress to out-tough each other was the widespread acceptance of the punitive paradigm by members and their constituents. These shared assumptions first set the contours of the debate and then helped narrow the political conflict over drug policy—until by the end of the decade there was little left for either side to contest.

Since the early 1980s the political battle over drug policy on Capitol Hill has been nominally framed as one of supply versus demand. Supply-side measures, as we have seen, rely on law enforcement, whereas efforts to reduce drug consumption by lowering the demand for drugs have traditionally included treatment and prevention. The party affiliations of the two sides in this political battle are by no means fixed: it was a tough Republican administration in the late 1960s, recall, that introduced the nation's first large-scale experiment with federally funded treatment efforts. Nonetheless, throughout the 1980s moderate Democrats generally defended demand-side measures as critical to the antidrug effort, while Republicans staked out an uncompromising supply-side position—and a pitched political battle ensued.

Yet the battle lines were not where they seemed to be. The real political struggle was a much narrower one, because both sides in the drug-policy battle embraced the law-enforcement emphasis embedded in the drug war paradigm. The Democrats, however, wanted to stake out a moderate position in the drug war: they wanted to win more money for treatment and prevention as a complement to law enforcement and to tame the excesses of enforcement, particularly constitutional abuses. Even in this more limited battle to change the drug-policy agenda the Democrats were trapped by the punitive assumptions they shared with the Republicans.

In the end, they were trapped on three fronts in pursuing their political agenda. First, they were stymied in the drive for a greater percentage of drug war funding for treatment and prevention. Second, they were drawn into a losing battle with hard-liners over the meaning of demand-reduction in drug control. And third, they steadily lost ground in the effort to contain what they saw as dangerous constitutional violations in the war on drugs.

The first trap emerged with the battle of the budget. With Presidents Reagan and Bush pushing to dramatically escalate enforcement spending, moderates in the 1980s faced two options in their quest for a shift in emphasis toward treatment and prevention in the drug budget. Each was untenable.

The Democratic majority in Congress could have rejected the president's proposed drug budget and insisted on shifting money from law enforcement to treatment, to achieve the fifty-fifty funding split they advocated. But many moderates were reluctant to take funds from law enforcement because, like the hard-liners, they believed that law enforcement was the front line of the drug war. They wanted more money for both. Others believed that enough had been invested in enforcement, and under different political circumstances they might have pushed to shift funds to the demand side. But they knew that the hard-liners would paint them into an untenable political corner with the voters. Rep. John Conyers, a strong supporter of treatment and prevention, explained: "Drug education and treatment have gained a name as a wimp activity. If you favor these things, you're a softy. When these proposals come up in Congress most members want to know, before they vote, which one is the toughest? It's sort of, 'I don't know if this is going to work, but nobody is going to blame me for not being tough.'"[26]

The moderate Democrats had a second option: to join in the Republicans' call for more enforcement funds and then ask for still greater increases in treatment and prevention. But this was a difficult political move. The common assumptions of the paradigm made it legitimate to ask for more money to get tough on drugs, but demanding vast new resources for treatment and prevention (neither of which was considered urgent or indispensable to fighting a punitive drug war) would have risked their being labeled tax-and-spend Democrats. Democrats feared the kind of conservative Republican criticism leveled by Rep. Mickey Edwards (R-Oklahoma) during one drug debate: "They [the Democrats] just want a tax increase. No matter what the issue—national defense, catastrophic health care, child care, now the war on drugs—their answer is always that we need more revenues."[27] But in the end, the Democrats did at least succeed in holding the line, maintaining about 30 percent of the drug budget for treatment and prevention.[28]

A second trap appeared in the late 1980s, when Republicans took advantage of the punitive assumptions most Democrats shared to claim the Democrats' banner symbol—demand reduction—for their own. The Republicans accomplished this feat by transforming the meaning of demand reduction from the moderates' long-standing definition— education and treatment to discourage use—to a new hard-line defini- tion—sanctions and threats to prevent use.

In mid-1988 a task force of House Republicans proposed several poli- cies demanding new levels of retribution against drug users, including the denial of federal benefits and the imposition of civil fines. Called user- accountability measures, they were packaged as a means of lowering de- mand. The Republicans, according to Rep. Bill McCollum (R-Florida), wanted to "go after drug users, to show them that there is a price to be paid."[29] Rep. Dan Lungren (R-California) explained that the drug user was to become as important a target as the dealer: "We want to con- centrate attention on middle-class users. You can't keep blaming the traf- ficker and excuse the user."[30]

Moderate Democrats, who had long been proclaiming the need to go after demand as well as supply (and using this to justify more emphasis on treatment and prevention), were trapped. The Republicans were now saying: we want to reduce demand too, but education and treatment are only two ways to do so; a more appropriate and efficient means would be to threaten users and potential users with sanctions and punishment. "Education and rehabilitation are not enough to stop demand for drugs," announced McCollum. "It is absolutely necessary that we enact user-accountability provisions that say that the user will pay some kind of a reasonable price" for taking drugs. Edwards elaborated the Re- publican definition of demand reduction in making the case for sanc- tions for drug possession: "Weekend cocaine snorters and joint smokers might think they have little in common with back-alley heroin and LSD addicts, but both create a demand for illegal drugs."[31]

Because the moderates accepted (or refused to challenge) the notion that drug use is a crime and because they had to be tough on crime, it was difficult for them to argue against increased enforcement against users. Although some moderates were genuinely alarmed by the new direction the drug debate was taking, most accepted enforcement against users as an appropriate demand-side strategy. The Democrats retreated, reduced to arguing that demand reduction necessitated treatment and prevention in addition to increased enforcement.[32]

Before long, Democrats and Republicans were united on the need for user-accountability measures—and the expanded definition of demand-side drug policies. Rep. William Hughes (D-New Jersey) cosponsored a Republican user-accountability proposal in 1988 with a rationale that joined Republican and Democratic responses to drug use. The measure, he explained, was intended to "drive people into treatment."[33]

The third trap appeared in the battle over the constitutional limits to drug enforcement. The liberal Democrats were vulnerable on this from the outset: conveying a concern for the constitutional rights of any criminal offender—whether or not the crime was drug related—risked the charge of being "soft on crime." Yet many liberal Democrats staked out constitutional protections as an important battleground in the fight over drug policy.

The trap was predictable. Unwilling or unable to challenge the drug-crime link at the heart of the paradigm, the Democrats were forced into a defensive posture. Had the Democrats argued convincingly that drug users and user-dealers were citizens with health problems in need of treatment—rather than criminals deserving punishment—they could more legitimately have sought to defend the constitutional rights of drug users. But the punitive paradigm sees no distinctions between drug users, small-time dealers, and major traffickers. All are criminals and deviants; all deserve punishment, not treatment, and the more the better. Without challenging this definition, the Democrats had no political ground on which to stand when Republican hard-liners demanded to know how they could justify being "soft" on drug-pushing or drug-using criminals by worrying about their constitutional rights.

With each successive vote of approval for tough strategies against all levels of use and dealing, the Democrats signaled their acceptance of the need to wage a full-scale war against suppliers and to take a tough stand against use. In this context, procedural arguments about fairness and constitutionality were repeatedly dismissed as a lack of commitment to these goals. The Democrats were reduced to one of two equally ineffective responses to the hard-liners: they resorted to arguments about inefficient policies rather than constitutional rights, or they made compromises. Either response led down a slippery slope, and the loser was the Constitution.

One of the clearest illustrations of this was the fate of moderate opposition to proposals for testing certain federal employees for drug use. In 1986 debates over the Reagan administration's antidrug package, Democrats such as Rep. Charles Schumer and Rep. Gary Ackerman of New York sought to prohibit employers from requiring tests without reasonable suspicion that an individual was using drugs. At stake were constitutional principles protecting individual rights to privacy. They tried to strengthen their case with pragmatic arguments about cost and effectiveness. "Testing is not only inappropriate for our society, but it is also impractical. We have found that innocent men and women will be incriminated with false positives while drug users will be able to cheat the testers—and that Reagan's program will cost hundreds of millions of dollars, money that could be better spent on education and eradication of drugs at the source."[34] But given the stigmatization of drug users and the Republican aim of eliminating any and all use—an aim few Democrats wanted to challenge—drug testing seemed a logical deterrent; and Democratic opposition was cast as mere quibbling over the social and fiscal costs of a necessary measure.

The Democrats caved in again in 1988 when they were confronted with an even more intrusive and extensive plan for drug testing, a drug-free workplace amendment. When amendment-sponsor Robert S. Walker (R-Pennsylvania) threatened to embarrass Democratic opponents with "soft-on-drugs" taunts, the Democrats "couldn't say no to Walker without losing ground in the we're tougher on drugs war then being waged across the House's center aisle," concluded the *Congressional Quarterly*.[35]

The Democrats' opposition to the federal death penalty revealed another pattern—one of gradual compromise in the face of effective Republican use of drug war symbolism. In this battle, as in others, Republicans successfully charged that Democrats shared the goal of reducing use but were simply unwilling to bite the bullet on the kind of measures that were necessary to meet this challenge. Long a Republican antidrug objective, the death penalty was proposed repeatedly as legislation: capital punishment was simply "a natural extension of the war on drugs we are waging," pointed out Rep. George Gekas (R-Pennsylvania).[36]

"Those who traffic in death should pay with their own death," argued Senator Alfonse D'Amato (R-New York).[37]

The Democrats managed to hold the Republicans at bay for most of the 1980s. Senate Democrats succeeded in defeating a death-penalty provision in 1986. But by 1988 the Democrats were forced into pushing "equally tough" measures for traffickers—such as life in prison—in order to hold the line on the death penalty. "Put them in jail and let 'em think about it for a lifetime," suggested Rep. James Oberstar (D-Minnesota). It was a losing battle, and by the time the debate was over, staunch opponents of the death penalty were reduced to arguing for limited controls on how—not whether—it would be used. Even then, some lost. A last-ditch effort by Senator Paul Simon (D-Illinois) to allow the death penalty for drug kingpins only if an innocent bystander or a police officer was killed (rather than for all drug-related murders) was overwhelmingly rejected in October.[38] Ultimately, the Democrats succeeded only in guarding against discriminatory use of the death penalty and in ensuring that condemned defendants had adequate legal representation.

The following year, Republicans sought an extension of the death penalty for drug offenses and other serious crimes. Rep. McCollum said he was seeking "an eye for an eye" in drug cases; Rep. Henry Hyde (R-Illinois) echoed, "We are not being serious about the drug problem until we provide the ultimate penalty." The measure came to the House floor with a list of ten crimes that should be subject to the death penalty. Three days of bellicose debate ensued, as members lined up with amendments to add to the list of death-penalty crimes. The list grew from ten to thirty, as dwindling numbers of liberal Democratic death-penalty opponents helplessly shouted "Kill! Kill! Kill!" from the floor in frustration. In the end, only time pressures and unrelated disputes led to the removal of the new death-penalty provision and several other controversial measures from the final 1989 bill. The state of antidrug politics on Capitol Hill, however, had been clearly established.[39]

Given the shared definition of the problem, the common goal, and the agreement about the primacy of enforcement, what the partisan battles of the 1980s came down to was a marginal struggle between hard-line and moderate drug warriors over the means, not the ends, of policy.[40] Beneath the sound and fury of the partisan conflict the moderates found themselves trapped, on the defensive, and losing ground fast. Their proposals to shift priorities from law enforcement to treatment were sidelined or dismissed, while spending for law enforcement and draconian measures—however unconstitutional—were escalated. Buying into the definition of the drug problem as a fight against crime, waged through a drug war, made it increasingly difficult for Democrats to hold to moderate means in the face of a "drug threat" that they themselves agreed demanded serious and decisive action.

HOW THE PARADIGM
DISTORTS TREATMENT AND PREVENTION

The logic of the paradigm does more than influence the debate and political battles over drug-policy priorities on Capitol Hill. It also shapes the ways in which drug policies are implemented. In particular, the punitive approach embedded in the paradigm shapes the two policies that are often advanced as alternatives to punishment: treatment and preventive education.

Treatment and preventive education, we argued in chapter 5, came to be accepted in the 1960s and 1970s as supplements to the central drug-policy instrument, punishment. Thus addicts were to be punished as well as treated; potential users were to be warned away from drug use through deterrents such as harsh laws as well as through preventive education. This two-track approach to drug control—combining the stick of law enforcement with the carrot of education and treatment—may make sense in theory, particularly to moderates who are anxious to balance out the approach to drug control. But those who attempt to implement treatment and prevention strategies often point to numerous contradictions and obstacles in practice.

Public support for treatment and prevention policies is undermined by the images and beliefs about drugs and drug users that are embodied in the paradigm. Drug-abuse problems are primarily defined not as personal medical or psychological problems, nor as symptoms of social problems, nor as public health problems, but as moral failings. The addict is portrayed as someone who has chosen to do wrong—not as someone in need of help and care. The punitive goal is to halt illicit drug use as quickly and completely as possible—"no use" or "zero tolerance" are the relevant catch phrases—and threats or punishment are held to be at least as effective and efficient as are treatment and education.

In practice, the dominant punitive approach has four effects on treatment and prevention. It discourages those who need treatment from seeking it. It undermines efforts to stem the spread of drug-related diseases like AIDS. It thwarts programs that could alleviate suffering and minimize crime. And it frustrates preventive-education programs that might otherwise help reduce the harms caused by drug use.

A disturbing example of the ways in which punitive law enforcement dissuades those who need help from seeking it is that of drug-dependent pregnant women. Medical experts point out that in many cases, their newborns could avoid a range of drug-related health problems if these mothers received prenatal treatment and care. But time and again legislators have responded to such reports with threats to punish these women to discourage their drug use. Some states criminalize women who use drugs during pregnancy. Some allow newborns who test positive for drugs to be taken (along with their siblings) from their mothers and placed in state custody.[41] Such punitive measures seriously undermine the prospects for treatment: fearing punishment and afraid to lose their children, many mothers may choose not to seek drug treatment or the prenatal care that could dramatically improve the life chances of their children.

The harm punitive measures may cause pregnant women and their children is only one instance of the ways treatment efforts are stymied by the current approach to drug control. Dr. David Lewis described his personal frustrations over the impact of punitive enforcement on treatment while he was working as chief of medicine at the Washingtonian Center for Addictions in Boston in the 1960s. Crucial to treatment was developing a "consistent therapeutic message that they [the patients] were not victims—not weak, helpless castaways—but people who could care for themselves, addicts who could take responsibility for and achieve freedom from their addiction." This demanded creating a safe haven at the center, a place with "rules distinct from the hunted/hunter mentality of the street." But, wrote Lewis,

> Bureaucratic events beyond our control seriously undermined our efforts. For example, during a routine program audit at a nearby Lowell, Massachusetts methadone maintenance program, the FDA [Food and Drug Administration] removed patient records. As soon as word got around, patients feared contact with treatment programs, thinking that their treatment records would be read and used for law enforcement purposes. State police routinely filmed our patients from a disguised bread truck. . . . The criminalized atmosphere of fear, suspicion, and punitive menace badly hindered our patients' ability to trust and participate in treatment.[42]

Treatment was also hindered by the signs required in all hospital emergency rooms under Massachusetts state law at the time: "Addicts Shall Be Reported." Lewis continued:

I have seen adolescents enter the emergency room, read the sign, turn on their heels and run. Physicians were required to report opiate, cocaine, and marijuana "addicts" through a telephone number assumed to be police-connected, although the calls actually went to the Food and Drug Division of the Public Health Department. . . . The major effect of the statute, originally designed to provide public health surveillance of addicts, was to erect a barrier to needed health care.[43]

Sociologist Elliott Currie contrasts this punitive disincentive to treatment with the approach used in the Netherlands:

One of the most crucial limitations of drug treatment in the United States is that only a minority of drug abusers—especially younger ones—ever make use of it, in part because they are afraid that doing so will deliver them into the clutches of the law. In Holland, on the other hand, a surprising—by our standards—proportion of addicts are routinely in contact with treatment programs or other agencies of help; in the city of Amsterdam, for example, about 60–80 percent are being reached by one form of assistance or another at any given time, and the proportion is probably even higher outside the largest cities.[44]

The attitudes and assumptions fed by the punitive paradigm do more than discourage those in need from seeking help. They also foil efforts to stem the spread of drug-related diseases. We know, for example, that intravenous heroin use spreads the AIDS virus when addicts share dirty needles. Yet many public officials do not search out ways to interrupt the mechanisms that spread the disease; they look instead to sanctions to try to stop all intravenous drug use (through laws punishing people who buy, sell, or possess syringes without a prescription, for example). In the end, such laws not only fail to stem intravenous drug taking but actually encourage more needle sharing—because poorer addicts cannot easily obtain clean needles—and thus exacerbate the AIDS crisis.

A number of community groups, public-health officials, and others in the treatment community have urged nonpunitive alternatives designed to interrupt the routes by which the virus is transmitted (dirty needles and unprotected sexual contact). Needle-exchange programs (NEPs) have emerged in parts of Europe and in some U.S. cities as one response: they are intended to encourage addicts to regularly turn in their used (dirty) needles in exchange for free sterile ones. Many programs do not simply exchange needles; they also use the opportunity to encourage addicts to seek health and social services, including drug treatment. Well-documented studies show that such programs can reduce the rate of HIV infection by as much as one-third.[45] Yet most states have laws that prohibit addicts from possessing injection equipment. And efforts to permit needle exchange often face fierce opposition.

Under three different administrations, Congress passed eight bills with provisions that barred or inhibited federal funding for needle-exchange programs.[46] Robert Martinez, ONDCP director in the final years of the Bush administration, argued strongly that distributing needles "undercuts the credibility of society's message that drug use is illegal and morally wrong. . . . We must not lose sight of the fact that illegal drugs still pose a serious threat to our nation. Nor can we allow our concern for AIDS to undermine our determination to win the war on drugs."

This opposition is predictable. If the primary commitment is to "no use," not to public health, distributing clean needles makes no sense. Unless officials are willing to publicly abandon this position and argue that reducing the harms caused by drug abuse (in this case, the spread of AIDS) is a goal so important that some use ought to be tolerated, it is impossible to join a debate on appropriate measures to reduce those harms. From the punitive perspective imposed by the paradigm, however, sending a condemnatory message about drug use in general is more important than addressing the public-health threat of drug-related AIDS.[47] "Many politicians," comments Mathea Falco, "remain fearful that they will be criticized for encouraging illegal, immoral behavior."[48]

The punitive paradigm not only loads the debate against the prevention of AIDS but also blinds citizens and public officials to hard evidence about the impact of needle-exchange programs on drug use. In fact, the assumption that such programs will encourage drug use turns out to be a myth. Needle-exchange programs not only radically curb the spread of HIV but also increase the number of addicts who seek treatment and succeed in managing or breaking their drug dependence. The National Commission on AIDS appointed by President Bush concluded:

> National drug policy must recognize the success of outreach programs which link needle exchange and bleach distribution [for needle disinfection] programs with drug treatment. The Commission has visited numerous programs throughout the country which distribute bleach and some that exchange clean needles. These programs have demonstrated the ability to get substance users to change injection practices. Most significantly, these programs, rather than encouraging substance use, lead substantial numbers of substance users to seek treatment.[49]

After less than two years of operation, a conservative estimate of the effects of the needle-exchange program in New Haven, Connecticut, concluded that the HIV transmission rate had dropped 33 percent. A comprehensive study of needle-exchange programs by the University of California recommended that all laws prohibiting the purchase or exchange of syringes be repealed and urged the federal government to provide funds for such exchange programs. Even the federal Centers for Disease Control and Prevention confirmed that needle exchange saves lives and does not increase drug use.[50] Despite the evidence produced by these studies, most public officials continue to reject such programs. It is, as New York City Health Commissioner Woodrow Meyers explained in 1990, an "ideological issue," and positions are not easily influenced by "data or evidence."[51]

The symbolic and political importance of insisting on "no use" not only thwarts efforts to curb the spread of diseases such as AIDS but also directly undermines drug-treatment programs that might ease the suffering and marginalization of those who are drug dependent. We saw, for example, that methadone maintenance, despite its problems (one of which is that it can create dependence on methadone) has a proven track record for weaning addicts from heroin, moving them into treatment and out of crime, and allowing them a chance to build healthier and more satisfying lives. Yet attempts by the Food and Drug Administration (FDA) to expand methadone clinics in 1988 met with opposition by elected officials such as Rep. Rangel, then chairman of the House Select Committee on Narcotics. Rangel wanted treatment programs that were designed to end drug use entirely; he derisively labeled maintenance clinics "juice bars."[52] The congressman also asked the General Accounting Office to review federally regulated methadone-treatment programs. The resulting report criticized uneven practices but concluded that this form of treatment offered substantial benefits. Rangel chose to ignore the evidence and to continue his attack.[53]

Such opposition to methadone programs is rooted in a punitive interpretation: because consumption of methadone is still drug use and because drug use is wrong, it must be eliminated. The consequence of the commitment to "no use" is that a treatment program that could bring a significant reduction in the suffering of many heroin addicts is less available to those who need it.

The presumptions of the paradigm also lead hard-liners to cut short serious consideration of many treatment alternatives. Research has shown that treatment works better than does prison in cutting drug abuse and addiction, for example. A 1994 RAND Corporation study showed that a dollar put into treatment is worth seven dollars put into the most successful law-enforcement efforts to curb the use of cocaine.[54] But the unquestioned assumption among hard-liners that addicts are criminals who deserve to be punished often makes it difficult to make the case for spending more on treatment.

This punitive assumption promotes a double standard. At budget time, elected officials are likely to press treatment providers to present evidence of the effectiveness of their programs and particularly to address recidivism rates. When considering funding for prisons, they are far less likely to ask about the effectiveness—including the recidivism rates—of incarceration. Mark Mauer, of the Sentencing Project in Washington, D.C., illustrated the double standard: "Say the corrections director in Michigan comes before a hearing asking for $300 million for next year. Someone trying to get 29 cents for an alternative sentencing program [which involves a nonjail alternative such as treatment] also testifies. This second guy gets grilled: 'how do you know it will work,' the committee wants to know. But the corrections director barely gets questioned."[55] Linda Lewis, a former deputy director for treatment and rehabilitation at ONDCP, explained, "Officials are willing to accept a high rate of prison recidivism and don't complain when it does not do anything"; they keep putting money into prisons even though "this is money down the tubes."[56]

This dual standard reflects the punitive orientation and dominant influence of the paradigm: it is assumed that jails are both appropriate and effective solutions to drug use. "People understand law enforcement," Lewis told us. "They know cops and robbers. If I say: 'We have a choice of therapy or a cell,' their brain says: 'I know what a cell is, but I'm not sure about this therapy business'—so they will choose the cell."[57]

Dr. Herbert D. Kleber, a deputy director of the ONDCP during the Bush years, reinforced this point. Political leaders, he said, fear that spending more on treatment and less on enforcement will hurt them politically: "There's still almost a moralistic feeling that, 'Why should we be putting tax dollars into treating something that people have brought on themselves?'"[58]

This dominant image of the addict—as a criminal who has no one to blame but himself—is one of the major obstacles to expanding opportunities for treatment. In Lewis's experience, there is an assumption that addicts continually "make a conscious choice to use drugs—and they can't understand how a pregnant woman could hurt her baby by smoking crack," unless of course these people are bad or are criminals. So when they hear the word treatment, "they say to themselves, 'We'll be helping criminals. What are we doing helping these people? We should be punishing them.'" In her efforts to promote treatment, Lewis concluded, it is "law enforcement that sells."[59]

Naya Arbiter, director of Amity, a therapeutic community in Tucson, Arizona, emphasized the impact of this stigmatization in an interview with Mathea Falco. Most Americans, she said, view addicts as "throwaway people" who should be ignored or locked up. "So much of this war on drugs has been spent identifying and rejecting the enemy, deepening the division between 'us' and 'them.' . . . Once we make drug addicts into the enemy, society has a tough time taking them back in. Why would the public want to pay for more treatment if they're dealing with the enemy?"[60]

The stigmatization encouraged by the punitive paradigm also undermines local support for treatment facilities—to the point that many citizens oppose decisions to locate clinics in their neighborhoods. Mark R. Bencivengo, the coordinator for municipal drug-abuse programs in Philadelphia, explained the ways in which attempts to win siting decisions for new treatment centers are often blocked by neighborhood groups that invoke zoning restrictions. "Try to put recovering substance abusers with AIDS in a neighborhood. . . . It's a political hot potato." Powerful political constituencies use their clout to fight "disenfranchised" former drug users.[61]

Occasionally this stigmatization extends into the treatment community. A director of a California methadone-maintenance clinic interviewed by Elliott Currie made his own views clear: "What you have to understand is that the clients are fuck-ups. They will always *be* fuck-ups. They don't even have it together enough to know they have to get their act together."[62] Such an attitude subverts treatment by corroding the confidence and dignity of those who need it. Geoffrey Pearson's research shows that

> it is a disturbing feature of the accounts which heroin users and ex-users give of their experiences in trying to secure assistance that they often felt that they were met with what they perceived as a mixture of indifference, incompetence, and sometimes even a malevolently punitive attitude. . . . The outcome of these unhappy exchanges was that heroin users and their families were often thrust back onto their own resources in trying to combat the problems in their lives.[63]

The deep assumptions of the punitive paradigm not only undermine treatment efforts but also warp preventive drug-education programs. There is now considerable evidence about what does and does not work in school programs that aim to dissuade teenagers from using or abusing substances like marijuana, heroin, cocaine, and alcohol. Most analysts agree that scare tactics (the fear-arousal approach) and moral appeals (preaching to students about the evils of drinking, smoking, and using drugs and exhorting them to abstain) do not work. Exaggerating the dangers of drugs undermines the credibility of the message and often backfires, encouraging experimentation.[64] But if scare tactics do not work, neither does the simple provision of factual information. Solely explaining the facts about the harms of different drugs is not effective at discouraging adolescent use, for example, in part because many adolescents see themselves as impervious to harm. Their decisions to use drugs reflect a complex range of influences—drug-dependent parents, disruptive homes, and peer pressure, to name a few. If preventive programs are to be effective, we see in chapter 10, they must not only provide factual information but also address such social influences.[65]

Yet parents and public officials often advocate prevention programs that do not work. Some may do so because of the overriding importance of the moral message within the paradigm—because conveying the message of total abstinence is more important than its effectiveness in altering the behavior of young people. Many public officials may do so because they fear the political consequences for their administrative positions or their next election if they support programs that draw distinctions between more or less harmful drugs or that advocate ways to reduce the harms of drug use.

One example of this is the insistence on abstinence by moral reformers within and outside government in the early 1980s. Parents' groups (many of which were eventually organized under the umbrella NFP— the National Federation of Parents for a Drug-Free Youth) were outraged by any message which suggested that some drug use was tolerable. In about 1980, parents' groups began "to monitor federal publications with the goal of weeding out comments favorable to drug use. As one high-ranking NIDA official put it, 'The NFP has reviewed most if not all of the NIDA publications in order to spot ambiguous messages that could be interpreted as being anything other than firmly against drug use. As a result of these efforts, several NIDA publications have been revised or removed from circulation.'"[66]

Such censorship efforts continued in the early 1990s among several federal treatment-and-prevention agencies. *Prevention Plus II: Tools for Creating and Sustaining Drug-Free Communities,* published by the Federal Office of Substance Abuse Prevention, lays out guidelines for choosing materials for community prevention programs that eschew any distinctions between use and abuse. The publication warns educators to reject materials that distinguish between soft drugs (marijuana) and hard drugs (heroin and cocaine) because they imply "that one is safe and the other is dangerous." The manual advises: "Look for 'red flag' phrases incorrectly implying that there is a 'safe' use of illegal drugs. For example, materials that use the term 'mood-altering' as a euphemism for 'mind-altering' drugs or imply that there are no 'good' or 'bad' drugs, just 'improper use, misuse, or abuse.'"[67] So anxious are some such publications to project an unambiguous commitment to abstinence that they recommend censoring any mention of designated drivers: "Materials recommending a designated driver should be rated unacceptable. They encourage heavy alcohol use by implying that it is okay to drink to intoxication as long as you don't drive."[68]

Similarly, in the late 1980s the Department of Education discouraged support for the Students Against Drunk Driving (SADD) program in public schools. The Department of Education opposed SADD's proposal that students and parents sign an agreement (called a contract for life) under which a youth who has been drinking and is unable to drive promises to contact a parent for a ride home. "Parents who engage in the contract acknowledge that their children may use alcohol," and this, argued opponents in the Department of Education, sends a mixed message.[69] Here again, rigid adherence to the no-use message thwarts education efforts to protect the safety of young users.

Treatment and prevention do hold much promise for improving the health of millions of Americans who suffer from drug abuse and addiction. But it is difficult to realize the promise as long as treatment and prevention are designed and implemented in the present punitive context.

PART THREE

Public Health and the Struggle for Reform

The politics of denial have created destructive dynamics that are diffi-cult to change. The drug war not only fails but also helps sustain itself by continually re-creating the very problems it is designed to solve. As we saw in Part 1, the war on supply helps create the high profits and eco-nomic incentives which ensure that drugs will continue to flow onto U.S. streets—and that crime will follow. The war on users, meanwhile, exerts further pressure on the criminal-justice system while doing little to abate crime. As the drug supply and crime rates continue to run high, the ra-tionale for the policy remains intact, and it is logical for legislators and administrators to argue for escalation. Said another way, the strategy perpetuates its own justification: by fueling a continual crisis of addic-tion, crime, and other drug-related problems, it demands a further in-vestment in the drug war policies designed to address these problems.

In Part 2 we saw that public officials confront the problems unsolved and even exacerbated by the drug war by denying the strategy's flaws and harms and by continuing the drug war—or at best tinkering around the edges. Part of the reason is that government officials have institu-tional interests that make it rational for them to continue the drug war: drug war bureaucrats have an interest in pressing for money to do their jobs, and presidents and members of Congress have an interest in com-peting with each other to win support for a popular policy, especially at election time.

But we cannot understand why it is rational for public officials to per-petuate and escalate an irrational policy unless we also understand the character of the punitive drug paradigm. This historically created frame-work—with its myths, symbols, and values—defines the drug problem in a way that makes it particularly difficult to question the goals and instruments of policy. The drug problem is so spiked with powerful symbols and emotionally charged concerns (crime, fear, toughness, and immorality) that it is difficult—for conservative, moderate, and liberal policymakers alike—to propose a change in direction.

For conservative antidrug crusaders, the central purpose of a war on drugs is reflected in the symbolic signals it sends about the threats to American values and the moral failings of drug users. Whether the signals are heard, whether behavior is changed, whether the tragedies of drug abuse and addiction are stemmed, and whether the drug war causes further harms are secondary concerns at best. To moderates and liberals, the drug war does seem costly and somewhat problematic, and, yes, perhaps a little more treatment and prevention should also be pursued. But they are reluctant to challenge the hard-line drug warriors head on, for fear of looking as though they are "soft on crime" or too tolerant of the demon drugs.

Thus despite differences and even heated debates between moderates and hard-liners, direct challenges to the guiding premises of the punitive paradigm rarely surface. Such challenges would be morally inadmissible to hard-liners and symbolically and politically costly to moderates and liberals. The fact that the punitive paradigm is so deeply rooted in the minds of many constituents, and perhaps in policymakers' own minds as well, keeps real challenges off the political agenda.[1] Only occasionally is the overt exercise of power actually necessary to curb such opposition: the dominance of the punitive paradigm is sufficient to preclude most challenges from ever penetrating the debate.

This entrenched dynamic will not change simply because analysts come up with some bright new policy ideas to add to the good ones already out there.[2] It will not change until there is a transformation in the way the drug problem itself is framed: it must become rational for policymakers and citizens to think and act differently. This will demand a new paradigm and a new political agenda.

9 Paradigm Shifts

In the 1960s, despite widespread environmental damage, few Americans saw an urgent need to protect the environment; it was difficult to envision such concerns guiding national and international policies. Today it is increasingly difficult to imagine *not* considering the environmental impact of our individual and public actions. Heated political battles continue, but the debate is no longer over whether but over which activities should be regulated for environmental reasons, and how, and when. In the 1950s, despite extensive harm and illness caused by smoking, most Americans considered cigarettes sources of pleasure, socially acceptable, and even sexually alluring. Today virtually all Americans understand the dangers of cigarettes, smoking is fast becoming socially unacceptable, and government regulation in the name of health is largely seen as legitimate.

Similarly, the drug war paradigm has been dominant for so many decades that it is difficult for many Americans to envision a different paradigm for dealing with today's drug problems. Even those who understand that the drug war strategy is flawed and harmful may find it difficult to abandon the strategy and its assumptions because they cannot imagine a better alternative. But other paradigms can be identified; we will explore two alternatives—the legalization paradigm and a public-health paradigm. Each draws on particular strands in American culture to offer a distinct definition of the drug problem; each reframes the public-policy debate on drugs. The legalization paradigm is familiar to many Americans and is commonly rejected, in part because it is misunderstood and in part because it threatens to create a new set of problems that could be as serious as those that are caused by other legal drugs, such as alcohol and cigarettes. The second, a public-health paradigm, would better confront the problems of abuse and addiction, regulate the availability of drugs, and avoid the harms inflicted by the drug war.

THE LEGALIZATION PARADIGM

The movement for the legalization of drugs has its roots in the marijuana-reform movement of the 1960s and 1970s, a campaign that rallied student protestors and libertarian conservatives alike under the banner of marijuana decriminalization. Those who favor drug legalization today often disagree on the form that legalization policies should take and on some of its justifications, but most "legalizers" do share certain values and concerns that together suggest a paradigm.

The central problem identified in this legalization paradigm is the harm caused by current drug policies—not by drug taking—and what to do about it. In particular, the concern is with the damage caused by drug prohibition to individuals' lives and freedoms. Drugs such as heroin, cocaine, marijuana, alcohol, and tobacco are not seen as good or bad in and of themselves. These are moral labels imposed by social forces and cultural assumptions. The paradigm recognizes that such drugs do have pharmacological effects on the user's moods and that they can negatively affect health. Citizens should therefore be provided with factual information about these effects. But adults should be allowed to choose freely whether to take such drugs, how frequently, and in what dosages. Whether drugs are good or bad is a personal judgment, a subjective evaluation, not something to be determined by government.

This notion of free choice in drug taking is central to the legalization paradigm. Yes, taking such drugs can lead to addiction—and many legalizers voice concern over the effects of drug dependence. But the choice should be left to the individual, and if addiction is the consequence, this is the individual's responsibility. Likewise, individuals are responsible for their behavior while they are using drugs: if they use drugs dangerously or irresponsibly and threaten their safety, then they must pay the consequences; if they hurt another person or behave in ways that could endanger someone else (driving while intoxicated, mishandling machinery on the job, becoming violent, committing a crime), then they deserve punishment. Individuals are responsible for behavior that is harmful to others or illegal, and laws exist to enforce this principle. But it is the harmful behavior, not the taking of drugs, that is to be punished. The use of drugs itself is not regarded as a criminal activity. Consequently, it is wrong to arrest people for drug possession or use if their actions are not harming anyone else.

The legalization approach is derived from a fundamental liberal principle, the protection of individual freedom and choice against the intrusion of the state.[1] Legalizers argue, for example, that the "right to choose how to live one's life includes the right to choose which drugs are to be ingested," and "the judgment of individuals about the value of their drug taking is far more reliable than the judgment of the state."[2] As harmful as such choices may be to the individual, the government has no right to interfere as long as the damage is limited to the user. Such actions are self-regarding, not other-regarding, and to allow the state to interfere because some citizens do not approve of the desires, tastes, preferences, or choices of particular individuals is to open the flood gates to authoritarianism. The drug war constitutes an invasion of privacy and a threat to constitutional rights. These claims resonate across the social and political spectrum: they are advanced not only by those who personally favor drug use but also by conservative political officials (such as former Secretary of State George Shultz),[3] authors (William F. Buckley),[4] and economists (Milton Friedman).

Challenging the Terms of Debate

The legalization paradigm frames a pragmatic and coherent critique of the drug war strategy. Prohibition artificially raises the price of drugs and creates an enormous black market with attendant damage to individuals and society. One consequence, legalizers argue, is the policy-induced crime we analyzed in chapter 3. Those who are drug dependent and impoverished may commit crimes for money to pay these high prices. Drug producers, traffickers, and dealers, attracted by the profits and unable to compete freely on the open market, resort to violence— against law enforcers who threaten their markets and against each other in the competition for market shares. This policy-generated crime and violence would be reduced dramatically by one fundamental policy change: removing the prohibition of drugs. Legalization would reduce other harms as well. Drug-dependent individuals would not be deterred by the fear of punishment from seeking treatment. And because they would not be criminalized by drug-control policies, it would be easier for them to find jobs during or after treatment and to lead more productive, law-abiding lives.

Milton Friedman put the case clearly to drug czar Bennett in a 1989 exchange in the *Wall Street Journal.* "Your mistake," he told Bennett,

> is failing to recognize that the very measures you favor are a major source of the evils you deplore. Of course the problem is demand, but it is not only demand, it is demand that must operate through repressed and illegal channels. Illegality creates obscene profits that finance the murderous tactics of the drug lords; illegality leads to the corruption of law enforcement officials; illegality monopolizes the efforts of honest law forces so that they are starved for resources to fight the simpler crimes of robbery, theft and assault.
>
> Drugs are a tragedy for addicts. But criminalizing their use converts that tragedy into a disaster for society, for users and non-users alike.[5]

Such critiques challenge the core assumptions of the punitive paradigm, and to many drug warriors they are heresy. The mere presentation of evidence that the drug war causes crime or the modest suggestion that the impact of prohibition on crime should be studied—regardless of whether the spokesperson advocates legalization—triggers knee-jerk rejection, not reflection. Drug war advocates may even attempt to burn such heretics at the political or rhetorical stake: the attacks on Surgeon General Elders discussed in the last chapter are only one example.[6]

The legalization paradigm thus shifts the focus of debate from how to stop drug use through coercion and punishment to how to confront the social costs of prohibition. Significant differences over the appropriate scope of legalization and other policy recommendations divide advocates of the legalization approach, however.

Ethan Nadelmann distinguishes "progressive legalizers" from the free-marketeers he calls the "conservative libertarians."[7] The central policy prescription for the free-market legalizers is to remove almost all legal restraints on the production, sale, and use of drugs. Restrictions on sales and use are justified only for children, who are unable to make a reasoned decision about taking drugs.

But if the central policy recommendation of the free-market legalizers is "just say no to prohibition," the question many concerned citizens have about drugs remains unanswered: what should be done about the harmful effects that drug addiction and dangerous drug use have on individuals and society? Progressive legalizers argue that a totally free market in drugs may not be desirable, that drug abuse and addiction are social, not simply individual, problems, and that the "government does have an important role to play in shaping and improving the lives of its citizens."[8] Because they are not as wedded to free-market principles, such progressive legalizers are willing to entertain government policies to regulate (not prohibit) the use and sale of dangerous drugs and are often committed to public policies—such as treatment and better drug education—to reduce or minimize the harm caused by drug use.[9]

Limits of the Legalization Paradigm

The regulatory and harm-reduction policies favored by progressive legalizers, however, are drawn from other, often unarticulated, paradigms and certainly are not derivative of the legalization paradigm itself. On its own, the legalization paradigm provides little or no guidance on issues outside the realm of individual autonomy and free choice: it does not, for example, give guidance as to which drugs should be controlled or regulated and for what ends.

Despite the legalizers' powerful critique of the harm done by the drug war and despite the deep roots of principles such as individual autonomy and free enterprise in American culture, this failure to offer guidance on the real problems of drug abuse and addiction makes many people leery of embracing legalization. Their concerns are exacerbated by the fact that legalization is likely to increase levels of drug use. Because some new users would become drug dependent, abuse and addiction would increase in turn. How great the increase would be is a contested question and depends in part on how tightly legal sales would be regulated.[10] But the underlying principles and values of the paradigm—individual responsibility for drug use and its consequences—offer no counsel regarding the appropriate bounds of public responsibility for regulating sales or for funding treatment, prevention, or harm-reduction schemes.

Public concern about legalization, even among pragmatists who are not wedded to the punitive paradigm, also reflects an often unarticulated rejection of the individualism at the heart of this free-choice thinking. Drug abuse and addiction not only affect individual users but also undermine social relationships. It is difficult to justify letting a husband or friend take heroin or crack because everybody has to make his or her own choices. Such individual choices can damage a friendship, a marriage, or a family: it is difficult to be a friend to someone who is always "stoned" or to raise children if one parent is abusing alcohol or drugs. And in neighborhoods where families are devastated by poverty and unemployment, where housing projects are crumbling and schools do not function well, drug abuse can have a particularly pernicious effect: it further demoralizes communities and saps the strength to confront already difficult problems. Not surprisingly, many residents of these communities oppose legalization.

The limits to the legalization paradigm are in part a consequence of its individualist assumptions, reflected not only in its defense of free choice against government intervention but also in its presumption that self-regarding actions should not be regulated by the government. Many people who are skeptical of legalization recognize that what actually constitutes a self-regarding action—the distinction between harm to oneself and harm to others—is highly questionable in the case of drugs.[11] Because all individuals live in a social world of families, friends, and communities, the seemingly private act of drug taking often does harm others—but the harm is much less direct than is the physical harm many legalizers have in mind when they use these categories. Implicit in many criticisms of the free-choice and free-market principles advocated by some legalizers is thus a recognition that there are areas of life that should not be governed by such principles.

DRUGS AS A HEALTH PROBLEM

Too often, public debate about drugs is paralyzed between the extremes of drug war or drug legalization, state control or the free market, collective moral condemnation or individual free choice. Lost in the fray is the possibility of seeking health, not condemnation or choice, as our common goal. Making the question of how to heal without harm the central problem would radically transform our thinking about drugs themselves, about drug use, and about the individuals who use them. But what does it mean to treat drugs as a health problem? And why a *public*-health problem?

Health and Individual Responsibility

In one sense, the answer is commonsensical: drug taking is a health problem because it leads to physical ailments such as addiction and other diseases. Many Americans, however, focus on the wrongful choices made by individuals who use drugs; it is these choices, they point out, that lead to drug users' health problems. Consider the reaction of Dodgers manager Tommy Lasorda when top hitter Darryl Strawberry admitted he had a drug problem and agreed to undergo treatment in April 1994: "I'm very upset because Darryl let the team down. . . . When you're weak enough to let something like that control you, it's disgraceful. How someone can be so dumb to put that substance in their body is beyond me. I get sick and tired of hearing people describe this as a sickness. It's not a sickness. It's a weakness. Sickness is cancer, a heart attack. Not substance abuse."[12]

On one hand, Strawberry was "dumb" and "weak" because he chose to use drugs. Lasorda's mockery of the word sickness condemns those who hide behind such claims to avoid responsibility for their actions. Such people are to be blamed or punished, not cared for and treated. On the other hand, as even Lasorda recognizes, drugs can "control you." Implicit is the notion that the health problem of addiction limits choice and responsibility. Like Lasorda, many people are torn by what seems to be a contradiction between seeing drug use (and its effects) as a matter of individual responsibility and approaching it as a health problem, for which an individual should be treated, not blamed.

In fact, understanding drug abuse—or any other problem—as a health problem does not deny a role for individual responsibility. There is an element of choice at every point in drug use—in the decision to experiment, to engage in casual use, to engage in heavy use, and even to seek treatment in order to moderate or abandon drug use. This is characteristic of many health problems.

Sexually transmitted diseases, AIDS, and illnesses related to tobacco, alcohol, and drug use are all in some respects self-imposed health risks, and choices can be made to reduce these risks. People with high cholesterol levels or weight problems, similarly, may have made choices that created or exacerbated these conditions. Even in the case of genetically related health problems—heart conditions, diabetes, and high blood pressure—individuals face choices to alter their behavior through diet, exercise, or medication in order to manage such problems.

To treat drugs first and foremost as a health problem would mean thinking of individuals who abuse drugs the same way we think about people with these other kinds of health problems. In each case, individual responsibility complicates our thinking. We may be frustrated, for example, when someone we know refuses to stop smoking or overeating or fails to exercise or drinks too much. But we still think about such problems and their consequences as health problems; we focus on how to prevent or treat them. If people try to make better choices and fail, we may chastise them, but we also support them in their efforts to try again instead of punishing them for failure or abandoning them. We continue to feel concern and empathy for those who are suffering despite the "stupid" choices or "weakness of character" that might have brought on their health problems.

The Medical Approach
and the Public-Health Approach

To argue that the drug problem is a health problem, however, still begs the question: what sort of health problem?

In the United States, health problems are generally equated with medical problems. An individual with a health problem is considered sick and in need of a doctor's attention. To "medicalize" the drug problem would be to define drug abuse and addiction as a disease of individuals; substance abusers would be thought of primarily as patients in need of medical treatment. The medical aim in many cases would be to cure abusers of their disease; thus success would be defined as ending the addiction and making the patients drug free. Such a medical model might instruct us, in short, to replace police officers with doctors in dealing with the drug problem.

A medical approach to the health problems of abuse and addiction—although less punitive than the present approach—is limited. One limit is obvious. Although medical treatment of addiction is important, no medical cure for problems of drug abuse and dependence is known: addiction does not have a specific cause, such as a microbe or a genetic defect, that can be targeted with a medicinal cure; no therapeutic strategy works for all people, and relapse is common.

Two other limits are less obvious. First, the medical model relies on individual doctors working with individual patients. Yet too often doctors are limited in their ability to understand or influence the social context that affects an individual's drug use. Second, medical doctors are rarely called in until the physical effects of addiction have set in. As is the case with many other health problems, emphasis is on treating problems once they have occurred, rather than averting them.

To define the drug problem as a public-health problem is to frame the issues of concern differently. Public health means many things to many people; the approach presented here draws on three hallmarks of the public-health tradition that distinguish it not only from other frameworks for thinking about drugs—the punitive paradigm or the legalization paradigm—but also from a strictly medical approach to drugs and other health problems.

The first hallmark of a public-health approach is its emphasis on drug use as a *public,* not an individual, health issue. Some health problems and illnesses are social in nature. They may be caused or exacerbated by social conditions over which individuals have limited control: for example, unsanitary city streets and impure water spread cholera. And they have social consequences: tuberculosis, for instance, cannot be conceived as a private matter, because one individual's illness can harm others. Such problems require public actions, including inoculation programs, quarantines, and treatment. A public-health approach to drugs emphasizes the social causes and consequences of drug problems.

The second hallmark follows from the first: a public-health approach to drugs focuses on the *social environment* in determining how to address health problems. Drug abuse and dependence are traced not simply to the drug itself or to the drug user but to factors in the user's environment: the subculture in a local neighborhood; the presence or absence of a home or a job or medical care; family and peer influences. Such conditions do not cause drug problems in any simple, mechanistic way; individual choice is always a factor. The social environment, however, shapes and constrains choice. A person whose family and friends use drugs is more likely to use drugs. Someone with a family, home, and job who becomes addicted is better able to make choices to break his or her addiction than is someone without these social supports. A public-health approach addresses the interaction among drugs, the individual user, and the social environment (in the jargon of some public-health experts: the agent, the host, and the environment).

The third hallmark of a public-health approach is its concern with *prevention* as well as treatment: it is far better for a person's health, and far cheaper for everyone, to prevent health problems such as drug abuse and dependence in the first place. Treatment is important when prevention fails and may also be important in preventing further harm—but prevention is the first line of defense. Because the social environment shapes choices about drug use and abuse, prevention requires attention to environmental conditions. Individuals must be enabled to better cope with or to change their immediate environments. These health-care tasks go far beyond what individual doctors or patients can do alone; they require public-policy action.

To think of drugs as a public-health problem, then, is to reconceive both the problem and the appropriate response: the aim would be to prevent drug abuse and addiction and, when they occur, to heal those who suffer from these problems and to minimize the harm they cause to themselves and others. In preventing and treating drug problems, attention would be paid not simply to individual patients but also to the social environments that encourage abuse and addiction and that thwart treatment.

Such an approach to health problems is not foreign to American thinking and habits, even if it is not dominant. A public-health paradigm for drugs would have its roots in a public-health tradition that emerged in the United States at the turn of the century.[13]

The Rise of a Public-Health Movement

The idea that the social and physical environment is connected to health is an old one. One of the major Hippocratic writings of fifth-century Greece, for example, was *Airs, Waters and Places*. The work explored the relationship between diseases and climate, soil, mode of life, and nutrition and provided guidance to Greek colonists as they established new communities.[14] Yet the effect of the environment on health has not always been recognized. It began to assume particular importance in the United States only in the second half of the nineteenth century,[15] as public officials struggled to prevent the rise and spread of epidemics in America's growing cities.

The rapid industrialization and expansion of major cities produced not only unprecedented levels of pollution but also urban slum areas. Poverty and overcrowding spread disease, increased infant deaths, and lowered life expectancy. New theories and techniques in epidemiology led to studies which demonstrated statistically that many diseases were linked to such environmental conditions. Public-health reformers used these reports and the example of European efforts in organizing to pressure city governments to address dangerous and unsanitary urban conditions. Public-health departments were established, and city governments gradually came to accept responsibility for public-health conditions. Over time, many of these responsibilities were passed on to new government agencies that few people today even associate with public health. By the turn of the century, municipal garbage-collection systems were improving. Sewage and water systems were being developed (although they often dumped wastes into nearby lakes and rivers). Regulations governing slaughterhouses, pollution, and ventilation in public buildings were established. And regulations evolved to control tenement conditions.[16]

The growing field of public health saw a major breakthrough in the late nineteenth century with the discovery (led by Louis Pasteur and others) of the specific bacteriological agents that were the causes of many infectious diseases. This knowledge expanded the scope of prevention and enabled scientists and doctors to determine and address very specific environmental conditions that caused disease and to develop immunizations against particular diseases. Prevention now demanded scientific research as the basis of public-health campaigns. State and local health departments created research laboratories to identify and combat dangerous microorganisms.

Although bacteriology spurred a new focus on the individual in efforts to prevent health problems—through immunizations and medical examinations—social and environmental conditions remained an important concern in prevention efforts. Public-health advocates launched successful campaigns to filter water to prevent typhoid, to test and supervise production of milk and other foodstuffs (inspectors were sent to restaurants, meat-packing plants, and dairies, for example), and to drain swamps and promote screening to reduce the malaria-carrying mosquito population.[17] Continued concern with the environment was perhaps most evident in occupational health, which by the 1920s had become a major public-health issue. As the nation saw increasing "health problems arising out of exposure to noxious substances and dangerous working conditions,"[18] public-health advocates and other reformers argued that social conditions beyond the control of the individual were harming the health of workers, and they demanded public action.[19]

Education became an increasingly important tool of prevention in the late nineteenth and early twentieth centuries, as advocates recognized that public health could be achieved not simply by "doing things *to* or *for* people" but by doing things "*with* people and to get people to accept an increasing responsibility for their own health."[20] The promotion of child health through education and nutrition led the way in the early 1900s; health education also aimed to teach people both general personal hygiene and specific steps to prevent particular health problems, such as tuberculosis.

In the early part of the twentieth century, efforts to immunize, examine, educate, and treat were manifested in the rapidly growing number of clinics—for child health, tuberculosis, and sexually transmitted disease, for example—particularly in poor urban areas.[21] By the 1920s and 1930s the scattered nature of these distinct clinics led some public-health advocates and administrators to argue that public health required a more comprehensive network of services. Neighborhood health centers were needed, they suggested, to bring together such services as maternal and child care, dentistry, treatment of venereal disease and tuberculosis, and local food inspection; such health services, moreover, should be integrated with welfare services. The ordinary citizen, argued a 1925 New York report on health-center experiments in Harlem, might find himself

> in trouble of some kind, his health failing, or one of the children backward at school, or running afoul of the police, or the family just could not make ends meet. . . . If his courage were strong, and his health not too bad, the needy person might persevere and by making the rounds, calling on one office and clinic after another, and being referred from one agency to another, he might finally arrive at the place where he should have gone in the first instance for real help for his particular trouble . . . [but more frequently] the fact of not knowing just what was needed, or just where to go, resulted on the part of the less enterprising, in not going anywhere. And, going nowhere and doing nothing meant that things went from bad to worse.[22]

New York City, Boston, and Buffalo led the way with citywide health networks. By the late 1920s hundreds of such centers had been established across the country.[23]

Public Health Is Institutionalized—and Marginalized

By the 1930s public health had come to represent an established approach to America's health problems at the municipal, state, and even national levels. Federal institutions—from the Public Health Service and the National Institutes of Health to the Children's Bureau—implemented and promoted public-health programs.[24] There was wide recognition that the prevention and treatment of many health problems demanded a public response: government intervention was needed to direct, regulate, or encourage actions to deal with social conditions that affected the public at large. The mission of public health had expanded from a largely defensive notion—protection against infectious diseases—to a proactive notion of, in C.-E. A. Winslow's words, "prolonging life" and "promoting health and efficiency through organized community effort."[25]

Despite its wide reach, the public-health approach was challenged and eventually eclipsed by a clinical, medical model of health care during the 1920s and 1930s. The growing dominance of the medical model was not due to its superiority over the public-health approach—

indeed, there was no scientific reason that prevention and treatment, attention to environmental conditions and to individuals, social reform and medicine, could not be merged into a comprehensive approach to health care. But the privatization and individualism of the medical model tapped the strong, liberal, individualist vein in American political culture, with its antistatist, antisocialist emphasis.[26] Furthermore, as doctors created powerful associations such as the AMA, this bias was supported by an increasingly well organized, self-interested profession. An approach to health in which patients (individual consumers of medical expertise and drugs) paid money to doctors (private suppliers) for treatment (medical expertise and medication) favored the interests of a profession that was anxious to guard its privileged role. Physicians committed to public health, who earlier had been at the forefront of public-health reforms, were not in control of the AMA.[27] The association was opposed to the government intervention implied by public health and had little interest in supporting public funds for social and environmental reform.[28]

Faced with such stiff opposition, many public-health authorities in local health departments—increasingly professionals themselves (engineers, chemists, biologists, as well as physicians)—retreated into research, epidemiology, and diagnosis. Not only were these public-health professionals reluctant to challenge the medical profession, they were far more hesitant than were reform-minded civic groups and volunteer agencies to engage in the rough-and-tumble of politics and to push for expensive programs of broader social reform. Explains John Duffy, "Science, by providing new means for identifying, curing, and preventing contagious diseases, was thought to offer health departments a way to promote health without the cost of major social changes."[29]

The Public-Health Legacy

The public-health movement may have been eclipsed by the medical approach, but it left an important legacy. A network of government institutions and community agencies remained in place. Perhaps more importantly, the public-health movement established and legitimized a particular approach to understanding and confronting certain health problems, one that remained available to health reformers and practitioners struggling to address new health problems.

The nation's post–World War II growth spurt—marked in part by a broad expansion in scientific and industrial development—brought in

its wake a range of new health problems that eluded standard medical science, demanding instead a public-health response. Radiation,
environmental hazards, and increased levels of smoking, alcoholism, and
drug addiction, for example, "could not be prevented by immunizing the
public through some new vaccine or providing laboratory diagnostic services, and public health found itself being pushed into the area of social
and behavior concerns."[30]

Convincing public-health professionals and government officials to
tackle these new problems often required difficult political struggles. In
some cases reformers were able to draw directly on earlier experiences
and traditions, particularly in campaigns for urban sanitation and occupational safety and health and against epidemics and chronic illnesses. In other cases, notably problems related to mental health and to
alcohol, tobacco, and drug use, reformers expanded public health into
new areas.

The environmental-health movement was perhaps the clearest example of the post–World War II public-health concern with prevention,
illness, and the social environment. Reformers increasingly focused
public attention on health problems (such as cancer or birth defects)
created by environmental dangers, including hazardous wastes and
toxic substances that pollute groundwater, air, soil, and food. This
led to regulation of polluting industries and to other forms of public
action.[31]

In poor inner-city areas, new neighborhood health centers created
in the late 1960s and 1970s drew on earlier urban experiences in
providing comprehensive and affordable preventive health care. The
new centers sought to provide integrated treatment and preventive care
to people in their own neighborhoods and, like some earlier efforts,
often strove for community participation in decisions about health-care
services.[32]

The response to the AIDS threat in the 1980s, slow and begrudging
at first, was a classic public-health campaign.[33] The fact that there was
no cure for AIDS underlined the importance of prevention. Prevention
demanded public action to educate individuals about how AIDS is spread
and about how to alter their behavior in order to avoid contracting it.
Prevention also required changing the social and cultural context in order to encourage individual awareness and responsibility. This required
major efforts by community groups (especially in the gay community)
and government public-health officials to shift the focus away from
blaming the victims—which was the initial response of some antigay con-

servatives—and toward promoting public health.[34] The initial public-health response to AIDS also triggered important if limited efforts to re-orient government and community approaches to intravenous drug use, a major mechanism for spreading the virus. The effort to minimize modes of intravenous drug use that might spread AIDS began to challenge the principle of zero tolerance for drug use, and small-scale campaigns were launched to teach safe intravenous drug use and to promote needle exchange.

The public-health approach to AIDS highlights the integral connection between prevention and treatment. It has emphasized a view of treatment as reducing harm and providing care, not curing. Efforts are made, for example, to find ways to slow the onset of AIDS among people who are infected with HIV and to minimize the chances that victims of AIDS will contract infectious diseases that their immune systems cannot combat. Prevention and treatment become inseparable: the goal of treating an HIV-infected patient with the drug azidothymidine (AZT), for example, is to prevent rapid onset of the disease.[35] Once AIDS sets in, treatment consists not in seeking a cure but in caring for someone with a chronic illness—as was the case with tuberculosis during most of the nineteenth century. Central health questions thus become how the life of a person with the AIDS virus can be prolonged, how the suffering of a person with AIDS can be minimized, and how the process of dying can be made more humane. Treatment in this case, as with tuberculosis before a cure was identified, requires paying attention not simply to medicine but also to "the problems of housing, long-term care, public education, and the financing of palliative care for people suffering from chronic infections."[36]

Expanding the Public-Health Agenda

The emergence of new health problems in the postwar period expanded the public-health agenda in entirely new directions.[37] One example was the widespread effort to redefine mental health not simply as a private problem but also as a public-health problem with social consequences and social roots. The effort became the community mental-health movement of the 1960s and 1970s.[38]

Before the 1960s those who suffered from mental illness and could not afford private care were confined to state-run mental institutions. Initially designed to provide humane care and to help cure mental illness, these institutions were generally underfunded and overcrowded, and humane treatment was scarce. In the 1960s federal grants encouraged the creation of community mental-health clinics that sought to focus on prevention and early intervention. Treatment was aimed at reducing the need for hospitalization and at preventing mentally ill persons from harming themselves or others. Those who were chronically ill needed a continuum of care, including not only clinical attention but also rehabilitation services, social support, and decent shelter.[39] By 1977 some six hundred community mental-health centers were serving an estimated two million people,[40] and hundreds more centers were being planned.

The community mental-health movement also focused attention on aspects of the social environment that were damaging to mental health. Advocates believed that "it was essential to consider the mentally ill person within the context of his total personal and social environment, rather than merely as an isolated human being incarcerated in a large institution."[41] This required attention not only to the individual but also to the community environment itself—and to the impact of stress factors, including poverty, broken homes, parental conflict, and marital problems. Returning patients with mental-health problems to an unsupportive environment after brief medical treatment, for example, achieved little.[42]

The political support for public-health and social reform did not survive the conservative revolution of the 1980s. Although the principles of a public-health approach to mental health survived, its institutional support was cut when the Reagan administration repealed Carter's Mental Health Systems Act, cutting funds for mental health and leaving thousands of indigent mentally ill to wander city streets, without access either to state mental hospitals or to community alternatives.[43]

In addition to addressing mental health, the public-health agenda in the 1960s expanded to confront health problems whose immediate causes were choices made by individuals to engage in pleasurable but potentially risky and addictive behaviors—such as drinking alcohol and smoking. Public-health advocates argued that these risky choices were made in social contexts that often encouraged such behavior. Furthermore, the harmful consequences of these private acts—for the individual and for others—were exacerbated by environmental factors. Here again, prevention was deemed crucial; the possibilities for treating chronic problems such as lung cancer, for example, were limited and costly. Prevention was aimed at changing a social context that tolerated or encouraged these dangerous practices, and great emphasis was placed on government regulation, not prohibition, for public-health purposes.

Following the repeal of alcohol prohibition in the 1930s, restrictions were imposed on the distribution and sale of alcohol. The primary aim of these early laws, however, was not promoting public health.[44] To the extent that alcoholism was seen as a health problem, it was considered an individual one, a disease to be handled through individually based treatment strategies.[45] But research beginning in the late 1960s and 1970s suggested that many alcohol-related problems—highway fatalities, spouse and child abuse, homicides and other violent acts, fetal alcohol syndrome, lost work time, early death—result not only from serious alcohol addiction but also from broader patterns of heavy drinking, including among people who are not alcoholics.[46] Alcohol, the new research showed, is a dependence-inducing, intoxicating, debilitating substance—one that is far more dangerous and harmful to society than are illicit drugs. Beginning in the 1960s and 1970s, the harmful social consequences of alcohol abuse gradually led public-health reformers to urge government regulation and community programs designed to prevent such harms.

The public-health aim of these prevention efforts was not simply "no use" (though abstinence was urged for adolescents), but responsible or safe use rather than heavy use; and when people did drink heavily, the goal was to minimize the harm they could cause themselves and others (by driving, for example). Public-health advocates sought (rather unsuccessfully) to limit sales outlets, to raise prices by raising taxes on alcoholic beverages, and to restrict advertising—but they faced fierce resistance from the alcohol industry.[47] And they sought (rather more successfully) to pass tough laws against drunk driving, backed by punitive sanctions. Community programs established to prevent alcohol abuse included an array of services, including counseling and treatment, acute detoxification, halfway houses, employee-assistance programs, and community and school education programs.[48] These campaigns laid solid groundwork for a continuing and far-reaching public-health response to alcohol problems.

Public-health concerns with tobacco have a longer history. The spread of tuberculosis through the spitting of chewing tobacco led, by the early 1900s, to public-health campaigns to discourage the habit. These, ironically, may have encouraged cigarette smoking. Smoking was prohibited by law in fourteen states by 1921, but the ban was widely disregarded. By 1927 all of these laws had been repealed, leaving in place only laws that prohibited minors from smoking—which were also widely ignored.[49] Promoted by aggressive tobacco-company advertising, annual production of cigarettes in the United States soared from some 4 billion at the turn of the century to well over 500 billion by the 1960s. Cases of lung cancer and other smoking-related illnesses, including coronary heart disease, chronic bronchitis, and emphysema, also soared. The harmful consequences of smoking were borne not only by smokers themselves but also by those around them who inhaled secondhand smoke, by the health-care system, and by the nonsmokers who paid the taxes and insurance premiums to finance the treatment and other costs of smoking. By the mid-1990s tobacco use was responsible for more than 420,000 American deaths, surpassing the combined deaths from suicide, homicide, AIDS, automobile accidents, and alcohol and drug abuse.[50]

Despite mounting evidence of the harmful effects of tobacco smoking, it took decades of effort by reformers before the public began to see smoking as a health problem and to support measures to reduce its risks. These efforts gathered steam after 1964, when the U.S. surgeon general's Advisory Committee on Smoking and Health issued its first warnings.[51] Every step in the antismoking campaign involved a battle against powerful, well-financed tobacco companies. Preventive-education efforts were developed by government health departments and not-for-profit advocacy groups like the American Cancer Society, the American Lung Association, and the American Heart Association. They included airing antismoking messages in the media and classrooms and developing school programs that emphasized peer influence and resistance skills.

Education was increasingly complemented by government regulations. New laws forced companies to place warning labels on their products and advertisements, banned cigarette advertisements on television and radio, and sought to protect nonsmokers from passive smoking first by prohibiting smoking in public buildings and then by extending restrictions to restaurants, public transportation, entertainment centers, and private businesses.[52]

Public-health concerns also led to measures aimed at helping nicotine addicts minimize the harms of smoking. Special gum and skin patches, for example, deliver nicotine to the body without smoke. Public-health advocates acknowledged that the nicotine still puts stress on the heart and the circulatory system by repeatedly constricting the arteries; but ingesting nicotine without smoke eliminates the carcinogenic harm of the tars, the harm to the lungs caused by the hot gases and particulates, and the harm to others caused by secondhand smoke.[53] Like methadone treatment for heroin addicts, such public-health measures recognize that prevention must take place at every stage of use: the aim is not only to prevent initial use but also to find ways to minimize the harm caused to, and by, addicts.

Public-health advocates launched an effort in 1994 to classify nicotine as the addictive drug it is. Government officials and others brought their case to Congress and the media. The emphasis was on further regulation; there was little support—even among public-health advocates—for the total prohibition of tobacco production, sales, or use, in part because of the negative consequences that would accompany the inevitable black market in cigarettes. Although the powerful tobacco lobby and proindustry members of Congress resisted the reclassification of nicotine, the FDA, with the public backing of President Clinton, for the first time determined in 1995 that "nicotine in cigarettes and smokeless tobacco products is a drug." Armed with this classification, the FDA moved to issue stiff drug-control regulations aimed at promoting public health—triggering a court battle with the tobacco companies. These regulations included outlawing tobacco brand-name sponsorship of sporting events, banning cigarette vending-machine sales to force over-the-counter sales where proof of age would be required, limiting advertisements, and requiring the tobacco industry to run an education campaign against underage smoking.[54]

Such campaigns, both past and present, demonstrate that concern with public health has been a prominent feature of the health-care tradition in the United States, despite the clear dominance today of a medical approach to health problems—and despite attempts to dismantle public hospitals, clinics, and other public-health institutions by conservatives in the mid-1990s.

Although the concerns of public-health advocates have varied over time, four central themes underlie such campaigns. First, a clinical, medical approach to many health problems is insufficient. Second, it is far more effective—and, in the case of health problems without a cure, absolutely imperative—to prevent rather than to treat many health problems. Third, prevention demands attention to the physical and social environment that causes or exacerbates health problems. And fourth, attention to the broader environment demands a response by the public: it is beyond the control of individuals alone and beyond the reach of physicians.

A PUBLIC-HEALTH PARADIGM FOR DRUGS

The principles and practice of America's public-health tradition offer a useful framework for envisioning a public-health paradigm for illegal drugs such as heroin, cocaine, and marijuana. How would the drug problem, its causes, and appropriate solutions be defined from a public-health perspective?[55] How would such an approach change the way of thinking about drugs created by the punitive drug war paradigm?

Under a public-health paradigm, an individual who abuses drugs or is addicted to them would be considered a person with a health problem in need of care, not a criminal in need of punishment. This health problem is a public one for two reasons. First, it is caused not simply by an individual defect—a weak will, a moral failing, a disease—but also by the social environment. Changing this environment or becoming empowered to cope with it is not something an individual can do alone. Thus drug abuse and addiction are public-health problems. Second, drug abuse and addiction have social as well as individual consequences: they harm others and impose social costs. This, too, makes them public-health problems. These twin public aspects of drug use and abuse deserve closer attention.

The Public Roots of Drug Use

Social and cultural conditions in any environment—whether in the inner city or the suburbs—influence the decisions individuals make about drugs: whether to try them, how often, what precautions to take, whether to seek treatment, how long to stay in it, and whether to continue recovery afterward. The importance of environmental factors was already evident to the 1973 National Commission on Marijuana and Drug Abuse, which rejected

> the facile notion that drug dependence is a disease as susceptible to cure as ordinary maladies of the body. Drug dependence is often an illness of the spirit, relating in large part to the individual's relationships with the total society. . . . Drug use is a behavior that is transmitted by circumstances, experiences, and ideas rather than by viruses or bacteria. Purely medical solutions cannot succeed. Unless we can change the circumstances, there is little that can be done that will radically alter the motivation and the behavior.[56]

Subsequent research has made it clear that certain environmental factors—beyond the availability and price of drugs—make substance abuse and addiction more likely. These include peer pressures, patterns of past parental abuse, marital problems, poverty, joblessness, and home-lessness.[57] These risk factors are spread throughout the population but are particularly prevalent among the economically disadvantaged in the inner cities, making damaging drug behavior a particularly serious problem there.

In a public-health paradigm, attention to the social environment would shift the focus away from exclusive attention on an individual's decision to use drugs. But it would not deny that an individual's choices are important in almost every pattern of drug use, from the decision to try drugs to the decision to seek treatment. However, in many cases an individual's capacity to choose may be affected by the drugs themselves: choosing to stop using crack or alcohol, for example, is far more difficult after one has become addicted. And in every instance, the individual choices made are shaped and constrained by social conditions—by the knowledge one has about the effects of drugs, by the patterns of drug use among one's family and friends, by advertising, by the legal sanctions on drug use, by the price and availability of drugs, by the availability of treatment, by the accessibility of clean needles, by available networks of social support, by the presence or absence of a job or a home. As a 1990 Institute of Medicine report on drug treatment points out:

> It is difficult to overstate the critical importance of the socioeconomic environment. Individuals make choices, but they always do so in a social and economic environment, and there is ample evidence that such environments exercise great influence over drug consumption. They can promote initiation of drug use, aggravate and amplify drug effects, and counteract the process of recovery from drug dependence. The capabilities necessary to change socioeconomic factors must be developed so that these environments will help channel more individuals away from rather than toward drug problems.[58]

Because a social environment that constrains or empowers positive individual choices about drugs is itself a product of social choices, government intervention is justified by a concern with public health. Just as public officials make choices about particular policies (such as environmental protection or regulating the purity of food), they also make numerous choices (through action or inaction) about the social environment that shapes patterns of drug use—decisions about the information available to children, for example, about the advertisements permitted in the media, and about the opportunities for health care and housing and employment offered to citizens. A public-health approach would open a new debate on the role and responsibility of government in shaping the social environment of drug use.

The Public Consequences of Drug Use

If the roots of drug use reach into the social environment, in what sense are the consequences of drug use a social or public concern? More specifically, when should the effects of drug use be thought of as a *public* health problem? Three public-health consequences of drug use, first suggested by the 1973 report of the National Commission on Marijuana and Drug Use, can be developed into foundational principles.[59]

One public-health concern is *individual well-being*—the ability of an individual to become fully human, to realize his or her potential and lead a productive life. When a pattern of drug use impairs an individual's faculties or retards development, it reduces the options for self-fulfillment. Certain patterns of drug use may lead to addiction, cause acute health crises (injuries while intoxicated or a serious overdose, for example), or cause physiological damage (such as cirrhosis, cancer, or AIDS among intravenous drug users). Heavy drug use, even without physical addiction, may cause acute psychological effects (such as impaired judgment and motor function, mood changes, decreased attention span, memory loss, and poor school or work performance), which imperil the normal processes of development by hindering the ability to think clearly, make choices, plan one's life, and be creative.[60] Heavy drug use can also damage spiritual and emotional well-being—the ability to have caring, loving relationships and to make moral choices. The public-health approach seeks to minimize the physical harm and the mental anguish experienced by drug-dependent persons and to give such people the support and opportunities to choose productive lives.

A second public-health concern is drug use that impairs an individual's *social and economic functioning*. Here the focus is not on the immediate danger to the user's safety but on the possibly harmful impact of drug abuse and addiction on a person's ability to function in social relationships—as a husband, as a mother, or as a breadwinner, for example. The public-health approach attempts to minimize the kind of harm a drug-dependent person may do to such social relationships and to seek ways to reintegrate him or her into family and community life. Isolation and alienation arising from drug abuse are problems to be addressed not only to help individuals with drug problems but because families, friendships, and communities are inherently valuable.

Third, drug use that poses a threat to the safety or welfare of others is a legitimate public-health concern. Certain patterns of drug taking threaten *public safety*—by encouraging violence, dangerous driving, irresponsible use of machinery in the workplace, and the spread of diseases such as AIDS. In the interest of public health, policies and programs need to be designed to minimize or reduce these risks.

This definition of the drug problem as a public-health problem is commonsensical in many respects, yet it transforms the entire approach to drug use embodied in the punitive paradigm. To begin with, in a public-health paradigm the very meaning of illicit or dangerous use would be changed. The effects of drugs on one's health and on one's behavior toward others would demand a classification based on scientific, empirical evaluation. Such a classification would evaluate all psychoactive substances—including tobacco (nicotine), alcohol, marijuana, cocaine, heroin, LSD—from the standpoint of their health effects, not of political expedience or a subjective moralism.

Such research has already shown that legal drugs such as alcohol and tobacco are far more damaging to health than is marijuana, that nicotine is more addictive than are many illegal hard drugs, that heroin is less likely to encourage violent or abusive behavior than is alcohol, and so on.[61] It has demonstrated that many of the dangers attributed to the drugs themselves are in fact caused by the ways in which drugs are sold (without labeling or without inspection of contents, purity, or dosage, for example) and the ways in which they are used. Contaminated needles, not heroin itself, spread AIDS, for example; smokable heroin is less dangerous in terms of spreading this particular disease than is injected heroin. A public-health approach would encourage such research and insist that drug policies aim to minimize the harms caused by various drugs.

A public-health perspective would also challenge the central notion of the punitive paradigm: that the overarching aim of drug control is to suppress drug use. For public health, preventing first-time use or achieving total abstinence are only two ways to change harmful patterns of drug use.

It is reasonable, however, to ask: why wouldn't total abstinence be the top priority of a public-health model, and why wouldn't a concern with health also lead to a commitment to stop all drug use? If even the casual use of drugs constitutes a potential health problem, why not simply eliminate the possibility of such a problem by making "no use" the primary goal? The public-health perspective provides three answers. First, millions of people who use certain drugs like alcohol or marijuana occasionally and at low or moderate dosages do not constitute a major health problem—certainly not one that would justify the resources that would be required to prohibit all such use. Furthermore, the majority of individuals who try illicit drugs, like most alcohol users, do not progress from use to abuse and addiction. Rather, they continue a pattern of occasional and mild use or return to abstinence after experimenting with drug use.[62] Second, as we saw in chapter 2, it is impossible for a war on supply and users to limit drug availability and raise prices enough to eliminate the widespread use of drugs; from a public-health perspective, the money spent on this futile effort would be better spent addressing those patterns of drug use that most seriously endanger public safety and health. Third, a single-minded focus on stopping drug use, as we saw in chapter 3, often ends up harming public health in other ways, by spreading disease, causing crime, and distorting treatment and education efforts, for example.

In a public-health paradigm, limiting drug use in general would thus become only one element in a multifront strategy to influence all patterns of drug use in order to promote health and minimize harm. A public-health model would try to discourage any use of the most dangerous drugs, to prevent casual use from developing into heavier use or into addiction, to encourage addicts to use less dangerous forms of certain drugs (nicotine patches, not cigarettes; methadone, not heroin); to teach people who insist on using drugs how to prevent or minimize the health hazards to themselves and others; and to design treatment strategies that help people lessen, manage, or end their drug use while minimizing the harm they may cause others.

A fundamental guiding principle behind a public-health paradigm is providing a *continuum of positive choice* for individuals who are facing decisions about drug use. From a public-health perspective, one never gives up on an individual for having made a misguided choice; nor does one assume that an individual—regardless of the seriousness of his or her drug problem—has ever lost all capacity to choose. At each stage in an individual's decision-making about drug use—for example, whether to experiment, which drugs to use, and how to use them—public health demands a strategy for prevention and treatment that encourages better choices,[63] that helps individuals cope with their social environments, and that changes these environments to offer individuals better choices.

Many people confuse general strategies of treatment and prevention with a public-health approach. But such strategies would have very different meanings under a public-health paradigm than they do under the dominant drug war paradigm. Their central aim would be to promote public health, not primarily to stop all use, to punish users, or to relieve pressure on overcrowded prisons; and their focus would be not simply on individuals and drugs but also on the social environment that encourages dangerous patterns of drug use. The role and meaning of law enforcement, too, would be different in a public-health model. How might such a public-health paradigm work?

10 Envisioning a Public-Health Paradigm

Today's policy debate on drugs would be transformed if our thinking were shaped by a public-health paradigm. So, too, would be the institutional apparatus for drug control and, indeed, the very way we think about drugs and about people who suffer from drug dependence.

Politicians would most likely still be "tough on crime," but drug use and addiction would be regarded primarily as health problems, not as crime problems. Members of Congress and the media would demand to know whether a particular program had attracted substance abusers into treatment, enabled them to find or keep jobs, or slowed the spread of AIDS and other drug-related diseases—instead of demanding to know how many tons of heroin were interdicted, how many drug users were arrested, and how many coca fields were destroyed. There would be little reason to inject venom or fear into the debate over drugs.

Many of the present targets for enforcement would become subjects for treatment and assistance. Police forces would shift their attention from rounding up users and petty dealers to addressing crimes such as murder, rape, and robbery, as well as violent drug-related crimes. Many current drug-control agencies—the Border Patrol, Customs Service, and Coast Guard, for example—would be relieved of their unrealistic drug war mandate to "seal the borders." Meanwhile, the fragile public-health system that exists today—the federal agencies, the private and nonprofit organizations, the community programs—would expand to provide substance-abuse prevention and treatment at the state and local levels. A public-health paradigm would justify shifting tax dollars wasted on the current war against supply and users to fund such programs.

To be sure, problems of abuse and addiction would not disappear. But drug dependence would be thought about differently—perhaps in the way that alcoholism has begun to be understood today. Increasingly, individuals who suffer from alcohol dependence are seen as deserving not punishment and contempt but compassion and assistance in confronting their addiction. They are able to seek and find help without shame and without the threat of arrest and punishment. A new paradigm for public health would do the same for other substance abusers.

To many Americans, such a model for dealing with drug problems may sound like a nice idea but entirely implausible. Yet a public-health vision currently guides drug policy in several nations. The Netherlands is a case in point. Drug policy in the Netherlands is often caught in the cross fire between prohibitionists and legalizers in today's drug debate, because Dutch policy includes decriminalization measures. As a result, U.S. commentators often miss what is most important about the case of the Netherlands: the fact that its drug policies are guided by the goal of improving public health, not by the goal of either punishing use or of protecting individuals' right to choose to use drugs. Former U.S. ambassador to the Netherlands, John Shad, explained that Dutch policy views the drug abuser

> primarily as an unfortunate with health and social problems rather than primarily as a criminal. It attempts to keep him "above ground" and it wants him within reach of medical authority. The policy attempts to stabilize his life and to limit the damage he causes to society, to family and to himself. It encourages and provides immediate therapy—virtually upon demand whenever he is ready for it—including methadone maintenance, free needle exchange to reduce the risk of AIDS and hepatitis infection if he is an intravenous abuser, counseling, and residential or out-patient long-term treatment. Finally, and when possible, it assists his eventual reintegration into society.[1]

The Dutch see the problem of drug abuse "as a matter of public health and well-being," according to a top health official, Eddy Engelsman. Responsibility for coordinating drug policy lies not with the criminal-justice system but with social-welfare institutions—specifically, in the Alcohol, Drugs and Tobacco branch of the Ministry of Welfare, Public Health and Cultural Affairs. "One of the most striking features" of the system for assisting addicts, Engelsman says, "is the wide range of treatment and counseling services, which is capable of reaching the major part of the population of addicts." He explains that "treatment approaches [are] primarily directed at improving addicts' physical and social functioning, without requiring abstinence immediately. . . . The care system has no waiting lists. It is easily accessible free of charge and it treats addicts respectfully as fellow-citizens." The result, he suggests, is that addicts indeed appear and function differently from their counterparts in the United States. "Field studies among methadone clients and 'street addicts' have shown that this approach has proved to be successful and that the 'typical' addict is in no way an antisocial 'junkie.'" The health of these heroin users is "reasonably good," and drug deaths in the Netherlands are low relative to those of other countries.[2]

The Dutch system of drug control, finally, recognizes the importance of a broader context of care: "Drug use does not stand alone. Poverty, discrimination of ethnic minorities, tensions between the rich and the poor, lack of access to social and health services, and dilapidated neighborhoods are all factors that could lead to substance abuse. In the Netherlands, demand-reduction programs are therefore being integrated with the social security system, which guarantees a minimum income to every citizen, and with an accessible general health care system."[3]

The Netherlands case was once unusual in Europe, but today there are a number of countries—Great Britain, Italy, Switzerland, and Germany—in which the public debate about drugs is increasingly dominated by concerns about health, AIDS, and the minimization of the harms caused by drugs rather than by punitive concerns about suppressing drug use. Drug abuse in these European countries "is far more likely to be regarded as a tragedy than a sin, a product of deprivation rather than of weakness. Protection from it, then, becomes more easily a matter of nurturance rather than of punishment. As a public-health problem, drug abuse is to be managed with the services (medical, psychological, and social) available for other disabilities."[4]

Such cases are important because they enable us to better envision a public-health paradigm in practice. These models cannot simply be imported into the United States, however, because of fundamental differences in social conditions. The Netherlands, for example, is far smaller than the United States; it does not suffer from ethnic and class tensions as sharp as those in the United States; its cities are not plagued by the degree of economic deterioration and crime found in many U.S. cities; it already has a sophisticated tradition and institutional structure of social welfare and health care; and a punitive paradigm that emphasizes moral condemnation and considers drug use a crime was never as deeply rooted there.

If a public-health system for drugs were ever to emerge in the United States, it would be shaped by political struggles fought in American circumstances. The possibilities for and limits to such struggles are the subject of the next chapter. In this chapter we examine specific ways in which a public-health approach would redefine drug problems and drug policies. Prevention and treatment would be the central strategies in pursuit of public health; law enforcement would also be important but would no longer be the keystone. More importantly, prevention, treatment, and law enforcement would all take on distinct meanings if the drug problem were redefined in terms of public health.

PREVENTION

Prevention under the punitive paradigm has a singular aim: to stop use. It would have a different meaning under a public-health paradigm. It would seek to promote healing and reduce harm, not simply to promote the goal of zero tolerance for drug use, and it would address not only the condition of the individual user but also the harmful social consequences of abuse and addiction.

Concern for an individual's health and well-being requires strategies for prevention at every level of use: to prevent individuals from turning to drugs, from slipping to heavier reliance on drugs, from moving from less harmful to more harmful drugs, and from shifting from less hazardous to more hazardous drug-use habits, such as sharing needles. Concern for the social consequences of abuse and addiction demands strategies to prevent harm to the physical safety of others—by deterring drug users from injuring others by driving while intoxicated or sharing contaminated needles, for example. But it also means addressing other serious, if less dramatic, harms. Because abuse can affect a person's ability to function in social relationships, prevention for public health seeks ways in which to prevent drug problems from destroying marriages and families, from disrupting school life, and from harming workplace relationships.

What would such prevention strategies look like? To begin with, drug education for public health would have a different message and reach a wider audience than do many of today's drug-education programs, most of which share with punitive strategies the primary aim of achieving total abstinence. The "Just Say No" campaign is a prominent example. A public-health approach would remove the incentive to exaggerate the harmful effects of drugs. The primacy of the current goal of "zero use" of drugs tempts educators to overstate the dangers of certain illicit drugs, such as marijuana, particularly in contrast to the effects of legal drugs such as alcohol and tobacco. It also encourages some drug educators to rely on fear, on the assumption that people are most likely to modify their behavior in response to the threat of punishment. This approach persists despite evidence that scare tactics and moral exhortations to abstain do not work well.[5] In the words of a 1990 congressional report, "Putting forth the idea that all illegal drugs are extremely dangerous and addictive, when young people subsequently learn otherwise through experimentation, discredits the message."[6] This means providing people with accurate information (much the way public-health efforts with respect to tobacco and alcohol do[7]) about the physical and psychological effects on individuals of all psychoactive drugs—as well as the effects that taking drugs can have on other things of value, such as work and relationships with friends and family.

Drug education for public health must also teach safer use—even while it discourages use. Although promoting safer use is contradictory under a punitive paradigm that has "zero use" as its goal, no such contradiction exists under a public-health paradigm. Because the goal is to promote health, a public-health approach seeks not only to reduce use but also to minimize the harm caused by use. It accepts that some use will persist despite the best efforts at prevention. And people who are unwilling or unable to quit need to know which drugs are more addictive; they need to know which combinations of drugs are particularly dangerous; they need to know how to prevent an overdose and what to do in the event of one; they need to know what kinds of conditions make drug use more or less dangerous and how to avoid dangerous behaviors while intoxicated (such as unsafe driving or sex).

Some preventive-education programs already tread on this politically sensitive ground. Many communities, for example, have sponsored programs that encourage the use of designated drivers, or contracts in which teenagers agree to call home for a ride if they are drunk and, in turn, parents agree to refrain from punishment. Communities have encouraged party hosts to gather the keys of all guests on arrival and to return the keys only to guests who are capable of driving on departure. They have convinced taxicab companies to offer free rides on prom nights to any young person who feels incapable of driving home.

Similarly, prevention advocates in some communities have sought to educate intravenous drug users about safer ways to use drugs in order to prevent the spread of blood-borne diseases. Some have combined education with offers of sterile needles that can be obtained in exchange for used ones. These programs often combine needle exchange with educational programs on sanitation and safe sex; some help addicts find treatment. Success is measured not simply by abstinence but also by the slowdown in the spread of AIDS and other diseases and by the increase in the number of addicts who seek treatment.

Designated-driver and needle-exchange programs are anathema to people who are wedded to the zero-use doctrine of the punitive paradigm, because such strategies imply that some use is acceptable as long as it is safe. Yet they are entirely consistent with public-health principles, which advocate intervention at every stage—not only to prevent use but also to prevent the harms that come with use.

Prevention demands more than educating drug users about how to change their behavior. Environmental factors that influence drug use must also be addressed. Explaining the dangers of different drugs to adolescents, for example, is inadequate because they often think of themselves as invulnerable and because their motivation to take drugs is often rooted not merely in misinformation but also in a complex array of social influences—messages delivered through the entertainment media, peer pressure, and substance-abusing parents. The "Just Say No" campaigns in schools, for example, "aren't sensitive to the number of kids living in environments where people they love and depend on are using and selling drugs," explained one child-health specialist.[8]

Many drug-education programs already recognize certain elements of the social environment. Some have drawn on social-influences models to teach young people to resist peer pressure or to pursue counseling and to engage them in positive community-based activities.[9] The Midwestern Prevention Program, an experimental program in Kansas City, had some success in lowering drug taking among both high-risk and low-risk young people. It moved beyond the often less successful school-based programs to work at multiple levels of the social environment, involving educational programs for youngsters and their parents, community-organization and health-policy components, and mass-media campaigns.[10]

Prevention under a public-health paradigm, however, demands strategies that reach well beyond drug education. Its broader role is to ensure that public values, institutions, and behaviors mirror and reinforce public-health messages. This requires regulation, not simply to prevent drug use but also to prevent drug abuse and addiction from harming users and those around them. Laws and sanctions must be designed to prevent people who are under the influence of behavior-impairing substances from engaging in public activities such as driving buses, controlling air traffic, or performing surgery. The proper disposal of contaminated needles would need to be ensured. It would be legitimate to have regulations forbidding the use of drugs in certain public areas, just as cigarette smoking is regulated today.

Finally, prevention for public health must confront the cultural and social environment of drug use. Taking the cultural environment of drug consumption seriously is a far more difficult task than that undertaken by those (such as former drug czar Bennett) who simply want to teach the evils of drugs and the importance of individual responsibility and traditional values. It means challenging the materialist and consumerist tenets of modern capitalism that feed—and are exploited by—the licit and illicit drug markets. Todd Gitlin, for example, observes that "in many ways American culture is a drug culture. . . . It cultivates the pursuit of thrills; it elevates the pursuit of private pleasure to high standing; and, as part of this ensemble, it promotes the use of licit chemicals for stimulation, intoxication, and fast relief. The widespread use of licit drugs in America can be understood as part of this larger set of values and activities."[11]

Advertising for legal drugs such as alcohol and tobacco reinforces a culture that glamorizes drug use, associating it with sexual attraction, rugged individualism, rewards for a job well done, humor, excitement, success, friendship, and fun. Over-the-counter drugs are sold—and consumed—as instant problem solvers. The "take-a-pill" message in the media (to make you feel better, to take away your headaches, backaches, and sleeplessness, to give you energy) creates and sustains a culture of drug consumption. One consequence is to encourage the use of illicit drugs—which many users, understandably, do not distinguish clearly from legal drugs.[12]

Reforming this broader drug culture is a considerable task, but there are many small steps that might be considered under a public-health paradigm. Advertising might be regulated to minimize the profit-driven commercialization and glamorization of psychoactive substance use. Coherent public-health campaigns against all substance abuse could warn of the varying dangers of addiction, of heavy use, and of dangerous

modes of drug use. They could explicitly attack the images (often promoted by legal drug manufacturers) that link pleasure to drug use. Television spots of the social smoker with the hacking cough and Spanish-
language New York City subway cartoon stories of friends who
unknowingly spread the AIDS virus to each other are examples of what
a vigorous, realistic public-health campaign might look like.

Because the problem of drug abuse and addiction is in part a symptom of larger health and social problems, a public-health approach to
prevention would also demand attention to social conditions that lie well
beyond the reach of a drug-policy paradigm. Changes in our nation's
health system, for example, would have an important effect on preventing substance abuse. Many of the most serious risk factors for abuse
would be addressed by making comprehensive health care accessible to
the poor and by making substance-abuse prevention and treatment part
of that system. From a public-health perspective, a national system that
provided prenatal and infant care in addition to treatment would have
far more success in preventing pregnant women with substance-abuse
problems from harming their babies than would stricter sanctions, which
discourage women from seeking help. Health-care programs aimed at
preventing sexually transmitted diseases or the spread of the AIDS virus
could deal with drug use and addiction as a daily part of health care.
Programs that deal with rape, sexual abuse, and incest could help lower
risk factors associated with abuse and addiction.

Changes in urban policy would also have a dramatic effect in preventing drug abuse and addiction. Inner-city conditions are particularly
pernicious in encouraging substance abuse: lack of employment and the
curtailment of publicly funded health care and of welfare payments have
shrunk social-support mechanisms; rates of homelessness are increasing
rapidly; public-housing projects in disrepair have become centers for
drug dealing and violence. Inner-city residents who seek alcohol and drug
treatment face long waiting lists, understaffed programs, and the threat
of sanctions. Such pressures have disrupted family and community life
and have caused a sense of despair and hopelessness.

The thought that we must rebuild our cities seems so overwhelming
that it is tempting to overlook the connection between drug problems
and urban conditions. But a concern for public health demands that
we confront this connection squarely.[13] This does not mean that
nothing can be fixed until everything is fixed. An urban public-health response would suggest, to the contrary, that a modest, intelligent policy
aimed at solving immediate inner-city problems would go a long way to-

ward promoting public health in general as well as toward preventing the problems of drug abuse. Small steps toward job creation, child-care opportunities, improved schools, adequate housing, and safer streets would make a significant difference. The concrete successes of some local community-development corporations demonstrate the real gains that can come from such steps.[14]

Drug problems, of course, are only one of the many reasons for instituting workable urban and health-care policies, and the impetus for such social reforms would have to come from a coalition far broader than those who are anxious to do something about drug problems. But just as drug problems in the inner cities are in part symptoms of larger social problems, so, too, those who seek a public-health approach to drug prevention must ally themselves with broader reform coalitions.

TREATMENT

Preventing any health problem is always preferable for public health than treating it after it occurs—it is far better for the health and well-being of both the individual and the public, and it is far less costly. But when a drug problem occurs, promoting public health and preventing further harm demands drug treatment. Ideas about treatment under a public-health paradigm—its purposes, methods, and measures of success— would be fundamentally different from the ways in which treatment is viewed through the lenses of the punitive paradigm.

Many drug-policy officials today talk about treatment as simply another instrument, in addition to force, to achieve "zero use." For them, the primary purpose of treatment is to "cure" abusers and addicts of their drug use (with cure defined as total and permanent abstinence). Treating for public health, in contrast, would seek to foster individual and social well-being and to promote public safety. Helping heavy users quit entirely would thus be one goal. But treating for public health would also mean helping individuals cut back to less dangerous levels of drug use and preventing them from taking the next step toward more hazardous drug use.

Equally important, treatment would demand helping people manage the effects of their drug use. This would mean helping them minimize the physical effects of drug use—by reducing the risk of disease or overdosing, for example. It would also mean minimizing harm to the social relationships of drug users—helping them manage work, family, and community obligations—and protecting public safety.

Under a public-health paradigm, treatment and prevention would thus go hand in hand: they are part of a continuum of care. This is a marked contrast to the approach encouraged by the punitive paradigm, in which the main purpose of prevention is to stop the first use of drugs and in which treatment is seen as an entirely separate strategy employed only when prevention programs fail. Prevention strategies for public health would not be abandoned when someone started using or abusing drugs and needed treatment: preventing heavier or more dangerous use would always be a concern, as would helping abusers prevent further harm to themselves and to others.

A public-health approach would also redefine success in drug treatment, by moving far beyond the narrow criterion of permanent abstinence. Dr. Douglas Anglin explains that today,

> many people assume that high dropout rates mean that treatment doesn't work, but research confirms that it does. . . . Though some addicts may succeed in staying off drugs the first time they try, most will go in and out of treatment a number of times. Each time they do, their drug use goes down, along with their criminal activity. Even if they never achieve abstinence, they may be able to reduce the size of their habits, or shift to less harmful drugs. These are positive gains, both for the addict and for society.[15]

Under a public-health paradigm, relapses would be considered a natural part of the recovery process—as they are in many treatment programs for alcohol or tobacco addictions.[16] Quitting drug use would be one measure of success, but others would also be important.

Job-based alcohol-treatment programs that fail to achieve total abstinence, for example, are nevertheless often successful in helping employees reduce or control their drinking and therefore work more safely and efficiently—and keep their jobs. If drug treatment helped a substance abuser use fewer and less dangerous drugs, to avoid harmful behavior, to secure and hold a job, or to be a better parent, these would be indicators of success under a public-health paradigm.

If total abstinence is the goal, the fact that some substance abusers may take years, even decades, to overcome their addictions—and that others may never entirely stop their drug use—encourages policymakers to give up on them. But from a public-health standpoint, to deny continued opportunities for treatment to these addicts amounts to giving up on the millions of people who have not, cannot, or will not stop taking drugs; it means giving up on helping them create socially productive lives, condemning many of them to the criminal underworld or to living as social pariahs; and it means giving up on the opportunity to prevent the harm they may cause themselves and others. From a public-health perspective, the willingness to give up on treatment and turn to punishment under the current system is evident in those treatment programs that consider participants who relapse as failures and force them out of treatment.

Although government policy aims at zero use, many treatment practitioners do, in fact, approach treatment with broader public-health goals in mind—although, for political reasons, they may be reticent to publicly advocate goals short of abstinence. A 1990 study by the Institute of Medicine reports that

> abstinence from illicit drug consumption is the central clinical goal of every kind of drug treatment, but it is not the complete goal. . . . Full recovery . . . can be realistically envisioned in some fraction of cases. . . . But full recovery is not a realistic goal for other individuals, and these others make up the majority of admissions to most drug programs. . . . In summary, the pragmatic objectives of treatment in most cases are modest: to reduce illicit drug consumption, especially of the primary drug of abuse, by a large percentage— perhaps to nothing for an extended period—*relative to the consumption one could expect in the absence of treatment;* to reduce the intensity of other criminal activity if present; to permit the responsible fulfillment of family roles; to help raise employment or educational levels if the client so desires and the program has the resources available for such an effort; and to make the client less miserable and more comfortable physically and mentally. These goals are incremental: instead of absolute success and failure, there are degrees of improvement.[17]

Under a public-health paradigm, then, helping people break their addictions and helping people live with their addictions would not be incompatible objectives but parts of a continuum of care. The continuum begins with policies to prevent the use of potentially dangerous drugs and ends with treating addicts to help them lead more healthy, productive lives and to minimize harm to those around them.

The different goals and measures of success for public-health treatment imply dramatically different strategies and priorities. As a policy, treatment would not simply be the small carrot to accompany the big stick of punishment but a well-funded centerpiece of a drug strategy committed to providing treatment on demand. Moreover, every effort would be made to encourage drug users to enter treatment—and to avoid the bureaucratic red tape and the threats of exposure and punishment that today often deter those who seek treatment.

If treatment were guided by primarily public-health considerations, its scope and character would expand. Medical or psychological treatment measures—such as detoxification programs and counseling—

aimed at getting individuals off drugs would only be one part of a broader continuum of care.

Consider one of the most difficult treatment challenges: the treatment of heroin addicts. A public-health response to heroin users would combine preventive measures (such as education about safer injection practices and access to sterile needles), treatment measures (methadone and counseling to deal with their heroin addiction, as well as medical measures for other common health problems among addicts, such as tuberculosis), and measures to address their social environments (from the unsanitary conditions of shooting galleries to the lack of homes, jobs, and hope they may face).

Such public-health principles have been employed on a small scale, with promising results. A New Haven needle-exchange program, for example, has served a vital outreach function by bringing addicts who distrusted and shunned the existing system into contact with treatment programs. One of every six addicts served by the exchange program subsequently entered treatment.[18]

The British approach to heroin addiction demonstrates how a more comprehensive public-health approach to treatment could be implemented. Since the 1920s British narcotics policy has largely been guided by a medical approach: for decades heroin, for example, could be legally prescribed to those who were addicted to it. Heroin policies became more restrictive in the 1960s, as responsibility for treatment was transferred from doctors to less lenient government health clinics, and by the 1980s a punitive approach had emerged to challenge the medical approach. The AIDS epidemic in the 1980s, however, spurred a reevaluation and encouraged a reemphasis on nonpenal methods of drug control, particularly public-health methods. In the late 1980s the National Advisory Council on the Misuse of Drugs concluded that "the spread of HIV is a greater danger to individual and public health than drug misuse. Accordingly, services which aim to minimize HIV-risk behavior by all available means should take precedence in development plans." It urged attracting as many drug users as possible and working to minimize the risky behavior of those who were not ready to stop drug use. And it argued that penal policies that might encourage drug users to stay underground needed to be changed if HIV infection rates were to be stemmed.[19]

A range of public-health strategies aimed at "harm-minimization for the individual and society" was put in place, including "regular health checks, open access services, free contraception, substitute drug therapy including the use of cocaine and amphetamines, heroin, injectable and oral drugs, and teaching safer injecting practices."[20]

The results were in many cases dramatic. In the mid-1980s officials in Edinburgh, Scotland, identified an average of 120 new HIV infections a year caused by contaminated needles. Acting under British law, local officials allowed physicians to prescribe, free and on demand, oral versions of the drugs that addicts used—if the users avoided needles and agreed to drug treatment. Heroin addicts were given methadone as well as other drugs. By 1991 there were only eight new cases of AIDS attributable to intravenous drug use. The programs were also successful in their goal of lowering drug use through regular drug and medical counseling. The Edinburgh police reported that heroin use and even local crime rates declined.[21]

This public-health response also challenged earlier British cultural images of drug users—as hedonistic, outlaw/rebels, sick, irrational—and instead advanced a view of drug users as capable of making rational choices about drug use and their lives. Health providers referred to the importance of "'enabling' and 'empowering' injectors to change their behavior by providing them with information, promoting motivation to change, and providing the means to make those changes (such as methadone, syringes, condoms). . . . One agency describes [this] as a 'consumer-oriented style of service delivery' where 'drug injectors' needs must dictate the direction of the service.'"[22]

The British case stands in sharp contrast to treatment programs shaped by a punitive drug war paradigm. It emphasizes a continuum of care, rather than a single-minded goal of "zero use." It aims to reduce social harm as well as to promote individual well-being. And it recognizes the importance of attracting or encouraging users to seek treatment.

Many treatment providers in the United States today echo the importance of finding ways to encourage those who need treatment to seek it. They point out that addicts are often uninterested in or repelled by treatment even when it is available because they do not think it serves their most important needs. The problem is particularly acute among certain segments of the substance-abusing population. Mexican American addicts, for example, are "especially unlikely to participate in traditional therapeutic communities and group psychotherapy" when treatment stresses confrontation and incessant self-revelation, strategies based on Protestant, middle-class models of the process of individual change.[23]

Treatment for women, to take another example, is not only scarce but ill designed under the current system; it often fails because it systematically neglects to take into account the social environment. Working women need clinic hours that are suited to their workdays. Women with children often need child care, and those who are enrolled in residential treatment also need facilities for their families. Pregnant women need comprehensive treatment facilities that offer not only drug treatment but also affordable prenatal and postnatal care. They need to be assured that they will not be sent to jail or have their babies taken from them if they enter drug treatment. Once they complete a treatment program, they may need assistance in finding work (job training and placement) and permanent housing.[24]

More generally, addicts today often "do not seek treatment, especially early in their drug careers, because they do not regard the drug itself as the problem that needs fixing in their lives: many, indeed, regard it as the solution."[25] The problems that need fixing in their lives are products of the social environment. "The research on what helps addicts succeed *in* treatment . . . points over and over again to the crucial importance of what we could call a social 'stake.' Addicts do better after treatment if they have social support and encouragement from families or spouses; if they have stable jobs; if they have others to care for; and if someone cares enough about what happens to them to consistently supervise their behavior and otherwise take on a caring and firm role in their lives."[26]

In congressional testimony Thelma Brown, of the Watts Health Foundation, described the need to deal with the social environment this way:

> One of the highest causes of recidivism occurs when a client leaves treatment. He or she is likely to be forced to return to the very same environment that contributed to the addiction in the first place. What awaits this individual is lack of employment—and the old cycle of hopelessness and helplessness. What does he or she do but seek out that which is known best—drugs. This escape through drugs is sometimes used to dull the pain of frustration, or, perhaps, as a way of survival. . . . Given the severity of the problem, simple "band-aid" attempts at treatment will lead only to a dead end. . . . Upon completion of these [treatment] programs, provisions should be made for follow-through; such as providing jobs, training and education. By providing a different way of life, we provide new hope and opportunities, to replace the drugs. One can say no to drugs, but we must provide something to which one can "say yes."[27]

Paying attention to the concrete problems that many drug-dependent individuals face suggests the need to confront and change some aspects of users' social environments—not simply to help them cope better with these conditions. If meaningful employment, for instance, helps drug-dependent people lead more productive lives and diminish their drug

dependence, then one treatment strategy would be to put chemically dependent people to work before or during treatment, not after recovery.

The Wildcat Service Corporation, organized in the early 1970s by the
Vera Institute of Justice in New York City, put hundreds of addicts to
work in responsible (not make-work) jobs, often in city agencies. More
than half of those who started stayed on the job for at least a year. About
one-third graduated to nonsubsidized jobs and held those jobs for at least
six months. Research on a sample of Wildcat workers compared them
over three years to a similar control group and showed that a smaller
proportion of Wildcat workers were arrested and that a larger proportion of them cut back on their drug use. A larger proportion of them
were also able to enter into common-law or marriage relationships, support dependents, and live with their children.[28]

Innovative programs developed by churches and local neighborhood
groups also illustrate what it would mean to take the overall social and
cultural environment seriously under a public-health approach. Consider Musica against Drugs, the drug-treatment and prevention program
organized in the Williamsburg section of Brooklyn.[29] The program had
its origins in a salsa band of the same name, an effort by local musicians
and community organizers to do something about drug problems in the
Latino (largely Puerto Rican) section of Williamsburg. Originally a vol-
untary organization but now funded by government and foundation
grants, it ties treatment and prevention efforts linked to Narcotics
Anonymous with workshops in dance, music, art, drama, poetry, mural
painting, video making, and other forms of artistic expression. Musica
tries to give people in the community—former addicts, people in recovery, and residents who are not on drugs—something creative in which
to engage and to encourage pride in their cultural identity.

Musica expanded its original work on drugs to include support groups
for people with HIV or AIDS and their families. Musica workers and
volunteers canvass heavy drug-trafficking areas, give users information
on AIDS, and provide referrals to detoxification and health-care programs. Musica works with Adapt, the local needle-exchange program,
to conduct outreach work among intravenous drug users. It has created
a community dining hall for people with AIDS, along with a nutrition-
ist and a van to provide food to people who are confined at home. It explicitly aims to connect persons with drug problems to a broader non-
drug-using community in an effort to provide alternatives to continued
drug use. It hosts large block festivals—clean and sober parties—and invites the community to participate in recreational alternatives.

Elements of programs such as these, which are responsive to the cultural and social environments, health problems, and other needs of substance abusers, can already be found in a wide variety of current treatment settings—such as some methadone-maintenance programs and therapeutic communities. In fact, many treatment providers and community programs would like very much to have the staff and facilities to provide the kind of counseling, child care, interagency coordination, job training, and continuing care that their patients need; and the public-health approach outlined here would be welcomed by many. But public and political support for the necessary funds is simply not there. As long as substance abuse is seen through the lens of a punitive paradigm, it is unlikely that such funds will be forthcoming.

Even the best treatment programs, moreover, will continue to be limited if opportunities are scarce after substance abusers complete programs. As long as there are not enough good jobs in the labor market to provide the level of involvement and challenge achieved in such experimental programs, there will be serious obstacles to success in realizing the values behind the public-health approach. The same can be said about the need for child care, housing, and health care. This conclusion again points toward broader social policies that would be necessary to fundamentally alter the environment in which treatment and recovery take place.[30]

THE ROLE OF LAW AND ENFORCEMENT

Like prevention and treatment, law and its enforcement take on a distinct meaning in the service of public health. Instead of being the centerpiece of the drug-control strategy, like law and enforcement under the punitive paradigm, they support the larger task of prevention: promoting health and minimizing harm.

The specific content of such legal regulations and their modes of enforcement are not dictated in any direct way by a public-health paradigm; laws and guidelines would emerge only after much debate among public-health advocates. But the public-health paradigm would set the broad terms of such a debate, and it is a very different debate from the one that is framed by the punitive paradigm.

The opening of the Hippocratic oath suggests one important guideline for the role of law: *primum non nocere*—first, do no harm. This means that under a public-health paradigm, laws that intentionally or unintentionally undermine public-health goals would have no place.

Laws and enforcement strategies that encourage harmful behavior—by forbidding access to sterile injection equipment, for example, or by discouraging addicts from seeking the treatment they need—would be unacceptable.

This Hippocratic principle also discourages drug laws that are more harmful to individual users than is drug consumption itself. To punish people with prison sentences solely because they use drugs is illogical from a public-health perspective; it is as questionable as putting heavy drinkers or heavy smokers into prison because they drink or smoke. It not only violates basic principles of justice to punish people who have committed no crime against the person or property of another, it also violates fundamental public-health principles by maximizing the harm to individual well-being and social functioning. Jailing people who are guilty only of drug use exposes them to a prison culture that all too often encourages further drug use and more serious crime after release. It leaves them with prison records that make it difficult to find employment or housing and to shape the kind of lives that might discourage drug abuse. Laws that criminalize drug use and punish possession for personal use would therefore be illogical and counterproductive under a public-health paradigm.

If the principle of *primum non nocere* clarifies what law should not do, what positive role should law play? From a public-health perspective, legal controls to promote health and prevent the harm caused by abuse and addiction could be pursued in two ways: the government could directly regulate the behavior of individuals, and it could regulate the social environment that shapes such individual choices—including the availability, price, and purity of drugs.

Regulating individual behavior in order to protect public safety would be one aim of a public-health approach. Laws should prohibit a person who is under the influence of drugs from engaging in activities that are potentially dangerous to others—such as driving or operating machinery. Similarly, a public-health regime would punish drug users who commit crimes against people or property: theft, for example, or child or spouse abuse while under the influence of a drug demands legal action and punishment.

If drug abuse or addiction is a factor in a crime, a public-health response would incorporate treatment into punishment. Drug treatment would be a central part of rehabilitation for substance abusers in prison, in order to prevent such crime in the future: experiments with such programs show promising results, but they are rare and often underfunded. For nonviolent criminals, compulsory treatment might be considered in lieu of prison. Such diversion-to-treatment programs are already under way in many places—although their objectives are more often to relieve prison overcrowding than to serve public health. Programs such as the Treatment Alternatives to Street Crime (TASC) program and local drug courts in places such as Miami, Florida, Oakland, California, and Portland, Oregon, now divert nonviolent drug-involved arrestees (after careful screening) into community-based treatment programs. Retention in the program is monitored by the court, and successful completion of treatment leads to dismissal of the pending charges or to probation. Evidence suggests that lower recidivism results from such programs—and many drug offenders avoid the damaging consequences of jail or prison time.[31]

Regulating for public health would also mean addressing the full range of noncriminal harms that drug abuse and addiction can do to users and to people around them. The degree and type of regulation would be the subject of much debate in a public-health paradigm: each case would raise contested questions over the severity of the harm, who is being harmed, and the potential harm caused by the regulation itself.

A student coming to school after having smoked marijuana, for example, might be well disciplined, polite, and not disruptive. However, the behavioral effects of use, especially if it is routine, are likely to harm this person's ability to learn and to hinder personal growth and development; it may also undermine the abilities of others to learn, especially if group dynamics are an integral part of the educational process and if a number of the students are using marijuana. On such grounds, it would be reasonable to strictly prohibit the use of marijuana in schools—just as smoking tobacco and drinking alcohol may be restricted today.

Similar arguments can be made for restricting certain kinds of drug use to the privacy of one's home or to designated areas and for prohibiting use in certain public areas and facilities. Where drug use is permitted, the public-health concern to minimize the harm caused by unsafe use would demand regulation—zoning, inspection, licensing—of particular premises. Such regulation has sometimes been used to control the consumption of alcohol in bars and taverns: their location, their hours, and the age limits on their clientele are restricted by law. Likewise, the conditions under which methadone is used in special clinics and programs are regulated—how much, to whom, and under what conditions. Under a public-health regime, the use of other drugs would also merit such regulation.

Heated debates over how far government should go to prevent drug users from harming themselves or others would be expected under a public-health paradigm. Does protection of the public's health justify compulsory treatment for users who have not broken laws against people or property but who may be doing serious harm to their own and others' well-being? Some public-health advocates would say yes: such treatment is justified, for example, for people who are mentally ill, although only under certain extreme circumstances. Others would point out that this system has often been misused.[32] California and New York, for instance, adopted civil-commitment laws in the early 1960s that "required only a finding of 'addiction' to sustain a commitment, abandoning any pretense of case-by-case determinations of dangerousness." The 1973 National Commission on Marijuana and Drug Abuse warned that such standards enabled the government

> to coerce conformity in many instances where the protection of society would neither require nor justify coercion. . . . Legislators and official spokesmen must realize that therapy is not a justification for assertion of control over the great majority of people who use prohibited substances. The person may have deviated from the prevailing norms of the larger group . . . but he is not necessarily sick, and, if he is not, treatment cannot be devised for him, much less provided. . . . Even when treatable . . . [drug dependence] is not subject to ready cure, if this means abstinence. Thus, a drug-dependent person subject to control until cured may never regain his liberty.[33]

Within a public-health paradigm, then, drug-control officials would agree that one critical role for law and enforcement is to regulate individual behavior to prevent harm and to promote health; precisely how much and what kind of regulation are open for debate.

A second role for law would be equally important and equally contentious: regulation of the social environment in pursuit of public health. Many of the environmental conditions that encourage drug abuse and addiction—and therefore merit regulation—can only be addressed by redefining and redirecting broader social and urban policies. Yet there is one aspect of the social environment that raises central and difficult questions regarding the role of law and enforcement under a public-health paradigm: the supply of drugs. Their availability and price are important factors that shape people's decisions to use, and abuse, drugs. What is the role of law and enforcement in controlling this aspect of the social environment? The question sets up an important debate under a public-health paradigm, one that is, in several respects, entirely different from the debate over the drug supply under the punitive paradigm.

Under a public-health paradigm, availability of drugs would be recognized as one element of the social environment that affects drug abuse and addiction, not the central element posited by the punitive paradigm. Similarly, controlling supply would be one part of a public-health prevention and treatment strategy, but not the central aim of policy as in today's drug war. Most important, the primary goal of supply regulation would be not to suppress all drug use but to promote health and minimize harm. This goal sets limits on an acceptable strategy for controlling supply.

The punitive strategy for controlling supply creates serious problems from a public-health perspective, as we saw in chapters 2 and 3. To take one compelling example, the effort to limit the availability of drugs by outlawing them and keeping black-market prices high makes it more likely that poor people who suffer from drug dependence will commit property crimes—such as stealing—as a result of their health problems.

This makes it tempting to argue that legalization would be in the interests of public health. Legalization would remove the incentives for drug users to cause the harms to themselves and others that result from going underground and turning to crime to obtain drugs: it would ensure that access to drugs was safe and relatively inexpensive. But public-health advocates would also argue that an environment in which potentially dangerous or addictive drugs are cheap and readily available increases the likelihood that they will be used more frequently by more people and that such increased use will raise the likelihood that a greater proportion of the population will abuse drugs or become addicted to them. How much more is contested: most users of illicit drugs do not progress beyond use to abuse or to dependence, just as most alcohol users do not become alcoholics.[34] But even a small percentage increase in drug dependence in a population of millions of users could mean tens of thousands more people with serious health problems.[35]

The two opposing strategies for confronting the problem of drug availability thus create an apparent dilemma for public health: a punitive, prohibitionist strategy causes harm by turning health problems into crime problems, but removing restrictions and creating a free market in drugs are likely to increase use, also harming public health.

A public-health paradigm makes it possible to confront the dilemma created by the current debate by reframing the central question. The issue for public health is not prohibition *or* legalization. Rather, it is the more difficult question of how the potential harms to health caused by drugs can be curbed, while the harms currently caused by drug-control strategies are simultaneously minimized. Although prohibition of certain drugs is not ruled out, the answer to this question is more likely to be neither prohibition nor the free market but some form of public regulation.

The argument for regulation is not that it is a compromise—a middle ground—between the two extremes of prohibition and legalization. Rather, the strong case for regulating the drug supply is that it will encourage far more healing and far less harm than prohibition or legalization will. Again, the concrete form that regulation would take is a matter for debate under a public-health paradigm—just as regulatory policies for alcohol and tobacco, even among people who are committed to public health, raise contested issues. We can, however, examine the kinds of considerations and alternatives that might be part of this debate.

To begin with, the basis for regulating the drug supply for public health would be a rational, scientific classification of drugs and their harmful effects. Pharmacology can tell us the physiological properties and psychological effects of specific drugs. However, the potential harm to individuals and their behavior is not simply a result of their chemical properties but also—as for nicotine and alcohol—a consequence of their dosage, the route of administration (injecting, inhaling, ingesting), and the social environment (a crack house, a bar, a clinic, a private living room, a street corner). Here research from clinicians who are helping people recover from dependence and from epidemiologists who are looking at the distribution of illness and death among the drug-taking population as a whole is critical.

Based on such a classification, regulations would be determined by the degree to which the use of a drug—or the dosage, route of administration, or drug-taking environment—is likely to be harmful to the individual or to cause behavior that endangers others.[36] Regulations could also be used to influence which drugs and which modes of use are favored, in ways that would promote public health.[37] The prohibition of certain very harmful substances would be one form of regulation; but before resorting to such measures, a public-health paradigm would demand that other issues be confronted—issues often excluded by the punitive paradigm. Would the prohibition measure actually work to promote health and reduce the harms caused by the drug? What other harms would the measure cause to individual health and well-being, to the drug users' ability to be socially responsible, and to public safety?

For example, the prohibition of nicotine theoretically would yield enormous health benefits for individuals and would lower many costs to society (insurance rates, government disability benefits, and health subsidies). But the creation of an enormous black market, the crime and the violence, and the impact on current addicts (who would be forced into the criminal underworld because of their addiction) would likely outweigh the benefits of prohibition and argue for other forms of regulation.[38] Similarly, the prohibition of certain kinds of alcohol (200 proof moonshine, for example) makes sense: it is enforceable and it creates only a small black market. But this prohibition is workable because it is part of an alcohol regime that also allows—and regulates—more benign, less potent alcoholic beverages such as beer and wine.

For those drugs that are regulated but not prohibited, difficult and contested questions would remain about the actual mechanisms of regulation. For example, where should decisions about regulation be made—at the local, state, or national level?[39] And what kinds of regulations would discourage the progression toward more serious drug involvement (from no use to casual use to abuse to addiction) and instead encourage less frequent and less dangerous forms of drug taking?

Should certain drugs be supplied only on the basis of prescription, thus placing the distribution of drugs in the hands of the medical profession? Should they be sold only in government-controlled facilities? Or should access to certain drugs (such as heroin) be handled by health centers that are designed to bring people who are seeking drugs into the health-care system to be monitored, counseled, and treated? (This is the way in which methadone-maintenance clinics currently distribute the legal opiate-based alternative to heroin.) Are there certain drugs, such as crack cocaine, for which there is no workable regulatory scheme except prohibition?[40] What kinds of restrictions could best keep drugs out of the hands of children and adolescents?[41]

Regulation of supply would allow a level of control over drug purity that does not exist under the present system. Current public-health concerns over the tar and nicotine content of cigarettes, the percentage of alcohol in a beverage, the amount of barbiturates in sedatives and sleeping pills, and the purity of ingredients in food products would logically extend to other drugs under a public-health regime. It would be possible to limit the amount of THC, the main psychoactive agent in marijuana, in a cigarette, for example, and to prevent the use of contaminated heroin.

Another critical regulatory issue would be that of price. Public-health principles of discouraging dangerous use and protecting public welfare clarify broad pricing goals but leave open questions of the price levels. Higher prices, for example, could help discourage use; but as we know from current experience, at some level these higher prices would generate a black market; at very high levels, this market would be widespread, costly to control, and violent. And how would prices be set? Would the government directly control production and sales, or would it leave this in private hands and regulate price through taxation? U.S. experience with alcohol and tobacco demonstrates the dangers of placing production and distribution in private hands: competition for profit leads producers and distributors to sell more of their product through lowering prices, mass advertising, and other promotional mechanisms. Moreover, their organized lobbying power has been a major obstacle to more extensive and effective government regulation. Yet government monopoly would pose other problems. The incentive to raise prices might be driven by a need for tax revenues, not a public-health concern, and that could generate black markets.

Under almost any regulatory scheme short of a legalized, free market, there will be an incentive for some level of black-market activity in drugs. Law enforcement to prohibit such illegal sales will be necessary, even though the black market is likely to be much less violent and widespread under a public-health regulatory regime than it is under the present regime. A public-health approach would not dictate any simple way of curtailing such black markets. But it would steer us away from current strategies that encourage more violent crime, threaten public safety, or simply shift drug markets to new locations. Instead, it might support neighborhood patrols or community policing efforts that work in cooperation with local treatment programs, social services, and drug courts to steer small-time black marketeers (who deal drugs to support their addictions) into treatment and other nonprison alternatives.

Under a public-health paradigm, confronting the availability of drugs in our communities would not be primarily a drug-law-enforcement problem, finally, but a broader social-policy problem.[42] Indeed, the problem of supply would be only one piece of a much broader strategy for prevention and treatment, not the centerpiece, as it is in today's drug war. Concretely, such a reduced role for law enforcement in drug control would dramatically relieve the criminal-justice system of many of its present responsibilities under the punitive system: police forces would not be overwhelmed by the need to arrest users and small dealers; courts and prisons would not be overflowing with drug offenders. As a result, punishment and prison would be reserved for their original intent: to punish and deter crimes against people and property.

Law enforcement, like prevention and treatment, would thus take on a very different meaning under a public-health paradigm than under the punitive paradigm. The roles of each instrument—prevention, treatment, and law—in pursuit of public health would imply different purposes, methods, and measures of success and failure. They would hold out greater promise to heal without harming, in several ways: by drawing those who have health problems into health-care and social-service networks, rather than forcing them underground and criminalizing them; by intervening at every stage of drug use to prevent or reduce harms, rather than insisting on total abstinence as the only legitimate goal; by promoting health campaigns against AIDS, rather than banning such programs in the service of the zero-use principle; and by returning the attention of police and courts to serious crime, rather than overloading the criminal-justice system and corrupting law enforcers. The concrete shape of such a public-health paradigm, and the drug strategy and policies that would flow from it, cannot be settled on paper. Like the dominant, punitive paradigm, it would only be given content by the political struggles of those who helped to forge it.

11 The Politics of Drug Reform

CONTRADICTIONS AND FAULT LINES

Overcoming the politics of denial will demand a paradigm shift. Eight decades of U.S. drug wars, however, make it difficult to imagine how such a shift might come about. It is tempting to believe that a clear presentation of a new paradigm, one that embodies public-health principles and a more promising response to America's drug problems, could shift public debate. But fundamental drug-policy reform will demand more than a new vision, coherent strategies, and intelligent ideas: no change will occur without political struggle. The politics of denial is so powerful that mere proposals for new paradigms or for transformative policies or programs are likely to be maligned, distorted, disregarded, or rejected. The current paradigm and the institutions it shapes were created and maintained only through protracted social and political conflicts that began early in the twentieth century; change will demand new political struggles.

Where might such struggles take place? At first glance the possibilities look bleak. The scope of the public-health tradition in the United States is little known outside scholarly and professional circles. There is no major social movement for progressive social reform, or even for health-care reform, let alone for the systemwide reforms that are implicit in a public-health model. In fact, in the mid-1990s conservative budget-cutting policymakers from both parties are more intent on dismantling many of the limited public-health and other social services that now exist. What is more, few politicians feel they can afford to be anything but tougher on drugs, treating drug problems as crime problems that demand ever more force and punishment.

Nevertheless, across the country small, halting efforts for drug-policy reform have cropped up. Many of these efforts are generated by the flaws and contradictions at the heart of the drug war and by the problems they have created for those on the front lines of the fight against drugs. Judges cannot dispense justice because their courts are clogged with drug cases. Police charged with eliminating drug dealers find that there is an endless supply of new dealers to take the place of those arrested. Providers of drug treatment cannot secure sufficient funds to keep their offices open—yet more and more people are knocking on their doors, seeking help. Local communities are paying more in tax dollars, but drug abuse and violence continue unabated in many neighborhoods. These contradictions can be thought of as fault lines in the current drug-control system. Modest struggles for change are under way along these cracks, each of which may open up a larger space for reform efforts that support a public-health approach to drugs.

The failures and contradictions of the drug war affect various groups differently. Some prominent drug warriors have "defected," and their criticism has made it more legitimate for others to question the current policies. Others who work daily on the "front lines" of the drug war—providing treatment, struggling with prevention efforts at the local level, or trying to make the criminal-justice system work—have engaged in a range of struggles that challenge the punitive paradigm and advance elements of a public-health approach. They are far from constituting a broad, coherent, or well-organized movement for fundamental reform, but they point to potential sources of such reform.

DRUG WAR DEFECTORS

Many people charged with designing and implementing the failed drug war have begun to expose its failures and flaws. Judges, policemen, federal and local officials, and military leaders—these dissenters are forming a growing corps of drug war defectors. Frustrated by what they see as the impossible task of arresting, prosecuting, and jailing an endless stream of dealers and users—while more serious crimes go unpunished and the drug problem rages unabated—many defectors have publicly criticized the drug war effort or have even chosen to withdraw from fighting the war. Such opposition indicates a loss of confidence in the present approach at the highest levels of government. It often attracts front-page media coverage and publicly raises questions about the power and legitimacy of the punitive paradigm.

In 1993, for example, fourteen New York City judges questioned the viability of imprisonment as a response to addiction-based crime. "As judges assigned to Manhattan Criminal Court, we are confronted daily with defendants who have committed quality-of-life crimes, such as shoplifting. . . . Many of these defendants are addicted to narcotics. . . . Imprisonment does not address the reasons they continue in their criminal conduct." The judges conclude with a call for continued funding for a local treatment program.[1]

Opposition from other judges has been even stronger. Two of New York City's most prominent federal judges announced in April 1993 that they would no longer preside over drug cases. Their public protest, according to the *New York Times,* drew attention to "what dozens of federal judges are doing quietly behind the scenes." The judges announced "that the emphasis on arrests and imprisonment rather than prevention and treatment has been a failure, and they are withdrawing from the effort." Court officials estimated that some 50 of the nation's 680 federal judges are refusing to hear drug cases.[2]

U.S. District Judge J. Lawrence Irving, a Reagan appointee in San Diego who resigned in 1990, is one of many who have raised objections to the mandatory drug-sentencing laws, under which a small-time drug dealer may receive a harsher sentence than an individual who is convicted for assault, rape, robbery, or murder. "I can't continue to give out sentences I feel in some instances are unconscionable. Every week, I get these cases of 'mules'—most of them Hispanics—who drive drugs across the border. Ninety percent of the time they don't even know how much they're carrying—they met somebody in a bar who paid them $500. If it's a couple of kilos, you hit these mandatory minimums and it's unbelievable. . . . You're talking 10, 15, 20 years in prison."[3] A U.S. magistrate in Florida, Peter Nimkoff, resigned because of his concern that the war on drugs was undermining the Constitution, leading police to behave like criminals, and threatening the presumption that citizens are innocent until proven guilty.[4]

Opposition in the military and police forces has underlined the futility of the drug war. Former Secretary of Defense Caspar W. Weinberger spoke for many in the military when he argued forcefully that U.S. troops should not be "drug cops" and that their deployment in an overseas drug war that lacked an explicit military objective—other than "a vague injunction to 'stop the drug traffickers'"—was unwise.[5] Similarly, retired chief detective Ralph Salerno, who worked in law enforcement for forty-two years, expressed the frustration of many police officers:

As someone who has been on the front-lines of the war on drugs, I know it will never work. . . . I have been here before. The same war was being fought in the 1960s, when the principal substance of abuse was heroin. I was a supervisor of Detectives in the New York City Police Department. . . . We were told by our political leadership that if the Turkish poppy crop was destroyed, the purification mills destroyed and the major mafiosi importers caught and convicted, there would be an end to the problem. While all of these things happened, the problem did not end. . . . What angers me is that today, police officers and all other Americans are being told by our political leaders that [reducing the cocaine supply will solve the drug problem]. . . . I am angry because the people I have spent my entire life with, the law enforcement community, are being lied to, just as I was lied to 20 years ago.[6]

Some of the most prominent drug war defectors have publicly shaken the central pillar of the punitive paradigm by calling for legalization of drug sales or for decriminalization of drug use. In 1989, for example, U.S. District Judge Robert Sweet came out for an end to drug prohibition. Sweet was "overwhelmed and frustrated by" the inability of the justice system to "control drug abuse." He argued that we need not only to turn our attention to treatment but also to address underlying social conditions: "We must alter society to eliminate, or at least substantially reduce, poverty and those conditions which result in drug use. . . . Our commitment to jobs, education, health and housing must be enhanced. If we are not willing to become our brothers' keepers, then we will have to become our brothers' jailers—and that is not an acceptable alternative to a nation which professes to prize personal liberty."[7] Sweet has been joined by other federal judges, such as Warren W. Eginton of Connecticut and James C. Paine of Florida, who have publicly backed drug legalization. Legalization of marijuana, cocaine, and heroin has also been supported by Superior Court Judge James P. Gray of Orange County, California, and by U.S. Magistrate for Orange County Ronald W. Rose.[8]

Less strident calls have come from former top-level government officials. The 1993 statements of Surgeon General Elders discussed in previous chapters are one example. Former Secretary of State George Shultz has also challenged assumptions of the punitive paradigm. "I have to tell you," Shultz told an alumni gathering at Stanford Business School:

It seems to me that the conceptual base of the current program is flawed and the program is not likely to work. The conceptual base—a criminal justice approach—is the same that I have worked through before, in the Nixon administration when I was budget director and secretary of the Treasury with jurisdiction over Customs. We designed a comprehensive program, and we

worked hard on it. In the Reagan administration we designed a comprehensive program; we worked very hard on it. Our international efforts were far
greater than ever before. . . . What we have before us now is essentially the
same program but with more resources ploughed into all the enforcement and
control efforts. These efforts wind up creating a market where price vastly
exceeds the cost. With these incentives, demand creates its own supply and a
criminal network along with it. It seems to me we're not really going to get
anywhere until we take the criminality out of the drug business and the incentives for criminality out of it. Frankly, the only way I can think of to accomplish this is to make it possible for addicts to buy drugs at some regulated
place at a price that approximates their cost. . . . We need at least to consider
and examine forms of controlled legalization of drugs. I find it very difficult
to say that. . . . But I feel that if somebody doesn't get up and start talking
about this now, the next time around, when we have the next start of these
programs, it will still be true that everyone is scared to talk about it. No politi-
cian wants to say what I just said, not for a minute.[9]

Similar positions are articulated by prominent individuals such as conservative writer and publisher William F. Buckley, Jr., economist Milton
Friedman, ACLU director Ira Glasser, and Harvard science professor
Stephen Jay Gould, and they receive a broad public hearing in journals
and the media.[10] Such critiques have played an important role in opening up the debate on drug policy to a broader range of policy alternatives. The head of one state association of substance-abuse programs,
for example, does not support legalization but recognizes the value of a
more open debate for a public-health alternative.

The legalization debate has been helpful. By creating debate, they are making it easier to negotiate a solution short of legalization that emphasizes health
and decriminalization. It makes people more willing to compromise, makes
it more possible to talk about health and decriminalization. It makes them
think that we need to stop arresting people and start treating them, and start
providing comprehensive treatment including habilitation, job placement,
comprehensive medical care, homes. People don't want legalization but think:
I better get off the dime on this and support something . . . other than more
arrests.[11]

Other drug war defectors who see the flaws of the punitive strategy,
such as Baltimore mayor Kurt L. Schmoke, have actively organized
local political coalitions to pursue a more public-health–oriented
approach. Arguing that the war on drugs is "doomed to failure" because
of its "internal and inescapable contradictions," Schmoke has argued
instead for the need to "[pull] addicts into the public health system." In
1993 he unveiled a drug program for his city which included support for
needle-exchange programs that incorporated doctors and other health-

care workers into an expanded treatment system and increased drug-maintenance options. The plan also called for a reordering of criminal-justice priorities to focus on major drug traffickers and violent crime instead of small-scale offenses and for creating a drug court to divert nonviolent drug offenders into drug treatment.[12]

The highly public critiques by drug war defectors are perhaps the best-recognized challenges to the drug war. The public statements and acts of defiance by prominent public officials keep the dominant drug war paradigm from becoming monolithic and open up political space, making it more legitimate and easier for others to speak out and organize in opposition. Yet because such challenges often come in the form of statements, not political battles, their impact is limited. Other challenges to the punitive approach, though less visible, have galvanized into modest but important struggles for public-health-oriented reforms.

POTENTIAL CHALLENGERS IN THE TREATMENT COMMUNITY

Thousands of health and social-welfare professionals—counselors, nurses, administrators, doctors, social workers—labor every day within the fault lines created by failed and harmful drug war policies.[13] What these front liners need in order to realize their goals, the drug war cannot deliver. In fact, the war on supply and users makes their efforts at treatment more difficult.

The services that treatment professionals provide constitute the only system available to absorb the harm caused by drug abuse and addiction—and by the drug war itself. Their job, always difficult, has become overwhelming in recent years. They confront the effects of the deterioration of conditions in the cities, aggravated by federal, state, and local cutbacks in social services and health care in the 1980s and 1990s. Against this backdrop they are facing the crack cocaine epidemic that began in the mid-1980s, the increase in heroin abuse, and the spread of AIDS and other diseases among drug users. The Reagan-Bush drug wars poured billions of dollars into law enforcement, which exacerbated urban violence and crime, led to the imprisonment of many individuals with substance-abuse problems, and aggravated health problems related to drug use.

Treatment budgets also increased, but the needs far outstripped the available resources. In 1995, according to the government's own figures, there were "more than 1 million people who need[ed] some type of drug treatment [but were] unable to access programs." For years, many programs have been badly underfunded, creating waiting-list delays of many months for those who seek treatment, discouraging others from even trying to get the help they need, straining staff, and limiting the quality of care provided. The experience of Jim David, the chief resident in psychiatry at Bronx Municipal Hospital, was common. By the late 1980s 60 percent of his patients were drug abusers. "I have been trained in the era of crack," he explained. "We bring people down, and then we send them back to the street. Most of them are in here again within a couple of weeks."[14]

The treatment community has organized to address these conditions. Hundreds of professional organizations have joined together in dozens of associations at the local, state, and national levels. Their objectives are ambitious. In addition to fighting for continued funding for their programs, they seek to expand treatment services so that assistance will be available to all who seek it; their goal is a system of treatment on demand. They organize support for new efforts to reach out and serve excluded, underserved, or high-risk populations (children, pregnant women, people with AIDS, the homeless, teenagers from poor urban areas or from drug-dependent families). They fight for more comprehensive and integrated programs that are designed to deal with the multiple alcohol and drug dependencies of many patients and with the complex health problems (such as AIDS and tuberculosis) and aftercare needs (such as counseling and job placement) that these patients face.

Many different types of treatment centers—including methadone clinics and therapeutic communities—are organized into state or national associations, such as the American Methadone Treatment Association and Therapeutic Communities of America. In their struggles for funding and expanded services, these treatment professionals have often also joined forces with drug-abuse prevention professionals. Local treatment and prevention associations have formed statewide coalitions that work to influence laws, policies, and spending in state capitols and in Washington. The New York State Association of Substance Abuse Programs, for example, includes not only statewide methadone and therapeutic-community associations among its fifteen members but also the State Association of Drug and Alcohol Abuse Prevention Professionals, the State Coalition for Children of Addictions, the Substance Prevention Intervention Network in Schools, and the Statewide Association of Latino Substance Abuse Agencies. Thousands of professional counselors are organized into the National Association of Alcoholism and Drug Abuse Counselors.

At the national level, nearly thirty state-level associations have joined forces in the National Coalition of State Alcohol and Drug Treatment and Prevention Associations. The coalition works closely with a Washington-based public-interest law firm, the Legal Action Center, to draft policy statements, analyze legislation, and press for new policies and increased funding. Another important nationwide coalition is the National Association of State Alcohol and Drug Abuse Directors (NASADAD), which represents alcoholism and drug-agency directors, the highest government officials in each state dealing with these problems. These state directors administer federal block grants to dozens of prevention and treatment organizations at the state and local levels. The National Prevention Network, affiliated with NASADAD, provides a national advocacy system for state alcohol- and drug-abuse prevention representatives.

If there were any place we might expect a challenge to the punitive paradigm and a political struggle for a public-health approach, this network of associations might seem to be the first place to look. It is in the interests of this community to challenge the punitive paradigm, not only because of the failure of the drug war to address the root problems of abuse and addiction but also because of the many ways in which the drug war complicates and increases their workload—by discouraging potential clients with threats and sanctions and by encouraging the spread of drug-related health problems, for example.

Furthermore, many treatment professionals share a public-health vision: they speak articulately about the importance of treating drug-dependent people as patients in need of care, not as criminals in need of punishment; about the fact that care must be provided along a continuum, with intervention at every point of drug use in order to minimize harm; and about the need for posttreatment programs that include job training and placement, health care, and housing assistance.

Yet those in the treatment community often find themselves hamstrung in their efforts to achieve their public-health goals. Part of the problem they face is a matter of time and resources. Treatment providers are continually tied down in the essential battle for funding. In a situation in which there are many more people in need of treatment than current facilities can absorb—and in which resources are continually under the threat of budget cuts—it is a full-time job for many treatment advocates simply to keep existing programs open. "We're scrambling to get more money, just to avoid cutting staff," explained the public-policy director of a national association.[15] One consequence is that treatment professionals are left with little chance to step back and consider broader questions of policy and strategy. "People on the front lines are so busy fighting for money that there's little time to reflect," the head of one state association of drug programs told us.[16]

Treatment and prevention advocates also face a second serious constraint in their struggle for reform: the terms of today's policy debate are set by the punitive paradigm. Although many treatment advocates believe that enforcement is an essential element of drug control, they are critical of many of the paradigm's core assumptions. They believe that a more effective strategy would put primary emphasis on treatment and prevention, not on a war against supply and users—and that the billions of dollars wasted on this war could make a real difference if they were shifted to treatment and prevention. But the broad acceptance of the punitive paradigm by policymakers and the public often makes treatment advocates reluctant to criticize this war and forces them to make difficult—but, they believe, necessary—compromises.

> As soon as you criticize law enforcement, you lose your credibility. They say to you: "So, you think we should close down the jails . . . you think we don't need to arrest these folks." Well, in fact the answer is yes. . . . If we had a new policy in place, we would not need to be arresting many of these people. . . . But if you say this, then they are going to come back at you. . . . You will have every enforcement group in the country all over you. These guys are organized. They go to their communities. You cannot win any kind of national campaign for treatment and prevention if you say federal dollars are wasted on law enforcement.[17]

Even more seriously, many treatment and prevention advocates find that the only way to win the funds they need to survive is to align themselves with law enforcement, presenting their own efforts as a necessary complement to an enforcement-oriented drug war. This dynamic is not new. Ever since the treatment and prevention community began to take shape in the 1960s, its funding has often been directly tied to the escalating war on drugs. Political leaders beginning with Richard Nixon have most ardently supported treatment and prevention when packaged in crime-fighting, not health-promoting, terms: methadone treatment, recall, was embraced by the Nixon administration as a way of reducing crime.

Despite their private misgivings about the drug war, many officials in treatment and prevention associations thus not only have been reticent to publicly criticize the policy but also have mined the punitive drug-crime connection for much-needed funding. A top executive in a national treatment association explained:

> You get resources to deal with the problem any way you can—and you get the resources for treatment with the connection to the crime problem. I wish it were not true. . . . I wish the concern out there was the health problem. . . . But if I can get more money for treatment by tying it to crime, then I should, because that money is badly needed to strengthen treatment facilities. The crime budget is not going away. . . . We might as well get money from it. If treatment were not tied to crime fighting, there would be no money.[18]

The head of a state organization of substance-abuse associations, a would-be critic of the punitive paradigm, put it more bluntly: "It's true. We're whores. But that's the only way we can get the money we need. . . . If riding the crime wave is the way to get money, I'll do it. There are a lot of folks out there who are trying to make ends meet, pay their staffs, keep their programs going. If this is the way to do it, they'll do it."[19]

A politics of financial necessity has thus shaped the political agenda of many people in the treatment and prevention community, influencing the ways in which they join the public debate on drugs, define their political objectives, and choose their battles. According to the director of one national treatment association: "There is a triad, prevention-treatment-enforcement. This is the way we always have to put the issue. We would consider it a victory if we could get 50–50 with enforcement—which shows you the negative bargaining position of the treatment community."[20]

Many in the treatment and prevention community recognize the irony of this funding trap: the immediate need for treatment and prevention funds leads public-health advocates to acquiesce to, or even support, the very drug war that misallocates funds and makes their treatment tasks more difficult.[21] The results of the battle for funding are a greater dependence on law enforcement and the entrenchment of a punitive politics as usual.

But this is only half of the story. Even in the face of such constraints, treatment advocates have often found ways to engage in struggles that begin to challenge the dominant assumptions of the punitive paradigm. They have demanded, for example, that money wasted on the failing war abroad be shifted to treatment at home, and they regularly advance ideas and policies that embody a public-health approach to drugs.[22] In particular, they are struggling to redefine the drug problem as primarily a health problem, to introduce health-based criteria for evaluating the success of drug policies, and to challenge the stigma that surrounds addiction.

One important struggle to redefine the drug problem has been the effort to link alcoholism and drug dependence under the notion of substance abuse. Defenders of the punitive paradigm have long sought to keep alcohol, a legal and socially acceptable—if health-endangering—substance, in a different category from illicit substances such as cocaine and heroin.

But those on the front lines of substance-abuse treatment know that all of these substances can be pharmacologically dangerous and addictive; that the distinction between licit and illicit abuse is a legal fiction; that many of their patients suffer simultaneously from abuse of alcohol and other drugs; and that some of the root psychological, social, and personal problems that cause or sustain these addictions are the same. Conceptually, front liners seek to redirect attention from the distinction between licit and illicit, to emphasize instead the dangers to health of cocaine, heroin, and alcohol abuse alike. Programmatically, state-government agencies and state-level substance-abuse programs increasingly address both alcohol and drug abuse. At the federal level, the Department of Health and Human Services has brought alcohol and other drugs together in the Substance Abuse and Mental Health Services Administration, the Center for Substance Abuse Treatment, and the Center for Substance Abuse Prevention. To the extent that this health-based conception of substance abuse becomes part of our conventional wisdom, it will begin to challenge the stigmatization of those who are drug dependent as criminals who deserve punishment and redefine them as substance abusers who need care and treatment.

The redefinition of drug abuse as a health problem has also informed some of the struggles waged by reformers in the halls of Congress and in the courts. One example is the organized opposition to specific punitive legislation to force those who need health care into the criminal-justice system or underground. In the early 1990s, for example, the National Council on Alcoholism and Drug Dependence helped organize the Coalition on Alcohol and Drug-Dependent Women and Their Children, which successfully fought against proposed legislation to punish women who use alcohol or drugs during pregnancy—and argued instead for treatment funds. In underlining the ways legal penalties deter such drug-dependent women from using the medical facilities that are indispensable to a healthy pregnancy, the coalition explicitly advanced public-health principles of health promotion and harm minimization.[23]

Such principled challenges have also been the basis of legal battles. In February 1994, for example, the Center for Reproductive Law and Policy in New York City, representing two Charleston, South Carolina, women, filed suit in federal court to end a Medical University of South Carolina program that threatened pregnant women who use drugs with jail or public exposure in order to force them into treatment programs.[24]

This struggle to redefine drug abuse as a health problem has also led to efforts to challenge the criteria of success used to evaluate drug-control policies. Under the drug war paradigm, the logic is simple: treatment that works cures addiction, and the measure of cure is abstinence. For years, however, many treatment advocates have challenged abstinence as the main measure of success and have introduced public-health goals as criteria instead.

In their published work and legislative testimony, such advocates have argued that success must be measured in broader public-health terms that consider social as well as individual consequences—enabling people in recovery to function socially as spouses, parents, jobholders, and community members, for example, and preventing or minimizing the harm to society caused by drug dependence. Treatment is successful, they have argued, if it improves the health of children born to a substance-abusing mother, if it helps preserve families, and if it enables a person in recovery to move off welfare and hold a job. Treatment is successful if it prevents child abuse and neglect or domestic violence and if it slows the spread of AIDS and other diseases.

Often such arguments are put in terms of dollars saved—to appeal to legislators who are concerned about wasting taxpayers' money and to the leaders of the large managed-care health organizations who are suspicious of long-term drug-treatment programs unless they see evidence of their cost-effectiveness.[25] Preventing drug-dependent people from requiring emergency-room care, stemming the spread of disease, saving money on foster care, saving employers money in terms of lost productivity and sick benefits can amount to billions of dollars. Alcohol and other drug-addicted individuals use medical benefits at rates ten times greater than do the rest of the population, for example. According to one Ohio-based study, worker absenteeism for drug users who completed a treatment program decreased by 89 percent, tardiness by 92 percent, and on-the-job injuries by 57 percent.[26] The economics of treatment provides a winning argument; but some reform advocates also emphasize the importance of reaching beyond a purely economic calculus, with images and testimony that underscore the ways in which successful treatment has made a difference in the lives of parents and children.[27]

Other drug-reform struggles have been framed in ways that challenge the punitive image of addicts as outcasts or criminals. Consider, for example, efforts to expand legal protections for people with drug problems, based on the 1990 Americans with Disabilities Act. The act prohibited discrimination in the workplace against recovered substance abusers and people in treatment. Treatment and prevention advocates have sought legislative avenues to extend these protections into the public-housing, social-security, and school systems: "We must always be vigilant to preserve the great gains that have been made in recent years to de-stigmatize and protect the rights of people who have histories of alcohol and drug problems. . . . It is senseless to spend substantial amounts of money on the rehabilitation of alcoholics and addicts and then turn around and not let a recovered person obtain a job or an education."[28] Such legal and policy fights represent modest but important steps toward redefining drug-dependent persons as citizens with disabilities who have rights deserving of respect.

Perhaps one of the boldest moves to redefine the image and role of addicts is reflected in efforts to help people in recovery, and their families, speak for themselves. The personal testimony of past and present substance abusers and their families has a significant impact on public perceptions. But it is very difficult to convince these individuals to speak out or to mobilize for drug reform. Many families of drug-dependent people are fragile or nonexistent, and families and abusers alike fear the stigma that comes with admitting drug dependence in the current punitive context. Anonymity is a condition for support groups such as Narcotics Anonymous.[29]

Nevertheless, some treatment advocates have successfully organized substance abusers and their families to speak out. In some cases this is done quietly and informally, with a potentially significant impact on policy but not on public perceptions. The director of one association of alcohol and drug programs, for example, relies on an informal network of individuals recovering from substance abuse in lobbying efforts at the state capitol. Recovering individuals know better than anyone, explained the director, that treatment works; they understand the importance of a continuum of care and the counterproductive effects of criminalizing addicted individuals; and occasionally, they are well positioned—chief executive officers in large firms, lawyers, prominent businessmen, even public officials. Such individuals can help by contacting committee chairs or key legislators. "I needed a letter from a well-known national figure to the state insurance commissioner supporting substance abuse treatment. I asked for assistance from the national recovering community. Within three weeks, the letter was on his desk. And it really helped."[30]

Some organizational efforts are much more public. The Society of Americans for Recovery, convened by former Iowa governor and senator Howard Hughes, has organized individuals who are in recovery to build political support for substance-abuse treatment. There have also been limited efforts to organize family members of people involved in treatment, many of whom can give eloquent testimony on the role of treatment in helping a son return to school or a parent find work and put food on the table once again. In New York, for example, family members of those in therapeutic communities such as Daytop have actively lobbied for treatment legislation at the state level.

Such efforts begin to redefine the drug problem as a health rather than a criminal problem and promote an understanding of drug-dependent people as citizens who deserve respect and care rather than stigmatization and condemnation. If these struggles for drug reform are to carry weight, however, they must be joined to broader reform efforts. Many treatment advocates point to the need for alliances with other health-care groups (people involved in mental health or in maternal and child care, for example), although competing organizational interests sometimes block such alliances. Beyond the health-care community, the harms caused by substance abuse and by the drug war create other potential allies.[31] Within local communities, for example, broad-based alliances have begun to form around drug problems.

POTENTIAL CHALLENGERS
IN LOCAL COMMUNITIES

The flaws and contradictions in the drug war are perhaps most deeply felt by citizens who live in drug-plagued communities. Despite tougher laws, despite increased arrests and the imprisonment of more drug users and dealers, their problems continue. The escalation of the drug war in the 1980s did little to stem hard-core drug abuse, and addiction-based and trade-based crime and violence have increased in many urban areas. In response, thousands of local community and neighborhood groups around the country have organized to confront drug problems.

Local coalitions often bring together sectors of the community that have not worked together before in an effort to develop nonpunitive approaches to common drug problems. Most coalitions include local schools, law-enforcement agencies, and alcohol- and drug-prevention agencies. They may also include treatment providers, parents, court and probation officers; labor, business, and civic groups; religious organizations; and the media.[32] Many of these coalitions formed in the late 1980s when the Reagan-Bush drug war was at its peak—and when its costs and constraints were most painfully evident.

Members of these local coalitions often understand the impact of the social environment on drug problems in ways that policymakers seeking quick-fix solutions fail to appreciate. The links are particularly clear in drug-ridden inner-city communities. Citizens there grasp in concrete terms the environmental factors that feed drug abuse and addiction—and the ways in which the drug war exacerbates them. They know the local economic conditions that lead addicts to steal to buy drugs and lead young people to deal drugs. They know the absence of social and health services that makes it difficult for those who want help to find it. And they know the world that those returning from treatment—or from prison—find, with its powerful incentives to slip back into patterns of abuse and dealing. The neighborhood context, moreover, humanizes the drug problem and makes it less abstract: the dealer who was shot is a friend's son; the addict who was just arrested is a neighbor whose two small children have been left behind.

Such understanding does not necessarily lead community members to reject the punitive approach to drugs. Some seek a tougher response to the problems they see. Local groups, particularly in high-crime, drug-ridden areas, have organized to demand more protection and intervention by law-enforcement officials. Some communities have organized local neighborhood watches or citizens' drug patrols. Such direct actions may result in an immediate improvement in the security and quality of life of their neighborhoods. But, as many of those who are involved recognize, such actions are at best stopgap measures that do not address the roots of drug abuse and dealing.

Other local efforts, however, reach well beyond short-term enforcement to address the deeper failings and contradictions of the drug war by focusing on prevention and early intervention programs. According to a 1992–1993 survey of thousands of these groups conducted by Join Together, a Boston-based nonprofit organization that provides assistance to local efforts,[33] most of the coalition leaders favor a dramatic shift in budget priorities from the war on supply to prevention and treatment.[34] Their emphasis is on community-based education, public-

awareness campaigns, parent education and training, school-based education, and after-school youth activities. Some coalitions (about 27 percent) focus on treatment. Their priorities reflect an understanding of the
drug war's neglect of the social environment and an effort to overcome
the current fragmented and individualistic approach to substance
abuse. Among the 2,200 community coalitions surveyed, reports Join
Together, there is a commitment to undertake "systemwide change,
rather than focusing their work on a single area," and the groups are
more likely to "focus on changing community environments than on
addressing individual needs."[35]

Like the prevention and treatment advocates, these coalitions are constrained. They can do little to alter the most fundamental and destructive features of their environments: they generally lack the means to create jobs, meaningful educational opportunities, and affordable health
care for their communities. But, like the efforts of people on the front
lines of treatment, their struggles within these constraints may challenge
and begin to undermine the assumptions and dominance of the punitive
paradigm. Such challenges take varying forms.

In some cases, local leaders have fought to change the terms of the debate in their communities by arguing for the primacy of treatment, care,
and prevention, rather than punishment, in dealing with drug users. In
other cases, groups have organized to create new and effective models
for drug control based on public-health principles. In still other instances, community leaders square off directly against those in their communities who defend a punitive approach.

The Fighting Back program, sponsored by the Robert Wood Johnson
Foundation in fourteen cities, is one example. In cities such as Worces-
ter, Massachusetts, Richmond, Virginia, Santa Barbara, California, and
Kansas City, these programs have helped build local citizens' networks
to encourage community prevention and treatment efforts. Many seek
to communicate a health-oriented approach to drug problems. The outreach materials produced by the Fighting Back group in New Haven,
Connecticut, for example, communicate a message about substance
abuse that embodies public-health rather than punitive values. "First
off, let's make one thing clear," one pamphlet begins: "'Fighting back'
has nothing to do with vigilantes or Hollywood's macho fantasies."
What fighting back means, the group explains through its materials, is
redefining and strengthening social relationships—to promote health,
well-being, and an ethic of care in the community. "Fighting back is the
spirit of the teen who tells his friends he'd rather study than get

stupid . . . the church that opens a basement soup kitchen . . . the child who says, 'Dad, I don't like you when you're high' . . . the cop who drives a junkie to detox instead of to jail . . . the mom who tells her kids she's going to a rehab . . . the counselor who knows relapse isn't 'failure'—it's part of recovery."[36]

Leaders of New Haven Fighting Back meet with community groups, make presentations, and provide services where they can. They have convened a Consortium for Substance Abusing Women and Their Children, a group of sixty state and local agencies that has developed a comprehensive approach to treatment for women. Emphasis is on providing a continuum of care that includes not only prevention and treatment but also posttreatment services and transportation and housing assistance. Fighting Back has also brought together the directors of various substance-abuse programs in New Haven to campaign for expanded facilities with an aim toward providing treatment on demand, and it is forging links with training and employment programs to help people in recovery overcome the difficult social conditions they face when they leave treatment.

Some local communities have organized comprehensive programs to provide direct services to people with drug problems. Often based on broad public-health principles, such models serve as powerful examples. Consider the programs of the Glide Memorial Church in San Francisco. Glide has helped bring together the local police, the housing authority, the health department, and other social-service agencies to create long-range programs for community residents who are struggling with substance-abuse problems. Glide's programs are multifaceted: individual and group counseling for drug treatment is part of a comprehensive array of programs that provide job training, anonymous HIV testing and counseling, and referrals to other social services.

Glide's Women on the Move program for victims of physical, emotional, or psychological abuse is an example of the church's efforts to address the varying environmental factors that discrete sectors of the community face. In addition to providing a twenty-week substance-abuse treatment program, Women on the Move provides child care, food, emergency shelter, and clothing and helps place women in crisis in shelters for battered or abused women. For pregnant teens, the program provides not only child care but also off-site activities to "enable these women to enjoy being teen-agers, while parenting classes and practical skills development give them tools for adulthood."

The underlying goal of the women's program is not simply to cure drug problems but also "to educate and empower women to make life-affirming choices that help to change their lives and the lives of their children." "Meaningful recovery" thus includes "economic recovery," a job-training program with courses in computer literacy, job-search skills, and self-esteem. Because health "is so integral to self-esteem and self-empowerment," the Glide program provides a series of lectures on health for women and modest health-care services.[37]

The Glide example challenges not only the methods but also the underlying values of the punitive approach. Glide's program seeks to heal, not to punish. Glide's Rev. Cecil Williams describes what a drug-ridden community needs: "Healing has to happen in that community, and that means you take time out and, rather than condemn, you put people in your bosom and you rock the pain away." Although its comprehensive programs draw on public-health principles, they are also grounded in both Christian faith and notions of empowerment rooted in the African American community that Glide serves. Its programs, Williams explains, speak to the particular condition, culture, and history of black men and women—to the shared experience of deep discrimination but also to the cultural roots of faith and resistance that can be tapped to empower them to change their lives and the world in which they live.[38]

At times, local struggles flare into overt conflicts with people who seek to defend or sustain the current punitive approach. Local battles over AIDS prevention are a case in point. The environmental factors that link intravenous drug use to the spread of AIDS have long been clear to many professionals in the health and social-services communities; drug war policies have helped spread the disease by prohibiting programs that encourage less dangerous forms of drug taking. The health problems created by this contradiction in the drug war have generated numerous local challenges. Alarmed by the spread of AIDS, some local groups have sought to change laws and create programs to encourage "safe use" of heroin—through needle exchanges, for example. Arguing the need to minimize harm and other public-health principles, they have found themselves struggling against people who are bound to a punitive approach and who insist that "zero use" must be the only goal of policy.

The battles over needle exchange in New York City and New Haven provide interesting examples of such struggles. In New York City, attempts by the Department of Health to institute a pilot needle-exchange program in 1985 faced stiff opposition, not only from some people in the law-enforcement community and from conservatives but also from leading black politicians who called the scheme "genocidal." Because needle exchange does not combat heroin use directly, it was seen by many black leaders as encouraging—or at least condoning—continued use.[39]

Rep. Charles Rangel and twelve other black politicians called the plan "a recklessly dangerous experiment" that would "legalize, condone, and encourage intravenous drug abuse." The plan was opposed with equal vehemence by the *Daily News*, which first called it "an act of surrender in the war on drugs" and then provided the previously undisclosed street addresses of the two proposed needle-distribution sites so that "the people in the vicinity would not sit quietly by while addicts waltz or slither in to pick up free needles."

The issue became mired in local politics. Mayor Koch ordered the planned project to be replaced by an even smaller pilot program run out of the Health Department's downtown headquarters, and the New York City Council (in a nonbinding resolution) voted 31–0 to cancel it completely. Professor Ernest Drucker of the Albert Einstein College of Medicine described the local politics of needle exchange as regrettable—but understandable. In a context of "huge new street markets" in crack, "increased territorial warfare among drug user-dealers and their network of local suppliers" and "soaring crime rates" related to drugs, this debate was not just about needles or AIDS. Rather, it "reflected the City's growing impatience with its drug problem and a new and ominous hostility to the drug user and his condition."[40]

When Mayor Dinkins took office in January 1990 he claimed that the pilot program, which was still in existence, sent the wrong message by condoning drug use. His health commissioner, Dr. Woodrow Meyers, closed the program down. When questioned by a *New York Times* reporter, Meyers explained that the matter was an "ideological issue" and said that he personally "could conceive of no data or evidence" that would lead him to a different position.[41] Only after similar programs proved successful in reducing the spread of AIDS in other cities (such as New Haven) were proponents finally able to convince Mayor Dinkins to withdraw his opposition and to support pilot projects.[42]

In New Haven, a much more broadly based coalition was more successful in starting a needle-exchange program and in convincing community residents that this approach could heal without harming. The New Haven coalition included the mayor, the police chief, the health department, community activists, experts from Yale University, the YMCA, and health-care and social-service personnel. They worked with others around the state to convince the Connecticut General Assembly—which engaged in emotional debates over the issue—to allow three demonstration projects.

Many of the people who were involved in the New Haven struggle sought explicitly to challenge elements of the punitive paradigm. They wanted to place care and health at the center of their drug strategy and to treat those who were drug dependent as people with dignity, capable of assuming responsibility for their lives and in need of social support and opportunities. The needle-exchange program (NEP) concept, the mayor's preliminary report explained,

> is based on the premise that IV drug users care about their health and will change behaviors to protect themselves and others against AIDS if given viable options. Relative to this concept is the belief that drug addiction is a disease that will not be remedied through punitive action. . . . To be effective, NEPs must embody a "user friendly" ethos. Addicts must be treated with understanding and in a nonjudgmental manner. The aim is to create a safe environment and foster trust and respect between those running the exchange and those who use the program.[43]

The New Haven program succeeded not only in slowing the spread of AIDS but also in drawing many heroin addicts into treatment programs—without increasing levels of use.

Similar local coalitions have waged successful struggles in Hawaii and other states.[44] In doing so, they have begun to challenge central elements of the punitive paradigm. Needle exchange itself, however, is only a very minimal public-health program: teaching safe use still fails to address the other harms caused by intravenous drug use and the sizable population of HIV-infected drug users who need comprehensive treatment. Guided by a public-health vision, however, leaders of such efforts can move—and have moved—beyond the reduction of harm to foster more comprehensive programs for hard-core drug users. Some needle-exchange projects have evolved into outreach or local clinic programs offering broader health services and drug treatment. In such cases the relationships of trust already established with intravenous drug users make it more likely that they will take advantage of these services. To the extent that such programs can demonstrate the benefits of changing the social-environmental factors that foster drug use, they may help create a local constituency for job training and placement, health care, and decent housing as integral parts of substance-abuse treatment programs. And to the degree that such programs provide evidence that hard-core users can be productive members of their communities, these programs can help transform dominant images of drug users.[45]

POTENTIAL CHALLENGERS
IN THE CRIMINAL-JUSTICE SYSTEM

One might least expect challenges to the war on drugs from the people who are charged with prosecuting it. But those on the front lines of law enforcement in the drug war daily face the fallout from the deep flaws and contradictions in the drug war.

New Haven police chief Nicholas Pastore described the problem. The department's "drug demand reduction activities, in particular the drug sting operations," he wrote in 1990, did not serve as a deterrent to drug buys or drug use but did create "a tremendous strain on police resources. . . . [They] caused a divisive rift between the police and the community; did not effectuate any substantial jail or prison time for those arrested; and did not create an avenue for getting users into treatment."[46]

Pastore is joined by other officers, lawyers, judges, and prison officials in condemning traditional enforcement methods, out of frustration over the contradictions of drug enforcement. The more they battle drug suppliers and users, the less time they have to combat more serious, violent crimes. The more they escalate the war, the more their own police forces are undermined by corruption. The more drug offenders they bring into court, the more other serious civil and criminal cases wait unheard. The more they imprison dealers and users for nonviolent crimes, the more violent criminals are released to make room for them. Worst of all, none of their efforts has any appreciable effect on reducing drug abuse or drug dealing.

Many people in the legal and criminal-justice systems still respond to such failures with calls for more force; and most simply do their best to do their jobs. But some have begun to argue for new directions.

Lawyers' associations have been among the most vocal critics. "Solutions must be found 'upstream' to prevent many of the drug-related problems from ever entering the justice system," wrote ABA president R. William Ide III.[47] Faced with the growing overload of drug cases in the courts and the impossibility of trying civil cases, the ABA created a Special Committee on the Drug Crisis in 1990. The criminal-justice system, argued the committee, "can only provide a 'holding action' until society addresses the root causes that fuel the distribution and use of drugs."[48] The committee works closely with local bar associations (about forty be-

tween 1992 and 1994) to create community antidrug coalitions, emphasizing local prevention programs, employee drug-assistance programs in
the workplace, and drug-court programs to divert nonviolent offenders
in drug-related cases to treatment instead of to prison.

In addition to such professional opposition, two explicit challenges
to the current system of drug enforcement have begun to emerge from
within the criminal-justice system. One contests existing methods of
policing the drug problem; the other questions current methods of punishing users and dealers. Each challenge embodies elements of a public-
health approach.

Confronted with the contradictions described above, several city police departments have sought alternatives to street sweeps and crack-
downs in drug-plagued communities. Dozens of cities, including New
York City, Houston, Texas, Oakland, California, and Chicago, Illinois,
have launched experiments with community-oriented policing by moving officers out of patrol cars and back to walking neighborhood beats.
Although the character and effectiveness of community policing efforts
vary enormously, many such programs represent a radical challenge to
the dominant approach to policing, particularly in drug enforcement.
Pastore suggests:

> A community-based police department will not be judged only on its ability
> to react to crimes, but also on its ability to prevent crime and improve the
> quality of life by providing unique services as warranted neighborhood by
> neighborhood. . . . [For example, in recognizing] urban blight as a precursor
> to crime . . . the neighborhood and officers will work together to combat the
> particular problem, whether by notifying the Office of Building Inspection
> and Enforcement or by referring substance abusers who are beginning to con-
> gregate in a park to treatment or by spending a weekend afternoon cleaning
> the neighborhood.[49]

In New Haven the break with traditional drug enforcement went further
than community-based policing. Pastore directed his police force to target upper-level drug dealers and drug gangs and discouraged arrests of
low-level street dealers and users. Instead, the police were instructed to
work more closely with social-service agencies to draw addicts and
addict-dealers into treatment. A partnership was formed with a local
mental-health organization to guarantee that the requisite number of
treatment slots would be available for referrals from the police department's community-outreach effort.[50]

The change in New Haven policing did not come without a struggle:
Pastore had to overcome opposition from a majority of his force and

from the police union. Turning around the force demanded, among other things, the careful recruitment of new officers who were willing and able to handle the local community-relations work implicit in the new approach to drug policing.[51]

Shreveport, Louisiana, has also struggled over the meaning of drug enforcement. Police Chief Charles Gruber argued that traditional policing is not a solution to drug problems. His search for a more effective response to the problem led to a focus on the environmental factors that fuel drug use and dealing: he embarked on what he called problem-oriented policing in an effort "to solve the underlying problems that create crime . . . unemployment, poverty, illiteracy, etc." He applied for a $3 million federal grant to establish seven community-action centers in low-income areas of the city. The centers, he told a congressional committee, aim to help young people find employment, provide health services such as prenatal care, offer educational opportunities, and help young people develop coping skills. "When youths do not have these skills, they often turn to the streets to find a living. . . . All too often . . . problems lead . . . residents to believe that a life of drugs and crime are the only option, or, in some cases, the best solution. Until we understand these problems and work to solve them, we will probably experience no more success in this war on drugs than we are presently experiencing."[52]

As police forces confront these problems on the streets, court and corrections officials face another set of problems that arises from the failure and contradictions of the drug war. Their daily task is to manage the onslaught of drug cases that arise from the thousands of arrests by police officers across the country; their frustrations mount as they see the distortions produced by overloaded court dockets and overflowing prisons and as they watch drug offenders move in and out through the system's revolving door. These problems have led many court and corrections officers to challenge a basic premise of the drug war paradigm—the role and effectiveness of punishment as a primary response to addiction. In their efforts to resolve the contradictions of the drug war, they have turned to treatment as an alternative or complement to punishment. The turn to treatment has taken three basic forms.

One form involves court-mandated diversion-to-treatment programs, in which drug offenders who have committed nonviolent crimes are given the option of choosing a court-monitored treatment program instead of prison: if they successfully complete the program they serve no time and may have the charges against them dismissed; if they do not complete the program they face the threat of incarceration. Pioneered on a small scale by government-funded Treatment Alternatives to Street Crime (TASC) programs beginning in 1972, the idea is rapidly expanding into what are known as treatment-oriented drug courts. These special courts—launched first in Miami in 1989, then in such cities as Oakland, California, and Portland, Oregon, and now in operation in many cities across the nation—not only conduct trials of and sentence drug offenders but also coordinate a broad system of monitoring and treatment. The system involves probation officers, treatment providers, public-health, housing, and social-service agencies, educational institutions, and job-training and placement providers.

The second form of the move toward treatment is the creation of special drug-treatment facilities, run by the criminal-justice system, to which nonviolent drug offenders are sentenced. These include the Substance Abuse Felony Punishment System in Texas and so-called boot camps in states such as Georgia, Oklahoma, and New York, in which military drills and physical labor are combined with drug treatment.[53] The third form involves in-prison treatment programs, which a few states, such as Texas, began to emphasize in the early 1990s. The Texas program aimed to offer drug offenders long-term treatment, education, and vocational training prior to their release and then followed up with a continuum-of-care program that would last up to fifteen months after an offender returned to the community.[54]

The turn to treatment has generated a powerful backlash among people who are committed to traditional punitive approaches or opposed to new spending on such experiments. "Some Hail Treatment Approach; Others Think It's Too Soft," reported a *New York Times* headline in April 1994. A spokesman for New York State's Senate majority leader opposed the diversion of offenders to treatment programs, on familiar grounds: "These are not the innocent drug addicts they are made to seem," he announced, adding, "If you're going to sink new spending into this area, we ought to deal with additional prison bed space."[55] When Texas governor Ann Richards, a Democrat, actively pushed diversion-to-treatment and in-prison treatment programs in the early 1990s, she met harsh criticism from her successful Republican challenger, George W. Bush, in the 1994 campaign. Calling for substance-abuse beds to be transferred to the juvenile-justice system to incarcerate violent youths, Bush argued that "so long as we've got an epidemic of crime, I think we ought to forget about rehabilitation and worry about incarceration. . . . I believe that most adult criminals are, sad to say, beyond much chance of rehabilitation." When he became governor in 1995, he severely cut back the funds for the programs Richards had created.[56]

In the face of such opposition, people who are struggling to create diversion-to-treatment programs have worked to build broad political and community coalitions in order to gain support. In planning the Miami drug court, for example, Judge Herbert M. Klein put together a team that drew on a wide range of public agencies, including representatives from the state attorney's, public defender's, and county manager's offices; from the human-services, corrections, and public-safety departments; and from local colleges and community organizations.[57] Crucial in generating political support was the Miami Coalition for a Drug-Free Community, a coalition with more than 1,500 volunteer members from the media and from business, labor, religious, and other community organizations. Without such an influential group, Judge Klein recognized, "we would never have been able to get all the different agencies to agree to the Drug Court. It takes real clout to overcome ingrained bureaucratic resistance to new ways of operating, and the Drug Court looks revolutionary."[58]

Even where such struggles to incorporate treatment do succeed, however, they are fundamentally constrained by the punitive context out of which they have emerged. Unquestionably, such programs will increase the number of drug-dependent individuals who receive treatment and will help prevent crime. But there is no guarantee that such efforts, even as they expand, will help facilitate a shift from a punitive approach to a public-health approach. Such programs, after all, are defined and managed by agencies that are charged with conviction and punishment, not with health and well-being. This can shape their purposes and operating principles in critical ways.

One of the strongest motives for the recent turn to treatment, recall, is economic. From a criminal-justice perspective, treatment pays. Diverting nonviolent drug offenders to treatment is less expensive than building more prisons. It eases overcrowding by keeping prison space open for the most violent criminals.[59] It reduces crime by relieving future budgetary pressures on the system: helping people overcome drug abuse prevents addiction-based crime in the future. Embracing treatment because it is more cost-effective and efficient than are existing modes of punishment may lead public officials to design drug-treatment programs as alternative forms of punishment—and to sell them to a skeptical public by making them harsh and mandatory.

Conceiving of treatment in this way has in some cases encouraged programs in which judges, not treatment professionals, determine whether and what kind of treatment is appropriate for a particular defendant and whether the defendant is making adequate progress. In other cases it has encouraged prison officials, instead of health-care professionals, to run in-prison treatment programs, thus destroying the trust and openness necessary for counseling or therapeutic communities to work. Often, it has led to criteria of success that measure the prisoner-patient's ability to remain drug free—regardless of the fact that frequent relapses are almost inevitable on the road to recovery. And it has sometimes led some program officials to disregard the need for alternative life opportunities—education, jobs, housing, medical care—that are necessary for long-term recovery. Over time, the result of such an approach might be to sustain a criminal-justice system that first criminalizes people largely because of health problems and then traps these substance-abusing patient-criminals into endless, court-mandated treatment, with little health promotion and minimal chances to find ways in which to lead healthy, productive lives—a critique made of civil-commitment programs in the 1960s.[60]

Yet even within these constraints, a number of reform advocates have begun to fight for change based on public-health principles, and their efforts may undermine the punitive approach to drug control by opening up debate on important questions. One such question is implicit in the small struggles over how the diversion-to-treatment programs are to be set up: many advocates are insisting that punitive procedures and principles are not appropriate for some program components. At the heart of this administrative issue is a critical debate over how to define the relationship between treatment and punishment.

Many law-enforcement officials with long experience in TASC programs, for example, have been struggling to shape the programs set up by the newly emerging drug courts. Their aim is to keep the treatment end of the program in the hands of treatment professionals, so that the criteria for who is admitted and whether the program is working are based on principles of treatment, not punishment. If the drug-court programs are to work, explained one TASC official, "the treatment programs need to control the door. The judges need to adopt the policy of giving a court order which demands assessment. But it's the treatment program that needs to do the assessment and decide who gets in—who is likely to benefit by such court-ordered treatment and what kind of treatment they need."[61]

One Washington advocate stressed the importance of convincing those in the criminal-justice system that "if treatment is done by the keeper of the keys—as opposed to having public health people come in and do it—it won't work. You need a staff of counselors, who are community based, who go into the prison on a consistent basis, who provide group and individual counseling to the inmates: this is the way to do it. These counselors need the trust of the inmates for treatment to work. You can't be keeper of the keys and be a person's confidante at the same time."[62]

A 1993 report on the Miami drug court indicated that the struggle over how to think about treatment has not yet been resolved and that there remains "an uneasy marriage of criminal justice and drug treatment goals." From a punitive perspective, for example, there is pressure to give drug users only a few chances to quit—with the threat of prison time if they do not.

> In contrast, a treatment perspective would probably not view a "three strikes and you're out" approach to program compliance as realistic. Indeed, treatment staff would understand that, to the extent that serious drug abusers are encouraged to enter the program, the road to progress is likely to be very difficult, with initial failures routinely to be expected. This difference in perspectives translates into differences in expectations about the performance of drug court defendants and, as a result, into potentially different ways to measure outcomes.[63]

Another important debate has emerged over the question of how much attention such criminal-justice programs should pay to aftercare. A concept of treatment as punishment is concerned only with ensuring that drug offenders have been adequately penalized; the focus is therefore on whether they have put in the time and met the requirements of the program. Some reformers, however, have begun to challenge this punitive concept by arguing for attention to the conditions that drug offenders face on release. Behind such calls lies an interest not (or not only) in punishing drug users but in enabling them to build healthy and satisfying lives.

Some people who have been involved in diversion-to-treatment programs, for example, have begun to advocate an expansive notion of aftercare that takes seriously a public-health emphasis on the social environment. One former detective explained to us how his own views were transformed after he began to work in treatment-alternative programs. He described his initial position as not "liberal on law enforcement"; "my mission was convicting these people and getting them as much time in prison as possible—even though I always knew that they would be out again, and I was always frustrated by this." The diversion-to-treatment experiment, he thought at first, was "a liberal program" designed "to give someone early release and make things easier on them." Yet over time, he explained, he became convinced that the treatment programs demanded hard work and were more effective in reducing recidivism than were traditional forms of punishment. And he came to see the young people who use and sell drugs very differently:

> I really admire the kids that grow up in a neighborhood like Roxbury [Boston] and make it. I understand why they are dealing drugs instead of getting a job at McDonald's for $4.00 an hour—and there isn't even a McDonald's in the area because it's so unsafe. These kids can't just pack up and move somewhere else. And there are no real economic opportunities in the area. Those in the diversion programs: think about the world you're asking them to make it in. A lot of these kids have got to use bus passes, and go all the way across the city to another location each day just to get the vocational training [required by the program]. And the environment they are going back into: you're not just asking them to work at keeping away from the gang on the corner, but their families—their mothers and sisters may be on drugs. John Q. Citizen who has not lived in these communities just does not understand that.[64]

James Swartz writes about lessons learned from TASC experiences and about the importance of a continuum of care that addresses elements of the social environment: "With relatively little modification, the TASC model can be extended to become not only a bridge between the criminal justice system and drug treatment but also a network between clients and a variety of service agencies, all specialized in one area or another where addicts require additional help . . . such as GED classes, vocational training, AIDS education and prevention, and medical and psychological care."[65]

Some designers of drug-court programs have demonstrated a concern with precisely these issues. Aftercare is an integral part of the Miami drug-court program. To provide literacy training, high-school degrees, apprenticeship, and training programs, it includes not only group-counseling programs but also classes at Miami-Dade Community College.[66] Judge Jeffrey S. Tauber of the Oakland, California, drug court underlined the importance of this approach to treatment: "Without adequate aftercare, an offender's sobriety may be short-lived when he or she faces the same problems that contributed to their drug usage in the first place. Aftercare should include ongoing treatment and counseling, as well as educational opportunities, job training and placement, and health and housing assistance."[67]

These debates over the meaning of treatment, its relationship to punishment, and the role of the social environment constitute a serious challenge to the current war on users by many of the people who are charged with conducting it. Despite the inherent limits of challenging the punitive drug-control system from within its primary apparatus, such struggles may have an important effect.

Drug courts guided by the principles that are advocated in Miami and Oakland could help legitimize the importance of comprehensive treatment programs that address the environmental factors emphasized by a public-health approach. Moreover, through the coordinating mechanisms of a drug court, prosecutors, judges, probation officers, prison officials, treatment centers, social agencies, and community groups that may formerly have been "uncooperative or even mutually hostile agencies"[68] might come to forge local programs that focus on treating drug abuse and addiction not mainly through the threat of punishment but by creating a continuum of care and decent educational, housing, and economic opportunities.

CONCLUSION

Important struggles for drug-policy reform are under way. They have emerged in response to the failures and contradictions of the drug war and to the tremendous burdens these contradictions have laid on the shoulders of people who seek to prevent and treat abuse and addiction, who are facing drug problems in their local communities, and, most ironically, who are charged with conducting the drug war itself. The outcome of these struggles is impossible to predict. It is conceivable that the next few decades will see the beginnings of a shift from a punitive paradigm to a public-health paradigm. This seems unlikely to us today—but so too would the politics of drug prohibition and condemnation of the 1930s have seemed inconceivable to Americans who could buy morphine from the Sears Roebuck catalog at the turn of the century.

If such a shift to a public-health paradigm were to take place, we might look back on the contradictions and struggles generated by the drug wars of the late twentieth century as a critical juncture, a fork in the road at which the human and economic costs of a failed strategy sparked a rethinking of the nation's approach to drug abuse and addiction. Today's scattered struggles might then appear to be precursors to a paradigm shift in much the same way as the various struggles by progressive reformers, moral zealots, and Treasury Department agents gradually forged a punitive paradigm in the first decades of the century. Such a new drug paradigm would appear to be a logical consequence of these struggles in much the same way that new ways of thinking about the environment or about smoking seem today to be the logical consequence of earlier challenges to previous paradigms.

But in thirty years we might also look back and find that little has changed; we might see better-funded treatment and prevention efforts but continuing commitment to a punitive war on drugs. Our dramatically expanded prison and court systems might still be overflowing with low-income drug offenders, a high percentage of them black or Hispanic. We might see periodic escalations of drug war efforts followed by periods of relative calm in drug war rhetoric and enforcement. Evidence of failure might still be confronted much as it is today, with drug warriors arguing that the solution is more force and punishment, with liberal pragmatists arguing for a better mix of tough enforcement and treatment, and with few people daring to argue that the war in pursuit of a drug-free America be abandoned for regulation in pursuit of public health.

Whether we look back at the present as the beginning of a paradigm shift or as one more chapter in the politics of denial will depend primarily on larger social and political trends and on their impact on U.S. social policies—whether and how America handles its larger health-care and other social problems, for example, and whether the broader political context is supportive of social reform. But it will also depend in some measure on the political struggle and the actions of individuals who are fighting for reform today—and of those who are battling against them. The lessons of the recent past are modest but, perhaps, important. They suggest that the more conscious reformers are about how the punitive paradigm distorts treatment and prevention, filters or marginalizes criticism, and supports a logic of escalation rather than reevaluation, the better able they will be to anticipate responses to their efforts and to design effective reform strategies. The more their short-term, pragmatic struggles are guided by clear public-health principles, the less the chances that their struggles will leave the entrenched assumptions of the paradigm untouched (or, worse, inadvertently reinforce them). And the more they are able to mobilize the potential power that exists in hundreds of organizations with tens of thousands of members and to bring it to bear on the political process, the less the probability of long-term marginalization and the greater the likelihood of gradual transformation to a strategy that promotes healing without harm.

Afterword

Illicit drugs and the war against them have great symbolic significance in American politics. Getting tough on drug users and dealers is political proof that one is anticrime, profamily, hard-nosed, practical, and realistic. Drug use as morally wrong, users as criminals, and the drug war as a righteous, moral crusade—such symbols dominate the policy debate and obscure the serious public-health problems that are caused by drug abuse and by our drug policy. Worse, broad public acceptance of these symbols has enabled well-organized and politically powerful conservatives to lead the charge for more force and punishment and has crippled would-be reformers who are concerned with healing and care.

In writing this book, we hope to help stem this rush into the abyss and to begin to shift the political debate from how to punish to how to heal. But we have no illusions about the difficulties of changing policy or broadening public debate. Distinguished commissions, some presidentially appointed, and respected and knowledgeable analysts have challenged the drug war solution time and again and have offered specific, alternative policy recommendations.

What we have learned is that real change will require far more than reasoned critiques and renewed calls for policy change. It will come only with a shift in the underlying drug war paradigm. Such a paradigm shift is difficult but not impossible.

In the 1950s, for example, a paradigm shift on environmental issues might have seemed inconceivable. Few Americans could have envisioned national policymakers winning votes for proposing tough new environmental laws; few could have predicted bipartisan support for national and local legislation forbidding certain forms of pollution, mandating door-to-door recycling programs, and halting major logging operations to protect endangered species.

In the 1960s a paradigm shift on smoking would have been equally unimaginable. Smoking was widely considered not only acceptable but glamorous and appealing. It would have been impolite to ask neighboring patrons in a restaurant or fellow passengers in a train to stop smoking; pregnant women did not think twice about smoking, and few smokers reflected on the serious risk to their own lives. The hallmarks of today's antismoking campaign would have been difficult to imagine a few decades ago: public declarations by the surgeon general about the health hazards of cigarette smoking, legislation requiring warnings on cigarette labels, bans on televised cigarette advertisements, federal and state requirements creating smoke-free public spaces to protect nonsmokers from secondary smoke, and the FDA classification of nicotine as an addictive drug.

Sweeping transformations in our thinking and policies on such issues show us that although paradigm shifts do occur, they are slow and arduous, and they are not easy to predict. We can suggest, however, that a politics of drug reform based on the kind of public-health paradigm we have discussed will probably need to satisfy three requirements.

First, it will require confronting the politics of denial—the multiple reasons for the persistence of failed and harmful drug policies. Until we do, calls for policy change will fall on deaf ears. The commitment to attacking drug problems through a war on supply and users is not simply the result of ignorance, hidden agendas, an irrational policy process, or a drug war mind-set; nor is it simply the outcome of presidential, congressional, or bureaucratic politics. It is the result of institutional patterns that involve all of these.

The punitive drug war paradigm created by struggles early in this century has become commonsensical. It defines certain facts about drugs and drug use: that drugs are morally wrong, that drug abuse and addiction are the fault of bad or ignorant individuals, that drug-dependent people are criminals, that drugs and crime are one and the same, and that so-called drug-related problems such as disease and crime are caused solely by drug use, not by antidrug policies.

The ideas, values, and symbols of the punitive paradigm persist not simply because they have become part of our political culture but because they are embodied in political institutions, from the DEA down to local police forces. The routine enforcement of drug war laws based on the punitive paradigm pushes drug dealers and users, many of whom have no prior criminal history, into the underworld and exacerbates crime and violence. When stories and images of this drug war are carried by nightly newscasts, the drug war strategy and the paradigm that informs it are reinforced; they seem plausible, indeed, necessary.

Within this context, partisan politics and electoral dynamics make the escalation of a failing and harmful drug war quite rational, as elected officials believe they must out-tough each other to win votes and public support for their policies. Their political rhetoric further reinforces the drug war and the punitive paradigm. Efforts to institute alternatives—treatment, education, social reform—are made to seem soft: an addict-criminal ought to be punished, not coddled. Such alternatives are underfunded or dismissed; when tried, they are often undermined and distorted by the punitive thinking and the law-enforcement institutions of the drug war. Politically powerful conservatives, meanwhile, are able to sustain the key symbols of the paradigm against challengers, viciously attacking and demeaning critics and sidelining pragmatic alternatives. Less zealous conservatives and liberals, many of whom are skeptics or closet critics, have been willing to go along or have chosen to remain silent.

Understanding this politics of denial—a phenomenon that experts in fields other than drug policy may recognize in slightly different versions—allows us to appreciate why many front-line advocates of treatment and prevention feel trapped politically. As long as the punitive paradigm is dominant, they know that funds for treatment and prevention can only be won by riding the antidrug-crime wave and by not challenging the basic principles of the drug war. Thus treatment and prevention are packaged as tools in the war effort. But as long as a war on supply and users is the central feature of the drug strategy, the illegality and high profits created by the war will assure continued crime and violence and will transform health problems into crime problems. And prevention and treatment, like law enforcement, are bound to fail if the criterion of success is quickly and significantly lowering the crime and violence fueled by today's drug policies.

Understanding the politics of denial also makes clear why this book will not easily turn the heads of most policymakers. Support for a dramatic change in direction would force officials to pay high political costs. Politically safe drug-policy reform is possible only within certain bounds.

Public officials can lower the rhetoric and can suggest increased funding for treatment and prevention. But it would be politically risky to condemn the current strategy for its fatal flaws and grave harms.

Finally, understanding the politics of denial makes clear a second requisite for meaningful change: an alternative vision about drugs, drug users, and drug problems to guide strategy and policies. Such a vision cannot simply be invented by policy analysts or reformers or even modeled on the often sound approaches adopted by other countries. To take hold, it must resonate: it must be rooted in accessible American traditions and accepted American values. Envisioning a new paradigm allows us to recognize and remove the blinders imposed by the punitive paradigm and to look at drug problems through new eyes. The problems and pitfalls of our current path become clearer. Most importantly, imagining a new paradigm gives us the confidence and guidance we need in order to choose a new direction.

A public-health paradigm for drugs provides one such vision. Based on principles rooted in a long-standing, if marginal, tradition of public-health practice in the United States, it can provide front liners, concerned citizens, and policymakers with an initial compass for plotting a new course. It envisions drugs as primarily a health problem, and it considers the goal of policy to be healing without harm. It conceives of drug abuse and addiction as public, not merely individual, problems for two reasons: their causes are rooted in social and cultural conditions as well as in individual choices; and their consequences harm families, neighborhoods, and schools as well as society at large. Because these causes and consequences are social as well as individual, government support and regulation are necessary to help individuals cope with their social environments and to change those environments that encourage drug abuse.

If we have helped convince concerned citizens, those on the front lines, and even some policymakers that breaking the cycle of drug war failure and escalation demands a paradigm shift and that something like a public-health paradigm is a plausible and worthy aim, we will have gone a long way toward meeting our goal. If we have helped people who are currently struggling for drug reform to see the need to search out ways in which to direct these struggles in order to open up possibilities for wider changes, we will have accomplished a great deal.

Beyond an understanding of the politics of denial and a vision of a new paradigm, however, there is a third requisite for fundamental change: political struggle. The reason a new vision alone is insufficient becomes clear when we recall the evolution of the punitive paradigm that is now so deeply rooted. Many people take the drug war paradigm as a given or perhaps a natural consequence of American political culture. But American culture can support—and has supported—other paradigms, ones that are based on pragmatism (try it and see if it works), on individual freedom and choice, or on a concern to care for the disadvantaged. The punitive paradigm became dominant only after a series of political struggles.

In the 1920s and 1930s social forces and government institutions fought political struggles over whether to medicalize the drug problem by giving doctors control of distribution and by regarding addicts as patients or to prohibit all sales and to criminalize users and sellers. In Congress, in municipal governments, and in the courts, battles were fought over what laws should regulate doctors and clinics and over how they should be enforced. Local neighborhoods struggled over whether to allow clinics to operate. Treasury Department agencies fought to reinterpret the 1914 Harrison Act and to consolidate the hegemony of the punitive, prohibitionist vision. When challenges to the punitive paradigm were placed on the public agenda—the decriminalization of marijuana in the 1960s and 1970s, for example—this, too, meant political struggle, through street demonstrations, petitions, and letter-writing campaigns and in state legislatures, courts, and the federal bureaucracy. These efforts were beaten back in part by powerful, conservative social forces who gained control of a wing of the Republican Party, sweeping into office two national administrations that refurbished the punitive paradigm, expanded the narco-enforcement complex, reversed attempts at reform, and escalated the drug war in the 1980s.

A new struggle for drug reform is unlikely to take hold—let alone succeed—in isolation: drug problems and their solutions are too much a part of deeper social issues and struggles—over health care, urban decay, racism, and economic underdevelopment in our cities. But if a paradigm shift is to be part of such struggles, concerned citizens and front liners with practical experience in treatment, prevention, criminal justice, and politics have a special responsibility.

Public officials will be reticent to change course as long as they fear the political costs of change. And as long as drug war politics is dominated by the voices of punitive prohibitionists, political leaders will find it reasonable to take the paths of least resistance: escalation when it serves a particular political agenda, maintenance of the drug war status quo when it does not, and occasional tinkering with treatment and education on the margins. Change will only come when pressure mounts from citizens and organized groups demanding an end to the politics of denial and a new commitment to a politics of reason, care, and collective responsibility.

Trends in Drug-Control Spending

Sources: Figures from 1970–78 from Peter Goldberg, "The Federal Government's Response to Illicit Drugs, 1969–1978," in Drug Abuse Council, *The Facts About Drug Abuse* (New York: The Free Press, 1980), 57; figures from 1979–1980 from Drug Abuse Policy Office, Office of Policy Development, the White House, *Federal Strategy For Prevention of Drug Abuse and Drug Trafficking 1982* (Washington, D.C.: U.S. Government Printing Office, 1982) 74–75; and figures from 1981–1995 from Office of National Drug Control Policy, *National Drug Control Strategy: Budget Summary* (Washington, D.C.: U.S. Government Printing Office, 1995), 235–38. Note that in most cases corresponding figures in the text have not been adjusted for inflation.

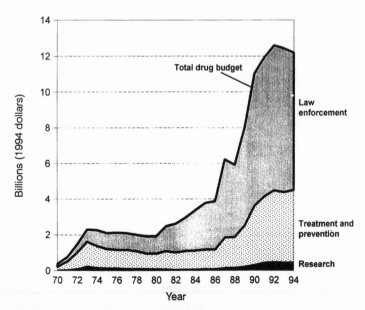

Figure 2.   Federal drug-control budget.

Trends in Drug Prices

The primary objective of drug law enforcement is to discourage consumption by raising the retail price of drugs. Between 1973 and 1994, the law-enforcement budget increased dramatically, yet the prices of heroin and cocaine did not; only marijuana prices rose significantly. Furthermore, the failure of drug enforcement to affect the prices of heroin and cocaine is often underestimated by government measures: prices are rarely adjusted for drug purity levels or for inflation. Prices of cocaine, for example, are generally reported as staying relatively constant over the past 15 years. Once adjusted for purity levels (which have risen), it becomes clear that prices have declined. If adjusted for inflation (using 1994 dollars), the decline is even more dramatic.

Figures are based on national range averages as calculated by the Drug Enforcement Administration. Although these figures suggest clear trends, estimates of illegal drug prices are not considered reliable market measures: drug prices vary widely across geographic regions in response to local conditions, including the level of enforcement.

Sources for Figure 3: Figures from 1970–78 from Peter Goldberg, "The Federal Government's Response to Illicit Drugs, 1969–1978," in Drug Abuse Council, *The Facts About Drug Abuse* (New York: The Free Press, 1980), 57; figures from 1979–1980 from Drug Abuse Policy Office, Office of Policy Development, the White House, *Federal Strategy For Prevention of Drug Abuse and Drug Trafficking* 1982 (Washington, D.C.: U.S. Government Printing Office, 1982), 74–75; and figures from 1981–1995 from Office of National Drug Control Policy, *National Drug Control Strategy: Budget Summary* (Washington, D.C.: U.S. Government Printing Office, 1995), 235–8.

Sources for Figures 4, 5, and 6: Figures for 1973–76 from Michael J. Handelang, Michael R. Gottfredson, and Timothy J. Flanagan, eds., *Sourcebook of Criminal Justice Statistics,* 1980, U.S. Department of Justice, Bureau of Justice Statistics (Washington, D.C.: U.S. Government Printing Office, 1981), 324.

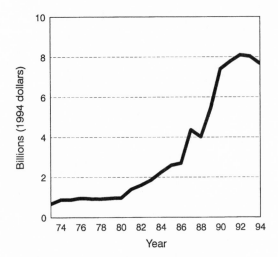

Figure 3.   Drug war spending: federal law enforcement budget.

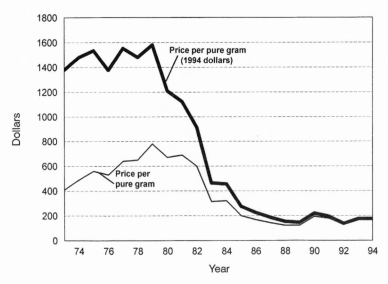

Figure 4.   Street price of cocaine.

Figures for 1977–1987 from Katherine M. Jamieson and Timothy J. Flanagan,
eds., *Sourcebook of Criminal Justice Statistics,* 1988, U.S. Department of Justice,
Bureau of Justice Statistics (Washington, D.C.: U.S. Government Printing Office,
1989), 372. Figures for 1988–1994 from U.S. Department of Justice, Drug Enforcement Administration, *Illegal Drug Price/Purity Report* (Washington, D.C.,

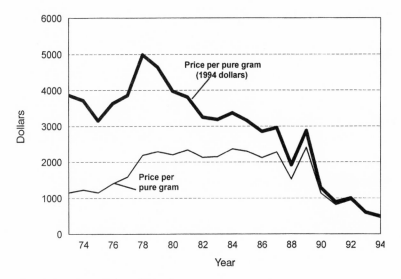

Figure 5.   Street price of heroin.

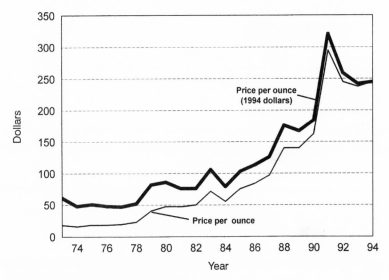

Figure 6.   Street price of marijuana.

March 1991), 3, 5, and 7; U.S. Department of Justice, Drug Enforcement Administration, *Illegal Drug Price/Purity Report* (Washington, D.C., April 1994), 1, 4, and 6; U.S. Department of Justice, Drug Enforcement Administration, *Illegal Drug Price/Purity Report* (Washington, D.C., June 1995), 1, 4, and 6. Note: Heroin prices are for powdered heroin, and purity adjustments are based on the average purity of heroin purchases as reported by the DEA. Marijuana prices are for the commercial grade.

Trends in Drug Use and Its Consequences

Sources for Figure 7: Office of National Drug Control Policy, *National Drug Control Strategy* (Washington, D.C.: 1995), 39. Data from National Household Survey on Drug Abuse (1979–1991), and Substance Abuse and Mental Health Services Administration (1992–1993). These data are drawn from self-reports of past-month drug use from members of the household population age 12 and over. "Any illicit drug use" includes use of marijuana, cocaine, heroin, hallucinogens, and other drugs. These estimates show a decline in overall casual drug use, most of which is attributable to a decline in marijuana use. As the next figure shows, there has been no such decline in heavy use. Note also that these data underestimate drug use, according to the ONDCP and other sources, not only because of the reluctance of some people to report use but also because many of the groups most likely to use drugs (including the homeless and school-age dropouts) do not reside in households and are not surveyed.

Source for Figure 8: Susan S. Eveningham and C. Peter Rydell, *Modeling The Demand for Cocaine* (Santa Monica, Calif.: RAND Corporation), 49. "Heavy users" are defined as those who use at least once a week. "Light users" are defined as those who use at least once a year, but less than weekly.

Sources for Figure 9: Office of National Drug Control Policy, *National Drug Control Strategy* (Washington, D.C.: 1995), 37, 143. Data from Drug Abuse Warning Network, National Institute on Drug Abuse (1988–91), and Substance Abuse and Mental Health Services Administration (1992–93). One indicator of serious drug abuse is the number of drug-related emergency-room visits. During 1990, for example, there were more than 635,000 mentions of drugs (illicit and over-the-counter) in the 371,208 emergency-room episodes in the hospitals in the 21 metropolitan areas nationwide that participate in the Drug Abuse Warning Network (DAWN). Almost half the episodes involved two or more drugs.

The drug mentioned most frequently was alcohol in combination with other drugs in 31 percent of the episodes, followed by cocaine in 22 percent of the episodes (80,355 mentions), and heroin in 9 percent of the episodes (33,884 mentions).

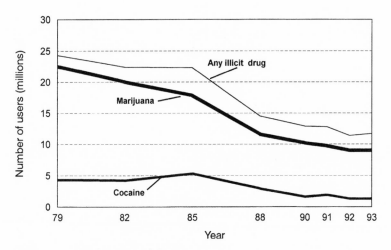

Figure 7.   Trends in casual drug use.

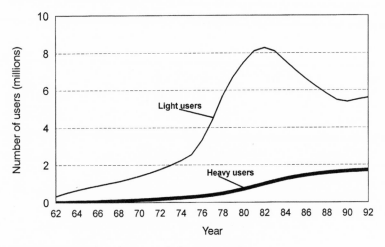

Figure 8.   Trends in heavy vs. light use: cocaine.

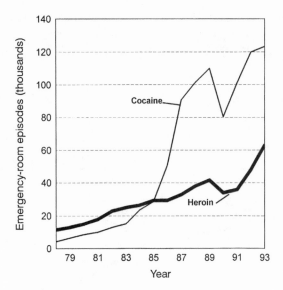

Figure 9.   Consequences of hard-core drug use:
trends in drug-related emergencies.

Notes

PREFACE

1. Peter Andreas et al., "Dead End Drug Wars," *Foreign Policy,* no. 85 (1991–1992):106–28.

2. Authors who have grappled with the problem of self-defeating policies include Barbara W. Tuchman, *The March of Folly: From Troy to Vietnam* (New York: Alfred A. Knopf, 1984); I. M. Destler, Leslie Gelb, and Anthony Lake, *Our Own Worst Enemy: The Unmaking of American Foreign Policy* (New York: Simon and Schuster, 1984); Loren Baritz, *Backfire* (New York: Ballantine Books, 1986); and D. Michael Shafer, *Deadly Paradigms: The Failure of U.S. Counter-insurgency Policy* (Princeton, N.J.: Princeton University Press, 1988).

3. U.S. Department of Health and Human Services, *National Household Survey on Drug Abuse: Population Estimates 1993* (Washington, D.C.: U.S. Government Printing Office, 1994).

CHAPTER 1

1. Our major focus here is on the politics of the wars on cocaine and heroin, although we will give some attention to marijuana. Synthetic drugs—amphetamines, barbiturates, lysergic acid diethylamide (LSD), and phencyclidine (PCP), for example—are also a serious problem in the United States but have received only very limited policy attention in national drug-control strategies.

2. Perhaps the most thorough and significant was the National Commission on Marihuana and Drug Abuse, *Drug Use in America: Problem in Perspective* (Washington, D.C.: U.S. Government Printing Office, 1973). The commission was appointed by President Nixon at the request of Congress and was chaired by Raymond P. Shafer, former governor of Pennsylvania.

CHAPTER 2

1. Office of National Drug Control Policy, *National Drug Control Strategy* (Washington, D.C.: U.S. Government Printing Office, 1995), 17–20.

2. Estimates are from President's Commission on Law Enforcement and Administration of Justice, *Narcotics and Drug Abuse* (Washington, D.C.: U.S. Government Printing Office, 1967), 2–8; and Office of National Drug Control Policy, *National Drug Control Strategy* (1995), 8–20. These statistics underestimate the number of hard-core users because the household survey data and high-school surveys do not include the homeless, persons in prisons or other institutionalized settings, or high-school dropouts, groups that account for many such users. Furthermore, the number of heroin addicts is expected to increase in coming years as heroin is increasingly marketed in forms that can be inhaled or smoked, removing the stigma and dangers of injection.

3. Office of National Drug Control Policy, *National Drug Control Strategy* (Washington, D.C.: U.S. Government Printing Office, 1994), 1, 12–14; Office of National Drug Control Policy, *National Drug Control Strategy* (1995), 138, 143.

4. CQ Researcher, "War on Drugs," *Congressional Quarterly,* 19 March 1993, 252.

5. "Gingrich on Drug Dealers," *New York Times,* 15 July 1995.

6. Figures for 1970–1978 are from Peter Goldberg, "The Federal Government's Response to Illicit Drugs, 1969–1978," in *The Facts About Drug Abuse,* by the Drug Abuse Council (New York: The Free Press, 1980), 57; figures for 1979–1980 are from Drug Abuse Policy Office, Office of Policy Development, the White House, *Federal Strategy For Prevention of Drug Abuse and Drug Trafficking 1982* (Washington, D.C.: U.S. Government Printing Office, 1982), 74–75; and figures for 1981–1995 are from Office of National Drug Control Policy, *National Drug Control Strategy: Budget Summary* (Washington, D.C.: U.S. Government Printing Office, 1995), 235–38. If state and local budgets for drug-law enforcement are included, the totals are far higher. In the early 1990s, for example, the annual state and local budgets for enforcement were about $12 billion a year. Office of National Drug Control Policy, *State and Local Spending on Drug Control Activities* (Washington, D.C.: U.S. Government Printing Office, 1993), 3.

7. Office of National Drug Control Policy, *National Drug Control Strategy* (1995), 45–47, 146; and testimony of Thomas Constantine, administrator, Drug Enforcement Administration, before the Senate Judiciary Committee, 14 February 1995.

8. Director of the Office of National Drug Control Policy, Lee Brown, Testimony before the Judiciary Committee, U.S. Senate, 10 February 1994. As the drug war intensified from 1988 to 1993, for example, the retail price (in constant 1994 dollars) of a gram of pure cocaine dropped from $146–$186 to $120–$151. The price of a gram of pure heroin dropped from $1,612–$3,007 to $837–$2,553 in 1993. Office of National Drug Control Policy, *National Drug Control Strategy* (1995), 146. Note that this failure of the drug war to achieve its stated objectives of reducing the availability and increasing the price of cocaine and heroin means that the observed decline in current use of these drugs cannot plausibly be attributed to these drug war strategies.

9. Mark H. Moore, "Supply Reduction and Drug Law Enforcement," in *Drugs and Crime*, ed. Michael Tonry and James Q. Wilson (Chicago: University of Chicago Press, 1990).

10. Steven Wisotsky, *Beyond the War on Drugs: Overcoming a Failed Public Policy* (Buffalo, N.Y.: Prometheus Books, 1990), 32–36 (quotation on p. 36); Edward M. Brecher and the editors of *Consumer Reports*, eds., *Licit and Illicit Drugs* (Boston: Little, Brown, 1972), 90–100; Mark A. R. Kleiman, *Against Excess: Drug Policy for Results* (New York: Basic Books, 1992), 104–26.

11. David Hoffman, "Proposal Is Marked Shift from Border Interdiction," *Washington Post*, 27 May 1988. In 1982 the Reagan White House asserted that the "elimination of illegal drugs at or near their foreign source is the most effective means to reduce the domestic supply of these substances." In 1971 Nixon promised to eliminate the drug supply by "literally cutting it off root and branch at its source." The quotations are from Peter Reuter, "Eternal Hope," *Public Interest* 79 (Spring 1985):79; and Franklin E. Zimring and Gordon Hawkins, *The Search for Rational Drug Control* (Cambridge, Mass.: Cambridge University Press, 1992), 46.

12. Clinton's drug czar, Lee Brown, explained: "We want to see if we can stop drugs at the source. It's easier to stop the drugs there than when they leave." Brown, Testimony. See also Office of National Drug Control Policy, *National Drug Control Strategy* (1995), 98.

13. U.S. Department of State, Bureau of International Narcotics and Law Enforcement Affairs, *International Narcotics Control Strategy Report* (Washington, D.C., 1995).

14. Office of National Drug Control Policy, *National Drug Control Strategy* (1994), 51.

15. James Brooke, "U.S. Aid Hasn't Stopped Drug Flow from South America, Experts Say," *New York Times*, 21 November 1993.

16. U.S. Department of Justice, Drug Enforcement Administration, Office of Intelligence, *Intelligence Trends: From the Source to the Street: Mid-1990 Prices for Cannabis, Cocaine, and Heroin* (Washington, D.C., 1990), 6. On the local economics of production, see Madeline Barbara Leons, "Risk and Opportunity in the Coca/Cocaine Economy of the Bolivian Yungas," *Journal of Latin American Studies* 25 (1993):121–57; and Edmundo Morales, "The Political Economy of Cocaine Production: An Analysis of the Peruvian Case," *Latin American Perspectives* 17, no. 4 (1990):91–109.

17. Michael Matza, "'Narc' No More," *Philadelphia Inquirer*, 2 April 1990.

18. Rensselaer W. Lee III, "Coca Growing Cannot Be Eradicated," in *Chemical Dependency*, ed. Bruno Leone (San Diego, Calif.: Greenhaven Press, 1989), 323.

19. Melvin Burke, "Bolivia: The Politics of Cocaine," *Current History* 90, no. 553 (1991):67.

20. *Latin American Weekly Report*, 22 February 1990, 1.

21. "The Cocaine Economies: Latin America's Killing Fields," *The Economist*, 8 October 1988, 24.

22. For more, see U.S. Congress, House, Committee on Government Operations, *United States Anti-Narcotics Activities in the Andean Region* (Washing-

ton D.C.: U.S. Government Printing Office, 1990), 56. See also Francisco E. Thoumi, "The Economic Impact of Narcotics in Colombia," in *Drug Policy in the Americas,* ed. Peter H. Smith (Boulder, Colo.: Westview Press, 1992).

23. Ibid., 91–92.

24. For a detailed analysis of this corruption, see Peter Andreas, "Profits, Poverty and Illegality: The Logic of Drug Corruption," *NACLA Report on the Americas* 27, no. 3 (1993):22–28.

25. U.S. Congress, House, Defense Policy Panel and Investigations Subcommittee, Committee on Armed Services, *The Andean Drug Strategy and the Role of the U.S. Military* (Washington, D.C.: U.S. Government Printing Office, 1990), 31.

26. Quoted in Clare Hargreaves, *Snow Fields: The War on Cocaine in the Andes* (New York: Holmes and Meier, 1992), 148.

27. Col. Robert Jacobelly, quoted in Washington Office on Latin America, *Clear and Present Dangers: The U.S. Military and the War on Drugs in the Andes* (Washington, D.C., 1991), 101.

28. "Inside the Cartel," *PBS Frontline,* 22 May 1990.

29. Diana Jean Schemo, "Colombia in Crisis as Drugs Tar Chief," *New York Times,* 13 August 1995.

30. See, for example, John Dinges, *Our Man in Panama* (New York: Random House, 1990); and Washington Office on Latin America, *Clear and Present Dangers,* 121–22.

31. James Brooke, "A Captain in the Drug War Wants to Call It Off," *New York Times,* 8 July 1994.

32. See, for example, Ethan Nadelman, "Drug Prohibition in the United States," *Science,* 1 September 1989, 940; Calvin Sims, "Defying U.S. Threat, Bolivians Plant More Coca," *New York Times,* 11 July 1995; U.S. Congress, House Committee on Government Operations, *United States Anti-Narcotics Activities in the Andean Region,* 35–37, 66–71; Kevin Healy, "Coca, the State, and the Peasantry in Bolivia, 1982–1988," *Journal of Interamerican Studies and World Affairs* 30, nos. 2–3 (1988):105–26; and Peter H. Smith, ed., *Drug Policy in the Americas* (Boulder, Colo.: Westview Press, 1992).

33. House Judiciary Committee, Subcommittee on Crime and Criminal Justice, February 1992, 93. A State Department official described the problem to Congress in 1994: "Since 1990, more coca cultivation has been eradicated in the Andean ridge than ever before in history, yet new cultivation is even greater. There have been more narcotics arrests, interdictions, and seizures than ever before, yet even more cocaine reaches the United States and the price on the street is not significantly changed." Cresencio S. Arcos, Statement of Cresencio S. Arcos, Principal Deputy Assistant Secretary of State for International Narcotics Matters, before the Subcommittee on Foreign Operations, House Appropriations Committee, 14 April 1994.

34. "Anti-Drug Effort Clogs Outside U.S.," *New York Times,* 25 November 1990.

35. David Clark Scott, "New Cooperation Seen in Anti-Drug Strategy," *Christian Science Monitor,* 16 March 1993.

36. U.S. Department of Justice, The United States Attorneys and The Attorney General of the United States, *Drug Trafficking: A Report to the President of the United States* (Washington, D.C., 1989), 16–17.

37. Douglas Farah, "Young Gangs Decentralize Drug Trade," *Washington Post*, 11 June 1995.

38. Ralph A. Weisheit, *Domestic Marijuana, A Neglected Industry* (New York: Greenwood Press, 1992), 31–39; Eric Schlosser, "Reefer Madness," *Atlantic Monthly*, August 1994, 59–62; Michael Pollan, "How Pot Has Grown," *New York Times Magazine*, 19 February 1995, 32.

39. Pollan, "How Pot Has Grown," 30–35, 44, 50, 56–57; and Schlosser, "Reefer Madness," 45–63.

40. Quoted in Washington Office on Latin America, *Clear and Present Dangers*, 95.

41. "War on Drugs," *Congressional Quarterly*, 19 March 1993, 243.

42. Mathea Falco, *The Making of a Drug-Free America: Programs That Work* (New York: Times Books, 1992), 8.

43. Peter Reuter, "Can the Borders Be Sealed?" *Public Interest* 92 (Summer 1988):57.

44. Quoted in Eric Weiner, "Airborne Drug War Is at a Stalemate," *New York Times*, 30 July 1989.

45. Statement of the Director, Systems Development and Production Issues, National Security and International Affairs Division of the General Accounting Office (Louis J. Rodriguez, Statement before the Legislation and National Security Subcommittee, House Committee on Government Operations, 5 October 1993).

46. Keith B. Richburg, "New Trafficking Routes Boost SE Asian Heroin Threat," *Washington Post*, 10 July 1995; Office of National Drug Control Policy, *National Drug Control Strategy* (Washington, D.C.: U.S. Government Printing Office, 1991), 102–3; and Silvana Paternostro, "Mexico as a Narco-Democracy," *World Politics Journal* 12, no. 3 (1995):41–48.

47. See, for example, Patricia A. Adler, *Wheeling and Dealing: An Ethnography of an Upper-Level Drug Dealing and Smuggling Community* (New York: Columbia University Press, 1985), 5–9.

48. Daniel K. Benjamin and Roger Leroy Miller, *Undoing Drugs: Beyond Legalization* (New York: Basic Books, 1991), 42.

49. Jessica Speart, "The New Drug Mules," *New York Times Magazine*, 11 June 1995, 44–45.

50. Rodriguez, Statement.

51. Transcript of the President's News Conference on Foreign and Domestic Matters, *New York Times*, 7 March 1981, 10.

52. Reuter, "Can the Borders Be Sealed?" See also Peter Reuter, Gordon Crawford, and Jonathan Cave, *Sealing the Borders: The Effects of Increased Military Participation in Drug Interdiction* (Santa Monica, Calif.: RAND Corporation, 1988). A similar argument holds for the ineffectiveness of drug war efforts against heroin. See, for example, Brecher et al., *Licit and Illicit Drugs*, 90–100.

53. CQ Researcher, "War on Drugs," 243.

54. Since the mid-1980s law enforcement officials have tried to interdict the billions of dollars a year in illegal profits, mostly paid in cash, that traffickers try to conceal (or launder) in legitimate businesses and bank accounts or transfer out of the country. Money launderers have been caught and banks fined, but the strategy is unlikely to raise prices enough to affect drug abuse and addiction. Enforcement is limited because there are so many ways of hiding and transferring money, because the financial system itself processes millions of transactions a day, because electronic banking allows traffickers to move vast sums around the globe in seconds, and because the international financial system is highly unregulated. See Stephen B. Duke and Albert C. Gross, *America's Longest War: Rethinking Our Tragic Crusade Against Drugs* (New York: G. P. Putnam's Sons, 1993), 208–11; and for a brief description of the many ways of concealing and transferring money, see U.S. Department of Justice, *Drug Trafficking*, 40–43. For an optimistic analysis of anti-money-laundering efforts, see David A. Andelman, "The Drug Money Maze," *Foreign Affairs* (1994):94–108.

55. Thus finding the major traffickers, not just the street dealers, and gathering sufficient evidence to prosecute them require time-consuming and expensive measures like systematic surveillance or "buy-and-bust" techniques.

56. This analysis of profit at each stage is based on similar calculations by Steven Wisotsky, who used earlier data. Wisotsky, *Beyond the War on Drugs*, 45–46.

57. Peter Reuter, Robert MacCoun, and Patrick Murphy, *Money from Crime: A Study of the Economics of Drug Dealing in Washington, D.C.* (Washington, D.C.: RAND Corporation, 1990), 59.

58. Jane Mayer, "In the War on Drugs, The Toughest Foe May Be Alienated Youth," *Wall Street Journal*, 8 September 1989.

59. Robert M. Stutman and Richard Esposito, *Dead on Delivery: Inside the Drug Wars, Straight from the Street* (New York: Warner Books, 1992), 225.

60. Enrique J. Gonzalez, "Discreet Dealers Dodge Drug Patrols," *Washington Times*, 5 August 1991.

61. Joseph McNamara, "Forum," KQED Radio, 2 December 1991.

62. Stutman and Esposito, *Dead on Delivery*, 226.

63. During most of the 1980s and early 1990s, only about 30 percent of the federal drug budget has been for prevention and treatment. Office of National Drug Control Policy, *National Drug Control Strategy: Budget Summary* (Washington, D.C.: U.S. Government Printing Office, 1995), 235–38. The percentage of state and local government spending on treatment and prevention has been even lower—about 20 percent of roughly $16 billion of drug-control expenditure in 1991. Office of National Drug Control Policy, *National Drug Control Strategy* (1994), 99.

64. Office of National Drug Control Policy, *National Drug Control Strategy* (Washington, D.C.: U.S. Government Printing Office, 1992), 115.

65. Alfred R. Lindesmith, *The Addict and the Law* (Bloomington: Indiana University Press, 1965), 239. Not surprisingly, sanctions against users have often been harshest against racial minorities. It is not insignificant that the defendant in this case was black.

66. Kleiman, *Against Excess*, 267, based on figures from U.S. Department of Justice, Bureau of Justice Statistics, *Federal Offenses and Offenders: Drug Law Violators, 1980–1986* (Washington, D.C., 1988), 4–5; and U.S. Department of Justice, Bureau of Justice Statistics, *Sourcebook of Criminal Justice Statistics—1989* (Washington, D.C., 1990), 500.

67. The quotations are from the Office of National Drug Control Policy, *National Drug Control Strategy* (Washington, D.C.: U.S. Government Printing Office, 1989), 11; but similar arguments are made, for example, in Office of National Drug Control Policy, *National Drug Control Strategy* (1992), 33–36.

68. Office of National Drug Control Policy, *National Drug Control Strategy* (1989), 25.

69. See, for example, Philip J. Hilts, "Hospital Is Object of Rights Inquiry," *New York Times*, 6 February 1994.

70. Denise B. Kandel, "The Social Demography of Drug Use," *Milbank Quarterly* 69, no. 3 (1991):404–7.

71. Office of National Drug Control Policy, *National Drug Control Strategy* (1995), 19–25.

72. U.S. Department of Health and Human Services, *National Household Survey on Drug Abuse, Population Estimates 1993* (Washington, D.C.: U.S. Government Printing Office, 1994).

73. Harry K. Wexler, Douglas S. Lipton, and Bruce D. Johnson, *A Criminal Justice System Strategy for Treating Cocaine/Heroin Abusing Offenders in Custody* (Washington, D.C.: National Institute of Justice, 1988), 5; Jeffrey Fagan, Prepared testimony, U.S. Congress, House, Subcommittee on Crime, Committee on the Judiciary; *Cocaine and Federal Sentencing Policy*, 104th Cong., 1st sess., 29 June 1995; and Patricia G. Erickson, "A Public Health Approach to Demand Reduction," *Journal of Drug Issues* 20, no. 4 (1990):565.

74. Joseph B. Treaster, "Drug Therapy: Powerful Tool Reaching Few Inside Prisons," *New York Times*, 3 July 1995; and Office of National Drug Control Policy, *National Drug Control Strategy* (1995), 39–40.

75. Benjamin and Miller, *Undoing Drugs*, 105. See also Matthew Purdy, "Bars Don't Stop Flow of Drugs into Prisons," *New York Times*, 2 July 1995.

76. Steven Jonas, "Public Health Approach to the Prevention of Substance Abuse," in *Substance Abuse: A Comprehensive Text*, ed. Joyce H. Lowinson, Pedro Ruiz, Robert B. Millman, and John G. Langrod, 2d ed. (Baltimore, Md.: Williams and Wilkins, 1992), 933.

77. Elliott Currie, *Reckoning: Drugs, the Cities, and the American Future* (New York: Hill and Wang, 1993), 154, from Barry S. Brown, Susan K. Gauvey, Marilyn B. Meyers, and Steven D. Stark, "In Their Own Words: Addicts' Reasons for Initiating and Withdrawing from Heroin," *International Journal of the Addictions* 6, no. 4 (1971):639–42.

78. Dan Waldorf, Craig Reinarman, and Sheila Murphy, *Cocaine Changes: The Experience of Using and Quitting* (Philadelphia: Temple University Press, 1991), 10. Peter K. Manning also stresses the importance of social ties in his work on the deterrent effects of police action. One critical error in the conventional reasoning is failure to recognize that "the 'choice' to use drugs (violate the law and thus risk arrest) depends on collective ties . . . and the social net-

work within which dealing and use occurs. The cost of loss of these ties, on the whole, far exceeds the risk entailed in the threat of arrest." Peter K. Manning, "The Criminal Justice System and the User," in Lowinson et al., *Substance Abuse,* 1028.

79. Isidor Chein, Donald L. Gerard, Robert S. Lee, and Eva Rosenfeld, *The Road to H: Narcotics, Delinquency, and Social Policy* (New York: Basic Books, 1964); and Norman Zinberg, *Drug, Set and Setting: The Basis for Controlled Intoxicant Use* (New Haven, Conn.: Yale University Press, 1984).

CHAPTER 3

1. This distinction is more common among policy analysts than in public debate. See, for example, Brecher et al., *Licit and Illicit Drugs,* 521; Ethan Nadelmann, "Drug Prohibition in the United States: Costs, Consequences, and Alternatives," *Science,* 1 September 1989, 939–47; and Kleiman, *Against Excess,* 12–16.

2. But even in this case, such behavior is not simply or solely due to the drugs themselves. Personality factors and social setting often determine whether or not intoxication with a particular drug will lead to aggression. See, for example, Jeffrey Fagan, "Intoxication and Aggression," in *Drugs and Crime,* ed. Michael Tonry and James Q. Wilson (Chicago: University of Chicago Press, 1990), 243.

3. R. S. Weppner and D. C. McBride, "Comprehensive Drug Programs: The Dade County, Florida Example," *Psychiatry* 132 (1975): 734–38.

4. Edward Jay Epstein, *Agency of Fear* (London: Verso, 1990), 127–28; and Arnold S. Trebach, *The Heroin Solution* (New Haven, Conn.: Yale University Press, 1982), 232–34.

5. James Q. Wilson, "Drugs and Crime," in *Drugs and Crime,* ed. Michael Tonry and James Q. Wilson (Chicago: University of Chicago Press, 1990), 522; Adler, *Wheeling and Dealing;* and P. J. Goldstein et al., "Crack and Homicide in NY City, 1988: A Conceptually Based Event Analysis," *Contemporary Drug Problems* 16 (1989):651–87.

6. Not every crime committed by those who are drug dependent is the result simply of needing money to finance their habits. See, for example, Jan M. Chaiken and Marcia R. Chaiken, "Drugs and Predatory Crime," in *Drugs and Crime,* ed. Michael Tonry and James Q. Wilson (Chicago: University of Chicago Press, 1990), 203–39; and Currie, *Reckoning,* 168–80.

7. "Can Clean Needles Slow the AIDS Epidemic?" *Consumer Reports,* July 1994, 466.

8. National Commission on Acquired Immune Deficiency Syndrome, *The Twin Epidemics of Substance Use and HIV* (Washington, D.C., 1991), 1.

9. "Can Clean Needles Slow the AIDS Epidemic?" 466.

10. Kleiman, *Against Excess,* 379.

11. Laws that prohibit possession also encourage poor heroin addicts to leave their equipment in the relative safety of shooting galleries (so they won't be caught with them on the street), a practice that also invites others to share contaminated needles.

12. In Britain, for example, the reported rate of AIDS cases is 2 per 100,000 people, well below the United States' rate of 18.5 per 100,000 in 1992. "Can Clean Needles Slow the AIDS Epidemic?" 467.

13. Infants born to mothers who abuse any of a range of substances—alcohol, nicotine, cocaine—face increased risks of fetal damage. These risks include low birth weight, respiratory problems, brain damage, later developmental problems, and increased likelihood of addiction.

14. U.S. Congress, House, Committee on Government Operations, *The Role of Demand Reduction in the National Drug Control Strategy*, 101st Cong., 2d sess., 30 November 1990, 75.

15. Jan Hoffman, "Pregnant, Addicted—and Guilty?" *New York Times Magazine*, 19 August 1990, 32–35.

16. Because of the risks imposed by the drug war, suppliers can maximize the profit on each risky transaction by minimizing the physical volume and maximizing the strength of a given drug. Seeking to maximize profits per pound smuggled encourages traffickers to favor drugs that are more potent, and profitable, per pound—harder and more dangerous drugs such as heroin and cocaine—instead of less dangerous, bulkier drugs such as marijuana. Drug war policies that kept the price of cocaine high to discourage use ended up encouraging dealers in the mid-1980s to reach lower-income users by marketing highly addictive crack-cocaine "rocks" that can be bought for $5 or $10 and smoked—thus creating a far more serious and widespread health problem. It is such black-market forces that have also dramatically pushed up the purity levels of heroin and cocaine and the potency of marijuana in the last fifteen years.

17. Ethan Nadelmann, "Legalization Is the Answer," *Issues in Science and Technology*, Summer 1990, 43.

18. Office of National Drug Control Policy, *National Drug Control Strategy* (1995), 34–35.

19. Office of National Drug Control Policy, *National Drug Control Strategy* (1992), 6–7.

20. By the early 1990s, African Americans accounted for 45 percent of the AIDS cases attributed to intravenous drug use and Hispanics accounted for 26 percent, for a total of 71 percent of all such AIDS cases. Centers for Disease Control, *AIDS/HIV Surveillance: U.S. AIDS Cases Reported Through May 1991* (Atlanta, Ga., 1991), 9–10. See also Stephen B. Thomas and Sandra Crouse Quinn, "The Burdens of Race and History on Black Americans' Attitudes Toward Needle Exchange Policy to Prevent HIV Disease," *Journal of Public Health Policy* 14, no. 3 (1993):325.

21. See, for example, Loic J. D. Wacquant and William J. Wilson, "The Cost of Racial and Class Exclusion in the Inner City," *Annals of the American Academy of Political and Social Science* 501 (1989):8–25; and John Kasarda, "Urban Industrial Transition and the Underclass," *Annals of the American Academy of Political and Social Science* 501 (1989):26–47.

22. In studying heroin addicts in Chicago's Puerto Rican community in the early 1970s, for example, Ronald Glick found that about "two-thirds of all the addicts, including dealers, who were interviewed . . . indicate that they began to

use drugs in addictive quantities not as part of a hip or romantic lifestyle, but rather because drugs offered escape from their depression and feelings of failure. . . . A substantial majority of addicts associate their discouragement principally with family problems." Ronald Glick, "The Chicago Puerto Rican Community," in *Drugs in Hispanic Communities*, ed. Ronald Glick and Joan Moore (New Brunswick, N.J.: Rutgers University Press, 1990), 86. For a review of recent studies, see also Currie, *Reckoning*, 103–23.

23. "Drug Use Down, Report Says," *USA Today*, 20 December 1990. The NIDA reports also show that the percentage of drug use for each group was more or less the same: 6.6 percent of whites, 8.6 percent of blacks, and 6.2 percent of Latinos. Note that such NIDA reports probably underestimate drug use among the poor and in the inner cities because they do not include people in prisons, those in mental institutions, or the homeless, and such people are more likely to be using drugs than are those who were surveyed. For a discussion of why serious drug abuse and addiction seem to be proportionately higher among blacks than whites despite the rough equality in the figures on drug use, see Kandel, "Social Demography of Drug Use," 395–403.

24. Sam Vincent Meddis, "Is the Drug War Racist?" *USA Today*, 23 July 1993.

25. *USA Today*'s analysis of the government's 1991 drug-arrest data showed that 16 blacks were arrested for every 1,000 blacks in the population and that 4 whites were arrested for every 1,000 whites in the population. Ibid.

26. Kenneth J. Meier, "Race and the War on Drugs: America's Dirty Little Secret," *Policy Currents* 2, no. 4 (1992):3.

27. Meddis, "Is the Drug War Racist?"

28. Stuart Taylor, Jr., "How a Racist Drug War Swells Crime," *Legal Times*, 22 February 1993.

29. Mike Tidwell, *In the Shadow of the White House* (Rocklin, Calif.: Prima Publishing, 1992), 199. See also Ron Harris, "Blacks Feel Brunt of Drug War," *Los Angeles Times*, 22 April 1990.

30. This 1991 study found that 15 percent were in prison; 21 percent, on probation or parole; 6 percent, out on bond or "sought by the police." By the age of thirty-five, 70 percent of the black men in the capital had been arrested; about 85 percent are arrested at some point in their lives. Lawrence M. Friedman, *Crime and Punishment in American History* (New York: Basic Books, 1993), 378.

31. Chris Black, "America's Lost Generation," *Boston Globe*, 4 March 1990.

32. Clarence Lusane, *Pipe Dream Blues: Racism and the War on Drugs* (Boston: South End Press, 1991), 49. See also Sam Staley, *Drug Policy and the Decline of American Cities* (New Brunswick, N.J.: Transaction Publishers, 1992), 126–28, 135, 170–72; Terry M. Williams, *The Cocaine Kids* (Reading, Mass.: Addison-Wesley, 1989), 132; and Philippe Bourgois, "In Search of Horatio Alger: Culture and Ideology in the Crack Economy," *Contemporary Drug Problems* 16, no. 4 (1989): 620–49.

33. Mayer, "In the War on Drugs." See also Williams, *Cocaine Kids*.

34. Kleiman, *Against Excess*, 300. The tendency for illicit activity to concentrate in urban poor and minority communities is not unique to the drug trade. Kornblum argues that similar social forces have historically thrust other vice

markets (such as gambling or prostitution) into stigmatized, segregated communities. He points, for example, to a pattern of collusion between corrupt authorities and illegal merchants that has encouraged this concentration. William Kornblum, "Drug Legalization and the Minority Poor," *Milbank Quarterly* 69, no. 3 (1991):415–36.

35. Sam Vincent Meddis, "No 'Conspiracy' in Black Drug Arrests," *USA Today,* 26 July 1993, final edition.

36. Ibid.

37. Sam Vincent Meddis, "In Twin Cities, A Tale of Two Standards," *USA Today,* 26 July 1993, final edition. Police Chief John Dale of Albany, New York, clarified the comparative ease of making arrests in inner-city areas where the trade is visible, contrasting it with a typical conspiracy investigation against upper- or middle-class whites that could last six months and yield fewer than six arrests. Meddis, "Is the Drug War Racist?"

38. Dan Weikel, "War on Crack Targets Minorities over Whites," *Los Angeles Times,* 24 May 1995.

39. Office of National Drug Control Policy, *National Drug Control Strategy* (1989), 25.

40. Jackson, Rangel, and Webster were quoted in Sam Vincent Meddis, "Drug War Claiming 'Entire Generation' of Young Blacks," *USA Today,* 27 July 1993, first edition; and Kramer and Williams were cited in the version of the article that appeared in the final edition.

41. Samuel L. Meyers, Jr., "Drugs and Market Structure: Is There Really a Drug Crisis in the Black Community?" in *The Great Issues of Drug Policy,* ed. Arnold S. Trebach and Kevin B. Zeese (Washington, D.C.: Drug Policy Foundation, 1990), 98.

42. Meddis, "Is the Drug War Racist?"

43. Meddis, "In Twin Cities."

44. Claude Brown, "They Can't Afford to Stay Out of Jail," *Los Angeles Times,* 17 March 1990.

45. Craig Reinarman and Harry G. Levine, "Crack in Context: Politics and Media in the Making of a Drug Scare," *Contemporary Drug Problems* 16 (1989):541.

46. These other dangerous classes include immigrants, cultural liberals, and young people. Diana G. Gordon, *The Return of the Dangerous Classes: Drug Prohibition and Policy Politics* (New York: W. W. Norton, 1994).

47. House Committee on Government Operations, *Role of Demand Reduction,* 17.

48. Meddis, "No 'Conspiracy' in Black Drug Arrests."

49. Derrick Z. Jackson, "Police Investigation Delivers an Open Denial of Racism," *Boston Globe,* 14 May 1994.

50. Mike Tidwell pieced together this account. See Tidwell, *In the Shadow of the White House,* 192–201.

51. Randy E. Barnett, "Curing the Drug-Law Addiction: The Harmful Side Effects of Legal Prohibition," in *Dealing with Drugs: Consequences of Government Control,* ed. Ronald Hamowy (Lexington, Mass.: Lexington Books, 1987), 95.

52. Drug-courier profiles are procedures devised by police trying to stop drugs from moving across borders and along interstate highways. A New Mexico profile instructed police to beware of "Hispanics or blacks between 20 and 35 . . . who appear to be foreign, [who are] driving too fast or too slow or too cautiously, [or who have] too much or too little luggage." "Looking directly into the eyes of a police officer" is grounds for suspicion; yet "not looking into the eyes of a police officer" is equally suspect. Paul Weingarten and James Coates, "Drugs Blaze New Paths," *Chicago Times*, 12 September 1989. In detaining travelers on these grounds, such profiles dramatically redefine probable cause, chipping away at Fourth Amendment protections.

The right to legal counsel, guaranteed by the Sixth Amendment, has also been undermined by the Justice Department's tactic of forbidding defendants to pay their lawyers unless they can prove the money comes from legal sources—a move that can make it difficult for defendants to hire attorneys to represent them. See, for example, Steven Wisotsky, "Crackdown: The Emerging 'Drug Exception' to the Bill of Rights," *Hastings Law Journal* 38, no. 5 (1987):889–926.

Another drug war tactic that threatens to undermine constitutional rights is the use of forfeiture laws. The 1984 Comprehensive Crime Control Act created a Customs Forfeiture Fund, which permits drug-law enforcement agencies to keep a portion of the money and goods they seize from drug offenders to equip or finance their drug operations. Such laws make good sense from the point of view of the police: why not make dealers and users foot the bill for the drug war by seizing their assets? But they often undermine the constitutional presumption that a person is innocent until proven guilty because police can seize a person's property with little more than suspicion, and the owner bears the burden of proving innocence to recover the property. The laws also lead to abuses of power. The possibilities of gains from forfeiture often encourage police to base their crime-fighting decisions on profit, not effectiveness (the more assets seized, the more funds for police budgets). Elected officials charged with controlling the purse strings of enforcement agencies (in order to check abuses of power in law enforcement) do not control these purse strings: the money comes right into police budgets with little public scrutiny and democratic accountability. See, for example, Jon Nordheimer, "Seizure of Assets by an Aggressive Drug Fighter Raises Eyebrows," *New York Times*, 2 August 1992.

53. Wisotsky, "Crackdown," 889.

54. *Turner v. United States*, 396 US 398, 426 (1979), quoted in ibid., 924.

55. Joseph B. Treaster, "Is the Fight on Drugs Eroding Civil Rights," *New York Times*, 6 May 1990.

56. Carroll Bogert and Gregory Beals, "When Cops Betray Their Communities," *Newsweek*, 19 December 1994, 32.

57. Tom Morganthau, "Why Good Cops Go Bad," *Newsweek*, 19 December 1994, 30–34.

58. Carl Hiassen, "Greed, Drug Dealers Bring Down Top Federal Agent," *Miami Herald*, 7 May 1983; Peter Slevin, "Ex-Guardsman: I Stole, Sold Drug-Fight Plans," *Miami Herald*, 3 March 1983; Joan Fleischman and Jim McGee, "Metro Police 'Lost' Drugs Stored in Property Room," *Miami Herald*, 29 Au-

gust 1982; Charles Babington, "Drug Probe in Navy Snares Nearly 40 Here; Cases Involved Some in Presidential Unit," *Washington Post,* 24 October 1991; and Andrea Ford, "Former DEA Agent Gets 5-Year Sentence," *Los Angeles Times,* 10 September 1991.

59. The pattern of incentives and temptations is the same as that facing Latin security forces, as we saw in chapter 1.

60. See, for example, John H. Langer, "Corruption of Public Officials: An Inevitable Consequence of International Drug Traffic," *Police Studies* 9, no. 1 (1986):34–41.

61. This comment, from hearings for the Subcommittee on Legal and Monetary Affairs of the House Committee on Government Operations in 1970, is quoted in Wisotsky, *Beyond the War on Drugs,* 145.

62. Morganthau, "Why Good Cops Go Bad," 34.

63. See David L. Carter, "Drug-Related Corruption of Police Officers: A Contemporary Typology," *Journal of Criminal Justice* 18 (1990):85–90.

64. Quoted in Clifford Krauss, "Corruption in Uniform: The Long View," *New York Times,* 8 July 1994. See also Bob Herbert, "In America: A Warning Shot," *New York Times,* 10 July 1994.

65. Quoted in Morganthau, "Why Good Cops Go Bad," 34.

66. Bogert and Beals, "When Cops Betray Their Communities," 32.

67. Joseph P. Armao and Leslie U. Cornfeld, "How to Police the Police," *Newsweek,* 19 December 1994, 34.

68. Stuart Taylor, "A Test of Reno's Courage," *Legal Times,* 9 August 1993, suppl., 36.

69. Critics in the legal community have questioned not only the severity of these sentences (claiming that they are out of proportion to the crime committed) but also the disparity in the sentence for possession of cocaine in the form of crack (which is cheap and distributed in poor, minority communities) as opposed to the powdered form (more likely to be possessed by wealthier users and midlevel dealers, generally whites). The sentence for the first is five years for one gram; to receive a five-year sentence for the second, one would have to be caught with 500 grams. See for example, Richard P. Conaboy, Testimony before the Subcommittee on Crime, Committee on the Judiciary, U.S. House of Representatives, 29 June 1995.

70. A recent study by researchers at Florida State University concluded that more than 75 percent of all persons arrested on drug charges lacked prior criminal records. Benjamin and Miller, *Undoing Drugs,* 104.

71. Dan Weikel, "War on Crack Targets Minorities over Whites"; and Dirk Johnson, "For Drug Offenders, How Tough Is Too Tough?" *New York Times,* 9 November 1993.

72. "Harper's Index," *Harper's,* May 1994, 15 (citing the U.S. House Subcommittee on Civil and Constitutional Rights).

73. Don J. De Benedictis, "How Long Is Too Long?" *ABA Journal* 79 (1993):74–75.

74. Curtis Stiner, "U.S. Legal Group Debates Reform as Drug Cases Inundate System," *Christian Science Monitor,* 12 February 1990.

75. Ronald J. Ostrow, "In Ranking Jailers, U.S. Easily No. 1," *Los Angeles Times,* 11 February 1992; and Mark Pazniokas, "Tough Stands on Crime May Ignore Reality," *Hartford Current,* 20 October 1994.

76. U.S. Department of Justice, Bureau of Justice Statistics, *Federal Criminal Case Processing, 1989–1990* (Washington, D.C., 1992), 17, table 17; and American Bar Association, *The State of Criminal Justice: An Annual Report* (Washington, D.C.,1993), ii.

77. Falco, *Making of a Drug-Free America,* 132.

78. Michael Hennessey, "Our National Jail Scandal," *American Jails* 7, no. 3 (1993):13.

PART 2

1. Lewis H. Lapham, excerpted in *Drug Prohibition and the Conscience of Nations,* ed. Arnold S. Trebach and Kevin B. Zeese (Washington, D.C.: Drug Policy Foundation, 1990), 39.

2. See, for example, Christina Jacqueline Johns, *Power, Ideology, and the War on Drugs* (New York: Praeger, 1992).

3. Lapham, excerpted in Trebach and Zeese, *Drug Prohibition,* 40.

4. Gordon, *Return of the Dangerous Classes.* For a good example of the literature on symbolic politics, see Murray Edelman, *Political Language: Words That Succeed and Policies That Fail* (New York: Academic Press, 1977).

5. See Thomas Kuhn, *The Structure of Scientific Revolutions* (Chicago: University of Chicago Press, 1970). Peter Hall ("Policy Paradigms, Social Learning, and the State: The Case of Economic Policymaking in Britain," *Comparative Politics* 25, no. 3 [1993]:279) notes that

> policy makers customarily work within a framework of ideas and standards that specifies not only the goals of policy and the kind of instruments that can be used to attain them, but also the very nature of the problems they are meant to be addressing. Like a Gestalt, this framework is embedded in the very terminology through which policy makers communicate about their work, and it is influential precisely because so much of it is taken for granted and unamenable to scrutiny as a whole.

For another excellent analysis of how paradigms help explain the persistence of failed policies, see Shafer, *Deadly Paradigms.*

6. On the importance of causal stories in public policy and the political struggles to create and maintain them, see Deborah Stone, "Causal Stories and the Formation of Policy Agendas," *Political Science Quarterly* 104, no. 2(1989):281–300.

7. David F. Musto, *The American Disease* (New York: Oxford University Press, 1987).

8. See, for example, David J. Langum, *Crossing over the Line: Legislating Morality and the Mann Act* (Chicago: University of Chicago Press, 1994).

CHAPTER 4

1. Musto, *American Disease,* 7.

2. James A. Inciardi, *The War on Drugs: Heroin, Cocaine, Crime, and Public Policy* (Palo Alto, Calif.: Mayfield Publishing Co., 1986), 6–7.

3. Troy Duster, *The Legislation of Morality: Law, Drugs, and Moral Judgment* (New York: Free Press, 1970), 7.

4. Ibid., 9, 10.

5. Brecher et al., *Licit and Illicit Drugs,* 7.

6. Quoted in Musto, *American Disease,* 18.

7. Samuel Hopkins Adams, writing in a series in *Collier's* between 1905 and 1907. Quoted in James Harvey Young, *The Medical Messiahs: A Social History of Health Quackery in Twentieth-Century America* (Princeton, N.J.: Princeton University Press, 1967), 31.

8. See, for example, Joseph R. Gusfield, *Symbolic Crusade: Status Politics and the American Temperance Movement* (Urbana: University of Illinois Press, 1963); David J. Pivar, *Purity Crusade: Sexual Morality and Social Control, 1868–1900* (Westport, Conn.: Greenwood Press, 1973); and Langum, *Crossing over the Line.*

9. Inciardi, *War on Drugs,* 94.

10. Ibid., 93.

11. Douglas Clark Kinder, "Shutting Out the Evil: Nativism and Narcotics Control in the United States," *Journal of Policy History* 3, no. 4 (1991):472–73.

12. Musto, *American Disease,* 6.

13. Kinder, "Shutting Out the Evil," 473.

14. John Helmer, *Drugs and Minority Oppression* (New York: Seabury Press, 1975), 13.

15. Richard Harvey Brown, "Drug Policies and Politics in Comparative Perspective: The Case of Opium in India, China, Britain and the United States" (paper presented to the Drug Policy Seminar, Institute for Latin American and Iberian Affairs, Columbia University, February 1993), 35.

16. Brecher et al., *Licit and Illicit Drugs,* 44.

17. Arnold H. Taylor, *American Diplomacy and the Narcotics Traffic, 1900–1939: A Study in International Humanitarian Reform* (Durham, N.C.: Duke University Press, 1969), 27.

18. Ibid., 37. The State Department backed the request, recognizing that it served other foreign-policy interests as well. In particular, it allowed the United States to increase its influence in the Pacific, notably against its major competitor, Britain, and to strengthen its relations with the Chinese government, which was strongly opposed to the British trade. Musto, *American Disease,* 39.

19. Quoted in Musto, *American Disease,* 34.

20. Ibid., 36, 44.

21. Quoted in Charles Reasons, "The Politics of Drugs: An Inquiry in the Sociology of Social Problems," *Sociological Quarterly* 15 (Summer 1974): 392–93.

22. Ibid., 393.

23. Brecher et al., *Licit and Illicit Drugs,* 49.

24. The actual level of opium use was highly contested, and reliable reports at the time gave estimates ranging from 2,000,000 to 246,000. See William Butler Eldridge, *Narcotics and the Law: A Critique of the American Experiment in Narcotic Drug Control* (New York: New York University Press, 1962), 7.

25. Ibid., 9.

26. Reasons, "Politics of Drugs," 394.

27. Brecher et al., *Licit and Illicit Drugs,* 49.

28. Musto, *American Disease,* 123. The Justice Department was a little more cautious than the Treasury Department: the district attorneys (who had to prosecute the cases brought by the Treasury Department) and the attorney general seemed to share the assumption that maintenance was an illegitimate medical practice, but they questioned "whether the Harrison Act could sustain violations of this morality as an illegal act" (p. 125).

29. "Only words from which there is no escape could warrant the conclusion that Congress meant to strain its powers almost if not quite to the breaking point in order to make the probably very large proportion of citizens who have some preparation of opium in their possession criminal or at least *prima facie* criminal and subject to serious punishment." *United States v. Jin Fuey Moy,* 241 US 402 (1916).

30. In the wake of the Bolshevik revolution in Russia, fears of communist subversion in the United States heightened and spread, triggering the Red Scare of 1919–1920.

31. *New York Times,* 18 December 1918, quoted in Rufus King, *The Drug Hang-up* (New York: W. W. Norton, 1972), 26.

32. Musto, *American Disease,* 190; and Inciardi, *War on Drugs,* 98.

33. U.S. Department of Justice, Drug Enforcement Administration, *A Chronicle of Federal Drug Law Enforcement* (Washington, D.C., 1977), 22, 24.

34. Musto, *American Disease,* 193.

35. H. Wayne Morgan, *Drugs in America: A Social History, 1800–1980* (Syracuse, N.Y.: Syracuse University Press, 1981), 116.

36. Musto, *American Disease,* 193.

37. Duster, *Legislation of Morality,* 15.

38. Musto, *American Disease,* 92, 107, and 218.

39. The Prohibition Bureau's regulations began: "It is well-established that the ordinary case of addiction will yield to proper treatment, and that addicts will remain permanently cured when drug addiction is stopped and they are otherwise physically restored to health and strengthened in will power." Quoted in King, *Drug Hang-up,* 38.

40. In 1918 the Treasury Department "reported that it had *dropped* charges against (that is, instituted and then terminated—or, in other words threatened) 14,701 persons registered under the Act." The following year the figure rose to 22,595, and in 1920 it leapt to 47,835. Ibid., 27.

41. U.S. Department of Justice, "Chronicle of Federal Drug Law Enforcement," 18.

42. Musto, *American Disease,* 139–41, 151–52.

43. Ibid., 167–69; see also chap. 7, "The Narcotic Clinic Era."

44. Physician and pharmacist lobbies were still strong enough to block sweeping new legislation in Congress. Reasons, "The Politics of Drugs," 398.

45. King, *Drug Hang-up,* 41.

46. *Webb et al. v. United States,* 249 US 96 (1918), cited in Musto, *American Disease,* 132.

47. See Jerald Cloyd, *Drugs and Information Control* (Westport, Conn.: Greenwood Press, 1982), 62.

48. *United States v. Behrman,* 258 US 288 (1922).

49. *United States v. Linder,* 268 US 5 (1925).

50. See Cloyd, *Drugs and Information Control,* 64.

51. Musto, *American Disease,* 143, 135–45.

52. Ibid., 144–45.

53. Ibid., 204–6, 235.

54. King, *Drug Hang-up,* 36.

55. "State legislatures also exercised considerable imagination in elaborating on the possession offense in an effort to give law enforcement officials new tools to root out users. All consumption-related activity, such as presence in a place where narcotics were being used, possession of hypodermic syringes, even the status of addiction itself, was punishable. In fact, under the 'narcotics vagrancy' laws and similar statutory catchalls, policemen could arrest someone who appeared to them likely to use narcotics." National Commission on Marihuana and Drug Abuse, *Drug Use in America,* 244–45.

CHAPTER 5

1. See John C. McWilliams, "Through the Past Darkly: The Politics and Policies of America's Drug War," *Journal of Policy History* 3, no. 4 (1991):365.

2. Kinder, "Shutting Out the Evil," 479.

3. Lindesmith, *The Addict and the Law,* 252–54.

4. U.S. Department of Justice, *Chronicle of Federal Drug Law Enforcement,* 28.

5. John C. McWilliams, *The Protectors: Harry J. Anslinger and the Federal Bureau of Narcotics, 1930–1962* (Newark: University of Delaware Press, 1990), 51. McWilliams also points out that when efforts were made to reorganize or dismantle the FBN, Anslinger mobilized support: "Letters from the National Association of Retail Druggists, the WCTU, Women's Clubs, and the National Congress of Parents and Teachers flooded the White House in protest of any reorganizational scheme that included dismantling the Bureau of Narcotics" (p. 91).

6. "At that time, and for at least a decade longer, the drug [pharmaceutical] trades saw no reason why a substance used chiefly in corn plasters, veterinary medicine, and nonintoxicating medicaments should be so severely restricted." Musto, *American Disease,* 216.

7. A. E. Fossier, "The Marihuana Menace," *New Orleans Medical and Surgical Journal* 84, no. 4 (1931):247–52, cited in Helmer, *Drugs and Minority Oppression,* 75.

8. This position was reflected in the U.S. Treasury Department's year-end report on dangerous drugs in 1931. Brecher et al., *Licit and Illicit Drugs,* 412.

9. Ibid., 413.

10. Quoted in ibid.

11. U.S. Department of Justice, *Chronicle of Federal Drug Law Enforcement,* 40.

12. Brecher et al., *Licit and Illicit Drugs,* 69, 77.

13. Ibid., 405, 418.

14. Cited in McWilliams, "Through the Past Darkly," 368.

15. Quoted in Musto, *American Disease,* 226.

16. McWilliams, *Protectors,* 71–74. McWilliams provides a fascinating account of the way a witness bearing the wrong message is abused in his discussion of the testimony of Dr. Woodward on 4 May 1937. See also Jerome L. Himmelstein, *The Strange Career of Marihuana: Politics and Ideology of Drug Control in America* (Westport, Conn.: Greenwood Press, 1983), 70–71; and Musto, *American Disease,* 227–28.

17. Some authors have argued that a crucial 1945 editorial in the *Journal of the American Medical Association* condemning the final report (after originally welcoming the early findings with some enthusiasm) was actually written by Anslinger. Himmelstein (*Strange Career,* 83–84) reviews these arguments.

18. Brecher et al., *Licit and Illicit Drugs,* 117.

19. All quotations of Coffee are from King, *Drug Hang-up,* 65.

20. Musto, *American Disease,* 231.

21. McWilliams, "Through the Past Darkly," 370.

22. Kinder, "Shutting Out the Evil," 484.

23. Trebach, *Heroin Solution,* 164.

24. Cited in McWilliams, "Through the Past Darkly," 371; and Musto, *American Disease,* 231.

25. This stepping-stone or gateway theory, first introduced by the FBN in 1949, became common thereafter despite lack of evidence that marijuana led to heroin use any more than alcohol or tobacco did. The theory was frequently mentioned by FBN officials in congressional testimony and was picked up in periodical articles that began to speak of the progression from marijuana to heroin as a "tragically familiar story." Himmelstein, *Strange Career,* 85.

26. Joint Committee of the American Bar Association and the American Medical Association on Narcotic Drugs, *Drug Addiction: Crime or Disease?* (Bloomington: Indiana University Press, 1961), 19.

27. Karl M. Bowman, "Some Problems of Addiction," in *Problems of Addiction and Habituation,* ed. Paul H. Hoch and Joseph Zubin (New York: Grune and Stratton, 1958), 171.

28. Chein et al., *The Road to H,* 371–72, 379.

29. Editorial, *Wall Street Journal,* 17 April 1963.

30. Editorial, *New York Times,* 27 February 1965.

31. Musto, *American Disease,* 235.

32. Ibid., 237.

33. Eldridge, *Narcotics and the Law,* 140–41.

34. Ibid., 133–34.

35. See critiques of this civil commitment in ibid., 143–44; and in National Commission on Marihuana and Drug Abuse, *Drug Use in America,* 261–67.

36. House Committee on Government Operations, *Role of Demand Reduction,* 46.

37. Trebach, *Heroin Solution,* 233, 241.

38. Musto, *American Disease,* 259.

39. House Committee on Government Operations, *Role of Demand Reduction*, 47.

40. About 80 percent of drug-abuse clients in the early 1970s were heroin addicts. Barry S. Brown, "The Growth of Drug Abuse Treatment Systems," in *Handbook of Drug Control in the United States,* ed. James A. Inciardi (New York: Greenwood Press, 1990), 59.

41. Ibid., 56; and George De Leon, "Treatment Strategies," in *Handbook of Drug Control in the United States,* ed. James A. Inciardi (New York: Greenwood Press, 1990), 118.

42. William J. Bukoski, "Federal Approach to Prevention," in *Handbook of Drug Control in the United States,* ed. James A. Inciardi (New York: Greenwood Press, 1990), 101.

43. Quoted in ibid., 102.

44. Brecher et al., *Licit and Illicit Drugs,* 137, 71.

45. Epstein, *Agency of Fear,* 127–28.

46. Nixon's SAODAP considered methadone maintenance a key weapon in the war against heroin addiction and crime, and Nixon selected a medical doctor, Dr. Jerome H. Jaffe, to head the office. It was Jaffe who first earned the title of "drug czar." Trebach, *Heroin Solution,* 232–34; and Musto, *American Disease,* 258.

47. For a discussion of the politics of LSD, see Jay Stevens, *Storming Heaven: LSD and the American Dream* (New York: Atlantic Monthly Press, 1987). LSD was not illegal in the early 1960s and was not then considered a serious problem. But by 1966 prohibition campaigns had succeeded in criminalizing its possession in every state.

48. Himmelstein, *Strange Career,* 105. See also Morgan, *Drugs in America,* 161.

49. Patrick Anderson, *High in America* (New York: Viking Press, 1981), 106.

50. Richard Cowan, "American Conservatives Should Revise Their Position on Marihuana," *National Review,* 8 December 1972, 1344–46. Cited in Himmelstein, *Strange Career,* 105.

51. Quoted in Anderson, *High in America,* 92.

52. Private distribution of small amounts of marijuana for no profit should be legal, and public use or possession of more than an ounce of marijuana should be punishable by a fine of up to $100.

53. Himmelstein, *Strange Career,* 104–5.

54. Among eighteen- to twenty-one-year-olds, 40 percent had tried marijuana. National Commission on Marihuana and Drug Abuse, *Marihuana: A Signal of Misunderstanding* (Washington, D.C.: U.S. Government Printing Office, 1972), 32–33.

55. Cited in Himmelstein, *Strange Career,* 109–14.

56. Morgan, *Drugs in America,* 164.

57. Himmelstein, *Strange Career,* 145.

58. Ibid., 103–4. The eleven states, with about a third of the U.S. population, were Oregon, Alaska, Maine, Colorado, California, Ohio, Minnesota, Mississippi, Nebraska, New York, and North Carolina.

59. For a discussion of these state struggles over decriminalization, see Anderson, *High in America*, 121–23, 150–68.

60. Musto, *American Disease*, 266.

61. Ibid., 267.

62. Decriminalization proposals were seriously considered in Congress, but they were sidelined, at least in part because of the fact and manner of Bourne's departure. Bourne resigned from the administration after allegations that he had used cocaine at a party given by a prolegalization group, NORML. The allegations were made by NORML's director, who was angry at Bourne for not stopping Mexican efforts to spray marijuana with paraquat and thus potentially endangering Americans who smoked the paraquat-laced marijuana. (These charges came in the context of another problem Bourne faced, when it was revealed that in July 1978 he had written a prescription for methaqualone tablets for an aide who was suffering from nervousness and sleeplessness. To keep her record clear of any indication of emotional problems, he wrote the prescription for a fictitious patient. His opponents turned this into a national scandal, and in this context, the NORML charges of cocaine use forced him to resign.) Bourne's resignation removed a key manager of the decriminalization legislative process, and the circumstances surrounding his departure made it difficult for the Carter administration to push for decriminalization, for fear of being considered soft on drugs. See Anderson, *High in America*, 274–91, 304; and Musto, *American Disease*, 268–69.

63. National Commission on Marihuana and Drug Abuse, *Marihuana*, 106.

64. In a 1968 memorandum to all field offices, Hoover wrote, "Since the use of marijuana and other narcotics is widespread among members of the New Left, you should be alert to opportunities to have them arrested by local authorities on drug charges." Anderson, *High in America*, 54.

65. See, for example, Morgan, *Drugs in America*, 164–65. The National Commission on Marihuana and Drug Abuse described the reactions of such conservatives: "Use of the drug is linked with idleness, lack of motivation, hedonism and sexual promiscuity. Many see the drug as fostering a counter-culture which conflicts with basic moral precepts as well as with the operating functions of our society. The 'dropping out' or rejection of the established value system is viewed with alarm. Marihuana becomes more than a drug; it becomes a symbol of the rejection of cherished values." National Commission on Marihuana and Drug Abuse, *Marihuana*, 8–9.

66. See, for example, Morgan, *Drugs in America*, 164–65.

67. John Kaplan, *Marijuana—The New Prohibition* (New York: World Publishing Co., 1970), 9.

68. Cited in Himmelstein, *Strange Career*, 132.

69. On the NFP and the mobilization of support for the Reagan antidrug offensive, see also Musto, *American Disease*, 270–73; and Gordon, *Return of the Dangerous Classes*, 130–33.

CHAPTER 6

1. Elaine B. Sharp, in *The Dilemma of Drug Policy in the United States* (New York: HarperCollins, 1994), examines this lack of reevaluation, drawing

on the academic literature on agenda setting and the policy process. Little of the "evaluative information" on drug policy seems to affect the drug-policy agenda, she argues, and she offers a number of explanations. One factor she emphasizes is the initial "problem definition," which continues to track policy toward failure. Another is the role of the "political stream," which is often more important than evaluative information in shaping drug policy. Sharp is particularly concerned with the role played by "enforcement-oriented interests" (and, more recently, by treatment and prevention interests). She points also to "blame avoidance" mechanisms that allow public officials to avoid responsibility for failed policies. In another perceptive study of the process of policymaking (including drug policymaking), Frank R. Baumgartner and Bryan D. Jones (*Agendas and Instability in American Politics* [Chicago: University of Chicago Press, 1993]) analyze how issues and agendas come to be defined, maintained, and changed.

2. Trebach, *Heroin Solution*, 231.

3. "Text of Nixon Message on Plan to Attack Drug Abuse," *Congressional Quarterly Almanac* 24 (1969):57A.

4. "President's Message on Drug Control Programs," *Congressional Quarterly Almanac* 26 (1971):94A.

5. Epstein, *Agency of Fear*, 178; see also pp. 165–72.

6. Ibid., 173–82.

7. "President's Message on Drug Control Programs," 95A.

8. Epstein, *Agency of Fear*, 83–92; Musto, *American Disease*, 256–57.

9. Peter Goldberg, "Federal Government's Response to Illicit Drugs, 1969–1978," in *The Facts About "Drug Abuse,"* The Drug Abuse Council (New York: Free Press, 1980), 57.

10. Musto, *American Disease*, 234, 239–41.

11. Goldberg, "Federal Government's Response," 29, 39.

12. See, for example, "Police Terror," *New York Times*, 2 July 1973. See also Epstein, *Agency of Fear*, esp. 18–20, 212–16.

13. Wisotsky, *Beyond the War on Drugs*, 250.

14. The treatment budget increased from about $34 million in fiscal 1970 to about $329 million in fiscal 1974. Goldberg, "Federal Government's Response," 57.

15. Ibid., 42.

16. Ibid., 45; and, more generally, 20–62.

17. Domestic Council Drug Abuse Task Force, "White Paper on Drug Abuse: A Report to the President from the Domestic Council Drug Abuse Task Force" (Washington, D.C.: U.S. Government Printing Office, 1975), 5.

18. "Drug Law Revision" [text of President Carter's message to Congress], *Congressional Quarterly Almanac* 32 (1977):41E.

19. Ibid.

20. "Senate-Passed Criminal Code Dies in the House," *Congressional Quarterly Almanac* 33 (1978):165–71.

21. Goldberg, "Federal Government's Response," 57; and Office of National Drug Control Policy, *National Drug Control Strategy: Budget Summary* (1995), 235–38.

22. Office of National Drug Control Policy, *National Drug Control Strategy: Budget Summary* (1995), 235–38.

23. Brecher et al., *Licit and Illicit Drugs*, 302–5. On pages 304–5 Brecher and his co-editors continue:

> The decade [of the 1960s] began with almost all stimulants being supplied by reputable manufacturers; their low-cost amphetamines had almost driven cocaine off the market. The withdrawal of intravenous amphetamines from the legal market opened the door for the illicit speed labs. The Drug Abuse Control Amendments of 1965 curbed the direct diversion of legal amphetamines to the black market; this opened the door for the smuggling of exported amphetamines back into the United States. By 1969, law-enforcement efforts had raised black-market amphetamine prices and curbed amphetamine supplies sufficiently to open the door for renewed cocaine smuggling.

24. According to NIDA, 4.4 million people had used cocaine within the past thirty days; at least 9.7 million, within the past year; and at least 15 million, at least once at some time in the past. These figures, which represent a 250 to 300 percent increase over the NIDA survey in 1977, were considered low by other official estimates. Wisotsky, *Beyond the War on Drugs*, 12–14.

25. Bruce D. Johnson and John Muffler, "Sociocultural Aspects of Drug Use and Abuse in the 1990s," in *Substance Abuse: A Comprehensive Text*, ed. Joyce H. Lowinson, Pedro Ruiz, Robert B. Millman, and John G. Langrod, 2d ed. (Baltimore, Md.: Williams and Wilkins, 1992), 124.

26. Ibid.

27. See Musto, *American Disease*, 274; and Wisotsky, *Beyond the War on Drugs*, 7.

28. See, for example, the discussion in Reinarman and Levine, "Crack in Context," 537–39, 555–59.

29. Wisotsky, *Beyond the War on Drugs*, 250; Office of National Drug Control Policy, *National Drug Control Strategy: Budget Summary* (Washington, D.C.: U.S. Government Printing Office, 1994), 23, 184–85.

30. Trebach, *Great Drug War*, 150–52.

31. Wisotsky, *Beyond the War on Drugs*, 99–100.

32. Trebach, *Great Drug War*, 152.

33. Leslie Maitland, "President Gives Plan to Combat Drug Networks," *New York Times*, 15 October 1982.

34. "Major Crime Package Cleared by Congress," *Congressional Quarterly Almanac* 40 (1984):213–24.

35. Wisotsky, *Beyond the War on Drugs*, 5. For a full discussion of the role of the media in the war against cocaine, see Jimmie L. Reeves and Richard Campbell, *Cracked Coverage: Television News, the Anti-Cocaine Crusade, and the Reagan Legacy* (Durham, N.C.: Duke University Press, 1994).

36. "Major Crime Package Cleared by Congress."

37. Trebach, *Great Drug War*, 184.

38. "Text of the Address by President Bush," *Washington Post*, 6 September 1989.

39. Kitty Dumas, "Weighing the Price of Enforcement Against the Record of Treatment," *Congressional Quarterly*, 6 April 1991, 860–61.

40. Jo Anne Kawell, "Drug Wars: The Rules of the Game," *NACLA Report on the Americas* 23, no. 6(1990):9.

41. "National Drug Control Strategy: Budget Summary" (Washington, D.C.: The White House, 1992), 23.

42. Office of National Drug Control Policy, *National Drug Control Strategy: Budget Summary* (Washington, D.C.: U.S. Government Printing Office, 1994), 184–85.

43. "Martinez to follow Bennett as Drug Czar," *Congressional Quarterly Almanac* 44 (1990):503.

44. Joseph B. Treaster, "Some Think the War on Drugs Is Being Waged on Wrong Front," *New York Times,* 28 July 1992.

45. Analysis by Robert Lichter, Center for Media and Public Affairs, cited in Michael Oreskes, "Drug War Underlines Fickleness of Public," *New York Times,* 6 September 1990.

46. "Off with Their Heads? Thoughts from the Drug Czar," *Washington Post,* 20 June 1989, 21.

47. Benjamin and Miller, *Undoing Drugs,* 179.

48. *Washington Post*/ABC News poll, cited in Tom Wicker, "The Wartime Spirit," *New York Times,* 3 October 1989.

49. Michael Kramer, "Clinton's Drug Policy Is a Bust," *Time,* 20 December 1993, 35.

50. William J. Bennett and John P. Walters, "Suddenly Losing the War Against Drugs," commentary, *Washington Times,* 7 February 1995. Walters was ONDCP's deputy director during the Bush administration.

51. Quoted in Francis Wilkinson, "A Separate Peace," *Rolling Stone,* 5 May 1994, 26.

52. Brown, Testimony.

53. "Top Cop in the War on Drugs," *San Francisco Chronicle,* 12 March 1995.

54. Office of National Drug Control Policy, *National Drug Control Strategy* (1994), 23.

55. "Top Cop in the War on Drugs."

56. De Benedictis, "How Long Is Too Long?" 75, 77.

57. U.S. Department of Justice, *An Analysis of Non-Violent Drug Offenders with Minimal Criminal Histories* (Washington, D.C., 1994), 1–12.

58. Michael Massing, "The Longest War," *Rolling Stone,* 20 April 1995, 44.

59. Douglas Jehl, "Clinton to Use Drug Plan to Fight Crime," *New York Times,* 10 February 1994.

60. Quoted in Massing, "The Longest War," 45.

61. "Appropriations: Treasury/Postal Service," *Congressional Quarterly Almanac,* 1993, 688.

62. "House Votes to Keep ONDCP on Short Leash," *Alcoholism and Drug Abuse Week,* 13 December 1993, 4.

63. Jerry Seper, "Criticism of FBI-DEA Merger Grows," *Washington Times,* 30 September 1993.

64. Ibid.; and Jerry Seper, "R.I.P. for the DEA?" *Washington Times,* 12 October 1993.

65. Office of National Drug Control Policy, *National Drug Control Strategy: Budget Summary* (1994), 50–51. Administration officials tried to reassure

Congress that the money saved would still go into the overseas war on drugs but argued it could be better used for the other element of the drug war abroad, the war against drug production—a dubious proposition, given the enormous evidence of the flaws in the war on drug producers in the Andes and elsewhere.

66. Office of National Drug Control Policy, *National Drug Control Strategy: Budget Summary* (1995), 235.

67. Office of National Drug Control Policy, *National Drug Control Strategy* (1994), 2.

68. Clinton did not press hard for his prevention initiatives either. As a result, Congress cut the fiscal 1995 request for $660 million for school-based prevention programs to $87 million. Office of National Drug Control Policy, *National Drug Control Strategy: Budget Summary* (1995), 17.

69. The quotations are from John Schwartz, "Reports Back Needle Exchange Programs," *Washington Post*, 16 February 1995; and Saabin Russell, "CDC Endorses Needle Swaps," *San Francisco Chronicle*, 8 March 1995.

70. The Crime Control Act provides that by 1997 all eligible inmates must receive six to twelve months of residential drug treatment. Office of National Drug Control Policy, *National Drug Control Strategy: Budget Summary* (1995), 17, 57.

71. Brown still said the new budget would open up treatment slots for another 140,000 people but claimed the extra funds would come through efficiency savings by consolidating treatment money into block grants for the states. Richard Whitmire, "Clinton Unveils Drug Strategy, Some Experts Disagree on Focus," *Gannett News Service,* 7 February 1995.

72. Office of National Drug Control Policy, *National Drug Control Strategy: Budget Summary* (1995), 12, 238. These figures do not include funds for research, nor do they include the funds for increased police forces that were included as a prevention item in the Clinton budget.

73. See John Dillon, "Clinton Adds an Ounce of Prevention to Drug War," *Christian Science Monitor,* 11 February 1994; Robert C. Bonner, Testimony before the Subcommittee on National Security, International Relations, and Criminal Justice, Committee on Government Reform and Oversight, U.S. House of Representatives, 9 March 1995; and Jerry Seper, "GOP Senators Vow to Give Priority to War on Drugs," *Washington Times,* 24 December 1994.

74. See William J. Bennett, Testimony before the Committee on the Judiciary, U.S. Senate, 10 February 1995; Penny Bender, "Biden: GOP-Led Congress, Clinton Fall Short in Drug War," *Gannett News Service,* 10 February 1995; Bonner, Testimony; and Michael Hedges, "Bipartisan Critics Rip Clinton's Drug Policy," *Washington Times,* 7 March 1995.

75. Dillon, "Clinton Adds an Ounce of Prevention to Drug War."

76. All figures are from Office of National Drug Control Policy, *National Drug Control Strategy* (1995), 144–45.

77. See U.S. Department of Justice, Drug Enforcement Administration, "A Chronicle of Federal Drug Law Enforcement," *Drug Enforcement* 7, no. 2 (1980):esp. 52–64.

78. Office of National Drug Control Policy, *National Drug Control Strategy: Budget Summary* (1994), 12.

79. See U.S. Department of Justice, Drug Enforcement Administration, *Briefing Book* (Washington, D.C., 1990), 7; and Office of National Drug Control Policy, *National Drug Control Strategy: Budget Summary* (1992), 90–92.

80. Office of National Drug Control Policy, *National Drug Control Strategy: Budget Summary* (1995), 228.

81. This is out of a total 1995 drug-control budget of about $13.3 billion. Ibid., 235–38.

82. Office of National Drug Control Policy, *National Drug Control Strategy: Budget Summary* (1994), 75–118.

83. Ibid., 159–60.

84. Ibid., 23.

85. Ibid., 184–85; and Office of National Drug Control Policy, *National Drug Control Strategy* (1995), 235–36. This military drug-enforcement budget is the sum of the Defense Department's budget for interdiction and its budget for assisting state and local law-enforcement agencies; we have not included in these figures its budget for treatment, prevention, or research and development.

86. Sid Balman, Jr., "An Electronic Picket Faces Smugglers," *Air Force Times,* 18 June 1990.

87. Washington Office on Latin America, *Clear and Present Dangers,* 67–87. Some other figures demonstrate how dramatic this escalation was. For example, Navy ship days devoted to antidrug activity in the Caribbean increased by 80 percent and flight hours by 220 percent from 1989 to 1990. Drug-dedicated days in the Pacific increased by 150 percent and flight hours by 25 percent. In 1989 the airplanes of the U.S. Atlantic Command flew 5,400 hours on drug missions; in 1991 this increased to more than 37,000 hours. Charles Lane, "The Newest War," *Newsweek,* 6 January 1992, 19. The number of military flying hours devoted to drug interdiction increased by 700 percent between 1990 and 1992. At one point in fiscal 1990, 48 percent of all AWACS flying hours were related to drug control. Balman, "Electronic Picket."

88. Office of National Drug Control Policy, *National Drug Control Strategy: Budget Summary* (1994), 63.

89. Ibid., 67.

90. Ibid., 140–41.

91. Ibid., 144.

92. Note that the number of drug defendants per case is estimated at 1.95. See ibid., 71–74.

93. Ibid.

94. National Commission on Marihuana and Drug Abuse, *Drug Use in America,* 282.

95. Lawrence Korb, Assistant Secretary of Defense, quoted in "Faced with Peace, Pentagon Wants to Enlist in Drug War," *The State* (Columbia, S.C.), 17 December 1989.

96. Ibid. Military officials have made other, similar arguments. For example, Lt. Charley L. Diaz explained: "DoD should consider expanding its funding justification to include increased federal funds for its 'new' drug detection and monitoring mission. . . . Shifting the emphasis of a portion of DoD's budget toward its new peace-time mission will help DoD retain certain resources and manpower

while satisfying domestic pressure to increase the drug interdiction effort."
Charley L. Diaz, "DoD Plays in the Drug War," *Proceedings/Naval Review* 116,
no. 5 (1990):84, 86.

97. David C. Morrison, "Police Action," *National Journal* 24, no. 5
(1992):267–70.

98. Ibid. Similarly, the North American Aerospace Defense Command
(NORAD), built in the 1960s and 1970s to track incoming Soviet bombers and
missiles, sustained its budget by tracking drug smugglers in the early 1990s. Eric
Schmitt, "Colorado Bunker Built for Cold War Shifts Focus to Drug Battle,"
New York Times, 18 July 1993.

99. Opening statement of Chairman Charles Rangel. U.S. Congress, House,
Select Committee on Narcotics Abuse and Control, *Drug Interdiction: Hearing
before the Select Committee on Narcotics Abuse and Control,* 100th Cong., 1st
sess., 30 April 1987, 55–56.

100. According to one report, "a high-level State Department field coordinator scathingly denounced to subcommittee staff DEA's ability to work with local anti-narcotics police and Peruvian naval forces in riverine operations and
later added that he wants DEA entirely out of anti-drug activities in the Upper
Huallaga Valley." U.S. Congress, Senate, Committee on Governmental Affairs,
Report of the Permanent Subcommittee on Investigation, 101st Cong., 2d sess.,
6 February 1990, 10–11.

101. Associate Attorney General Stephen B. Trott. U.S. Congress, House, Select Committee on Narcotics Abuse and Control, *Drug Interdiction,* 46.

102. Warren G. Woodfork, Sr., Superintendent of Police, New Orleans Po-
lice Department, Prepared remarks. U.S. Congress, House, Select Committee on
Narcotics Abuse and Control, *The Drug Enforcement Crisis at the Local Level:
Hearing before the Select Committee on Narcotics Abuse and Control,* 101st
Cong., 1st sess., 31 May 1989, 183–205.

103. Joseph E. Kelly, Prepared testimony, U.S. Congress, House, Subcommittee on Legislation and National Security, Committee on Government Operations, *The Drug War: Colombia Is Implementing Antidrug Efforts, but Impact
Is Uncertain,* 103d Cong., 1st sess., 5 October 1993.

104. National Commission on Marihuana and Drug Abuse, *Drug Use in
America,* 282.

105. Ibid., 227.

106. To name one example: the futility of earlier efforts to stop drug dealers
from hiding their profits in legitimate banks and businesses led the Treasury Department to develop a broad-ranging "financial crimes enforcement strategy" in
1989. As part of its plan, the Treasury Department convinced Congress to create yet another agency in April 1990 to try to stop drug traffickers, through attacking money-laundering operations: the Financial Crimes Enforcement Network. It was to serve as "the central source for systematic identification,
collation, and analysis of financial and other information to assist in the investigation and prosecution of drug-related financial crimes." By 1994 its budget
had increased from $10.6 million to about $14.6 million. Office of National
Drug Control Policy, *National Drug Control Strategy: Budget Summary* (1994),
156.

107. Office of National Drug Control Policy, *National Drug Control Strategy* (1991), 102–3.

108. Woodfork, Remarks. At the national level, the Bush administration publicly recognized this problem in its 1991 *National Drug Control Strategy.* The success of the drug war meant that "prison overcrowding is likely to continue, posing difficult policy choices." Its solution: more prisons and more funds for technical assistance and training programs for state and local corrections staff. Office of National Drug Control Policy, *National Drug Control Strategy* (1991), 39–40.

CHAPTER 7

1. "Congress Clears Massive Anti-Drug Measure," *Congressional Quarterly Almanac* 42 (1987):92–106; and "Election-Year Anti-Drug Bill Enacted," *Congressional Quarterly Almanac* 44 (1989):85–111.

2. "Election-Year Anti-Drug Bill Enacted."

3. U.S. Congress, House, Select Committee on Narcotics Abuse and Control, *Implementation of Provisions of the Anti-Drug Abuse Act of 1986,* 100th Cong., 1st sess., 1987.

4. Tom Kenworthy, "Liberals Call House Drug Bill an Assault on the Constitution," *Washington Post,* 19 September 1988.

5. A review of *Congressional Quarterly Almanac* from 1968 through 1995 establishes this pattern. Two exceptions (1971 and 1979) involved the extension of additional moneys and the reauthorization of funding for existing programs, respectively. A third exception was 1989, when increased funding for law enforcement in the war on drugs was approved through the midyear supplemental spending bill, and two presidential initiatives cleared Congress: the Drug Free Schools and Communities Act and the president's Andean Initiative.

6. "Four Major Crime Bills Cleared 91st Congress," *Congressional Quarterly Almanac* 26 (1970):125.

7. Polls indicate that the drug issue topped the list of public concerns in 1986, 1988, and 1989; drugs and crime ranked second, after the economy, in 1992. See, for example, Julie Rovner, "Reagan, Senate Republicans Join Drug War," *Congressional Quarterly,* 20 September 1986, 2191–97; "Election-Year Anti-Drug Bill Enacted" *Congressional Quarterly Almanac;* Richard Morin, "Drug Abuse Leads Nation's Worries," *Washington Post,* 23 August 1989; and discussion with Richard Morin, 25 March 1992.

8. On the general dynamics of credit claiming and blame avoidance, see David Mayhew, *Congress: The Electoral Connection* (New Haven, Conn.: Yale University Press, 1974); Morris P. Fiorina, *Congress: Keystone of the Washington Establishment* (New Haven, Conn.: Yale University Press, 1977); and R. Kent Weaver, "The Politics of Blame Avoidance," *Journal of Public Policy* 6, no. 4 (1987):371–98.

9. "Congress Clears Massive Anti-Drug Measure."

10. Ibid.

11. Ibid.

12. Ibid.

13. Rovner, "Reagan, Senate Republicans Join Drug War" *Congressional Quarterly.*

14. "Congress Clears Massive Anti-Drug Measure."

15. Ibid. Remarkably, this was a year of great caution in congressional spending (Congress was acting under the constraints of the 1985 Gramm-Rudman antideficit law), yet Congress approved full funding for the drug bill even though this funding pushed the bill over budget for the year.

16. "Four Key Issues Playing Role in Congressional Contests," *Congressional Quarterly,* 18 October 1986, 2599.

17. Ibid.

18. McWilliams, "Through the Past Darkly," 376.

19. Phil Kuntz, "Anti-Drug Plan: Surviving the Legislative Wringer," *Congressional Quarterly,* 17 December 1988, 3516–21.

20. "Second Thoughts on the Military as Narcs," *Washington Post,* 15 June 1988.

21. "Republican Party Issues Detailed, Long Platform," *Congressional Quarterly Almanac* 44 (1989):46A–75A.

22. Ibid. Point 13 reads: "In addition to our enforcement activities, we encourage drug education in our schools. . . . Cutting down on the demand for drugs will be of great assistance as we increase our enforcement efforts to reduce drug supply."

23. "Text of 1988 Democratic Party Platform," *Congressional Quarterly Almanac* 44 (1989):87A–90A.

24. "Republican Party Issues Detailed, Long Platform."

25. "Election-Year Anti-Drug Bill Enacted"; and Christine C. Lawrence, "Parties Fighting Hard for Lead on Drug Issue," *Congressional Quarterly,* 18 June 1988, 1680–81.

26. "Smaller Anti-Drug Measures Pass in 1990," *Congressional Quarterly Almanac* 46 (1991):502–6.

27. Dumas, "Weighing the Price of Enforcement."

28. For most of the 1980s, the Democrats controlled both houses of Congress. Republican control of the Senate in the early 1980s was an exception.

29. "Election-Year Anti-Drug Bill Enacted."

30. U.S. Congress, House, Select Committee on Narcotics Abuse and Control, *National Drug Policy Board Strategy Plans,* 100th Cong., 2d sess., 14 April 1988, 27.

31. "Election-Year Anti-Drug Bill Enacted."

32. "Bush Signs Stripped-Down Crime Bill," *Congressional Quarterly Almanac* 46 (1991):486–99.

33. "Bush and Dukakis: Face to Face on Key Issues," *Congressional Quarterly Almanac* 44 (1989):91A–101A.

34. "Key Votes in 1988 Reflect a Partisan Standoff," *Congressional Quarterly Almanac* 44 (1989):3B–21B; and "Law/Judiciary," *Congressional Quarterly Almanac* 44 (1989):61–62.

35. "Legislative Summary: Surprisingly Busy Year for the 100th Congress," *Congressional Quarterly Almanac* 44 (1989):10–29.

36. After caving in on the issue of stiff fines for possession of personal-use amounts, for example, the Democrats were able to ensure that persons who were

caught had the right to a jury trial rather than a civil hearing, as the Republicans had proposed. And penalties for possession (loss of federal benefits, for example) were left up to a judge; they were not mandatory, as many Republicans would have preferred.

37. There were always some Democrats who challenged the get-tough orthodoxy. For example, when Bush nominated Bob Martinez to replace William Bennett as drug czar, Edward Kennedy and about a dozen other senators publicly opposed it, pointing to the escalation of harsh, punitive drug-control measures promoted by Martinez when he was governor of Florida and to his marginalization of drug treatment.

38. Joan Biskupic, "Bush's Anti-Drug Campaign Emphasizes Enforcement," *Congressional Quarterly*, 9 September 1989, 2312.

39. "Bush Signs Stripped-Down Crime Bill."

40. Joe Frolik, "Recession, War Divert Interest in Drug Problem," *Cleveland Plain Dealer*, 20 February 1994.

41. Statement of Senator Joseph R. Biden Jr., U.S. Senate, Committee on Judiciary, 10 February 1994.

42. Dillon, "Clinton Adds an Ounce of Prevention."

43. Peter J. Boyer, "Whip Cracker," *New Yorker*, 5 September 1994, 38.

44. Seper, "GOP Senators."

45. U.S. House of Representatives, Committee on Government Reform, "Clinton Drug Policy," 14 February 1995, press release.

CHAPTER 8

1. U.S. Ambassador to Bolivia Charles Bowers, interviewed by Peter Jennings of ABC News, "Special Report, The Cocaine War: Lost in Bolivia," 28 December 1992.

2. Office of National Drug Control Policy, *National Drug Control Strategy* (1991), 94.

3. George F. Will, "Our Harmful Drug Policy," *Washington Post*, 27 June 1993.

4. Robert C. Bonner, Letter to the Editor, *Washington Post*, 15 July 1993.

5. Daniel Patrick Moynihan, "Neutralizing 19th-Century Science," *Washington Post*, 26 July 1993.

6. Michael Hedges, "GOP: Spend More on Drug Interdiction," *Washington Times*, 15 June 1989.

7. Michael Isikoff, "Aerial Anti-Drug Plan Called Flawed," *Washington Post*, 9 June 1989.

8. U.S. Congress, House, Select Committee on Narcotics Abuse and Control, *Legalization of Illicit Drugs: Impact and Feasibility*, 100th Cong., 2d sess., 29 September 1988, part I, 47–48.

9. Douglas Waller, "Risky Business," *Newsweek*, 16 July 1990, 18.

10. U.S. Congress, House, Committee on Foreign Affairs, *Operation Snowcap: Past, Present and Future*, 101st Cong., 2d sess., 23 May 1990, 27.

11. John Dillin, "Congress Drafts Military to Battle Drug Traffickers," *Christian Science Monitor*, 23 March 1989.

12. House Select Committee on Narcotics Abuse and Control, *Legalization of Illicit Drugs*, Part I, 15.

13. Ibid., 81–84.

14. Mark Thomson, "Pentagon Questions Its Ability to Play Big Role in Drug War," *Philadelphia Inquirer*, 13 September 1989.

15. "Pentagon Drug War Called Expensive," *St. Louis Post Dispatch*, 17 September 1989; and Dillin, "Congress Drafts Military to Battle Drug Traffickers."

16. Sen. Pete Wilson (R-California), quoted in John M. Broder, "Wider Anti-Drug Role Announced for Pentagon," *Los Angeles Times*, 19 September 1989.

17. Brecher et al., *Licit and Illicit Drugs*, 57.

18. Ibid., 57.

19. Ira Eisenberg, "Elders Has the Idea: Just Say Maybe," *San Francisco Examiner*, 16 February 1994.

20. *Addiction Letter*, 6.

21. David Tuller, "Surgeon General's Remarks: Debate Changing in War on Drugs," *San Francisco Chronicle*, 11 December 1993.

22. "GOP Demands Elders Quit," *Rocky Mountain News*, 25 June 1994.

23. Thomas Brazaitis, "Elders Dares 'Heresy': Drug Quote Sets Off Stampede," *Cleveland Plain Dealer*, 12 December 1993.

24. "Elders Still Seeks Study on Legalizing Drugs," *New York Times*, 15 January 1994.

25. An excellent example of the difficulties many citizens have in seeing how drug policy—as opposed to crime itself—creates problems such as an overloaded criminal-justice system is provided by a 1987 focus-group study prepared for the Edna McConnell Clark Foundation in 1987. Respondents had difficulty seeing any connection between mandatory sentencing and prison overcrowding, and many were resistant to seeing the connection when it was explained to them. John Doble, *Crime and Punishment: The Public's View* (New York: Public Agenda Foundation, 1987), esp. 33–34.

26. Joseph B. Treaster, "Some Think the War on Drugs Is Being Waged on Wrong Front," *New York Times*, 28 July 1992. Reuter concludes that the "owls" (the moderates) always lose to the "hawks" (the hard-liners) because they accept "the need for vigorous enforcement" and concede that enforcement budgets must be maintained at current levels. Their "timidity" in criticizing punitive policies precludes their "consideration of the negative consequences of that enforcement" and limits "their contribution to drug policy discussions." Peter Reuter, "The Punitive Trend of American Drug Policy," *Daedalus* 121, no. 3 (1992):17, 43–44.

27. "More Anti-Drug Bills Cleared in 1989," *Congressional Quarterly Almanac* 45 (1990):252–58.

28. Although treatment and prevention budgets were dwarfed by the increases in law-enforcement spending in the 1980s and early 1990s, the increased overall spending on drug control did mean that spending on treatment and prevention also expanded, from about $780 million in 1986 to about $4 billion in 1994. Office of National Drug Control Policy, *National Drug Control Strategy: Budget Summary* (1995):237–38.

29. "Election-Year Anti-Drug Bill Enacted"; and Lawrence, "Parties Fighting Hard for Lead on Drug Issue."

30. "Election-Year Anti-Drug Bill Enacted."

31. Ibid., 102.

32. Ibid.; and Lawrence, "Parties Fighting Hard for Lead on Drug Issue." Rep. Charles Rangel called it "hypocritical to go after drug users when there are no real government resources to help with drug treatment or rehabilitation." "Election-Year Anti-Drug Bill Enacted," 93.

33. "Election-Year Anti-Drug Bill Enacted," 102.

34. Rovner, "Reagan, Senate Republicans Join Drug War."

35. Kuntz, "Anti-Drug Plan."

36. "Congress Clears Massive Anti-Drug Measure."

37. "Election-Year Anti-Drug Bill Enacted."

38. "Conservative Coalition: Still Alive, But Barely," *Congressional Quarterly Almanac* 44 (1989):42B–48B.

39. "Bush Signs Stripped-Down Crime Bill."

40. Policymakers holding moderate or hard-line positions have never divided neatly or consistently along party lines. A tough Republican administration in the late 1960s introduced the nation's first large-scale experiment with federally funded treatment efforts, and even today each party has its hard-liners and its moderate advocates. However, the loudest advocates for the moderate position in the 1980s were the liberal Democrats; most of the hard-liners tended to be Republicans in the administration and in Congress.

41. For example, a program at the Medical University of South Carolina in Charleston employs the twin threats of jail time and public exposure to coerce pregnant women on drugs into treatment: "When pregnant women seek prenatal treatment at the hospital, staff members choose those whom they suspect of being drug users and, without informing the women, test them for drug use. If the test is positive, the woman is threatened with jail unless she signs up for treatment, agrees to have continuing drug tests and agrees to complete both drug treatment and prenatal care that the hospital prescribes." Philip J. Hilts, "Hospital Is Object of Rights Inquiry," *New York Times,* 6 February 1994.

42. David C. Lewis, "Medical and Health Perspectives on Failing U.S. Drug Policy," *Daedalus* 121, no. 3 (1992):169–71.

43. Ibid.

44. Currie, *Reckoning,* 194.

45. The federal government's first comprehensive study, authored by a panel led by Peter Lurie, confirmed this earlier research in a 1993 report. Philip J. Hilts, "Giving Addicts Clean Needles Cut Spread of AIDS, U.S. Study Finds," *New York Times,* 1 October 1993. For a review of recent research, see "Can Clean Needles Slow the AIDS Epidemic?"

46. "Can Clean Needles Slow the AIDS Epidemic?" 467. When members of a congressional committee argued in 1988 that "it was more of a priority to fight AIDS than to fight drug use," the committee "did not want to appear to condone illegal drug use by saying that if you are going to use drugs at least use a clean needle." "Election-Year Anti-Drug Bill Enacted." There were, however, some small victories for needle-exchange advocates. Moderates were able to in-

troduce language in the 1992 Alcohol, Drug Abuse, and Mental Health Association Reorganization Act (Public Law 102–321) that allowed the surgeon general to make a finding that needle exchange does not exacerbate drug use but does stop the spread of AIDS; such a finding would then allow federal money to go for needle exchange.

47. This opposition is particularly vocal in the African American community, including Rep. Charles Rangel (D-New York) and other black legislators. Other African American leaders, including past and present mayors of Baltimore, New Haven, New York City, and Washington, and some black legislators in California support NEPs. "Can Clean Needles Slow the AIDS Epidemic?" 466. For an analysis of black attitudes toward needle exchange, see Thomas and Quinn, "Burdens of Race and History," 320–347.

48. Falco, *Making of a Drug-Free America,* 30.

49. National Commission on Acquired Immune Deficiency Syndrome, *Twin Epidemics,* 10.

50. "Can Clean Needles Slow the AIDS Epidemic?"; and Russell, "CDC Endorses Needle Swaps."

51. Ernest Drucker, "Drug Policy, Drug Treatment and Public Health" (report prepared for the American Foundation for AIDS Research, 15 September 1991), 119.

52. Ibid., 125. See also House Committee on Government Operations, *Role of Demand Reduction,* 63.

53. For example, when DEA agents bought methadone in a sting operation outside two New York City clinics (demonstrating that methadone was leaking into the black market), Rangel praised the DEA, declaring that methadone had become "part of the problem instead of part of the solution." He vowed to close down clinics that permitted such "diversion" of controlled drugs. (This example is presented in Drucker, *Drug Policy,* 125–26.)

54. Joseph B. Treaster, "Study Says Anti-Drug Dollars Are Best Spent on Treatment," *New York Times,* 19 June 1994. According to Treaster, the study said that "for every $34 million allocated to treatment, cocaine consumption would be reduced by 1 percent, or a little more than three tons. To achieve the same effect with enforcement . . . the Government would have to spend $246 million on domestic law enforcement or $366 million on anti-smuggling programs or $783 million for anti-drug programs in countries where cocaine was produced."

55. Interview with Mark Mauer, Assistant Director, Sentencing Project, Washington, D.C., 6 May 1993.

56. Interview with Linda Lewis, Director of Public Policy, National Association of State Alcohol and Drug Abuse Directors, 6 May 1992.

57. Interview with Lewis.

58. Treaster, "Study Says Anti-Drug Dollars Are Best Spent on Treatment."

59. Interview with Lewis.

60. Falco, *Making of a Drug-Free America,* 109.

61. W. John Moore, "Rethinking Drugs," *National Journal,* 2 February 1991, 271.

62. Currie, *Reckoning,* 244.

63. Quoted in ibid., 231.

64. Gilbert J. Botvin, "Substance Abuse Prevention: Theory, Practice, and Effectiveness," in *Drugs and Crime,* ed. Michael Tonry and James Q. Wilson (Chicago: University of Chicago Press, 1990), 475–76. Botvin does argue that moral appeals might have some effect on individuals who are highly religious. Falco points out the 1960s reaction to the movie *Reefer Madness,* made by Anslinger's Federal Bureau of Narcotics in 1937. A successful, young, white middle-class man turns violent and abusive after a puff of marijuana and ruins his life. The movie may have reflected prevailing attitudes toward drugs, but by the 1960s this kind of information was so completely at odds with the actual effects of marijuana that it became a cult movie among young drug users. Falco, *Making of a Drug-Free America,* 33.

65. For a discussion of the research on what works and fails and on some of the promising prevention programs being tried, see Falco, *Making of a Drug-Free America,* 32–70; and Botvin, "Substance Abuse Prevention," 488–89.

66. Musto, *American Disease,* 270, 272.

67. U.S. Department of Health and Human Services, Office for Substance Abuse Prevention, *Prevention Plus II: Tools for Creating and Sustaining Drug-Free Communities* (Rockville, Md., 1989), 391, 392.

68. Ibid., 392.

69. House Committee on Government Operations, *Role of Demand Reduction,* 40.

PART 3

1. This subtle exercise of power—how ruling ideas keep problems from ever even getting on the political agenda—is explored by Steven Lukes, *Power: A Radical View* (London: Macmillan, 1974).

2. Among the recent books that present thoughtful alternatives are Kleiman, *Against Excess;* Falco, *Making of a Drug-Free America;* Currie, *Reckoning;* and Zimring and Hawkins, *Search for Rational Drug Control.* See also National Commission on Marihuana and Drug Abuse, *Drug Use in America.*

CHAPTER 9

1. Many legalization advocates cite as the touchstone for such arguments John Stuart Mill's essay *On Liberty.*

2. Duke and Gross, *America's Longest War,* 152.

3. *Wall Street Journal,* 27 October 1989.

4. See, for example, William F. Buckley Jr., "Drug Talk Across the Way," *National Review,* 5 May 1989, 63.

5. Milton Friedman, "An Open Letter to Bill Bennett," *Wall Street Journal,* 7 September 1989.

6. Not all debate on legalization is unreasoned and rhetorical. See, for example, Rod L. Evans and Irwin M. Berent, *Drug Legalization: For and Against* (La Salle, Ill.: Open Court, 1992); Melvyn B. Krauss and Edward P. Lazear, eds.,

Searching for Alternatives: Drug-Control Policy in the United States (Stanford, Calif.: Hoover Institution Press, 1991).

7. Ethan Nadelmann, "Thinking Seriously About Alternatives to Drug Prohibition," *Daedalus* 121, no. 3 (1992):90–91. Articulate examples of the case for free-market legalization include Thomas Szasz, *Our Right to Drugs: The Case for a Free Market* (New York: Praeger, 1992); Douglas N. Husak, *Drugs and Rights* (New York: Cambridge University Press, 1992); David Boaz, *The Crisis in Drug Prohibition* (Washington, D.C.: Cato Institute, 1990); and Milton Friedman, "The War We Are Losing," in *Searching for Alternatives: Drug-Control Policy in the United States,* ed. Melvyn B. Krauss and Edward P. Lazear (Stanford, Calif.: Hoover Institution Press, 1991).

8. Nadelmann, "Thinking Seriously About Alternatives," 93.

9. See, for example, Baltimore Mayor Kurt L. Schmoke, "Foreword," in Staley, *Drug Policy,* xiii–xvi. Many of the policies suggested by our public-health approach below would be embraced by pragmatists like Nadelmann and Schmoke.

10. Evidence shows, for example, that repeal of alcohol prohibition did increase the harm caused by alcohol abuse. See, for example, Mark H. Moore, "Actually, Prohibition Was a Success," *New York Times,* 16 October 1989. But Levine and Reinarman emphasize that prohibition was replaced by regulation, not a free market, and "post prohibition regulatory policies kept alcohol use sufficiently low that it was not until the end of the 1960s, 35 years after repeal, that per capita alcohol consumption rose to the [preprohibition] levels of 1915." They also point to research in Australia and England which showed that tighter regulation substantially reduced consumption and cirrhosis mortality in the absence of prohibition in comparison with the laxer regulations in the United States. Harry G. Levine and Craig Reinarman, "From Prohibition to Regulation: Lessons from Alcohol Policy for Drug Policy," *Milbank Quarterly* 69, no. 3 (1991):470.

11. See, for example, Mark H. Moore, "Drugs, the Criminal Law, and Administration of Justice," *Milbank Quarterly* 69, no. 4 (1991):529–60.

12. Rick Weinberg, "Dodgers Suspected Strawberry's Drug Use," *New York Times,* 6 April 1994.

13. Useful histories of public health in the United States include John Duffy, *The Sanitarians: A History of American Public Health* (Urbana: University of Illinois Press, 1990); George Rosen, *A History of Public Health* (Baltimore, Md.: Johns Hopkins University Press, 1993); Judith Walzer Leavitt and Ronald L. Numbers, eds., *Sickness and Health in America: Readings in the History of Medicine and Public Health,* 2d rev. ed. (Madison: University of Wisconsin Press, 1985); and Mazyck P. Ravenel, *A Half Century of Public Health* (New York: Arno Press and the *New York Times,* 1970). Like any tradition, public health cannot be defined simply or easily: its advocates often emphasize different elements in its history, and it cannot be understood merely as what health departments do today.

14. Rosen, *History of Public Health,* 9–10.

15. Duffy traces even earlier public-health measures against epidemics like Asiatic cholera, yellow fever, and smallpox in the early 1800s. Duffy, *The Sanitarians,* chaps. 1–6.

16. A detailed account of these reforms can be found in ibid., esp. chaps. 9, 10, and 12.

17. Rosen, *History of Public Health,* 296–302.

18. Ibid., 395.

19. Ibid., 409. See also David Rosner and Gerald Markowitz, "The Early Movement for Occupational Safety and Health, 1900–1917," in *Sickness and Health in America: Readings in the History of Medicine and Public Health,* ed. Judith Walzer Leavitt and Ronald L. Numbers, 2d rev. ed. (Madison: University of Wisconsin Press, 1985), 513.

20. George Pickett and John J. Hanlon, eds., *Public Health: Administration and Practice,* 9th ed. (St. Louis, Mo.: Times Mirror/Mosby College Publishing, 1990), 293.

21. These clinics were themselves successors to the nineteenth-century dispensaries that had provided medical care for urban lower-income groups in the late nineteenth century. Duffy, *The Sanitarians,* 158–59.

22. Quoted in George Rosen, "The First Neighborhood Health Center Movement," in *Sickness and Health in America: Readings in the History of Medicine and Public Health,* ed. Judith Walzer Leavitt and Ronald L. Numbers, 2d rev. ed. (Madison: University of Wisconsin Press, 1985), 478–79.

23. For a discussion of these neighborhood health centers, see ibid., 482–83; and Alice Sardell, *The U.S. Experiment in Social Medicine: The Community Health Center Program, 1965–1986* (Pittsburgh, Pa.: University of Pittsburgh Press, 1988), 34–36.

24. Federal institutions entered into public health in the early decades of this century. Congress passed the Food and Drug Act in 1906 to regulate the manufacture, labeling, and sale of foods. The Marine Hospital Service was renamed the Public Health Service in 1912, and its modest programs in research, rural health, and venereal disease were expanded to include drug treatment for federal prisoners in the early 1930s. The Public Health Service began to expand more rapidly after 1939, when it was taken out of the Treasury Department and given a lead role in federal public health. The major public-health emphasis of the federal government before World War II was on funding public-health research, first through the National Hygienic Laboratory (founded in 1887) and then, more importantly, through its successor, the National Institutes of Health, created in 1930. The Children's Bureau was formed in 1912, and in 1922 it began to administer federal funds to provide assistance for states to promote maternal and child health—a forerunner of later federal-state partnerships during the New Deal (e.g., for campaigns against venereal disease and for training public-health personnel) and Johnson's Great Society programs of the 1960s (which created community health centers across the country and which provided block grants for state and county activities in general health, tuberculosis control, mental health, home health, and dental health). For summaries of the federal role in public health, see Institute of Medicine, *The Future of Public Health* (Washington, D.C.: National Academy Press, 1988), 66–71, 165–72. A summary of state and local public-health institutions can be found in Institute of Medicine, *Future of Public Health,* 172–90; and Pickett and Hanlon, *Public Health,* 97–120.

25. C.–E. A. Winslow, "The Untilled Field of Public Health," *Modern Medicine* 2 (1920):183, quoted in Pickett and Hanlon, *Public Health,* 5.

26. See, for example, the discussion of the "mobilization of bias" against social medicine in Sardell, *U.S. Experiment in Social Medicine,* chap. 2.

27. Duffy, *The Sanitarians,* 136.

28. These physician opponents of public health also fought against public treatment of the sick, requirements for reporting cases of tuberculosis and venereal disease, and attempts by public-health authorities to establish health centers to coordinate preventive and curative medical services. Paul Starr, *The Social Transformation of American Medicine* (New York: Basic Books, 1982), 181. This book provides an excellent social history of the emergence of the medical profession and its path to dominance over health care.

29. Duffy, *The Sanitarians,* 206.

30. Ibid., 273–75.

31. See, for example, Pickett and Hanlon, *Public Health,* 317–41.

32. Sardell, *U.S. Experiment in Social Medicine,* 34–36, 53–56. Some Office of Economic Opportunity health centers also helped community residents tackle economic and environmental issues. A clinic in Mississippi tackled malnutrition by constructing wells and establishing a farm cooperative to grow food, and in Brooklyn help was given to rehabilitate housing in the area. Sardell also analyzes the success of these centers; see pp. 225–33.

33. For a good introduction, see the collection of essays in Elizabeth Fee and Daniel M. Fox, eds., *AIDS: The Making of a Chronic Disease* (Berkeley: University of California Press, 1992).

34. Public-health measures were often particularly sensitive because the disastrous social consequences of AIDS were spread through the most private of acts: sexual intercourse, drug taking, and childbearing. For an excellent discussion of such issues, see Ronald Bayer, *Private Acts, Social Consequences: AIDS and the Politics of Public Health* (New Brunswick, N.J.: Rutgers University Press, 1991).

35. AZT also appears to prevent the transmission of the virus from infected mothers to their newborn children. Lawrence Altman, "In Major Finding, Drug Curbs H.I.V. Infection in Newborns," *New York Times,* 21 February 1994.

36. Elizabeth Fee and Daniel M. Fox, "Introduction: The Contemporary Historiography of AIDS," in *AIDS: The Making of a Chronic Disease,* ed. Elizabeth Fee and Daniel M. Fox (Berkeley: University of California Press, 1992), 4. Importantly, there were different interpretations of AIDS, even by those who took a public-health approach, when the epidemic was first identified in the early 1980s. Initially, many approached AIDS not as a chronic illness that would be with us for a long time but as a plague, "a sudden, time-limited, outbreak of infection" that needed to be ended with quarantine, isolation, and mass testing for the disease. That view had largely disappeared by the late 1980s.

37. In addition to those mentioned are public-health concerns with teen pregnancy, health care for the indigent, control of high blood pressure, Alzheimer's disease, and various injuries. See for example, Institute of Medicine, *Future of Public Health,* 21–32.

38. The public-health approach to mental illness had its origins in the 1920s and 1930s, but it only became prominent after World War II, which drew attention to the problem because about 1,750,000 men were rejected by the military for neuropsychiatric reasons. Several small groups pushed the National Mental Health Act through Congress in 1946. This led to the establishment of the National Institute of Mental Health in 1949 to conduct research. Federal spending for mental health jumped from $4.25 million in 1948 to about $176.4 million in 1964. Duffy, *The Sanitarians*, 267, 284.

39. Such sheltered care was once provided by state hospitals; with their decline and the move toward community mental health, a new form of sheltered care was needed. But attempts to create institutions like halfway houses, board-and-care homes, and family-care homes were severely restricted, especially after the early 1980s, due to cutbacks in federal funding, and many of the mentally ill who were poor were left without homes.

40. Henry A. Foley and Steven S. Sharfstein, *Madness and Government: Who Cares for the Mentally Ill?* (Washington, D.C.: American Psychiatric Press, 1983), 102, 111.

41. Robert H. Connery et al., *The Politics of Mental Health: Organizing Community Mental Health in Metropolitan Areas* (New York: Columbia University Press, 1968), 477.

42. For a review of some of the research on these stress factors, see Bernard L. Bloom, *Community Mental Health: A General Introduction* (Monterey, Calif.: Brooks/Cole Publishing Co., 1975), 79–95. For discussions of the importance of changing the social environment in preventing and treating mental illness, see, for example, Nolan Zane, Stanley Sue, Felipe G. Castro, and William George, "Service System Models for Ethnic Minorities," in *Reaching the Underserved, Mental Health Needs of Neglected Populations*, ed. Lonnie R. Snowden (Beverly Hills, Calif.: Sage Publications, 1982), 245–47; and M. B. Smith, "The Revolution in Mental Health Care—A 'Bold New Approach'?" *Trans-Action* 5 (1968):21.

43. On the relationship between such cuts and the expansion of drug treatment, see Keith Humphreys and Julian Rappaport, "From the Community Mental Health Movement to the War on Drugs: A Study in the Definition of Social Problems," *American Psychologist* 48, no. 8 (1993):892, 896.

44. Levine and Reinarman, "From Prohibition to Regulation," 470–75, 480. This article reviews alcohol control in the postprohibition period and examines lessons for drug control. In countries like Australia, where regulations were stricter than in the United States, the health damage of alcohol was reduced far more than in the United States. See, for example, Robin Room, "The Dialectic of Drinking in Australian Life: From the Rum Corps to the Wine Column," *Australian Drug and Alcohol Review* 7 (1988):413–37.

45. For a critique of the disease model, see Herbert Fingarette, *Heavy Drinking: The Myth of Alcoholism as a Disease* (Berkeley: University of California Press, 1988).

46. Pickett and Hanlon, *Public Health*, 480. See also Robin Room, "Alcohol Control and Public Health," *Annual Review of Public Health* 5 (1984):293–317.

On the comparative dangers of alcohol and illicit drugs, see Gordon, *Return of the Dangerous Classes,* 106–9.

47. See, for example, Levine and Reinarman, "From Prohibition to Regulation," 482.

48. For a discussion of public-health measures, see Pickett and Hanlon, *Public Health,* 479–82; Fingarette, *Heavy Drinking;* and Mark H. Moore and Dean R. Gerstein, *Alcohol and Public Policy: Beyond the Shadow of Prohibition* (Washington, D.C.: National Academy Press, 1981).

49. Brecher et al., *Licit and Illicit Drugs,* 229–31.

50. Roger Rosenblatt, "How Do They Live with Themselves," *New York Times Magazine,* 20 March 1994, 36.

51. For a review of public-health efforts and their impact, see U.S. Department of Health and Human Services, *U.S. Public Health Service: Reducing the Health Consequences of Smoking: 25 Years of Progress. A Report of the Surgeon General* (Washington, D.C., 1989).

52. Concern with the continued prevalence of smoking among teenagers, and how to regulate cigarette-industry advertisements and teenage access to cigarettes, is still a strong public-health focus. "Hooked on Tobacco: The Teen Epidemic," *Consumer Reports,* March 1995, 142–46.

53. Kleiman, *Against Excess,* 336–38.

54. Ann Devroy and John Schwartz, "Clinton Moves to Limit Teenage Smoking," *Washington Post,* 11 August 1995.

55. Among sources that explicitly outline a public-health agenda for drugs, the following were useful sources for us: James F. Mosher and Karen L. Yanagisako, "Public Health, Not Social Warfare: A Public Health Approach to Illegal Drug Policy," *Journal of Public Health Policy* 12, no. 3 (1991):278–323; and Jonas, "Public Health Approach," 928–43. Note that our aim here is not to come up with a list of new policies or a detailed drug strategy. A number of thoughtful reports and books have been written on this subject, many of which are cited below. A few explicitly base their policy suggestions on a public-health approach. See, for example, the National Commission on Marihuana and Drug Abuse, *Drug Use in America.* Others often include certain public-health considerations like measures to reduce the harm caused by drugs.

56. National Commission on Marihuana and Drug Abuse, *Drug Use in America,* 263, 407.

57. Johnson and Muffler, "Sociocultural Aspects of Drug Use and Abuse in the 1990s," 118–30; Richard Jacobson and Norman E. Zinberg, *The Social Basis of Drug Abuse Prevention* (Washington, D.C.: Drug Abuse Council, 1975); Chien et al., *The Road to H,* 1–319; Norma Finkelstein, "Treatment Programming for Alcohol and Drug-Dependent Pregnant Women," *International Journal of the Addictions* 28, no. 13 (1993):1275–1309; Dean R. Gerstein and Lawrence W. Green, *Preventing Drug Abuse: What Do We Know?* (Washington, D.C.: National Academy Press, 1993), 32–37; and, for a review of the literature, Mosher and Yanagisako, "Public Health, Not Social Warfare," 303–8.

58. Dean R. Gerstein and Henrick J. Harwood, ed., *Treating Drug Problems,* vol. 1 (Washington, D.C.: National Academy Press, 1990), 38–39.

59. National Commission on Marihuana and Drug Abuse, *Drug Use in America*, 205–6.

60. Gerstein and Green, *Preventing Drug Abuse*, 18–20.

61. For an early review of the research literature, see James V. DeLong, "The Drugs and Their Effects," in *Dealing with Drug Abuse: A Report to the Ford Foundation* (New York: Praeger, 1972), 62–122. For a more recent review, see Kleiman, *Against Excess*, 203–382; and Philip Hilts, "Is Nicotine Addictive? It Depends on Whose Criteria You Use," *New York Times*, 2 August 1994.

62. L. D. Johnston, P. M. O'Malley, and J. G. Bachman, *Drug Use, Drinking, and Smoking: National Survey Results from High School, College, and Young Adult Populations: 1975–1990, 1. High School Seniors* (Rockville, Md.: National Institute on Drug Abuse, 1991).

63. Gerstein and Green, for example, concluded: "Even in the case of a drug with as fearsome a popular reputation for inducing dependence as cocaine, most users do not progress to the point of dependence. It is sensible, then, to consider that every transition—nonuse to use, use to abuse, abuse to dependence—is an opportunity for preventive factors to operate, which both encourages and complicates the task of designing prevention interventions and measuring their effects." Gerstein and Green, *Preventing Drug Abuse*, 18.

CHAPTER 10

1. Quoted in Trebach and Zeese, *Drug Prohibition and the Conscience of Nations*, 47–48.

2. Eddy L. Engelsman, "The Pragmatic Strategies of the Dutch 'Drug Czar,'" in *Drug Prohibition and the Conscience of Nations*, ed. Arnold S. Trebach and Kevin B. Zeese (Washington, D.C.: Drug Policy Foundation, 1990), 51, 54. Engelsman directed the Alcohol, Drugs and Tobacco Branch of the Ministry of Welfare, Public Health and Cultural Affairs. See also Gordon, *Return of the Dangerous Classes*, 217.

3. Eddy L. Engelsman, "Drug Policy in the Netherlands from a Public Health Perspective," in *Searching for Alternatives: Drug-Control Policy in the United States*, ed. Melvyn B. Krauss and Edward P. Lazear (Stanford, Calif.: Hoover Institution Press, 1991), 171.

4. Gordon, *Return of the Dangerous Classes*, 217–23. See her discussion of European policy on pp. 211–24.

5. Botvin, "Substance Abuse Prevention," 475–76.

6. House Committee on Government Operations, *Role of Demand Reduction*, 3.

7. Jonas, "Public Health Approach," 937.

8. Patricia Bush, director of the Division of Children's Health Promotion at Georgetown University's Department of Community and Family Medicine, quoted in Amy Goldstein, "The Young in D.C. Meet Drugs Early," *Washington Post*, 31 August 1993.

9. For a discussion of the research on what works and fails and on some of the promising prevention programs being tried, see Gerstein and Green,

Preventing Drug Abuse; Falco, *Making of a Drug-Free America,* 32–70; and Botvin, "Substance Abuse Prevention," 488–99.

10. Johnson and Muffler, "Sociocultural Aspects of Drug Use and Abuse," 447–56. For a cautious evaluation, see Gerstein and Green, *Preventing Drug Abuse,* 100–102.

11. Todd Gitlin, "On Drugs and Mass Media in America's Consumer Society," quoted in Jonas, "Public Health Approach," 933.

12. See, for example, Jonas, "Public Health Approach," 933–34.

13. For an excellent analysis of this issue, see Currie, *Reckoning,* chap. 6.

14. See, for example, Nicholas Lemann, "The Myth of Community Development," *New York Times Magazine,* 9 January 1994, 54, 60.

15. Dr. Douglas Anglin, director of the Drug Abuse Research Center at the University of California at Los Angeles, interviewed by Falco in *Making of a Drug-Free America,* 111.

16. Even people who stop smoking often relapse three or four times before they succeed.

17. Gerstein and Harwood, *Treating Drug Problems,* 129.

18. Of those who left the program to seek treatment, 41 percent were black, 25 percent were Hispanic, and 34 percent were white—a far different racial and ethnic mix from that found among drug-dependent persons already in treatment in New Haven at the time (63 percent white, 27 percent black, and 9 percent Hispanic). "Can Clean Needles Slow the AIDS Epidemic?" 469.

19. *AIDS and Drug Misuse, Part 1: Report by the Advisory Council on the Misuse of Drugs* (London: HMSO, 1988); *AIDS and Drug Misuse, Part 2: Report by the Advisory Council on the Misuse of Drugs* (London: HMSO, 1989), quoted in David Turner, "Pragmatic Incoherence: The Changing Face of British Drug Policy," in *Searching for Alternatives: Drug-Control Policy in the United States,* ed. Melvyn B. Krauss and Edward P. Lazear (Stanford, Calif.: Hoover Institution Press, 1991), 184. On British approaches to heroin, see also Virginia Berridge, "AIDS, Drugs and History," *British Journal of Addiction* 87 (1992):363–70; and Edgar May, "Narcotics Addiction and Control in Great Britain," in *Dealing with Drug Abuse, A Report to the Ford Foundation* (New York: Praeger, 1972), 345–94.

20. Turner, "Pragmatic Incoherence," 186.

21. William E. Schmidt, "To Battle AIDS, Scots Offer Oral Drugs to Addicts," *New York Times,* 8 February 1993.

22. Gerry V. Stimson and Rachel Lart, "HIV, Drugs, and Public Health in England: New Words, Old Tunes," *International Journal of the Addictions* 26, no. 12 (1991):1266, 1269.

23. David P. Desmond and James F. Maddux, "Mexican-American Heroin Addicts," quoted in Currie, *Reckoning,* 246.

24. See, for example, Finkelstein, "Treatment Programming," 1275–1309.

25. Currie, *Reckoning,* 239; and, for a discussion of why addicts resist treatment, 226–37.

26. Ibid., 239, and, for a discussion of the literature on this issue, 226–41.

27. Statement of Thelma Brown, representative, Watts Health Foundation, Inc., before the Subcommittee on Legislation and National Security, 2 July 1990,

quoted in House Committee on Government Operations, *Role of Demand Reduction*, 71, 94.

28. Currie, *Reckoning*, 254–55.

29. The following account is drawn from Cathy Schneider, "Using Culture to Fight AIDS: Political Struggle in Williamsburg and the Origins of 'Musica against Drugs,'" (unpublished paper, 1994).

30. See Currie, *Reckoning*, chap. 6.

31. For a discussion of such programs, see Gerstein and Harwood, *Treating Drug Problems*, 114–19; L. F. Cook et al., "Treatment Alternatives to Street Crime," in *Compulsory Treatment of Drug Abuse: Research and Clinical Practice*, ed. C. G. Leukefeld and F. M. Tims, NIDA Research Monograph 86 (Rockville, Md.: National Institute on Drug Abuse, 1988), 99–105; and U.S. General Accounting Office, *Drug Control: Treatment Alternatives Program for Drug Offenders Needs Stronger Emphasis* (Washington, D.C., 1993).

32. For an overview of the legal and political history of civil commitment and a justification of it from a public-health perspective, see Lawrence O. Gostin, "Compulsory Treatment for Drug-dependent Persons: Justifications for a Public Health Approach to Drug Dependency," *Milbank Quarterly* 69, no. 4 (1991):561–93.

33. National Commission on Marihuana and Drug Abuse, *Drug Use in America*, 262.

34. Gerstein and Green, *Preventing Drug Abuse*, 18.

35. Estimates of the increase of such problems under a free-market drug regime vary widely. See, for example, Mark A. R. Kleiman, "Neither Prohibition nor Legalization," *Daedalus* 121, no. 3 (1992):70–71, 76; and Nadelmann, "Thinking Seriously About Alternatives," 105–8. See also James F. Mosher, "Drug Availability in a Public Health Perspective," in *Youth and Drugs: Society's Mixed Messages*, ed. H. Resnick (Rockville, Md.: Department of Health and Human Services, Public Health Service, Alcohol, Drug Abuse and Mental Health Administration, Office of Substance Abuse Prevention, 1990); and Room, "Alcohol Control and Public Health," 293–317.

36. Such a public-health classification, for example, would probably consider marijuana's harmful effects more like those of alcohol or tobacco and not place marijuana, as it is today, in the most dangerous category (so-called Schedule I drugs), with heroin and LSD. It would certainly allow marijuana to be used for medical purposes—to prevent nausea in cancer patients undergoing chemotherapy, for example. See American Medical Association, Council on Scientific Affairs, "Marijuana: Its Health Hazards and Therapeutic Potentials," *Journal of the American Medical Association* 246, no. 16(1981):1823–27; and Lester Grinspoon, *Marihuana, the Forbidden Medicine* (New Haven, Conn.: Yale University Press, 1993).

37. Postprohibition regulatory schemes, for example, encouraged the drinking of beer rather than hard liquor by making beer more widely available. See Levine and Reinarman, "From Prohibition to Regulation," 479, 482.

38. The full range of such alternatives is discussed in Kleiman, *Against Excess*, 335–58.

39. Benjamin and Miller offer a strong argument that national drug-prohibition statutes should be repealed and that each state should develop its own drug-regulatory policies. Benjamin and Miller, *Undoing Drugs,* chap. 11.

40. Kleiman, among others, argues that there may be no workable regulatory scheme for administering a drug like crack cocaine. See, for example, Kleiman, "Neither Prohibition nor Legalization," 72–78. Nadelmann argues that a regulatory scheme for crack cocaine might be impossible to administer but that such a scheme could be worked out for powdered cocaine which, if snorted, is far less likely to lead to compulsive use. He agrees with Kleiman that the powdered cocaine thus obtained could be converted to crack cocaine with minimal effort and expense—a fatal flaw, for Kleiman, in any scheme that tries to regulate distribution of powdered cocaine and prohibit crack. But Nadelmann argues that the availability of cocaine under a regulatory regime would have the same effect on crack that the availability of beer, wine, and liquor had on moonshine when prohibition was replaced by regulation. Crack, the moonshine of the cocaine world, would still be available, though prohibited; but its use would become much less significant and the prohibition much easier to enforce. Interview with Ethan Nadelmann, 2 August 1994.

41. For an insightful discussion of the problems and possibilities for such regulation, see Zimring and Hawkins, *Search for Rational Drug Control,* 119–31.

42. Zimring and Hawkins write: "The apparatus of drug law enforcement is one of a wide range of alternative resource investments that may be deployed in an effort to shore up neighborhoods. A drug control agency not only has drug control tools at its disposal; it also has a bias in favor of its drug control apparatus. It has been said that if the only tool one has is a hammer, an awful lot of problems will appear to call for nails. Efficient urban policy might require other tools." Ibid., 171.

CHAPTER 11

1. Laura E. Drager et al., "Drug Treatment Referral in Criminal Courts Must Continue," letter to the editor, *New York Times,* 5 August 1993.

2. The judges were Jack B. Weinstein and Whitman Knapp. Joseph B. Treaster, "Two Federal Judges, in Protest, Refuse to Accept Drug Cases," *New York Times,* 17 April 1993.

3. Michael Isikoff and Tracy Thompson, "Getting Too Tough on Drugs," *Washington Post,* 4 November 1990.

4. Karen Payne, "Upset with Court Trends, Top-Rated Nimkoff to Quit," *Miami News,* 4 January 1986.

5. Caspar W. Weinberger, "Our Troops Shouldn't Be Drug Cops," *Washington Post,* 22 May 1988.

6. Ralph F. Salerno, "The Anger of a Retired Chief Detective," in *Drug Prohibition and the Conscience of Nations,* ed. Arnold S. Trebach and Kevin B. Zeese (Washington D.C.: Drug Policy Foundation, 1990), 208–10.

7. Judge Robert W. Sweet, Speech to the Cosmopolitan Club in New York City, 12 December 1989, quoted in ibid., 205–6.

8. Joyce Price, "Nobel Winner, 2 Judges Want Drugs Made Legal," *Washington Times,* 17 November 1991; Peter J. Howe, "Meeting Endorses Legalized Drug Use; Advocates Vary on Means, Extent," *Boston Globe,* 10 May 1992; "Judge Besieged After All for Legalized Drugs," *Los Angeles Times,* 10 April 1992; and Matt Lait, "Make Drugs Legal, U.S. Judge Urges," *Los Angeles Times,* 25 April 1992.

9. George P. Shultz, "The Conceptual Base of Drug Prohibition Is Flawed," in Trebach and Zeese, *Drug Prohibition and the Conscience of Nations.*

10. Many of these positions are brought to public attention in the publications, conferences, and lobbying efforts of research and advocacy groups that favor legalization, such as the National Drug Strategy Network, the Drug Policy Foundation, the Alfred R. Lindesmith Center, and the Cato Institute. Some legalization advocates support public-health measures. The executive director appointed to the Drug Policy Foundation in 1994, for example, was David C. Condliffe, who had served as New York City's director of drug-abuse policy under Mayor Dinkins. A number of major policy analysts favoring legalization have begun to argue for treatment and prevention measures that would reduce the harm caused by drugs. See, for example, the discussions in Nadelmann, "Thinking Seriously," and in Duke and Gross, *America's Longest War,* 279–306.

11. Interview with the head of a state association of drug-treatment programs, 18 May 1994.

12. Kurt L. Schmoke, "The Mayor of Baltimore Continues His Challenge," in *Drug Prohibition and the Conscience of Nations,* ed. Arnold S. Trebach and Kevin B. Zeese (Washington, D.C.: Drug Policy Foundation, 1990); and "Cities Agree to Become 'Laboratories' of Change," *Action News* (Canadian Centre on Substance Abuse, Ottawa) 5, no. 1 (1994):2.

13. This was not unusual in earlier struggles for public health. The lead role was played not by those who suffered—immigrants, slum residents, and laborers—but by middle-class professionals—doctors, sanitary engineers, chemists, microbiologists, and statisticians—who were needed by the new public-health field. But their political clout came, in part, from being part of the larger Progressive Movement for social reform and good government at the turn of the century. See, for example, *The Sanitarians,* 129–30, 199.

14. Figures are from the Office of National Drug Control Policy, *National Drug Control Strategy* (1995), 38. The drug-abuse treatment budget increased from roughly $636 million in 1986 to some $2.4 billion in 1994. Office of National Drug Control Policy, *National Drug Control Strategy: Budget Summary,* (1995), 237–38. The quotation is from Michael Spencer and Howard Kurtz, "Modern Epidemics Threaten New York Hospital System," *Washington Post,* 11 February 1989.

15. Interview with Linda Lewis, Director of Public Policy, NASADAD, 6 May 1992.

16. Interview with the head of a state association of substance-abuse associations, 18 May 1994.

17. Interview with the director of a national treatment association, 15 March 1994.

18. Interview with the executive director of a national treatment association, 10 March 1994.

19. Interview with the executive director of a state association of drug-abuse programs, 18 May 1994.

20. Interview with Mark Parrino, President, American Methadone Treatment Association, 17 March 1994.

21. Another example of how immediate funding necessities lead treatment advocates to support measures that end up further entrenching the drug war is the struggle over who is to benefit by asset-forfeiture laws. Such laws allow police who seize the assets of suspected drug dealers and users to keep a percentage of the assets to fund more antidrug efforts. The treatment and prevention community, not surprisingly, saw this as an attractive pot of money generated by the drug war. It waged political struggles against sectors of the law-enforcement community (anxious to monopolize these funds) and in some states succeeded in having a portion of the seized assets assigned to treatment and prevention. But what seems so pragmatic and smart in the short term could have a long-term downside: it ties the interests of the treatment and prevention community to the continued, and escalating, prosecution of the drug war. The more the war is escalated, the more the assets seized and the more the money for treatment and prevention.

22. See, for example, National Coalition of State Alcohol and Drug Treatment and Prevention Associations, *The War on Drugs: Failure and Fantasy: An Alternate Drug Strategy Endorsed by 52 National Organizations* (Washington, D.C.: Legal Action Center, 1992); and National Coalition of State Alcohol and Drug Treatment and Prevention Associations, *1993 Federal Alcohol and Drug Policy Agenda* (Washington, D.C.: Legal Action Center, 1993).

23. See, for example, Coalition on Alcohol and Drug-Dependent Women and Their Children, *Drug and Alcohol-Related Issues and Pregnancy* (Washington, D.C., 1991).

24. "Judge Won't Halt Program for Pregnant Drug Users," *The State* (Columbia, S.C.), 17 February 1994. Meanwhile, a subcommittee in the South Carolina House was sharply divided in a debate on whether to pass legislation that would toughen penalties on pregnant drug addicts and allow doctors to turn over information on them to law-enforcement authorities. "House Panel Debates Treatment for Pregnant Addicts," *The State* (Columbia, S.C.), 10 February 1994.

25. Treatment advocates point out that managed care may work well for biomedical care, but its emphasis is very much a traditional medical one—treating diseases and other illnesses with medical or surgical cures. They fear it represents a move away from public health and from the kinds of considerations that are important in dealing with substance-abuse problems (and many mental-health problems too)—prevention, a continuum of long-term care, attention to social, cultural, and spiritual factors in the environment. Its criteria for cost-effectiveness can often be very short term—and that can create a rationale for minimizing the kind of long-term treatment involved in substance abuse. It will be an uphill battle for advocates of treatment and prevention to prove their efficiency in terms of outcome-based criteria and obtain continued funding. Articulating the public-health criteria against which success needs to be judged will be criti-

cal in the immediate fight to transform or challenge managed care, and if done successfully, this will further help to transform the punitive paradigm.

26. President's Commission on Model State Drug Laws, *Treatment* (Washington, D.C.: The White House, 1993), B–45; and The National Association of State Alcohol and Drug Abuse Directors, *Invest in Treatment for Alcohol and Other Drug Problems: It Pays* (Washington, D.C.: NASADAD, 1994).

27. In an interview on 26 February 1995 Mark Parrino explained:

> We need to use the current context to repackage information, but to do so in such a way that it does not sell out what we stand for. The first argument we need to make is the human argument for what we do—the real impact treatment has on helping people lead more decent lives. Then we need to make the argument about the benefits of what we do to the families of those with drug problems. If our audience rejects the humane argument, if you reject the family argument, then here is the cost argument: it will cost your city X million dollars if you keep these people out of treatment.

28. National Coalition of State Alcohol and Drug Treatment and Prevention Associations, *1993 Federal Alcohol and Drug Policy Agenda*, 11.

29. "I have trouble getting people to sit on my board," explained one director of an association of alcohol and drug programs in an interview on 27 February 1995. "They're afraid others will think they are recovered substance or alcohol abusers. This stigma is a powerful thing. The drug war really did us in. We were just getting to the point where addiction was seen as a public-health problem in the late 70s and the drug war turned it back into a crime problem—so many people are reticent to come out."

30. Interview with a director of an association of alcohol and drug programs, 11 June 1995.

31. An idea of the range of possible alliances is indicated by the array of groups that has sometimes been brought together by the Legal Action Center on important drug issues. Among the groups are the Academy of Family Physicians, the American Academy of Pediatrics, the American Association for Marriage and Family Therapy, the AIDS Action Council, the American Federation of State, County and Municipal Employees, the American Nurses Association, the American Public Health Association, the Association of Maternal and Child Health Programs, the Latino Council on Alcohol and Tobacco, the National Association of Addiction Treatment Providers, the National Association of Black Substance Abuse Workers, the National Black Police Association, the National Council of Community Mental Health Centers, the National Health Care for the Homeless Council, the National PTA, the United Methodist Church, the March of Dimes, the American Council on Alcohol Problems, the American Society of Addiction Medicine, the American Hospital Association, the National Consortium of TASC (Treatment Alternatives to Street Crime) Programs, Catholic Charities USA, the National Association of State Boards of Education, the National Association of Criminal Defense Lawyers, and the Women's Legal Defense Fund.

32. Many of the coalitions are still fragile, insecure in their funding, overly dependent on the federal government, and sometimes weak in leadership and organization. But they are receiving advice, training, technical assistance, and sometimes financial support from federal agencies like the Center for Substance

Abuse Prevention, foundations like the Robert Wood Johnson Foundation, and nonprofit organizations like Join Together, the Community Anti-Drug Coalitions of America in Alexandria, Virginia, the Center for Addiction and Drug Abuse in New York, and the American Bar Association's Special Committee on the Drug Crisis.

33. Join Together is based at the Boston University School of Public Health and is funded by the Robert Wood Johnson Foundation. The organization surveyed 15,000 community coalitions dealing with substance abuse in 1992 and 1993 and received 5,500 responses. This report draws on the 2,196 respondents that identified themselves as groups that lead or sponsor coalitions. See Join Together, 1993 *Report to the Nation: Community Leaders Speak Out Against Substance Abuse* (Boston, 1993).

34. They want 73 percent spent on prevention and treatment, 18 percent spent on local law enforcement, and 9 percent spent on interdiction. Ibid., 33–34. This does not, however, mean that they support less law enforcement against drug users or drug sellers. Community coalitions "hold firm and consistent views in support of stronger laws against drugs and excessive alcohol. More than 90% want stronger law enforcement and 51% strongly support increased penalties for drug sales. Eighty-six percent strongly oppose de-criminalizing the sale of drugs. . . . The majority of coalitions (79%) favor increased penalties for illegal drug possession, and the same majority is against de-criminalizing possession of drugs." Ibid, 34.

35. See ibid., 9.

36. New Haven Fighting Back, *We Won't Let Drugs and Alcohol Waste Our City* (New Haven, Conn., 1994).

37. The quotations are from Glide Memorial United Methodist Church, "Glide: Terms of Faith and Resistance" (San Francisco, 1992, mimeographed).

38. Kirsten A. Conover, "A Preacher Acts Against Crack," *Christian Science Monitor,* 27 March 1990.

39. A major objection to needle exchange in both African American and Latino communities derives from a history of persistent government neglect of the drug-abuse problem: needle exchange is seen as a stopgap measure that avoids investing resources in treatment. Other objections are based on the reluctance of many in these communities to admit the severity of the AIDS problem for fear of being stigmatized as a population. Furthermore, given the widespread belief in these communities that HIV is a manmade virus that was spread in black communities as a form of genocide, the image of black intravenous drug users "reaching out for drug treatment, only to receive clean needles from public health authorities, provides additional wind for the genocide mill." See Thomas and Quinn, "Burdens of Race and History," 333.

40. Drucker, *Drug Policy,* 113–17.

41. Ibid., 119.

42. Mireya Navarro, "New York Needle Exchanges Called Surprisingly Effective," *New York Times,* 18 February 1993.

43. Elaine O'Keefe et al., *Preliminary Report: City of New Haven Needle Exchange Program* (New Haven, Conn., 1991), 9.

44. See Aaron Peak, "A Community-Based Effort to Establish Legal Needle Exchange in the State of Hawaii," in *The Great Issues of Drug Policy,* ed. Arnold S. Trebach and Kevin B. Zeese (Washington, D.C.: Drug Policy Foundation, 1990), 214–16. Other states that have experimented with legal needle exchanges include Washington, Colorado, Oregon, and New York. As early as the mid-1980s such exchanges were begun in England, Scotland, Scandinavia, Italy, Australia, and Canada.

45. For discussions of such an expanded public-health approach, see Ernest Drucker, "AIDS and Addiction in New York City," *American Journal of Drug and Alcohol Abuse* 12, nos. 1–2 (1986):165–81.

46. Nicholas Pastore, "Combatting Substance Abuse in Inner Cities: A Proactive Police Perspective on New Initiatives Concerning Demand Reduction Strategies," in *The Great Issues of Drug Policy,* ed. Arnold S. Trebach and Kevin B. Zeese (Washington, D.C.: Drug Policy Foundation, 1990), 59.

47. American Bar Association, Special Committee on the Drug Crisis, *New Directions for National Substance Abuse Policy* (Washington, D.C., 1994), 5.

48. American Bar Association, Special Committee on the Drug Crisis, *The Community Anti-Drug Coalition Initiative* (Washington, D.C., 1991), 1.

49. Nicholas Pastore, "Community Police Policy Implementation in the City of New Haven," in *New Frontiers in Drug Policy,* ed. Arnold S. Trebach and Kevin B. Zeese (Washington, D.C.: Drug Policy Foundation, 1991), 308–9.

50. Pastore, "Combatting Substance Abuse," 60.

51. CBS News, *60 Minutes,* 9 January 1994.

52. U.S. Congress, House, Select Committee on Narcotics Abuse and Control, *National Drug Strategy Goals and the Root Causes of Drug Addiction and Drug Crime: Hearing before the Select Committee on Narcotics Abuse and Control,* 101st Cong., 1st sess., 15 November 1989, 80–83.

53. See, for example, Ian Fisher, "Prison Boot Camps Prove No Sure Cure," *New York Times,* 10 April 1994.

54. Texas, Department of Criminal Justice and Commission on Alcohol and Drug Abuse, "Texas Criminal Justice Treatment Initiative" (1994, mimeographed), 2.

55. James Dao, "For Addicts, Alternatives to Prison," *New York Times,* 4 April 1994.

56. David Elliot, "Emphasis on Rehabilitation Puts State on Cutting Edge of Corrections Theory," *Austin American-Statesman,* 16 January 1994; and Sam Howe Verhouek, "A Change in Governors Stalls Model Drug Program in Texas," *New York Times,* 4 July 1995.

57. Peter Finn and Andrea K. Newlyn, *Miami's "Drug Court": A Different Approach* (Washington, D.C.: National Institute of Justice, 1993), 11.

58. Quoted in Falco, *Making of a Drug-Free America,* 160. Judge Jeffrey S. Tauber, who heads the drug court in Oakland, California, has organized a national association of drug-court judges. In giving advice to judges he underlines the political importance of organizing coalitions to create and sustain drug courts—bringing together necessary agencies, developing "good relations with your local print and electronic media," raising funds. "You can expect a con-

siderable amount of opposition to any proposal to change existing systems. Don't be discouraged by the reluctance of some to change. Remember that important innovations don't come easily, but require persistence as well as vision to succeed." Jeffrey S. Tauber, "A Judicial Primer on Unified Drug Courts and Court-Ordered Drug Rehabilitation Programs" (paper presented to the California Continuing Judicial Studies Program, Dana Point, Calif., 10 August 1993), 5.

59. In New York, for example, TASC-like programs cost less than $16,000 per year for one treatment bed, compared with $25,000 a year to maintain one prison bed. Furthermore, by reducing prison overcrowding the programs allow the state to avoid new prison construction, which costs $100,000 per cell. Dao, "For Addicts, Alternatives to Prison."

60. See, for example, National Commission on Marihuana and Drug Abuse, *Drug Use in America,* 262–65. The "awkward and undesirable features" of the therapeutic approach under such mandatory diversion-to-treatment programs "reflect the fact that the therapeutic approach to drug use and dependence is still a stepchild of the criminal process" (p. 265).

61. Interview with an official in the National Consortium of TASC Programs, 10 March 1994.

62. Interview with Susan Galbraith, codirector of the Washington office of the Legal Action Center, 9 March 1994.

63. John S. Goldkamp and Doris Weiland, *Assessing the Impact of Dade County's Felony Drug Court* (Washington, D.C.: National Institute of Justice, 1993), 2–4.

64. Interview with an official in the National Consortium of TASC Programs, 10 March 1994.

65. James Swartz, "TASC—The Next 20 Years, Extending, Refining, and Assessing the Model," in *Drug Treatment and Criminal Justice,* ed. James A. Inciardi, Sage Criminal Justice System Annuals 7 (Beverly Hills, Calif.: Sage Publications, 1993), 131–32.

66. Finn and Newlyn, *Miami's "Drug Court,"* 8–9.

67. Tauber, "Judicial Primer," 12.

68. Tauber, "Community Judging," 8.

Bibliography

BOOKS, ARTICLES, REPORTS, PAPERS, AND STATEMENTS

Addiction Letter, January 1994.

Adler, Patricia A. *Wheeling and Dealing: An Ethnography of an Upper-Level Drug Dealing and Smuggling Community.* New York: Columbia University Press, 1985.

Air Force Times, 18 June 1990.

Alcoholism and Drug Abuse Week, 13 December 1993.

American Bar Association. *The State of Criminal Justice: An Annual Report.* Washington, D.C., 1993.

——. Special Committee on the Drug Crisis. *The Community Anti-Drug Coalition Initiative.* Washington, D.C., 1991.

——. *New Directions for National Substance Abuse Policy.* Washington, D.C., 1994.

American Medical Association. Council on Scientific Affairs. "Marijuana: Its Health Hazards and Therapeutic Potentials." *Journal of the American Medical Association* 246, no. 16 (1981):1823–27.

Andelman, David A. "The Drug Money Maze." *Foreign Affairs* 73, no. 4 (1994):94–108.

Anderson, Patrick. *High in America.* New York: Viking Press, 1981.

Andreas, Peter. "Profits, Poverty and Illegality: The Logic of Drug Corruption." *NACLA Report on the Americas* 27, no. 3 (1993):22–28.

Andreas, Peter, Eva Bertram, Morris Blachman, and Kenneth Sharpe. "Dead End Drug Wars." *Foreign Policy,* no. 85 (1991–1992):106–28.

Arcos, Cresencio S. Statement of Cresencio S. Arcos, Principal Deputy Assistant Secretary of State for International Narcotics Matters, before the Subcommittee on Foreign Operations, House Appropriations Committee, 14 April 1994.

Armao, Joseph P., and Leslie U. Cornfeld. "How to Police the Police." *Newsweek,* 19 December 1994, 34.

Austin American-Statesman, 16 January 1994.

Baritz, Loren. *Backfire.* New York: Ballantine Books, 1986.

Barnett, Randy E. "Curing the Drug-Law Addiction: The Harmful Side Effects of Legal Prohibition." In *Dealing with Drugs: Consequences of Government Control,* edited by Ronald Hamowy. Lexington, Mass.: Lexington Books, 1987.

Baumgartner, Frank R., and Bryan D. Jones. *Agendas and Instability in American Politics.* Chicago: University of Chicago Press, 1993.

Bayer, Ronald. *Private Acts, Social Consequences: AIDS and the Politics of Public Health.* New Brunswick, N.J.: Rutgers University Press, 1991.

Beauchamp, D. *Beyond Alcoholism: Alcohol and Public Health Policy.* Philadelphia: Temple University Press, 1981.

Benjamin, Daniel K., and Roger Leroy Miller. *Undoing Drugs: Beyond Legalization.* New York: Basic Books, 1991.

Bennett, William J. Testimony before the Committee on the Judiciary, U.S. Senate, 10 February 1995.

Berridge, Virginia. "AIDS, Drugs and History." *British Journal of Addiction* 87 (1992):363–70.

Biden, Joseph R., Jr. Statement before the U.S. Senate, Committee on the Judiciary, 10 February 1994.

Bloom, Bernard L. *Community Mental Health: A General Introduction.* Monterey, Calif.: Brooks/Cole Publishing Co., 1975.

Boaz, David. *The Crisis in Drug Prohibition.* Washington, D.C.: Cato Institute, 1990.

Bogert, Carroll, and Gregory Beals. "When Cops Betray Their Communities." *Newsweek,* 19 December 1994, 32.

Bonner, Robert C. Testimony before the Subcommittee on National Security, International Relations, and Criminal Justice, Committee on Government Reform and Oversight, U.S. House of Representatives, March 1995.

Boston Globe, 4 March 1990, 10 May 1992, 14 May 1994.

Botvin, Gilbert J. "Substance Abuse Prevention: Theory, Practice, and Effectiveness." In *Drugs and Crime,* edited by Michael Tonry and James Q. Wilson. Chicago: University of Chicago Press, 1990.

Bourgois, Philippe. "In Search of Horatio Alger: Culture and Ideology in the Crack Economy." *Contemporary Drug Problems* 16, no. 4 (1989):620–49.

Bowman, Karl M. "Some Problems of Addiction." In *Problems of Addiction and Habituation,* edited by Paul H. Hoch and Joseph Zubin. New York: Grune and Stratton, 1958.

Boyer, Peter J. "Whip Cracker." *New Yorker,* 5 September 1994, 38–54.

Brecher, Edward M., and the editors of *Consumer Reports,* eds. *Licit and Illicit Drugs.* Boston: Little, Brown, 1972.

Brown, Barry S. "The Growth of Drug Abuse Treatment Systems." In *Handbook of Drug Control in the United States,* edited by James A. Inciardi. New York: Greenwood Press, 1990.

Brown, Barry S., Susan K. Gauvey, Marilyn B. Meyers, and Steven D. Stark. "In Their Own Words: Addicts' Reasons for Initiating and Withdrawing from Heroin." *International Journal of the Addictions* 6, no. 4 (1971):639–42.

Brown, Lee. Testimony before the Judiciary Committee, U.S. Senate, 10 February 1994.

Brown, Richard Harvey. "Drug Policies and Politics in Comparative Perspective: The Case of Opium in India, China, Britain and the United States." Paper presented to the Drug Policy Seminar, Institute for Latin American and Iberian Affairs, Columbia University, February 1993.

Buckley, William F., Jr. "Drug Talk Across the Way." *National Review*, 5 May 1989, 63.

Bukoski, William J. "Federal Approach to Prevention." In *Handbook of Drug Control in the United States*, edited by James A. Inciardi. New York: Greenwood Press, 1990.

Burke, Melvin. "Bolivia: The Politics of Cocaine." *Current History* 90, no. 553 (1991):65–68, 90.

"Can Clean Needles Slow the AIDS Epidemic?" *Consumer Reports*, July 1994, 466–69.

Carter, David L. "Drug-Related Corruption of Police Officers: A Contemporary Typology." *Journal of Criminal Justice* 18 (1990):85–90.

Chaiken, Jan M., and Marcia R. Chaiken. "Drugs and Predatory Crime." In *Drugs and Crime*, edited by Michael Tonry and James Q. Wilson. Chicago: University of Chicago Press, 1990.

Chein, Isidor, Donald L. Gerard, Robert S. Lee, and Eva Rosenfeld. *The Road to H: Narcotics, Delinquency, and Social Policy*. New York: Basic Books, 1964.

Chicago Times, 12 September 1989.

Christian Science Monitor, 23 March 1989, 12 February 1990, 27 March 1990, 16 March 1993, 11 February 1994.

"Cities Agree to Become 'Laboratories' of Change," *Action News* (Canadian Centre on Substance Abuse, Ottawa) 5, no. 1 (1994):1–2.

Cleveland Plain Dealer, 12 December 1993, 20 February 1994.

Cloyd, Jerald. *Drugs and Information Control*. Westport, Conn.: Greenwood Press, 1982.

Coalition on Alcohol and Drug-Dependent Women and Their Children. *Drug and Alcohol-Related Issues and Pregnancy*. Washington, D.C., 1991.

Conaboy, Richard P. Testimony before the Subcommittee on Crime, Committee on the Judiciary, U.S. House of Representatives, 29 June 1995.

Congressional Quarterly, 20 September 1986, 18 October 1986, 18 June 1988, 17 December 1988, 9 September 1989, 6 April 1991, 19 March 1993.

Congressional Quarterly Almanac 23 (1968)–49 (1994).

Connery, Robert H., et al. *The Politics of Mental Health: Organizing Community Mental Health in Metropolitan Areas*. New York: Columbia University Press, 1968.

Cook, L. F., et al. "Treatment Alternatives to Street Crime." In *Compulsory Treatment of Drug Abuse: Research and Clinical Practice,* edited by C. G.

Leukefeld and F. M. Tims. NIDA Research Monograph 86. Rockville, Md.: National Institute on Drug Abuse, 1988.

Cowan, Richard. "American Conservatives Should Revise Their Position on Marihuana." *National Review,* 8 December 1972, 1344–46.

Currie, Elliott. *Reckoning: Drugs, the Cities, and the American Future.* New York: Hill and Wang, 1993.

De Benedictis, Don. J. "How Long Is Too Long." *ABA Journal* 79 (1993):74–79.

De Leon, George. "Treatment Strategies." In *Handbook of Drug Control in the United States,* edited by James A. Inciardi. New York: Greenwood Press, 1990.

DeLong, James V. "The Drugs and Their Effects." In *Dealing with Drug Abuse: A Report to the Ford Foundation.* New York: Praeger, 1972.

Destler, I. M., Leslie Gelb, and Anthony Lake. *Our Own Worst Enemy: The Unmaking of American Foreign Policy.* New York: Simon and Schuster, 1984.

Diaz, Charley L. "DoD Plays in the Drug War." *Proceedings/Naval Review* 116, no. 5 (1990):76–86.

Dinges, John. *Our Man in Panama.* New York: Random House, 1990.

Doble, John. *Crime and Punishment: The Public's View.* New York: Public Agenda Foundation, 1987.

Domestic Council Drug Abuse Task Force. "White Paper on Drug Abuse: A Report to the President from the Domestic Council Drug Abuse Task Force." Washington, D.C.: U.S. Government Printing Office, 1975.

Drucker, Ernest. "AIDS and Addiction in New York City." *American Journal of Drug and Alcohol Abuse* 12, nos. 1–2 (1986): 165–81.

———. "Drug Policy, Drug Treatment and Public Health." Report prepared for the American Foundation for AIDS Research, 15 September 1991.

Drug Abuse Council. *The Facts About "Drug Abuse."* New York: Free Press, 1980.

Duffy, John. *The Sanitarians: A History of American Public Health.* Urbana: University of Illinois Press, 1990.

Duke, Steven B., and Albert C. Gross. *America's Longest War: Rethinking Our Tragic Crusade Against Drugs.* New York: G. P. Putnam's Sons, 1993.

Duster, Troy. *The Legislation of Morality: Law, Drugs, and Moral Judgment.* New York: Free Press, 1970.

The Economist, 8 October 1988.

Edelman, Murray. *Political Language: Words That Succeed and Policies That Fail.* New York: Academic Press, 1977.

Eldridge, William Butler. *Narcotics and the Law: A Critique of the American Experiment in Narcotic Drug Control.* New York: New York University Press, 1962.

Engelsman, Eddy L. "Drug Policy in the Netherlands from a Public Health Perspective." In *Searching for Alternatives: Drug-Control Policy in the United States,* edited by Melvyn B. Krauss and Edward P. Lazear. Stanford, Calif.: Hoover Institution Press, 1991.

———. "The Pragmatic Strategies of the Dutch 'Drug Czar.'" In *Drug Prohibition and the Conscience of Nations,* edited by Arnold S. Trebach and Kevin B. Zeese. Washington, D.C.: Drug Policy Foundation, 1990.

Epstein, Edward Jay. *Agency of Fear.* London: Verso, 1990.

Erickson, Patricia G. "A Public Health Approach to Demand Reduction." *Journal of Drug Issues* 20, no. 4 (1990):563–76.

Evans, Rod L., and Irwin M. Berent. *Drug Legalization: For and Against.* La Salle, Ill.: Open Court, 1992.

Fagan, Jeffrey. Prepared testimony. U.S. Congress. House. Subcommittee on Crime. Committee on the Judiciary. *Cocaine and Federal Sentencing Policy,* 104th Cong., 1st sess., 29 June 1995.

————. "Intoxication and Aggression." In *Drugs and Crime,* edited by Michael Tonry and James Q. Wilson. Chicago: University of Chicago Press, 1990.

Falco, Mathea. *The Making of a Drug-Free America: Programs That Work.* New York: Times Books, 1992.

Fee, Elizabeth, and Daniel M. Fox. "Introduction: The Contemporary Historiography of AIDS." In *AIDS: The Making of a Chronic Disease,* edited by Elizabeth Fee and Daniel M. Fox. Berkeley: University of California Press, 1992.

————, eds. *AIDS: The Making of a Chronic Disease.* Berkeley: University of California Press, 1992.

Fingarette, Herbert. *Heavy Drinking: The Myth of Alcoholism as a Disease.* Berkeley: University of California Press, 1988.

Finkelstein, Norma. "Treatment Programming for Alcohol and Drug-Dependent Pregnant Women." *International Journal of the Addictions* 28, no. 13 (1993):1275–1309.

Finn, Peter, and Andrea K. Newlyn. *Miami's "Drug Court": A Different Approach.* Washington, D.C.: National Institute of Justice, 1993.

Fiorina, Morris P. *Congress: Keystone of the Washington Establishment.* New Haven, Conn.: Yale University Press, 1977.

Foley, Henry A., and Steven S. Sharfstein. *Madness and Government: Who Cares for the Mentally Ill?* Washington, D.C.: American Psychiatric Press, 1983.

Fossier, A. E. "The Marihuana Menace." *New Orleans Medical and Surgical Journal* 84, no. 4 (1931):247–52.

Fox, Daniel M. "The Politics of HIV Infection." In *AIDS: The Making of a Chronic Disease,* edited by Elizabeth Fee and Daniel M. Fox. Berkeley: University of California Press, 1992.

Friedman, Lawrence M. *Crime and Punishment in American History.* New York: Basic Books, 1993.

Friedman, Milton. "The War We Are Losing." In *Searching for Alternatives: Drug-Control Policy in the United States,* edited by Melvyn B. Krauss and Edward P. Lazear. Stanford, Calif.: Hoover Institution Press, 1991.

Gannett News Service, 7 February 1995, 10 February 1995.

Gerstein, Dean R., and Lawrence W. Green. *Preventing Drug Abuse: What Do We Know?* Washington, D.C.: National Academy Press, 1993.

Gerstein, Dean R., and Henrick J. Harwood, eds. *Treating Drug Problems.* Vol. 1. Washington, D.C.: National Academy Press, 1990.

Glick, Ronald. "The Chicago Puerto Rican Community." In *Drugs in Hispanic Communities,* edited by Ronald Glick and Joan Moore. New Brunswick, N.J.: Rutgers University Press, 1990.

Glick, Ronald, and Joan Moore, eds. *Drugs in Hispanic Communities*. New Brunswick, N.J.: Rutgers University Press, 1990.

Glide Memorial United Methodist Church. "Glide: Terms of Faith and Resistance." San Francisco, 1992. Mimeographed.

Goldberg, Peter. "The Federal Government's Response to Illicit Drugs, 1969–1978." In *The Facts About "Drug Abuse,"* by the Drug Abuse Council. New York: Free Press, 1980.

Goldkamp, John S., and Doris Weiland. *Assessing the Impact of Dade County's Felony Drug Court*. Washington, D.C.: National Institute of Justice, 1993.

Goldstein, Herman. *Problem-Oriented Policing*. Philadelphia: Temple University Press, 1990.

Goldstein, P. J., H. H. Brownstein, P. J. Ryan, and P. A. Bellucci. "Crack and Homicide in NY City, 1988: A Conceptually Based Event Analysis." *Contemporary Drug Problems* 16 (1989):651–87.

Gordon, Diana G. *The Return of the Dangerous Classes: Drug Prohibition and Policy Politics*. New York: W. W. Norton, 1994.

Gostin, Lawrence O. "Compulsory Treatment for Drug-dependent Persons: Justifications for a Public Health Approach to Drug Dependency." *Milbank Quarterly* 69, no. 4 (1991):561–93.

Grinspoon, Lester. *Marihuana: The Forbidden Medicine*. New Haven, Conn.: Yale University Press, 1993.

Gusfield, Joseph R. *Symbolic Crusade: Status Politics and the American Temperance Movement*. Urbana: University of Illinois Press, 1963.

Hall, Peter. "Policy Paradigms, Social Learning, and the State: The Case of Economic Policymaking in Britain." *Comparative Politics* 25, no. 3 (1993):275–96.

Hargreaves, Clare. *Snow Fields: The War on Cocaine in the Andes*. New York: Holmes and Meier, 1992.

"Harper's Index," *Harper's,* May 1994, 15.

Hartford Courant, 20 October 1994.

Healy, Kevin. "Coca, the State, and the Peasantry in Bolivia, 1982–1988." *Journal of Interamerican Studies and World Affairs* 30, nos. 2–3 (1988):105–26.

Helmer, John. *Drugs and Minority Oppression*. New York: Seabury Press, 1975.

Hennessey, Michael. "Our National Jail Scandal." *American Jails* 7, no. 3 (1993):13.

Himmelstein, Jerome L. *The Strange Career of Marihuana: Politics and Ideology of Drug Control in America*. Westport, Conn.: Greenwood Press, 1983.

Hoch, Paul H., and Joseph Zubin, eds. *Problems of Addiction and Habituation*. New York: Grune and Stratton, 1958.

Hoffman, Jan. "Pregnant, Addicted—and Guilty?" *New York Times Magazine,* 19 August 1990, 32–35.

"Hooked on Tobacco: The Teen Epidemic." *Consumer Reports,* March 1995, 142–46.

Houston Chronicle, 10 March 1995.

Humphreys, Keith, and Julian Rappaport. "From the Community Mental Health Movement to the War on Drugs: A Study in the Definition of Social Problems." *American Psychologist* 48, no. 8 (1993):892–901.

Husak, Douglas N. *Drugs and Rights.* New York: Cambridge University Press, 1992.

Inciardi, James A., ed. *Drug Treatment and Criminal Justice.* Sage Criminal Justice System Annual, 7. Beverly Hills, Calif.: Sage Publications, 1993.

———. *Handbook of Drug Control in the United States.* New York: Greenwood Press, 1990.

———. *The War on Drugs: Heroin, Cocaine, Crime, and Public Policy.* Palo Alto, Calif.: Mayfield Publishing Co., 1986.

Institute of Medicine. *The Future of Public Health.* Washington, D.C.: National Academy Press, 1988.

Jacobson, Richard, and Norman E. Zinberg. *The Social Basis of Drug Abuse Prevention.* Washington, D.C.: Drug Abuse Council, 1975.

Johns, Christina Jacqueline. *Power, Ideology, and the War on Drugs.* New York: Praeger, 1992.

Johnson, Bruce D., and John Muffler. "Sociocultural Aspects of Drug Use and Abuse in the 1990s." In *Substance Abuse: A Comprehensive Text,* edited by Joyce H. Lowinson, Pedro Ruiz, Robert B. Millman, and John G. Langrod. 2d ed. Baltimore, Md.: Williams and Wilkins, 1992.

Johnston, L. D., P. M. O'Malley, and J. G. Bachman. *Drug Use, Drinking, and Smoking: National Survey Results from High School, College, and Young Adult Populations: 1975–1990, 1. High School Seniors.* Rockville, Md.: National Institute on Drug Abuse, 1991.

Join Together. *1993 Report to the Nation: Community Leaders Speak Out Against Substance Abuse.* Boston, 1993.

Joint Committee of the American Bar Association and the American Medical Association on Narcotic Drugs. *Drug Addiction: Crime or Disease?* Bloomington: Indiana University Press, 1961.

Jonas, Steven. "Public Health Approach to the Prevention of Substance Abuse." In *Substance Abuse: A Comprehensive Text,* edited by Joyce H. Lowinson, Pedro Ruiz, Robert B. Millman, and John G. Langrod. 2d ed. Baltimore, Md.: Williams and Wilkins, 1992.

Kandel, Denise B. "The Social Demography of Drug Use." *Milbank Quarterly* 69, no. 3 (1991):365–413.

Kaplan, John. *Marijuana—The New Prohibition.* New York: World Publishing Co., 1970.

Kasarda, John. "Urban Industrial Transition and the Underclass." *Annals of the American Academy of Political and Social Science* 501 (1989): 26–47.

Kawell, Jo Anne. "Drug Wars: The Rules of the Game." *NACLA Report on the Americas* 23, no. 6 (1990):9–10.

Kelly, Joseph E. Prepared testimony. U.S. Congress. House. Subcommittee on Legislation and National Security. Committee on Government Operations. *The Drug War: Colombia Is Implementing Antidrug Efforts, but Impact Is Uncertain,* 103d Cong., 1st sess., 5 October 1993.

Kinder, Douglas Clark. "Shutting Out the Evil: Nativism and Narcotics Control in the United States." *Journal of Policy History* 3, no. 4 (1991):468–93.

King, Rufus. *The Drug Hang-up.* New York: W. W. Norton, 1972.

Kleiman, Mark A. R. *Against Excess: Drug Policy for Results*. New York: Basic Books, 1992.

———. "Neither Prohibition nor Legalization." *Daedalus* 121, no. 3 (1992):53–83.

Kobler, J. *Ardent Spirits: The Rise and Fall of Prohibition*. New York: G. P. Putnam, 1973.

Kornblum, William. "Drug Legalization and the Minority Poor." *Milbank Quarterly* 69, no. 3 (1991):415–36.

Kramer, Michael. "Clinton's Drug Policy Is a Bust." *Time*, 20 December 1993, 35.

Krauss, Melvyn B., and Edward P. Lazear, eds. *Searching for Alternatives: Drug-Control Policy in the United States*. Stanford, Calif.: Hoover Institution Press, 1991.

Kuhn, Thomas. *The Structure of Scientific Revolutions*. Chicago: University of Chicago Press, 1970.

Kyvig, D. E. *Repealing National Prohibition*. Chicago: University of Chicago Press, 1979.

Lane, Charles. "The Newest War." *Newsweek*, 6 January 1992: 18–23.

Langer, John H. "Corruption of Public Officials: An Inevitable Consequence of International Drug Traffic." *Police Studies* 9, no. 1 (1986):34–41.

Langum, David J. *Crossing over the Line: Legislating Morality and the Mann Act*. Chicago: University of Chicago Press, 1994.

Latin American Weekly Report, 22 February 1990.

Leavitt, Judith Walzer, and Ronald L. Numbers, eds. *Sickness and Health in America: Readings in the History of Medicine and Public Health*. 2d ed. rev. Madison: University of Wisconsin Press, 1985.

Lee, Rensselaer W., III. "Coca Growing Cannot Be Eradicated." In *Chemical Dependency*, edited by Bruno Leone. San Diego, Calif.: Greenhaven Press, 1989.

Legal Action Center. *A New Drug Budget: Recommendations for New Funding Priorities*. Washington, D.C., 1993.

Legal Times, 22 February 1993, 9 August 1993.

Lemann, Nicholas. "The Myth of Community Development." *New York Times Magazine*, 9 January 1994, 26–31.

Leone, Bruno, ed. *Chemical Dependency*. San Diego, Calif.: Greenhaven Press, 1989.

Leons, Madeline Barbara. "Risk and Opportunity in the Coca/Cocaine Economy of the Bolivian Yungas." *Journal of Latin American Studies* 25 (1993):121–57.

Levine, Harry G., and Craig Reinarman. "From Prohibition to Regulation: Lessons from Alcohol Policy for Drug Policy." *Milbank Quarterly* 69, no. 3 (1991):461–94.

Lewis, David C. "Medical and Health Perspectives on Failing U.S. Drug Policy." *Daedalus* 121, no. 3 (1992):165–94.

Lindesmith, Alfred R. *The Addict and the Law*. Bloomington: Indiana University Press, 1965.

Los Angeles Times, 19 September 1989, 17 March 1990, 22 April 1990, 10 September 1991, 11 February 1992, 10 April 1992, 25 April 1992, 25 May 1995.

Lowinson, Joyce H., Pedro Ruiz, Robert B. Millman, and John G. Langrod, eds. *Substance Abuse: A Comprehensive Text.* 2d ed. Baltimore, Md.: Williams and Wilkins, 1992.

Lukes, Steven. *Power: A Radical View.* London: Macmillan, 1974.

Lusane, Clarence. *Pipe Dream Blues: Racism and the War on Drugs.* Boston: South End Press, 1991.

MacKenzie, Doris L., and Craig Uchida, eds. *Drugs and the Criminal Justice System: Evaluating Public Policy Initiatives.* Beverly Hills, Calif.: Sage Publications, 1992.

Manning, Peter K. "The Criminal Justice System and the User." In *Substance Abuse: A Comprehensive Text,* edited by Joyce H. Lowinson, Pedro Ruiz, Robert B. Millman, and John G. Langrod. 2d ed. Baltimore, Md.: Williams and Wilkins, 1992.

Massing, Michael. "The Longest War." *Rolling Stone,* 20 April 1995, 44–45.

May, Edgar. "Narcotics Addiction and Control in Great Britain." In *Dealing with Drug Abuse: A Report to the Ford Foundation.* New York: Praeger, 1972.

Mayhew, David. *Congress: The Electoral Connection.* New Haven, Conn.: Yale University Press, 1974.

McWilliams, John C. *The Protectors: Harry J. Anslinger and the Federal Bureau of Narcotics, 1930–1962.* Newark: University of Delaware Press, 1990.

———. "Through the Past Darkly: The Politics and Policies of America's Drug War." *Journal of Policy History* 3, no. 4 (1991):356–92.

Meier, Kenneth J. "Race and the War on Drugs: America's Dirty Little Secret." *Policy Currents* 2, no. 4 (1992):1–4.

Meyers, Samuel L., Jr. "Drugs and Market Structure: Is There Really a Drug Crisis in the Black Community?" In *The Great Issues of Drug Policy,* edited by Arnold S. Trebach and Kevin B. Zeese. Washington, D.C.: Drug Policy Foundation, 1990.

Miami Herald, 29 August 1982, 3 March 1983, 7 May 1983.

Miami News, 4 January 1986.

Moore, Mark H. "Drugs, the Criminal Law, and Administration of Justice." *Milbank Quarterly* 69, no. 4 (1991):529–60.

———. "Supply Reduction and Drug Law Enforcement." In *Drugs and Crime,* edited by Michael Tonry and James Q. Wilson. Chicago: University of Chicago Press, 1990.

Moore, Mark H., and Dean R. Gerstein. *Alcohol and Public Policy: Beyond the Shadow of Prohibition.* Washington, D.C.: National Academy Press, 1981.

Morales, Edmundo. "The Political Economy of Cocaine Production: An Analysis of the Peruvian Case." *Latin American Perspectives* 17, no. 4 (1990):91–109.

Morgan, H. Wayne. *Drugs in America: A Social History, 1800–1980.* Syracuse, N.Y.: Syracuse University Press, 1981.

Morganthau, Tom. "Why Good Cops Go Bad." *Newsweek,* 19 December 1994, 30–34.

Morrison, David C. "Police Action." *National Journal* 24, no. 5 (1992):267–70.

Mosher, James F. "Drug Availability in a Public Health Perspective." In *Youth and Drugs: Society's Mixed Messages,* edited by H. Resnick. Rockville, Md.: Department of Health and Human Services, Public Health Service, Alcohol, Drug Abuse and Mental Health Administration, Office of Substance Abuse Prevention, 1990.

Mosher, James F., and Karen L. Yanagisako. "Public Health, Not Social Warfare: A Public Health Approach to Illegal Drug Policy." *Journal of Public Health Policy* 12, no. 3 (1991):278–323.

Musto, David F. *The American Disease.* New York: Oxford University Press, 1987.

Nadelmann, Ethan. "Drug Prohibition in the United States: Costs, Consequences, and Alternatives." *Science,* 1 September 1989, 939–47.

———. "Legalization Is the Answer." *Issues in Science and Technology,* summer 1990, 43–46.

———. "Thinking Seriously About Alternatives to Drug Prohibition." *Daedalus* 121, no. 3 (1992):85–132.

National Association of State Alcohol and Drug Abuse Directors. *Invest in Treatment for Alcohol and Other Drug Problems: It Pays.* Washington, D.C.: NASADAD, 1994.

National Coalition of State Alcohol and Drug Treatment and Prevention Associations. *1993 Federal Alcohol and Drug Policy Agenda.* Washington, D.C.: Legal Action Center, 1993.

———. *The War on Drugs: Failure and Fantasy: An Alternate Drug Strategy Endorsed by 52 National Organizations.* Washington, D.C.: Legal Action Center, 1992.

National Journal, 2 February 1991.

New Haven Fighting Back. *We Won't Let Drugs and Alcohol Waste Our City.* New Haven, Conn., 1994. Pamphlet.

New York Times, 18 December 1918, 27 February 1965, 2 July 1973, 7 March 1981, 15 October 1982, 30 July 1989, 16 October 1989, 6 May 1990, 8 June 1990, 6 September 1990, 25 November 1990, 28 July 1992, 2 August 1992, 8 February 1993, 18 February 1993, 17 April 1993, 18 July 1993, 5 August 1993, 15 August 1993, 14 October 1993, 9 November 1993, 21 November 1993, 15 January 1994, 6 February 1994, 10 February 1994, 21 February 1994, 4 April 1994, 6 April 1994, 10 April 1994, 19 June 1994, 8 July 1994, 10 July 1994, 2 August 1994, 2 July 1995, 3 July 1995, 4 July 1995, 11 July 1995, 15 July 1995, 13 August 1995.

O'Keefe, Elaine, et al. *Preliminary Report: City of New Haven Needle Exchange Program.* New Haven, Conn., 1991.

Pastore, Nicholas. "Combatting Substance Abuse in Inner Cities: A Proactive Police Perspective on New Initiatives Concerning Demand Reduction Strategies." In *The Great Issues of Drug Policy,* edited by Arnold S. Trebach and Kevin B. Zeese. Washington, D.C.: Drug Policy Foundation, 1990.

———. "Community Police Policy Implementation in the City of New Haven." In *New Frontiers in Drug Policy,* edited by Arnold S. Trebach and Kevin B. Zeese. Washington, D.C.: Drug Policy Foundation, 1991.

Paternostro, Silvana. "Mexico as a Narco-Democracy." *World Politics Journal* 12, no. 3 (1995):41–48.

Peak, Aaron. "A Community-Based Effort to Establish Legal Needle Exchange in the State of Hawaii." In *The Great Issues of Drug Policy*, edited by Arnold S. Trebach and Kevin B. Zeese. Washington, D.C.: Drug Policy Foundation, 1990.

Philadelphia Inquirer, 13 September 1989, 2 April 1990.

Pickett, George, and John J. Hanlon, eds. *Public Health: Administration and Practice*. 9th ed. St. Louis, Mo.: Times Mirror/Mosby College Publishing, 1990.

Pivar, David J. *Purity Crusade: Sexual Morality and Social Control, 1868–1900*. Westport, Conn.: Greenwood Press, 1973.

Pollan, Michael. "How Pot Has Grown." *New York Times Magazine,* 19 February 1995, 30–35, 44, 50, 56–57.

Ravenel, Mazyck P. *A Half Century of Public Health*. New York: Arno Press and the *New York Times,* 1970.

Reasons, Charles. "The Politics of Drugs: An Inquiry into the Sociology of Social Problems." *Sociological Quarterly* 15 (Summer 1974): 392–93.

Reeves, Jimmie L., and Richard Campbell. *Cracked Coverage: Television News, the Anti-Cocaine Crusade, and the Reagan Legacy.* Durham, N.C.: Duke University Press, 1994.

Regier, D. A., et al. "Comorbidity of Mental Disorders with Alcohol and Other Drug Abuse." *Journal of the American Medical Association* 264 (1990):2511–18.

Reinarman, Craig, and Harry G. Levine. "Crack in Context: Politics and Media in the Making of a Drug Scare." *Contemporary Drug Problems* 16 (1989):535–77.

Reuter, Peter. "Can the Borders Be Sealed?" *Public Interest* 92 (Summer 1988): 51–65.

———. "Eternal Hope." *Public Interest* 79 (Spring 1985):79–95.

———. "The Punitive Trend of American Drug Policy." *Daedalus* 121, no. 3 (1992):15–52.

Reuter, Peter, Gordon Crawford, and Jonathan Cave. *Sealing the Borders: The Effects of Increased Military Participation in Drug Interdiction*. Santa Monica, Calif.: RAND Corporation, 1988.

Reuter, Peter, Robert MacCoun, and Patrick Murphy. *Money from Crime: A Study of the Economics of Drug Dealing in Washington, D.C.* Washington, D.C.: RAND Corporation, 1990.

Rocky Mountain News, 25 June 1994.

Rodriguez, Louis J. Statement before the Legislation and National Security Subcommittee, House Committee on Government Operations, 5 October 1993.

Room, Robin. "Alcohol Control and Public Health." *Annual Review of Public Health* 5 (1984):293–317.

———. "The Dialectic of Drinking in Australian Life: From the Rum Corps to the Wine Column." *Australian Drug and Alcohol Review* 7 (1988):413–37.

Rosen, George. "The First Neighborhood Health Center Movement." In *Sickness and Health in America: Readings in the History of Medicine and*

Public Health, edited by Judith Walzer Leavitt and Ronald L. Numbers. 2d rev. ed. Madison: University of Wisconsin Press, 1985.
————. *A History of Public Health.* Baltimore, Md.: Johns Hopkins University Press, 1993.
Rosenblatt, Roger. "How Do They Live With Themselves." *New York Times Magazine,* 20 March 1994, 36–41, 55, 73–76.
Rosner, David, and Gerald Markowitz. "The Early Movement for Occupational Safety and Health, 1900–1917." In *Sickness and Health in America: Readings in the History of Medicine and Public Health,* edited by Judith Walzer Leavitt and Ronald L. Numbers. 2d rev. ed. Madison: University of Wisconsin Press, 1985.
Salerno, Ralph F. "The Anger of a Retired Chief Detective." In *Drug Prohibition and the Conscience of Nations,* edited by Arnold S. Trebach and Kevin B. Zeese. Washington D.C.: Drug Policy Foundation, 1990.
San Francisco Chronicle, 11 December 1993, 8 March 1995, 12 March 1995.
San Francisco Examiner, 16 February 1994.
Sardell, Alice. *The U.S. Experiment in Social Medicine: The Community Health Center Program, 1965–1986.* Pittsburgh, Pa.: University of Pittsburgh Press, 1988.
Schlosser, Eric. "Reefer Madness." *Atlantic Monthly,* August 1994, 45–63.
Schmoke, Kurt L. "The Mayor of Baltimore Continues His Challenge." In *Drug Prohibition and the Conscience of Nations,* edited by Arnold S. Trebach and Kevin B. Zeese. Washington, D.C.: Drug Policy Foundation, 1990.
Schneider, Cathy. "Using Culture to Fight AIDS: Political Struggle in Williamsburg and the Origins of 'Musica against Drugs.'" Unpublished paper, 1994.
Shafer, D. Michael. *Deadly Paradigms: The Failure of U.S. Counterinsurgency Policy.* Princeton, N.J.: Princeton University Press, 1988.
Sharp, Elaine B. *The Dilemma of Drug Policy in the United States.* New York: HarperCollins, 1994.
Shultz, George P. "The Conceptual Base of Drug Prohibition Is Flawed." In *Drug Prohibition and the Conscience of Nations,* edited by Arnold S. Trebach and Kevin B. Zeese. Washington, D.C.: Drug Policy Foundation, 1990.
Smith, M. B. "The Revolution in Mental Health Care—a Bold New Approach?" *Trans-Action* 5 (1968):19–23.
Smith, Peter H., ed. *Drug Policy in the Americas.* Boulder, Colo.: Westview Press, 1992.
Snowden, Lonnie R., ed. *Reaching the Underserved, Mental Health Needs of Neglected Populations.* Beverly Hills, Calif.: Sage Publications, 1982.
Sparrow, Malcolm, Mark H. Moore, and David Kennedy. *Beyond 911: A New Era for Policing.* New York: Basic Books, 1990.
Speart, Jessica. "The New Drug Mules." *New York Times Magazine,* 11 June 1995, 44–45.
Staley, Sam. *Drug Policy and the Decline of American Cities.* New Brunswick, N.J.: Transaction Publishers, 1992.
Starr, Paul. *The Social Transformation of American Medicine.* New York: Basic Books, 1982.

The State (Columbia, S.C.), 17 December 1989, 10 February 1994, 17 February 1994.

Stevens, Jay. *Storming Heaven: LSD and the American Dream.* New York: Atlantic Monthly Press, 1987.

Stimson, Gerry V., and Rachel Lart. "HIV, Drugs, and Public Health in England: New Words, Old Tunes." *International Journal of the Addictions* 26, no. 12 (1991):1263–77.

St. Louis Post Dispatch, 17 September 1989.

Stone, Deborah. "Causal Stories and the Formation of Policy Agendas." *Political Science Quarterly* 104, no. 2 (1989):281–300.

"S.T.O.P., Sanction-Treatment-Opportunity-Progress. An Early Drug Intervention and Case Management Program, August 1991–January 1993, 18 Months of Progress and Change." Mimeographed report of the Circuit Court, District Attorney, and Public Defender officers of Multnomah County, Oregon, 1993.

Stutman, Robert M., and Richard Esposito. *Dead on Delivery: Inside the Drug Wars, Straight from the Street.* New York: Warner Books, 1992.

Swartz, James. "TASC—The Next 20 Years, Extending, Refining, and Assessing the Model." In *Drug Treatment and Criminal Justice,* edited by James A. Inciardi. Sage Criminal Justice System Annual, 7. Beverly Hills, Calif.: Sage Publications, 1993.

Szasz, Thomas. *Our Right to Drugs: The Case for a Free Market.* New York: Praeger, 1992.

Tauber, Jeffrey S. "Community Judging: A National Strategy for the Development of Coordinated Drug Court Systems." Paper presented at the American Bar Association's "Just Solutions" Conference, Washington, D.C., May 1994.

———. "A Judicial Primer on Unified Drug Courts and Court-Ordered Drug Rehabilitation Programs." Paper presented to the California Continuing Judicial Studies Program, Dana Point, Calif., 10 August 1993.

Taylor, Arnold H. *American Diplomacy and the Narcotics Traffic, 1900–1939: A Study in International Humanitarian Reform.* Durham, N.C.: Duke University Press, 1969.

Texas Department of Criminal Justice and Commission on Alcohol and Drug Abuse. "Texas Criminal Justice Treatment Initiative." 1994. Mimeographed.

Thomas, Stephen B., and Sandra Crouse Quinn. "The Burdens of Race and History on Black Americans' Attitudes Toward Needle Exchange Policy to Prevent HIV Disease." *Journal of Public Health Policy* 14, no. 3 (1993):320–47.

Thoumi, Francisco E. "The Economic Impact of Narcotics in Colombia." *Drug Policy in the Americas,* edited by Peter H. Smith. Boulder, Colo.: Westview Press, 1992.

Tidwell, Mike. *In the Shadow of the White House.* Rocklin, Calif.: Prima Publishing, 1992.

Tonry, Michael, and James Q. Wilson, eds. *Drugs and Crime.* Chicago: University of Chicago Press, 1990.

Trebach, Arnold S. *The Great Drug War.* New York: MacMillan Publishing, 1987.

Trebach, Arnold S. *The Heroin Solution.* New Haven, Conn.: Yale University Press, 1982.

Trebach, Arnold S., and Kevin B. Zeese, eds. *Drug Prohibition and the Conscience of Nations.* Washington D.C.: Drug Policy Foundation, 1990.

———. *The Great Issues of Drug Policy.* Washington, D.C.: Drug Policy Foundation, 1990.

———. *New Frontiers in Drug Policy.* Washington, D.C.: Drug Policy Foundation, 1991.

Tuchman, Barbara W. *The March of Folly: From Troy to Vietnam.* New York: Alfred A. Knopf, 1984.

Turner, David. "Pragmatic Incoherence: The Changing Face of British Drug Policy." In *Searching for Alternatives: Drug-Control Policy in the United States,* edited by Melvyn B. Krauss and Edward P. Lazear. Stanford, Calif.: Hoover Institution Press, 1991.

USA Today, 20 December 1990, 23 July 1993, 26 July 1993, 27 July 1993.

Wacquant, Loic J. D., and William J. Wilson. "The Cost of Racial and Class Exclusion in the Inner City." *Annals of the American Academy of Political and Social Science* 501 (1989):8–25.

Waldorf, Dan, Craig Reinarman, and Sheila Murphy. *Cocaine Changes: The Experience of Using and Quitting.* Philadelphia: Temple University Press, 1991.

Walker, William O., III. *Drug Control in the Americas.* Rev. ed. Albuquerque: University of New Mexico Press. 1989.

Wall Street Journal, 17 April 1963, 7 September 1989, 8 September 1989, 27 October 1989.

Waller, Douglas. "Risky Business." *Newsweek,* 16 July 1990, 16–19.

Washington Office on Latin America. *Clear and Present Dangers: The U.S. Military and the War on Drugs in the Andes.* Washington, D.C., 1991.

Washington Post, 15 May 1988, 22 May 1988, 27 May 1988, 15 June 1988, 19 September 1988, 11 February 1989, 9 June 1989, 20 June 1989, 23 August 1989, 6 September 1989, 4 November 1990, 24 October 1991, 27 June 1993, 15 July 1993, 26 July 1993, 31 August 1993, 16 February 1995, 11 June 1995, 10 July 1995, 11 August 1995.

Washington Times, 15 June 1989, 5 August 1991, 17 November 1991, 30 September 1993, 12 October 1993, 24 December 1994, 7 February 1995, 7 March 1995.

Weaver, Kent R. "The Politics of Blame Avoidance." *Journal of Public Policy* 6, no. 4(1987):371–98.

Weber, Ellen. "Testimony before the Subcommittee on Trade of the House Committee on Ways and Means. U.S. Congress, 30 April 1992." Mimeographed.

Weisheit, Ralph A. *Domestic Marijuana: A Neglected Industry.* New York: Greenwood Press, 1992.

Weppner, R. S., and D. C. McBride. "Comprehensive Drug Programs: The Dade County, Florida Example." *Psychiatry* 132 (1975):734–38.

Wexler, Harry K., Douglas S. Lipton, and Bruce D. Johnson. *A Criminal Justice System Strategy for Treating Cocaine/Heroin Abusing Offenders in Custody.* Washington, D.C.: National Institute of Justice, 1988.

Wilkinson, Francis. "A Separate Peace." *Rolling Stone,* 5 May 1994, 26–28.

Williams, Terry M. *The Cocaine Kids.* Reading, Mass.: Addison-Wesley, 1989.

Wilson, James Q. "Drugs and Crime." In *Drugs and Crime,* edited by Michael Tonry and James Q. Wilson. Chicago: University of Chicago Press, 1990.

Wisotsky, Steven. *Beyond the War on Drugs: Overcoming a Failed Public Policy.* Buffalo, N.Y.: Prometheus Books, 1990.

———. "Crackdown: The Emerging 'Drug Exception' to the Bill of Rights." *Hastings Law Journal* 38, no. 5 (1987):889–926.

Wrobleski, Ann. Memorandum from the Assistant Secretary of State for International Narcotics Matters to Sherman Funk, Inspector General, attachment to Department of State Inspector General Report, March 1989.

Young, James Harvey. *The Medical Messiahs: A Social History of Health Quackery in Twentieth-Century America.* Princeton, N.J.: Princeton University Press, 1967.

Zane, Nolan, Stanley Sue, Felipe G. Castro, and William George. "Service System Models for Ethnic Minorities." In *Reaching the Underserved: Mental Health Needs of Neglected Populations,* edited by Lonnie R. Snowden. Beverly Hills, Calif.: Sage Publications, 1982.

Zimring, Franklin E., and Gordon Hawkins. *The Search for Rational Drug Control.* Cambridge: Cambridge University Press, 1992.

Zinberg, Norman. *Drug, Set and Setting: The Basis for Controlled Intoxicant Use.* New Haven, Conn.: Yale University Press, 1984.

GOVERNMENT DOCUMENTS

Centers for Disease Control. *AIDS/HIV Surveillance: U.S. AIDS Cases Reported Through May 1991.* Atlanta, Ga., 1991.

Constantine, Thomas. Testimony of the Administrator, Drug Enforcement Administration, before the Senate Judiciary Committee, 14 February 1995.

Drug Abuse Policy Office. Office of Policy Development. The White House. *Federal Strategy For Prevention of Drug Abuse and Drug Trafficking 1982.* Washington, D.C.: U.S. Government Printing Office, 1982.

National Commission on Acquired Immune Deficiency Syndrome. *The Twin Epidemics of Substance Use and HIV.* Washington, D.C., 1991.

National Commission on Marihuana and Drug Abuse. *Drug Use in America: Problem in Perspective.* Washington, D.C.: U.S. Government Printing Office, 1973.

———. *Marihuana: A Signal of Misunderstanding.* Washington, D.C.: U.S. Government Printing Office, 1972.

Office of National Drug Control Policy. *National Drug Control Strategy.* Washington, D.C.: U.S. Government Printing Office, 1989–1995.

———. *National Drug Control Strategy: Budget Summary.* Washington, D.C.: U.S. Government Printing Office, 1991–1995.

———. *State and Local Spending on Drug Control Activities.* Washington, D.C.: U.S. Government Printing Office, 1993.

President's Commission on Law Enforcement and Administration of Justice. *Narcotics and Drug Abuse.* Washington, D.C.: U.S. Government Printing Office, 1967.

President's Commission on Model State Drug Laws. *Treatment.* Washington, D.C.: The White House, 1993.

U.S. Congress. House. Committee on Foreign Affairs. *Operation Snowcap: Past, Present and Future.* 101st Cong., 2d sess., 23 May 1990.

U.S. Congress. House. Committee on Government Operations. *The Role of Demand Reduction in the National Drug Control Strategy.* 101st Cong., 2d sess., 30 November 1990.

———. *United States Anti-Narcotics Activities in the Andean Region.* Washington D.C.: U.S. Government Printing Office, 1990.

U.S. Congress. House. Committee on Government Reform. "Clinton Drug Policy." 14 February 1995. Press Release.

U.S. Congress. House. Defense Policy Panel and Investigations Subcommittee. Committee on Armed Services. *The Andean Drug Strategy and the Role of the U.S. Military.* Washington, D.C.: U.S. Government Printing Office, 1990.

U.S. Congress. House. Select Committee on Narcotics Abuse and Control. *The Drug Enforcement Crisis at the Local Level: Hearing before the Select Committee on Narcotics Abuse and Control.* 101st Cong., 1st sess., 31 May 1989.

———. *Drug Interdiction: Hearing before the Select Committee on Narcotics Abuse and Control.* 100th Cong., 1st sess., 30 April 1987.

———. *Implementation of Provisions of the Anti-Drug Abuse Act of 1986.* 100th Cong., 1st sess., 1987.

———. *Legalization of Illicit Drugs: Impact and Feasibility.* 100th Cong., 2nd sess., 29 September 1988, parts I and II.

———. *National Drug Policy Board Strategy Plans.* 100th Cong., 2d sess., 1988.

———. *National Drug Strategy Goals and the Root Causes of Drug Addiction and Drug Crime: Hearing before the Select Committee on Narcotics Abuse and Control.* 101st Cong., 1st sess., 15 November 1989.

U.S. Congress. Senate. Committee on Governmental Affairs. *Report of the Permanent Subcommittee on Investigation.* 101st Cong., 2d sess., 6 February 1990.

U.S. Department of Health and Human Services. *National Household Survey on Drug Abuse: Population Estimates 1993.* Washington, D.C.: U.S. Government Printing Office, 1994.

———. *U.S. Public Health Service: Reducing the Health Consequences of Smoking: 25 Years of Progress.* A Report of the Surgeon General. Washington, D.C., 1989.

———. Office for Substance Abuse Prevention. *Citizen's Alcohol and Other Drug Prevention Directory.* Washington, D.C., 1990.

———. *Prevention Plus II: Tools for Creating and Sustaining Drug-Free Communities.* Rockville, Md., 1989.

U.S. Department of Justice. *An Analysis of Non-Violent Drug Offenders with Minimal Criminal Histories.* Washington, D.C., 1994.

U.S. Department of Justice. Bureau of Justice Statistics. *Federal Criminal Case Processing, 1989–1990.* Washington, D.C., 1992.

———. *Federal Offenses and Offenders: Drug Law Violators, 1980–1986.* Washington, D.C., 1988.

————. *Sourcebook of Criminal Justice Statistics—1989*. Washington, D.C., 1990.

U.S. Department of Justice. Drug Enforcement Administration. *Briefing Book*. Washington, D.C., 1990.

————. *A Chronicle of Federal Drug Law Enforcement*. Washington, D.C., 1977.

————. "A Chronicle of Federal Drug Law Enforcement." *Drug Enforcement* 7, no. 2 (1980):52–64.

————. Office of Intelligence. *Intelligence Trends: From the Source to the Street: Mid-1990 Prices for Cannabis, Cocaine, and Heroin*. Washington, D.C., 1990.

U.S. Department of Justice. The United States Attorneys and The Attorney General of the United States. *Drug Trafficking: A Report to the President of the United States*. Washington, D.C., 1989.

U.S. Department of State. Bureau of International Narcotics and Law Enforcement Affairs. *International Narcotics Control Strategy Report*. Washington, D.C., 1995.

U.S. General Accounting Office. *Drug Control: Treatment Alternatives Program for Drug Offenders Needs Stronger Emphasis*. Washington, D.C., 1993.

INTERVIEWS

The following are the names of individuals we interviewed for this book, along with their affiliations at the time of the interview. The affiliations are given for identification purposes only.

Camile T. Barry, Deputy Director, Center for Substance Abuse Treatment.

Michael Beachler, Senior Program Officer, The Robert Wood Johnson Foundation, Princeton, New Jersey.

Deborah Beck, President, Drug and Alcohol Service Providers Organization of Pennsylvania.

Carol Bergman, Associate Counsel, Committee on Government Operations, U.S. House of Representatives.

Bill Butynski, Executive Director, National Association of State Alcohol and Drug Abuse Directors, Washington, D.C.

Shirley Coleman, Resident, Maryland.

John Daigle, Executive Director, Florida Alcohol and Drug Abuse Association.

Susan Galbraith, Co-Director of the Washington office of the Legal Action Center, Washington, D.C.

Barbara Geller, Project Director, Fighting Back, New Haven, Connecticut.

John Gustafson, Executive Director, National Association of State Alcohol and Drug House Directors, Washington, D.C.

Earl C. Huch, Program Manager, National Consortium of TASC Programs, Washington, D.C.

Paul Jellinek, Vice President, The Robert Wood Johnson Foundation, Princeton, New Jersey.

Robin Kimbrough, Project Director, Special Committee on the Drug Crisis, American Bar Association, Washington, D.C.

Linda Lewis, Director of Public Policy, National Association of State Alcohol and Drug Abuse Directors, Washington, D.C.

Ira J. Marion, Co-President, New York Association of Substance Abuse Programs.

Mark Mauer, Assistant Director, Sentencing Project, Washington, D.C.

Robert L. May, Executive Director, National Consortium of TASC Programs, Washington, D.C.

Don McConnell, Prevention Consultant, National Volunteer Training Center for Substance Abuse Prevention, Bethesda, Maryland.

Ethan Nadleman, Director, The Lindesmith Center, New York.

Mark Parrino, President, American Methadone Treatment Association, New York, New York.

Peter Reuter, RAND Corporation, Washington, D.C.

David Rosenbloom, Program Director, Join Together, Boston, Massachusetts.

Lisa Scheckel, Acting Director, Center for Substance Abuse Treatment, Washington, D.C.

Kathleen Sheehan, Director of Public Policy, National Association of State Alcohol and Drug Abuse Directors, Washington, D.C.

Eric Sterling, President, Criminal Justice Policy Foundation, Washington, D.C.

Sarah Vogelsburg, Counsel to the Secretary for Drug Abuse Policy, Department of Health and Human Services, Washington, D.C.

Scott Wallace, Legislative Director, National Association of Criminal Defense Lawyers, Washington, D.C.

Ellen Weber, codirector of the Washington office of the Legal Action Center, Washington, D.C.

Ronald Weich, General Counsel to the Committee on Labor and Human Resources, U.S. Senate.

Index

Eva Bertram has worked for ten years as a public policy analyst and organizational consultant in Washington, D.C., most recently with the government Accountability Project; she is writing her doctoral dissertation in Political Science at Yale University.

Morris Blachman is Associate Professor of Government and International Studies at the University of South Carolina and consults on management issues in the health field.

Kenneth Sharpe is Professor and Chairman of Political Science at Swarthmore College.

Peter Andreas is a research fellow in the Foreign Policy Studies program at the Brookings Institution and an SSRC-MacArthur Fellow on Peace and Security in a Changing World; he is writing his doctoral dissertation in Government at Cornell University.

Compositor: BookMasters, Inc.
Text: 10/13 Sabon
Display: Sabon
Printer and Binder: Haddon Craftsmen, Inc.